PENGUIN CLASSICS

THE SONGS OF THE SOUTH

QU YUAN was a minister of King Huai of Chu, who reigned from 328 to 299 BC. He was banished from the court because of a scandal or intrigue and wrote the poem *Li sao* in protest at his treatment, before committing suicide by throwing himself in the Mi-luo, a tributary of the River Xiang.

DAVID HAWKES, who was born in 1923, was one of the greatest translators of Chinese literature of his time. In 1942, he went up to Christ Church, Oxford to study Classics, before spending the rest of the war teaching Japanese to code-breakers. He returned to Oxford to study Chinese, and in 1948 he left for Peking, then in the last throes of civil war. From 1959 to 1971 Hawkes was Professor of Chinese at Oxford University and subsequently became Research Fellow of All Souls College, Oxford. For many years, it had been Hawkes's dream to work on *The Story of the Stone*, the eighteenth-century novel generally regarded as the greatest work of traditional Chinese fiction. His translation of the first three volumes of the novel, completed over ten years after he resigned from his chair at Oxford, is now regarded as his crowning achievement. David Hawkes died in Oxford in 2009.

T0201084

The Songs of the South

*An Ancient Chinese Anthology of Poems
by Qu Yuan and Other Poets*

Translated and introduced by
DAVID HAWKES

PENGUIN BOOKS

PENGUIN CLASSICS

Published by the Penguin Group
Penguin Books Ltd, 80 Strand, London WC2R ORL, England
Penguin Group (USA) Inc., 375 Hudson Street, New York, New York 10014, USA
Penguin Group (Canada), 90 Eglinton Avenue East, Suite 700, Toronto, Ontario, Canada M4P 2Y3
(a division of Pearson Penguin Canada Inc.)
Penguin Ireland, 25 St Stephen's Green, Dublin 2, Ireland (a division of Penguin Books Ltd)
Penguin Group (Australia), 250 Camberwell Road, Camberwell, Victoria 3124, Australia
(a division of Pearson Australia Group Pty Ltd)
Penguin Books India Pvt Ltd, 11 Community Centre, Panchsheel Park, New Delhi – 110 017, India
Penguin Group (NZ), 67 Apollo Drive, Rosedale, Auckland 0632, New Zealand
(a division of Pearson New Zealand Ltd)
Penguin Books (South Africa) (Pty) Ltd, 24 Sturdee Avenue, Rosebank, Johannesburg 2196, South Africa

Penguin Books Ltd, Registered Offices: 80 Strand, London WC2R ORL, England

www.penguin.com

First published in Penguin Classics in 1985
This edition published 2011

014

Copyright © David Hawkes, 1985

The moral right of the translator has been asserted

Set in Linotron Plantin
Printed and bound in Great Britain by Clays Ltd, Elcograf S.p.A.

ISBN: 978-0-140-44375-2

www.greenpenguin.co.uk

To J. R. Hightower

Contents

Preface

The translations published in this volume first appeared in *Ch'u Tz'u, The Songs of the South: An Ancient Chinese Anthology*, which the Clarendon Press, Oxford, published in 1959 and the Beacon Press of Boston reproduced as a paperback in 1962. They were originally part of a doctoral dissertation, 'On the Problem of Date and Authorship in Ch'u Tz'u', submitted to the Oriental Studies faculty of the University of Oxford in 1955. Most of them were made while I was a student at the old National Peking University between 1948 and 1951. *Li sao* was translated even earlier, in the first half of 1948, when I had been studying the Chinese language for considerably less than three years.

In preparing this completely new edition of *The Songs of the South* (of which both the hardback and paperback editions have long been out of print), I have altered the translations as little as possible, not so much because I am confident that they are right, as from a feeling that they were made by a young man whom I should perhaps scarcely recognize if I met him today and whose work I am therefore not entitled to deface. Either I must make a new translation, which I have neither the time nor the energy to do, or I must present them more or less as they were, altering only what I am fairly certain was incorrect.

A major difference in the translations as they now appear is that I have substituted Pinyin for the old Wade–Giles spellings. For the reader's convenience I have modified the conventions of Pinyin slightly by introducing hyphens. And since Pinyin normally has no hyphens, I have felt free to use them according to rules of my own. In the case of personal names I write two-syllable names without a hyphen but with a capital letter at the beginning of each syllable; names of more than two syllables I hyphenate where appropriate: Si-ma Xiang-ru, Bo-li Xi, Guan Long-feng, etc. Two-syllable place-names I invariably hyphenate. Bo Yong is a personal name, Bo-zhong is a place.

The Chinese text of *The Songs of the South* is full of ambiguities and uncertainties. About one of them I have found my opinion changing even as I have been preparing this new edition for the press. The 'Nine Songs', it now seems to me – although some of the material contained in it is much earlier – cannot have been put together any earlier than the second century B.C. In Si-ma Qian's biography of the Prince of Huai-nan the Great Spirit whom the Chinese magician meets while travelling at sea refers to the Chinese emperor as 'the Emperor of the West'. The idea that Tai Yi, the master of the spirit world, was the Emperor of the East and the Chinese emperor, the master of the human world, was the Emperor of the West cannot have existed before the beginning of the imperial era.

I am grateful to the Oxford University Press for allowing me to recycle *The Songs of the South* in this new edition. Perhaps it would not be amiss to thank Dan Davin, twenty-five years after the event, for seeing that first edition into print. I am indebted to the heirs of James Frazer for a substantial quotation from *The Golden Bough* on pp. 220–21, and to the Chinese scholar Lu Kanru for having pointed out its relevance. Finally I should like to thank Mrs Betty Radice for her unfailing encouragement, without which I doubt if this book would ever have got finished.

DAVID HAWKES

Note on Spelling

Chinese proper names in this book are spelled in accordance with a system invented by the Chinese and used internationally, which is known by its Chinese name of *Pinyin*. A full explanation of this system will be found overleaf, but for the benefit of readers who find systems of spelling and pronunciation tedious and hard to follow a short list is given below of those letters whose Pinyin values are quite different from the sounds they normally represent in English, together with their approximate English equivalents. Mastery of this short list should ensure that names, even if mispronounced, are no longer unpronounceable.

c	=	*ts*
q	=	*ch*
x	=	*sh*
z	=	*dz*
zh	=	*j*

Note on Spelling

Chinese Syllables

The syllables of Chinese are made up of one or more of the following elements;

1. an initial consonant (b.c.ch.d.f.g.h.j.k.l.m.n.p.q.r.s.sh.t.w.x.y. z.zh)
2. a semivowel (i or u)
3. an open vowel (a.e.i.o.u.ü), *or*
   a closed vowel (an.ang.en.eng.in.ing.ong.un), *or*
   a diphthong (ai.ao.ei.ou)

The combinations found are:

      3 on its own (e.g, *e*, *an*, *ai*)
      1 + 3 (e.g. *ba*, *xing*, *hao*)
      1 + 2 + 3 (e.g. *xue*, *qiang*, *biao*)

Initial Consonants

Apart from c = *ts* and z = *dz* and r, which is the Southern English *r* with a slight buzz added, the only initial consonants likely to give an English speaker much trouble are the two groups

j q x   and   zh ch sh

Both groups sound somewhat like English *j ch sh*; but whereas j q x are articulated much farther *forward* in the mouth than our *j ch sh*, the sounds zh ch sh are made in a 'retroflexed' position much farther *back*. This means that to our ears j sounds halfway between our *j* and *dz*, q halfway between our *ch* and *ts*, and x halfway between our *sh* and *s*; whilst zh ch sh sound somewhat as *jr chr shr* would do if all three combinations and not only the last one were found in English.

Semivowels

The semivowel i 'palatalizes' the preceding consonant: i.e. it makes a *y* sound after it, like the *i* in *onion*) (e.g. Bian He)

The semivowel u 'labializes' the preceding consonant: i.e. it makes a *w* sound after it, like the *u* in *assuages* (e.g. Zhuang Ji)

Vowels and Diphthongs

i. Open Vowels

a   is a long *ah* like *a* in *father* (e.g. Fu Cha)

e   on its own or after any consonant other than y is like the sound in French *oeuf* or the *er*, *ir*, *ur* sound of Southern English (e.g. He Bo, E-zhu)

e   after y or a semivowel is like the *e* of *egg* (e.g. Jie, Fu Yue)

i   after b.d.j.l.m.n.p.q.t.x.y is the long Italian *i* or English *ee* as in *see* (e.g. Zhang Yi)

i   after zh.ch.sh.z.c.s.r is a strangled sound somewhere between the *u* of *suppose* and a vocalized *r* (e.g. Xun Zi, Qiong-shi)

i   after semivowel u is pronounced like *ay* in *sway* (e.g. Kuai Gui)

o   is the *au* of *author* (e.g. Jing Cuo, Bo Yi)

u   after semivowel i and all consonants except j.q.x.y is pronounced like Italian *u* or English *oo* in *too* (e.g. Fu Fei)

u   after j.q.x.y and ü after l or n is the narrow French *u* or German *ü*, for which there is no English equivalent (e.g. Zi Xu, He Lü)

ii. Closed Vowels

an   after semivowel u or any consonant other than y is like *an* in German *Mann* or *un* in Southern English *fun* (e.g. Han Zhong, Guan Long-feng)

an   after y or semivowel i is like *en* in *hen* (e.g. Yan-zi, Jian Di)

ang   whatever it follows, invariably has the long *a* of *father* (e.g. Gao Yang)

en, eng   the e in these combinations is always a short, neutral sound like *a* in *ago* or the first *e* in *believe* (e.g. Chen, Feng Hou)

in, ing   short *i* as in *sin*, *sing* (e.g. Qin, Hong Xing-zu)

ong   the o is like the short *oo* of Southern English *book* (e.g. Guan Zhong)

un   the rule for the closed u is similar to the rule for the open one: after j.q.x.y it is the narrow French *u* of *rue*; after anything else it resembles the short English *oo* of *book* (e.g. Yun-zhong, Gun)

iii. Diphthongs

ai   like the sound in English *lie*, *high*, *mine* (e.g. Huai)

ao   like the sound in *how* or *bough* (e.g. Tai Hao)

ei   like the sound in *day* or *mate* (e.g. Fu Fei)

ou   like the sound in *old* or *bowl* (e.g. Gou Mang)

The syllable er which occurs in the name Chong **Er** is a peculiarity of the Pekingese dialect which lies outside this system. It sounds somewhat like the word *err* pronounced with a broad West Country accent.

General Introduction

The first thing to be lost when Chinese poetry is translated is not some subtle nuance of the meaning but the poetic form. The traditional forms of Chinese poetry are most of them extraordinarily antique. Some of those used by the late Mao Tse-tung in his occasional verse – some, for that matter, used by the thousands of amateurs who continue to write traditional-style Chinese poetry today – had already been perfected by the time of Charlemagne, and some were developed even earlier, in the second century A.D. Before the second century A.D. Chinese poetry was formally very different – at least as different as Old English alliterative verse from the poetry of Chaucer, Milton and Pope. Yet if we look beyond the superficialities of form and seek to understand the spirit of Chinese poetry – the Chinese poet's way of looking at the world, his vocabulary of images, and the various assumptions that he makes – it is to the ancient poetry that we must turn. In the ancient poetry of China we may, indeed, find clues to the dual origin of all poetry: the expression of men's feelings as social beings and the expression of their feelings as isolated individual souls.

North and South

For Chinese poetry has a dual ancestry, a Northern and a Southern, corresponding in some respects to these two poetic functions. The Southern ancestor is less ancient than the Northern one and can, in a very roundabout sort of way, be derived from it; but the differences between them are so great that it is more convenient to think of them as two separate sources, contributing in equal measure to the new kind of poetry that began to emerge in the second century A.D. The Northern of these two ancestors is *Shi jing*, the 'Book of Songs'; the Southern one is *Chu ci*, the 'Plaints of Chu' or 'Songs of the South'. In these two anthologies is contained all that we know of ancient Chinese poetry.

'Northern' and 'Southern' are relative terms and therefore apt to be misleading. The people who produced the songs of *Shi jing*, many of which date from the ninth and eighth centuries B.C., certainly did not think of themselves as Northerners, though they lived in what we should nowadays call North China: the North China Plain and the loess plateaux to the west of it. On the other hand, they would certainly have regarded the Chu noblemen who wrote the early *Chu ci* poems in the fourth and third centuries B.C. as Southerners, though the kingdom of Chu occupied what to us is Central China: the lakelands of the central valley of the Yangtze and the lands traversed by its tributaries, the Han and the Xiang.

Terms like 'China' and 'Chinese' can be as misleading as 'Northern' and 'Southern' when they are applied to the very ancient societies in which this early poetry was born. If we call 'Chinese' only those who can be shown to have spoken a language identifiable as Chinese, then we have to say that Chinese history begins with the dynasty of Shang kings who ruled in Henan from about the middle of the second millennium B.C. Theirs was, as far as we know, the earliest literate culture in that part of Asia, and the language they wrote in was certainly Chinese. Bushels of tersely inscribed fragments of bone and turtle shell which they used in divination testify to their literacy; but they left behind no literature. Chinese literature begins with the Zhou dynasty, founded towards the end of the second millennium by a rebellious vassal of the Shang kings who lived on the western marches of their empire.

The Zhou were a wordy people, justifying themselves and haranguing the defeated Shang princes with the victor's self-righteous confidence that God is on his side. Even their bronze ritual vessels are wordy, with long inscriptions taking the place of the uninformative 'X his tripod', which is the most we find on even the most magnificent and elaborate Shang bronzes. Until 771 B.C., when an alliance of rebellious vassals and barbarian invaders compelled them to move eastwards, nearer to the old Shang capital in Henan, the Zhou kings controlled their empire from a capital in Shaanxi. The period of about two and a half centuries from their conquest of Shang until the fall of their capital in Shaanxi is called Western Zhou. During it were produced the most ancient parts of *Yi jing* (the 'Book of Changes'), *Shu jing* (the 'Book of History') and a substantial part of *Shi jing* (the 'Book of Songs').

After their move to the east the lackland Zhou kings sank into powerlessness and their feudatories began to behave each as an independent kinglet in his own domain. Total anarchy was averted partly by the residual respect that the feudal lords still had for the religious and ritual functions of the 'Son of Heaven' or 'Heavenly King', as the Zhou king was called, and partly by the emergence during the seventh century B.C. of the Hegemons, rulers of one or other of the most powerful states who, acting as nominal deputies of the Son of Heaven, organized the other feudatories into a confederation of Zhou states for mutual assistance in times of flood, famine and pestilence and collaborative military action against internal defaulters and foreign foes. Some of the later songs of *Shi jing* – for example, the poignant dirge for three young warriors who followed Duke Mu of Qin to the grave in 621 B.C. – appear to belong to this Age of the Hegemons.

But the Hegemons' attempt to create a measure of stability in the anarchic political world of Eastern Zhou had little lasting success. Great social and political changes were taking place. Smaller states were continually being conquered and absorbed by their larger neighbours, and the administration of these new, enlarged states was becoming increasingly bureaucratic and centralized. By the beginning of the fifth century B.C. only six great states, each one of them as large as a medieval European kingdom, remained in place of the dozens of little duchies and baronies of Western Zhou. Soon, as their rulers began openly to flout the old convention which reserved the royal title for the Son of Heaven, they were kingdoms in name as well.

One of the greatest political changes which took place during these centuries was the rise to power of a seventh kingdom beyond the southern limits of the old Shang and Zhou empires and its gradual acceptance as an equal and sometimes as an ally by the other states. This was the kingdom of Chu, already powerful enough to meddle with its Northern neighbours by the beginning of the sixth century B.C. and at the peak of its greatness in the fourth century B.C. when a nobleman at the court of one of its kings wrote the remarkable poem which stands first in the *Chu ci* collection and was to be the pattern and inspiration of later generations of Chu poets.

Other powers besides Chu appeared in the South during the fifth century B.C. and made a brief impact on Northern affairs: Wu in the lower valley of the Yangtze, roughly corresponding to present-day Anhui and Jiangsu, and Yue in what is nowadays Zhejiang; but Wu, after a mere decade of dazzling military success, was conquered and absorbed by Yue, and Yue in its turn was extinguished by Chu in the fourth century B.C. Chu was therefore the sole Southern rival of Qin when Qin embarked on the policy of subversion and military conquest which culminated in the elimination of all six of its rivals in the latter part of the following century and the bestowal of its name on the empire it had thus created. The name survives to this day in our 'China', which is no more than a mispronunciation of 'Qin'.

The political history of Chu reads like a disaster, since it ends with the extinction of Chu, along with the five Northern kingdoms, and its absorption into the Qin empire. Yet in a sense the ultimate victory was Chu's. It was men of Chu who played a major part, as prophecy had said they would,[1] in overthrowing the Qin empire, and it was Chu poets and craftsmen who provided the new Han era with its art and letters when Qin was no more than a hated memory of harsh oppression and cruel, tyrannical laws.

The first-century historian Ban Gu concludes a brief survey of Chu history with these words:

> Watered by the Yangtze and the Han, Chu is a land of lakes and rivers, of well-forested mountains and of the wide lowlands of Jiangnan, where burning and flooding make the labours of ploughing and hoeing superfluous. The people live on fish and rice. Hunting, fishing and wood-gathering are their principal activities. Because there is always enough to eat, they are a lazy and improvident folk, laying up no stores for the future, so confident are they that the supply of food and drink will always be replenished. They have no fear of cold or hunger; on the other hand, there are no rich households among them. They believe in the power of shamans and spirits and are much addicted to lewd religious rites.

The riverine and lacustrine landscape of Chu which Ban Gu here refers to is something we are constantly being reminded of in *Chu ci*. Water goddesses are the subjects of two of its most beautiful songs, several of the longer poems recall journeys made by river, and even when the poets are on dry land, the lakes and rivers of this watery kingdom are seldom long out of mind. One of the most remarkable Chinese archaeological discoveries of the fifties was a set of inscribed bronze tallies dating from the late fourth century B.C. giving long itineraries of river journeys made for trading purposes throughout the length and breadth of Chu, some of them along waterways referred to by the Chu poets in these poems.

The slash-and-burn type of agriculture which Ban Gu refers to (literally 'ploughing by fire and hoeing by water') was still being practised by the more backward inhabitants of this area hundreds of years later when observers from the metropolitan area visited it in the ninth century A.D. It is interesting to note that the kings of Chu and most of the Chu aristocracy traced their lineage from a fire god called Zhu Rong whom one ancient authority identified with Curly

---

1. 'As long as three Chu households remain, Chu will be Qin's undoing'. The prophecy, which became proverbial, was made during the period of national outrage following King Huai of Chu's death in captivity in Qin in 296 B.C.

Sprout, the green god of springtime who pushed the green shoots up through the fertile, fire-blackened fields. To Northerners, whose ancestor was King Millet and who cultivated the loess soil with ploughs, the connection between fire and agriculture would have been incomprehensible.

As for the men of Chu's superstitious belief in spirits, their addiction to shamanism and fondness for 'lewd rites', these were already notorious when the *Chu ci* poems were being written and remained so for centuries afterwards. Suppression of shamans and destruction of their holy places were part of the 'civilizing' policy vigorously prosecuted by Confucian administrators in this area in the early years of the Tang dynasty. To judge from the numerous poetical accounts of shaman shrines and shaman ceremonies dating from the eighth and ninth centuries, it does not look as if they were altogether successful. Relics of the old shamanism are to be found even today among the Chinese settler communities of South-East Asia.

The impression given by Confucian historians that the shamanism of Chu was an outlandish regional aberration is misleading. Shamanism was the Old Religion of China, dethroned when Confucianism became a state orthodoxy and driven into the countryside, where it fared much as paganism did in Christian Europe: sometimes tolerated and absorbed, sometimes ferociously suppressed. Under the Shang kings shamans were sometimes great officers of state. Zhou society was more secular and its religious impulses more restrained. To give only two examples of this: human and even animal sacrifices on a scale that was common throughout the Shang dynasty were quite unknown under the Zhou; and divination seems to have played nothing like as important a part in the day-to-day running of affairs as it manifestly did under the Shang. One consequence of this changed attitude towards religion was that shamans ceased to be employed as counsellors or officials in the courts of kings or even to play a part in the ceremonial worship of the ancestors. From being honoured members of a ruling caste they became professionals of somewhat inferior status occasionally consulted by it: for exorcism or medication in time of sickness, for rain-making in time of drought, or for advice about particularly disturbing dreams. It was the Zhou society's changed attitude towards religious professionals and a growing scepticism among the more highly educated members of its élite which in the fourth and third centuries B.C. was beginning to make the shamanism of Chu seem outlandish and bizarre to its Northern neighbours. Far from being a 'foreign' culture from the South as European sinologists used sometimes to imagine, Chu was much more likely an offshoot of a Northern culture which, with the

conservatism commonly found in colonial societies, had retained
some of its ancient features long after the metropolitan culture had
discarded them. It is for this reason that we are, I think, justified in
looking for the ancient sources of Chinese poetry as much in the
poems of *Chu ci* as in the songs of the very much earlier *Shi jing*.

There are quite a number of indications that Chu and the other
Southern kingdoms were early colonies of a metropolitan Northern
culture rather than aboriginal dynasties or early invaders from the
South. Ancient tradition held that the kings of Wu were descended
from Zhou princes who had gone into voluntary exile in this remote
area two generations before the Zhou conquest of Shang. The Chu
king-list begins in the same period with an ancestor called Yu
Xiong, who was said to have been a friend and adviser of the first
Zhou king's father. Archaeological evidence, though not plentiful, is
entirely consistent with the existence of colonies of 'metropolitan'
culture in these areas in the late Shang period. But if Yu Xiong's
forebears did indeed come from the North, it would certainly have
been many generations before his time. The Chu royal surname was
Mi, and Shang oracle bone inscriptions mention campaigns against a
rebellious tributary people called Mi on the southern or south-
western borders of the Shang empire – a people who have plausibly
been identified with the ancestors of the ruling class of Chu.

According to tradition this Mi clan to which the kings of Chu
belonged was one of eight clans called the Eight Lineages of Zhu
Rong. Both the Zhou aristocracy and their Southern neighbours
believed that before the Shang kings there had been a Xia empire
founded by a semi-divine being called Yu who, by indefatigable
travelling and heroic feats of engineering, controlled a great flood
and created the Chinese landscape as it is today. In the Eastern
Zhou era there were only two tiny states left whose rulers claimed
to be directly descended from the Xia kings, yet 'Xia' had somehow
stuck as a name by which people who spoke the language and
shared the customs of these early ancestors of the Chinese
distinguished themselves from the 'barbarians' who surrounded
them, just as 'Han', the name of the dynasty which succeeded the
Qin at the end of the third century B.C., survives today as a term by
which ethnic Chinese distinguish themselves from Mongols,
Tibetans and other eastern races. People of the Eastern Zhou era
could recite the names of the Xia kings and claimed to know the
lengths of their reigns and where their various capitals had been,
but that was as far back as they could go. Before that was the Age
of the Ancestors, a sort of Australian aboriginal 'dream time' when
there was no chronology or even any very clear distinction between
heavenly and earthly happenings. In this nebulous period were
placed the First Ancestors of the dozens of noble lineages which

still survived and many more which had died out but whose memory was faithfully preserved. King Millet, the First Ancestor of the Zhou kings, the Shang First Ancestor, Xie, and Zhu Rong, the fire god from whom the kings and nobles of Chu were descended, were all contemporaries of Yu in the sense that they all belonged to the same timeless period in which everyone's genealogy began. Yu's father, Gun, seems originally to have been a water god, and in one version of the flood myth it was Zhu Rong the fire god who 'killed' Gun (being a demigod he did not really die but merely changed his shape). Gun and Zhu Rong were both sons of the sky god Gao Yang, from whom the kings of Qin also were descended, whereas the First Ancestors of the Shang and Zhou kings were the sons of virgin mothers, each of whom was thought to have been impregnated by a sky god called Ku or Gao Xin.

Ku, or 'Di Ku', is associated with a Sun Hero called Yi, a Mighty Archer whom Ku sent down to deal with various noxious monsters who were harassing mankind and to shoot down several superfluous suns which had appeared in the sky and were burning up the earth. In other legends he reappears as a dissolute tyrant who contended with the early Xia kings for possession of the North China Plain. Some Chinese scholars have suggested that the Mighty Archer represents the Yi peoples, who still had settlements in Shandong and other parts of East China in the historical period, and that the legendary struggle between the Mighty Archer and the early Xia kings represents a struggle between two groups of people in ancient times. Some go even further and identify the eastern group represented by the Mighty Archer with the neolithic Longshan culture, whose smooth black pottery has been found at sites in Shandong, Jiangsu, Anhui and Henan, and the Xia or western group with the Yangshao or Painted Pottery culture, which overlaps the Longshan sites but extends much farther west and never reached as far east as Shandong.

Whether or not these latter-day interpretations of ancient legend are to be believed, it is a fact that the Chu aristocracy were extremely tenacious of what they believed to be their Xia connection. The story of the struggle between the Xia kings and the Mighty Archer is several times referred to in the Chu poems and by a nobleman of Chu in one of the early chronicles; and we hear of a seventh-century king of Chu attacking and annexing two tiny neighbouring states on the grounds that their rulers, who were, like the kings of Chu, descended from one of the sons of Gao Yang, had 'gone over to the Eastern Yi'.

The 'Northern' pedigree of the kings of Chu could at times serve them in good stead politically. In 530 B.C. King Ling of Chu discussed with one of his ministers the possibility of laying claim to some land in southern Henan on the grounds that it had been occupied by his ancestor Kun Wu. Kun Wu's was the eldest of the Eight Lineages of Zhu Rong, and his line was believed to have died out in the course of the Xia dynasty. He was therefore as remote from King Ling, who, as a member of the Mi clan, was descended from the youngest of Kun Wu's seven brothers, as King Arthur and his knights are from us, yet King Ling could speak of him familiarly as 'my elder-uncle ancestor' and evidently thought the relationship a good enough one to base a claim on.

One ancient authority, in the course of enumerating the Eight Lineages of Zhu Rong and their various ramifications, mentions that one of the several branches of the Mi clan had gone native and were known as the 'Mi Man' (the 'barbarian Mi'). A sceptic might find an inverse reading of these facts – if facts they are – more plausible and infer that the entire Mi clan was originally barbarian and the Chu royal lineage merely a part of it which had acquired a veneer of Northern culture and a fake pedigree to go with it; yet there are some indications to the contrary.

First of all there are the Northern traditions, some of which I have already referred to, indicating a southward colonizing movement in very ancient times. In the Age of the Ancestors the god-king Shun, later idealized by the Confucians as the model of what a Sage Ruler ought to be, is said to have ended his days while campaigning against the Miao tribes in southern Hunan and to have been buried in a mountain near the source of the Xiang, a river of which his sorrowing wives became the tutelary deities. And Yu, the flood hero, not only travelled extensively in the South but was said to have died there and to have been buried at Guiji, near the modern Shaoxing in Zhejiang province.

It is true that the archaeological evidence is somewhat non-committal, partly because of the difficulty of distinguishing between imported and locally manufactured artefacts and partly because the presence of cultural objects tells us nothing about the ethnic or cultural origins of the people who enjoyed them; but at least there is nothing in it inconsistent with early colonization from the North; it could even be said that the distribution of Shang and Western Zhou sites in Central China, particularly those in the Xiang river valley and at Changxian and Yuhang in Zhejiang, shows a remarkable correspondence with the legends.

Among various bits of onomastic evidence that could be adduced is the presence of the word 'Xia' in Chu place-names, the most important being the ancient name of a water-course beginning in the Yangtze somewhat west of Jiangling (the old Chu capital), linking up later on with the lower course of the River Han, and finally joining the Yangtze again at Hankou, the ancient name of which was

Xiakou. But the most interesting onomastic evidence has been preserved for us thanks to the pictorial nature of the Chinese script, without which it would have been lost.

The most characteristic pottery form found among the remains of Late Neolithic and Early Bronze cultures in North China is a curious hollow-legged tripod called a *li* which looks rather like three conical pots that have fused together. Now, it so happens that the names of the fire god Zhu Rong, who was the First Ancestor of the Chu kings, and of the early king Yu Xiong, who in the royal ancestral cult of Chu was an object of almost equal veneration, are both written with characters which include the symbol for *li* – an easily recognizable representation of the vessel. The same symbol is found in the name of one of the Eight Lineages of Zhu Rong. The 'Book of Seas and Mountains', a strange topographical work full of gods and monsters and scraps of mythology, parts of which may have been written by Chu shamans at about the same time as the earliest of the *Chu ci* poems, contains a quaint genealogy which makes Zhu Rong the son of Play-with-Pots and the grandfather of Skilful Pot, 'whose head had a square top to it'. It is as if the writer had wished to give allegorical expression to the important part played by firing in the evolution of a new and sophisticated kind of pottery. When we are told elsewhere in the same book that God sent down the fire god Zhu Rong to punish the water god Gun for stealing his magic earth to soak up the flood-water with, we can perhaps detect another allegory of the part that fire plays in the manufacture of pottery.

If the early ancestors of the Chu kings were to be distinguished from other folk by their manufacture and use of *li* cauldrons, it follows not only that they were of Northern origin but that their colonization of the Han, Xiang and Yangtze valleys must have taken place very early indeed. The relationship of Chu with the 'metropolitan' area of North China was in some respects similar to that of Scotland and England in the Middle Ages. A substantial part of South Scotland, Lothian, was part of the original Anglo-Saxon settlement: i.e. by the seventh century it was as much 'English' as Norfolk or Kent; and by the time of the Norman Conquest, Scotland had an English-speaking court and many English institutions. And just as the kings of Scotland occasionally acknowledged the overlordship of a powerful Norman king but remained on the whole independent when not actually hostile to the southern kingdom, so the kings of Chu acknowledged the suzerainty of the early Zhou kings but forgot all about it when the Zhou kings lost their power. 'We have no more to do with you Northerners,' said the Chu king's herald to an army of confederate Zhou states invading Chu territory under the leadership of the hegemon Duke

Huan of Qi in 656 B.C., 'than cattle with horses when they are in heat.' And just as the English language and literature of medieval Scotland, developing on its own independently of the 'metropolitan' English of the South, retained a distinctive regional flavour, to the extent that Lallans is often incomprehensible to a Southern reader, so did the language and literature of Chu, as exemplified in the earlier *Chu ci* poems, exhibit strong regional differences which were in part due to the retention of archaic elements that had disappeared in the North.

Strictly speaking, these earlier poems of *Chu ci*, which date from the late fourth and early third centuries B.C., are not the earliest 'Southern' poetry. The 300-odd songs of *Shi jing*, which owe their present arrangement to court musicians of the Eastern Zhou period, include two groups entitled 'Zhou's South' and 'Shao's South', several of which contain references to 'the Jiang and the Han' – i.e. the Yangtze and Han rivers – and evidently emanate from an area that was subsequently part of the Southern kingdom of Chu.

The 'Zhou' and 'Shao' of these titles refer to the Dukes of Zhou and Shao, great officers at the Zhou court who seem to have shared between them responsibility for administering the precariously held southern territories conquered by royal armies in the Western Zhou period. A Duke of Shao believed to have been a contemporary of Kings Xuan and You of Zhou in the early eighth century B.C. is the subject of a praise-poem found elsewhere in the collection. In it a bard describes a great host of chariots and footsoldiers setting out to repulse a horde of Southern tribesmen, and the Duke marking out new lands 'on the banks of the Jiang and Han' and tithing the settlers who had gone out to cultivate the conquered territory. Elsewhere a soldier who fought in these campaigns and who describes himself as 'a gentleman who made this song in order to express his grief' complains bitterly of the hardships suffered by those who had to protect these outposts of empire in 'the southern land'.

It seems that the Zhou presence in this area did not immediately disappear after the collapse of royal power in the West, since one of the songs in the 'Shao's South' group celebrates a royal wedding in which the bride was 'granddaughter of King Ping', the first of the Eastern Zhou kings; but it did not long outlast the eighth century B.C. In 632 B.C. an officer in the army of the great hegemon Duke Wen of Jin complained that Chu had absorbed 'all the Ji states north of the Han river', i.e. all the 'southland' settlements ruled by members of the Ji clan to which the Zhou kings and most of the Zhou aristocracy belonged. It is clear that these southern outposts of Zhou power were little more than garrisons which were bound to succumb when military reinforcement from the North was no longer forthcoming. The mystery is that they held out so long and produced so rich a variety of songs.

Of course, the court musicians may sometimes have been mistaken in their classification of these songs, and their classification of them would in any case have been influenced as much by musical as by historical considerations. In a lament for a fallen warrior, found not among the twenty-five 'South' songs but elsewhere in the collection, the singer calls on the musicians to 'strike the bells with solemn note, strike the greater and the lesser zither, and with stone-chimes and reed-organs sounding in unison, and with the flute's unwavering sound, play the music of the capital, the music of the Southland'. The word for 'music' does not appear in the Chinese text of this, but it looks very much as if what the singer is referring to is a type of music rather than a set of song-words.

Nevertheless, even after due allowances have been made, it looks as if many of the 'South' songs must have emanated from the Zhou 'Southland' and that they were composed over quite a long period of time – probably not less than two centuries. The marriage-song of the Zhou king's granddaughter already mentioned was probably composed towards the end of the eighth or even as late as the seventh century B.C.; on the other hand, a stanza from a love-song in the 'Shao's South' section is 'quoted' elsewhere in *Shi jing* in a praise-song celebrating the exploits of a warrior of the mid ninth century – in a way, moreover, which suggests that the song was already old, dating, therefore, at the very latest from the early ninth century B.C.

But in spite of their long history, the 'South' songs of *Shi jing* do not differ significantly either in form or content from the other songs in the collection. Except for the occasional topographical reference, they might just as well have been composed in the Zhou heartland of the North. Looking for 'Southern' influences in the 'Zhou's South' and 'Shao's South' sections of *Shi jing* is about as profitable as looking for Red Indian influences in the folk-songs of Tennessee.

If *Shi jing* contains no traces of a distinctive Southern culture, it cannot be said that the Southern *Chu ci* poetry was uninfluenced by the Northern *Shi jing*. The 'Three Hundred Songs',[2] some of which are in fact hymns or odes intended to be played, sung and in some cases danced to in the worship of the divine ancestors, were not only being constantly performed in religious and secular ceremonials at the courts of Zhou kings and nobles and as an accompaniment to their feasting and leisure; they were also an indispensable part of

2. This, or simply 'the Songs', was the way in which the ancient Chinese invariably referred to *Shi jing*.

every Zhou nobleman's education. He was expected to be able to make appropriate quotations from them on public occasions, particularly those connected with inter-state diplomacy, in which sometimes quite long exchanges took place entirely through the medium of the 'Songs'. The birds and flowers which provided the background of so many of these poems and the lovesick maidens and anxious wives who appeared so often to be their subjects could be understood allegorically as symbols of something more appropriate to the serious business in hand.

The Chu noblemen who wrote the early *Chu ci* poems would, like all educated noblemen of their day, have been thoroughly familiar with the songs of *Shi jing* and with the various ways of interpreting them allegorically. The main substance of their own poetry was entirely original, but their somewhat bizarre use of symbolism, though it looks at first sight original, may derive from the thoroughly Northern habit of looking for allegorical meanings in the *Shi jing*.

As a teacher of young gentlemen training to become public servants (several of his star pupils subsequently held quite important posts in the administrations of one or other of the Northern states), Confucius naturally gave the *Shi jing* poems an important place in his curriculum. 'Study the "Songs", my children,' he would tell his students. 'The "Songs" can be used to enforce a point, to judge a man's character, to ease social intercourse, or to express a grievance. They can be used either at home in the service of one's father, or abroad in the service of one's prince. Moreover they will familiarize you with the names of birds, beasts, plants and trees.' And to his own son he once said, 'Have you done "Zhou's South" and "Shao's South" yet? A man who has not studied "Zhou's South" and "Shao's South" is as one standing with his face against a wall.'

To later generations Confucius was a divinely inspired sage and the textbooks he had used in his curriculum were sacred scriptures in which all that we can hope to know of Truth was somewhere or other enshrined. And because *Shi jing* was the only one of these canonical books which seemed to have any bearing on the processes and problems of literary creation, it was in *Shi jing* that poets and critics sought the principles that should inspire their art and guide their judgement. The *Chu ci* poems, however popular, belonged to no canon, dealt in matters that were outlandish and unorthodox, and originated outside the area of sanctified Western Zhou tradition. Critics who wished to justify their admiration for them had to do so in terms of principles derived from a distorted scholastic interpretation of *Shi jing* which was in any case irrelevant to this wholly different kind of poetry. Even as perceptive a critic as Liu Xie in the late fifth century A.D. approaches the Chu poems in a slightly defensive manner and seems more concerned to fudge the differences between the *Shi jing* and *Chu ci* types of poetry than to subject them to a serious analytical investigation.

Perhaps the biggest of the differences which the Confucian apologists overlooked was the great gulf separating the oral, anonymous nature of the *Shi jing* songs from the personal, essentially literary character of the *Chu ci* poems.

Of the 305 songs of *Shi jing* there are exactly three in which the singer identifies himself by name.

> Ji Fu made this song
> Clear and cool as a breeze.
> Lord, long worn by care,
> May it bring your heart ease

concludes one of them at the end of several stanzas celebrating the achievements of a nobleman called Zhong-shan Fu. We know that Zhong-shan Fu was a great officer at the court of King Xuan of Zhou at the end of the ninth century B.C., but 'Ji Fu' means nothing to us; the name was as common as 'Thomas' or 'Peter' is today. Was he an amateur or a professional, a squire in Zhong-shan Fu's employment or a bard? We have no means of knowing. No hint of his own personality is revealed to us in his poem. We have even less idea of him than of the anonymous footsoldier who sings, elsewhere in the 'Songs', about the hardships of campaigning, or of the disillusioned wife who sings about her betrayal by a faithless husband. But all the songs, with their short stanzas and frequent refrains, are oral poetry, circulating, in some cases perhaps, for centuries before they were committed to writing.

The *Chu ci* poetry is quite different. Qu Yuan, whose great poem *Li sao*, 'On Encountering Trouble', stands at the head of the collection, thrusts himself from the very first line on our attention:

> Scion of the high lord Gao Yang,
> Bo Yong was my father's name.
> When She Ti pointed to the first month of the year
> On the day *geng-yin* I passed from the womb . . .

And throughout the whole of the long poem he remains in the forefront: 'I . . . I . . . I . . .' He bares his breast to us, examines his motives, admits his doubts, reveals his aspirations, argues, cites historical precedents in defence of his opinions – in short, he is no mere bard or song-maker like Ji Fu, but a *poet*. China's First Poet we can with some justice call him. Other Chu poets followed him and their names are known to us, but the personality of the great founder and Archpoet Qu Yuan eclipsed them all, so that later

generations tended to ascribe any old Chu poetry to him, and what
started off as a collection of the works of Qu Yuan and his School
came in time to be thought of as consisting entirely or almost
entirely of the works of the Master.

The Chu ci *Anthology*

The poetry of Qu Yuan and his immediate successors has reached
us as part of an anthology of Chu poetry edited and annotated by
Wang Yi, a librarian employed in the Imperial Library at Luoyang
by the Later Han emperor Shun Di in the second century A.D. The
anthology consists of seventeen works, of which about half are
ascribed by Wang Yi to Qu Yuan whilst the other half are mostly
imitative works in the Chu style written by poets of the Han
dynasty. Later 'Chu ci' anthologies, like that of the great Song
scholar Zhu Xi, omit some or all of these Han poems, but all are
based ultimately on the original edition by Wang Yi. The
seventeenth and last work in Wang Yi's anthology is a set of not
very inspired verses of his own composition. The anthology includes
his general introduction, his introductions to the separate works in
it, and a line-by-line commentary on the text, which in some
sections is in rhyming doggerel. It used to be thought that the
commentary on Wang Yi's own verses was, like all the rest, by him,
until someone noticed that it contains a gross misinterpretation of
the text and must therefore have been added by some anonymous
later editor.

Wang Yi's birthplace was a town which some four centuries
before his time had been a sort of secondary, northern capital of the
kings of Chu. In his commentary on *Chu ci* he was therefore in a
position to explain the occasional word of Chu dialect or Chu
custom that had survived into his own day. Apart from that,
however, he is a very unreliable guide. The Later Han was an age
of great scholars and exegetes, but Wang Yi was emphatically not of
their number. This would not have mattered but for the fact that in
the majority of cases he is the only authority we have for attributing
the works in the anthology to one or another author.

Chu ci, the title that Wang Yi gave his anthology, means literally
'Words of Chu'. (The term '*ci*' was used to denote an oral or written
text: the words of a song, an oath, a treaty, a speech, a poem, and
so forth.) Long before Wang Yi used it as the title of his anthology
it was in use as a vague collective title for the various works
associated with Qu Yuan and the early Chu poets, just as *Matière de
Bretagne* was used in medieval Europe as a collective title for the
vast corpus of prose and verse woven round the legend of King

Arthur and his knights and the quest of the grail. *Chu ci* was, as it were, the *Matière de Chu*, the name of a literary tradition.

It was a tradition that did not die out with the political extinction of Chu. During the early reigns of the Han dynasty, when political devolution gave the Han imperial princes almost sovereign power over their separate 'kingdoms', Chu poets continued to write poems in the Chu style at one or other of the Southern princely courts. One of the southern princes, Liu An, Prince of Huai-nan, had his court at Shou-chun, which had been the last capital of the Chu kings, and was himself a poet. When his young nephew, the brilliant Wu Di, became emperor, the imperial court itself became a patron of this kind of poetry. We hear of a poor Southern scholar being offered a place at the imperial court because of his ability to discuss *Chu ci* with the emperor, and of Liu An himself being commissioned to write an introduction to Qu Yuan's famous poem 'On Encountering Trouble'.

In the course of Wu Di's long and glorious reign, interest in the Chu poetry gave place to other literary fashions. Its eclipse was no doubt in part due to the appearance on the scene of Si-ma Xiang-ru, the greatest poet of the Han dynasty, who started off by writing in the Chu style but soon broke away from it in pursuit of new and more exciting models. When a revival of interest in Chu poetry occurred in the latter part of the emperor Xuan Di's reign some half a century later, the tradition was all but dead. We hear of an aged 'Mr Pi of Jiujiang' being summoned to court to recite and expound *Chu ci* to the emperor. He was so frail, we are told, that he had to be sustained with gruel at the end of each recital. The poet Wang Bao, who, like Si-ma Xiang-ru, came from Sichuan, and the great bibliographer and editor Liu Xiang, whose catalogue of the Han Imperial Library, completed by his son Liu Xin, is preserved in Ban Gu's 'History of the Former Han Dynasty', both began their careers at court during that reign and both became *Chu ci* enthusiasts and wrote poems in this style. Liu Xin's great contemporary, the philosopher, poet and lexicographer Yang Xiong, wrote an 'Anti-*Li sao*' in the Chu style, which has survived, and other imitations of early Chu poems which have not. In the latter half of the first century A.D. the historian Ban Gu and the scholar Jia Kui are both said to have written commentaries on *Li sao* ('On Encountering Trouble') which have unfortunately not survived – apart, that is, from a somewhat ungenerous appraisal of Qu Yuan's character by Ban Gu which must have been part of his Commentary. Wang Yi stands, therefore, at the end of a long tradition; but, except for a few fragments, all of it is lost. He is our only authority and we are obliged to make the best we can of what he tells us.

In Wang Yi's day there were two kinds of book: those written on rolls of silk called *juan* and the more old-fashioned kind written on thin, flat strips of bamboo pierced and threaded together like a miniature picket fence and rolled up in bundles called *pian*. Since the *pian* were made up of individual strips each carrying only a single column of writing, they were of very variable length. A long text might be divided for ease of handling (for example, we know that the Taoist classic *Lao zi* was always in two parts, an 'upper' and a 'lower' *pian*) but apart from that a *pian* could be of any length: there was no particular reason why you should not have a short essay or a poem of only a dozen or so lines written in a separate *pian* of its own. A *juan*, on the other hand, was not economical to make unless it was of a certain length. It therefore often happened that when old books were copied on to silk, the contents of several *pian* might be copied into a single *juan*. In its original format Wang Yi's anthology was written on seventeen silk *juan*.

But perhaps we should not call it 'Wang Yi's anthology'. In his general introduction, which in the original format would have appeared as a colophon at the end of the roll containing *Li sao*, he tells us that the anthology was not in fact compiled by him but by Liu Xiang nearly two centuries before his time. All he, Wang Yi, did, he tells us, was to add the seventeenth roll containing his own poems in the Chu style and, of course, his Commentary.

The way in which Wang Yi imparts this information is puzzling. When Liu Xiang was cataloguing the books in the Imperial Library, he tells us, he edited the original twenty-five *pian* of Qu Yuan's Collected Works into sixteen *juan*. Now it is true that if we look at the beginning of the 'Poetry' section of Liu Xiang's Catalogue in Ban Gu's 'History of the Former Han Dynasty' we find 'Collected Works of Qu Yuan in 25 *pian*'; and if we turn from that to the table of contents of Wang Yi's anthology and add up the titles of all the poems in it which he unhesitatingly ascribes to Qu Yuan (omitting 'The Great Summons', about which he says there was uncertainty), we do in fact arrive at a total of twenty-five:

1.	'On Encountering Trouble'	1 title
2.	'Nine Songs'	11 titles
3.	'Heavenly Questions'	1 title
4.	'Nine Pieces'	9 titles
5.	'Far-off Journey'	1 title
6.	'Divination'	1 title
7.	'The Fisherman'	1 title

$$1 + 11 + 1 + 9 + 1 + 1 + 1 = 25$$

But these twenty-five *pian* are contained in only seven *juan*. The sixteen *juan* of the anthology (i.e. the number of *juan* left after subtracting Wang Yi's own contribution to it) contain very much more than the collected works of Qu Yuan. A suspicion that Wang Yi is deceiving either himself or us begins to deepen when we look at the original order of the pieces.

The order in which the seventeen titles included in the anthology are found in all modern editions (which is the order followed in this translation) is the result of an editorial rearrangement dating from no earlier than the tenth or eleventh century. It represents a not very accurate attempt at placing the pieces in chronological order. An alternative order, which we know must have been Wang Yi's original one because of a cross-reference in his Commentary, is preserved in the textual notes of a twelfth-century editor:

1. *Li sao* ('On Encountering Trouble') by Qu Yuan
2. *Jiu bian* ('Nine Changes') by Song Yu
3. *Jiu ge* ('Nine Songs') by Qu Yuan
4. *Tian wen* ('Heavenly Questions') by Qu Yuan
5. *Jiu zhang* ('Nine Pieces') by Qu Yuan
6. *Yuan you* ('Far-off Journey') by Qu Yuan
7. *Bu ju* ('Divination') by Qu Yuan
8. *Yu fu* ('The Fisherman') by Qu Yuan
9. *Zhao yin shi* ('Summons for a Recluse') by Liu An
10. *Zhao hun* ('Summons of the Soul') by Song Yu
11. *Jiu huai* ('Nine Regrets') by Wang Bao
12. *Qi jian* ('Seven Remonstrances') by Dong-fang Shuo
13. *Jiu tan* ('Nine Laments') by Liu Xiang
14. *Ai shi ming* ('Alas That My Lot') by Zhuang Ji
15. *Xi shi* ('Sorrow for Troth Betrayed') by Jia Yi
16. *Da zhao* ('The Great Summons') by Qu Yuan, some say by Jing Cuo: authorship uncertain
17. *Jiu si* ('Nine Longings') by Wang Yi

If the first sixteen *juan* did in fact represent an anthology originally compiled by Liu Xiang, it is unthinkable that he would have put his own poems anywhere other than at the very end of the book. The question is then: was Wang Yi himself the compiler of this anthology and did he merely drag in Liu Xiang's name in order to lend a spurious air of authority to it, or did he really find the anthology in the imperial collection and assume that his famous predecessor, who edited and compiled so many other ancient texts, must have been the compiler of this one as well? As a matter of fact, there is one very good reason for thinking that Wang Yi was *not* himself the compiler but only the annotator of the anthology.

In the Chinese text of the anthology, though in almost no other source, Qu Yuan's great poem 'On Encountering Trouble' is called not '*Li sao*' but '*Li sao jing*'. Now this word '*jing*' is not part of the original title of the poem but is evidently one that was added by an early editor. It is the same '*jing*' that is found in '*Shi jing*' in the sense of 'scripture' or 'classic' or 'canonical text'. It was used by the Chinese schoolmen to distinguish the ancient master-text in which they specialized from the exegetical and amplificatory parts of the 'tradition' (*zhuan*) which they had to memorize along with it. The *zhuan* could be a commentary, like Mao's *zhuan* on *Shi jing*, or it could consist of material which was thought to be relevant but was only very tenuously connected with the master-text, like Han's *zhuan* on *Shi jing*, which is a collection of illustrative anecdotes, or Zuo's *zhuan* on the 'Spring and Autumn Annals', which is a chronicle history of contemporary events. One editor of *Chu ci* realized that the '*jing*' of '*Li sao jing*' was being used in this way, because in addition to printing the '*jing*' after '*Li sao*' he printed a '*zhuan*' after every one of the titles which follow it.

Since *Li sao jing* was immediately followed by a work which everyone confidently attributed to Qu Yuan's 'disciple' Song Yu, it follows that whoever compiled the original anthology must have thought of *Li sao* as the master-text written by the Archpoet himself and all the works which followed as merely 'School of Qu Yuan'. Of this school Song Yu alone is named because he was the greatest and best-remembered of the 'disciples'; the others remain anonymous, eclipsed by the shadow of their great Master. Much the same sort of thing happened – to name only one of many examples – in the case of the book *Zhuang zi*. Only the first few *pian* are likely to have been written by Zhuang Zhou himself; the rest, brilliant though some of them are, were written by anonymous philosophers of his 'school'.

Now in his introduction to *Li sao* Wang Yi not only misinterprets the words '*Li sao*' but then proceeds to misinterpret '*jing*' as though it were part of the title. (He says it means 'path', which of course it does not.) This proves beyond any doubt that he cannot have compiled the collection. The editorial attitude which the use of the word '*jing*' implies is one that he manifestly did not share.

If neither Liu Xiang nor Wang Yi himself was the compiler of this anthology, then who was? I do not think there is much hope of our being able to come up with an answer to this question, but by studying the (at first sight) haphazard order in which the pieces were originally arranged I believe we can go some way towards one.

First of all, though, it must be emphasized that the idea of Qu Yuan as author of one single great poem and not of the numerous other works that Wang Yi attributes to him, far from being a modern or revolutionary one, was probably the view of him most widely current at the beginning of the Han dynasty.

> Qu Yuan, a virtuous minister of Chu, was banished because of a slander. He wrote the poem *Li sao*, ending with the words 'Enough! there are no true men in the state: no one understands me.' Then he threw himself into the river and was drowned.

This brief account of him is found in the first-century biography of Jia Yi in the 'History of the Former Han Dynasty', but is almost certainly based on material more nearly contemporary with Jia Yi (early second century B.C.). Early Han references to Qu Yuan invariably speak of his writing the *Li sao* after being banished by King Huai and of his throwing himself into the river after its completion. It was only later that a somewhat more elaborate curriculum vitae was worked out for him in which allowance was made for his having written various other works. The late Guo Mo-ruo took this process to an extreme by giving him more than twenty years of busy, creative life between his estrangement from King Huai and his final suicide, at the age of sixty-two according to Guo's computations, in the River Mi-luo.

If we now re-examine the table on p. 31 bearing all this in mind, I think it will seem a not unreasonable assumption that the first nine titles in it represent a '*Chu ci*' anthology compiled by Liu An, Prince of Huai-nan – probably in about 135 B.C., when the Prince was spending a good deal of time at the imperial court. The collection begins with the master-text *Li sao* (for which the emperor commissioned Liu An to write an introduction), follows with seven works belonging to the School of Qu Yuan (beginning with one by his most famous 'disciple') and concludes with a piece by Liu An himself.

Lighting on this collection some century or so later, Liu Xiang had only to abstract the pieces ascribed to Song Yu and Liu An in order to arrive at the 'Works of Qu Yuan in 25 *pian*' listed in his catalogue of the Imperial Library and several times referred to by Wang Yi. Besides doing that, however, he would almost certainly have had Liu An's collection (including the pieces by Song Yu and Liu An) copied on to silk rolls; and while he was about it, it would be quite natural that he should want to amplify it and bring it up to date.

Consider the first thirteen titles of the table on p. 31, which I take to be Liu Xiang's enlargement of the Prince of Huai-nan's anthology. Assuming, not unreasonably, that the criterion governing Liu An's selection had been that the works selected should be either *by* or *about* Qu Yuan (regardless of genre or style), Liu Xiang would have included Song Yu's 'Summons of the Soul' in his enlarged anthology probably because he was under the (mistaken) impression that the soul being summoned in it was Qu Yuan's. Liu An's anthology already has something by Song Yu in it, he would have argued: in that case, if it is to retain Liu An's own rather slight 'Summons' (No. 9), surely it ought also to include the much more important 'Summons' by Song Yu?

Dong-fang Shuo's 'Seven Remonstrances' – if they really are by Dong-fang Shuo – were written by a contemporary of Liu An at the court of the emperor Wu Di. Their subject is Qu Yuan: indeed, Qu Yuan is the persona through which the poet in them speaks. That would be sufficient grounds for Liu Xiang's including them on the 'by or about' principle.

Wang Bao, author of No. 11, was one of the poets of the *Chu ci* revival which took place in the second half of Xuan Di's reign when Liu Xiang, too, started his career at the imperial court. Liu Xiang could scarcely append his own poems to the anthology without including the 'Chu' poems of this well-known contemporary poet. He would have had Liu An's precedent for doing so, of course; but Liu An was an imperial prince and Liu Xiang was not. A cynic might say that Nos. 10–12 were included by Liu Xiang only as an excuse for appending his own masterpiece to the collection.

One modern Chinese scholar continues to insist that Liu Xiang *was* the compiler of Wang Yi's anthology, i.e. of *juan* 1–16 of the anthology we read today, explaining the three final *juan* (14–16) as a sort of appendix which Liu Xiang put at the very end, after his own 'Nine Laments', because he regarded their authorship as uncertain. I very much doubt this. Wang Yi always repeats whatever he has been told. In the case of No. 16, 'The Great Summons', he tells us that some people attributed it to Qu Yuan and some to Jing Cuo and concludes by leaving the matter open; but that is the only title of the three about which he expresses any uncertainty. We may not ourselves find the attribution of 14 and 15 very convincing, but Wang Yi shows no uncertainty on the subject whatsoever. His authority, whoever it was, must have been equally dogmatic. The case for Liu Xiang's appendix of queried items does not really stand.

And of course what finally eliminates Liu Xiang as the compiler of the sixteen-roll collection is the fact that he did not, any more than Wang Yi, think of *Li sao* as *jing* and all the other works as *zhuan*. To him the order of pieces in Liu An's collection must have seemed merely eccentric, since it is clear from the entry in his Catalogue that he regarded Nos. 1–8 as consisting not of No. 1 by Qu Yuan and Nos. 2–8 by disciples of Qu Yuan (of whom Song Yu, the author of No. 2, was the most famous), but of No. 1 by

Qu Yuan, No. 2 by Song Yu, and Nos. 3–8 by Qu Yuan. (The '25 *pian*' of Qu Yuan's works in the Catalogue consist of No. 1 plus the contents of Nos. 3–8.) Whoever added the three *juan* of extra material to Liu Xiang's enlargement of Liu An's little anthology to produce the 16-*juan* anthology on which Wang Yi based his Commentary was more sceptical than either Liu Xiang or Wang Yi on the subject of Qu Yuan's authorship, since he was prepared to put Nos. 3–8 in the same category as Nos. 2 and 10 by Song Yu; whereas Liu Xiang and Wang Yi regarded Nos. 3–8 as belonging to the same category as *Li sao*.

That there were people in Liu Xiang's day and even after it who were more sceptical about the 'Works of Qu Yuan' is made abundantly clear by the example of Yang Xiong, which we shall presently be examining. And Ban Gu and Jia Kui, both of whom wrote commentaries (now lost) on Qu Yuan's *Li sao* but on no other part of *Chu ci*, may have been consciously following Liu An's example, in which case they may have shared his views about the relative authenticity of the different 'works'. It is indeed not impossible that one or other of them may have been responsible for the 16-*juan* anthology.

The only Former Han source which mentions works by Qu Yuan other than *Li sao* (apart from Liu Xiang's single reference to *Jiu zhang* in one of his *Jiu tan* poems) is the double biography of Qu Yuan and Jia Yi by the historian Si-ma Qian (145–86 B.C.). Several of Si-ma Qian's biographies are linked ones, like those in Plutarch's *Lives*. Those of Qu Yuan and Jia Yi (?–168 B.C.) are linked because Jia Yi shared with Qu Yuan the fate of being a prescient statesman who was wrongfully banished and because, while on his way into banishment, he wrote a 'Lament for Qu Yuan', a copy of which he dropped into the River Xiang as an offering to the earlier poet's ghost.

In the section of the double biography devoted to Qu Yuan, Si-ma Qian cites the fifth of the *Jiu zhang* poems, 'Embracing Sand', in its entirety; and in the Appraisal, with which the double biography concludes, he mentions the third of them: 'When I read the works of Qu Yuan – the "Heavenly Questions", "A Lament for Ying" and "Summons of the Soul" – I get an impression of the kind of man he was.' He has already mentioned *Li sao* in the biography itself and does so again in the Autobiographical Preface to his 'History', where 'Qu Yuan writing the *Li sao* after his banishment' is one of the examples of literary creativity being born out of affliction with which he comforts himself for his own misfortune. (He had suffered the horrible and humiliating punishment of castration for having stood up to the emperor Wu Di in one of his

rages and continued to write his 'History' after undergoing it.) If we
collate all that Si-ma Qian says about works written by Qu Yuan,
we come up with this rather peculiar list:

> *Li sao*
> *Tian wen*
> *Ai Ying* ⎫
> *Huai sha* ⎬ Nos. 3 and 5 of *Jiu zhang*
> *Zhao hun* ⎭

Modern Chinese scholars have made somewhat heavy weather of the
fact that Si-ma Qian attributed *Zhao hun* to Qu Yuan, whereas
Wang Yi – and, it may be inferred, Liu Xiang – ascribed it
unhesitatingly to Song Yu; and the fact that the *Jiu zhang* poems
have individual titles, that Si-ma Qian ascribes only two of them to
Qu Yuan, and that Yang Xiong, in his imitations of Qu Yuan, used
only five of them as models has suggested to some scholars that Liu
Xiang, whose reference to *Jiu zhang* in one of his own poems[3] is the
earliest mention of that name in any text, was himself the person
who first put those nine poems together and gave them their
collective title.

In fact, if the 'early', i.e. pre-Han, *Chu ci* was thought of as a
collection comprising Qu Yuan's *Li sao* and other works by Qu
Yuan and his School, it would have been a matter of mere personal
caprice to decide whether the author of one of the 'other works' was
to be identified as Qu Yuan himself, as a particular 'disciple', or as
Anon. Si-ma Qian probably assumed – correctly – that the object of
the summons was a king and could therefore see no reason why its
author should not have been Qu Yuan himself; Liu An *et al.*
assumed that the object of the summons was Qu Yuan, in which
case the author had to be Qu Yuan's most important disciple.

As for the *Jiu zhang* poems, Liu Xiang is most unlikely to have
been their original compiler or even the first person to give them
their collective title. *Jiu zhang* is not the only *Chu ci* title which
represents a later compilation of originally independent poems; *Jiu
ge*, *Jiu bian* and *Jiu zhang* are, all three of them, compilations. All
three – the first manifestly, since it contains eleven titles – comprise
more than nine poems or parts of poems, and all three were
arranged in their present form with a view to some kind of
performance. Their titles are related. Those of *Jiu ge* and *Jiu bian*

---

3. The sixth of the 'Nine Laments': 'Sadly I sang the *Li sao* to give vent to my
feelings/ But I could not get to the end of *Jiu zhang*/ For the long sobs
rose in my throat and choked me . . .' See p. 294, *ll.*33–5.

are legendary and are referred to as such in *Li sao*.[4] *Jiu bian* ('Nine Changes') was the music brought down from heaven by the legendary Xia king Qi, and *Jiu ge* were the songs which were sung to it. 'Nine' in antiquity meant 'many', 'several' or 'various', and the 'changes' are presumably 'modes'. It is, therefore, quite likely that the '*Jiu bian*' of the legend originally meant no more than 'the modes' or 'modal music'. Musicians of a later, more sophisticated age no doubt understood it in a literal sense and attempted to 'reconstruct' nine-part modal sequences believed to have existed in ancient times.[5]

This almost certainly explains the use of the titles *Jiu ge* and *Jiu bian* in *Chu ci*. The poems existed prior to the music and the music probably existed prior to the arrangement of the poems in their present form. In any case it would only have been after their editing and arrangement for musical performance that the poems would have acquired their collective titles.

The editing of the constituent parts of *Jiu zhang* ('Nine Musical Pieces') into a single cycle would certainly have been later than that of *Jiu bian*; on the other hand, it would certainly have taken place long before Liu Xiang's day. To Liu Xiang, *Jiu zhang* were nine poems written by Qu Yuan. To the compiler of *Jiu zhang*, they were Chu poems, one or two of which might have been written by Qu Yuan, suitable for arrangement as a nine-part musical suite. The *raison d'être* of *Jiu zhang*'s compilation, in other words, has to do with musical requirements rather than with theories of authorship. It belongs to a period when *Chu ci* was still a lively and flourishing tradition, not to a period of antiquarian literary revival. It cannot, in short, belong to an age later than that of the Prince of Huai-nan, whose editorial activities, I have already suggested, provided the basis for Liu Xiang's '25 *pian*'.

Some of the twenty-five *pian*, it has long been recognized, cannot possibly have been written by Qu Yuan himself. *Bu ju* ('Divination') and *Yu fu* ('The Fisherman') are anecdotes *about* Qu Yuan. The second of them is actually incorporated by Si-ma Qian –

---

4. *Jiu ge* ('Nine Songs'), *Jiu bian* ('Nine Changes') and *Jiu zhao* or *Jiu shao* ('Nine Summonings') are different components of the same liturgy: *Jiu bian* refers to the music played, *Jiu ge* to the words sung to it, and *Jiu zhao* to the accompanying dances. Cf. *Li sao*, *l.*145, which links the Nine Songs with the Nine Changes, and *id.*, *l.*363, which links the Nine Songs with the Shao Dances. In the legends, as the modern scholar Jiang Liang-fu has pointed out, these titles were used almost interchangeably.

5. For a late example of this sort of thing, see 'Chiang K'uei's Nine Songs for Yüeh' by Laurence Picken in *The Musical Quarterly* 43 (1957), pp. 201–19.

without acknowledgement – into the narrative of Qu Yuan's biography. And *Yuan you* ('Far-off Journey') is a Taoist poem obviously inspired by *Li sao*, from which it makes frequent borrowings. At the same time it bears marked similarities to the Han poet Si-ma Xiang-ru's 'Rhymeprose of the Great Man', of which, indeed, the late Guo Mo-ruo believed it to be an early draft. It cannot, at all events, be by the author of *Li sao*.

If we forget these somewhat arid wrangles about authorship, which occupy so disproportionate an amount of the time and energy of modern *Chu ci* experts, and consider only the nature of the contents of this anthology, we find that the 'early' poems in it, i.e. those traditionally believed to be of pre-Han provenance, divide quite naturally into two classes: those which are functional, explicitly shamanistic and in which the presence of the poet – if there is one – is unseen; and those which are personal, confessional or self-revelatory, in which the poet speaks to us in his own voice and the shamanism, if there is any, is incidental, a mere part of the background of received ideas and beliefs on which the poet draws for his materials. Suppose we call these two classes 'Category A' and 'Category B'; omitting the two short narratives *Bu ju* and *Yu fu*, we arrive at the following table:

Category A

Jiu ge ('Nine Songs'):	invocations by shamans used in the public worship of various gods.
Zhao hun ('Summons of the Soul'): *Da zhao* ('The Great Summons'):	invocations by shamans used in the public summoning back of wandering souls.
Tian wen ('Heavenly Questions'):	a shamanistic (?) catechism consisting of questions about cosmological, astronomical, mythological and historical matters.

Category B

Li sao ('On Encountering Trouble'):	an autobiographical poem, representing real persons and events allegorically, in which the poet complains of undeserved rejection by his king, consults shamans, and embarks on a shamanistic 'flight' in an unsuccessful quest for a divine mate.

Jiu bian ('Nine Changes'):	complaints of a rejected courtier, using much the same imagery as *Li sao*, the concluding section being a shamanistic 'flight' of the poet through the heavens attended by minor deities.
Jiu zhang ('Nine Pieces'):	complaints, similar to those of *Jiu bian* and *Li sao*, of a loyal minister wrongfully rejected by his prince; some of the poems contain accounts of actual journeys made by the poet on the way to, or in the course of, his banishment.
Yuan you ('Far-off Journey'):	long poem obviously influenced by *Li sao*, most of it an account of a shamanistic 'flight' through the heavens; rather like a development of the last section of *Jiu bian*.

Whatever the age or the authorship of the different pieces in these two lists, it seems obvious that the *type* of poem found in Category A must have existed long before the *type* of poem found in Category B. That is not, of course, to say that the actual poems in the Category A list are earlier than those in the Category B one. The Category A texts may be later literary 'improvements' on, or imitations of, earlier shamanistic originals. This is, in fact, what Wang Yi – though perhaps it was no more than an inspired guess – says about the genesis of the present text of *Jiu ge*.[6] The fact remains that, in principle, *Chu ci* represents the cannibalization by a new, secular, literary tradition of an earlier, religious, oral one. Hence the title. For what these heterogeneous works have in common is not, as later editors came to believe, that they were all written by Qu Yuan or that they all belong to a particular genre or that they are written in a similar sort of verse, but that, whether traditional shaman songs or imitations of shaman songs or examples of the new secular poetry which developed out of them, they all, in one way or another, have their origins in Chu shamanism.

Two factors seem to strengthen this hypothesis. First of all, the works in these two categories are distinguished not only by the nature of their contents, but also by metrical differences. *Zhao hun*, *Da zhao* and *Tian wen* in Category A are all three of them written in what appears to be a development of the quadruple metres of *Shi*

6. For a discussion of Wang Yi's explanation of the origins of *Jiu ge*, see pp. 96–7.

jing. The typical song line of *Shi jing* is one of four equally accented syllables:

> *Guan guan ju jiu*   'Guan, guan,' the ospreys cry
> *Zai he zhi zhou*   On the island in the river

are the opening lines of the first song in the first section of *Shi jing*, and all four lines of the first stanza have the same *tum tum tum tum* beat. The monotony of this heavy, thumping measure can be varied, however, by weakening the fourth beat in alternate lines. This is done by placing a pronoun or a nonce-word refrain in the fourth position:

> tum tum tum tum
> tum tum tum ti
> tum tum tum tum
> tum tum tum ti

Tian wen, of the above-mentioned poems, is prosodically just like *Shi jing*: quadrisyllabic lines, mostly arranging themselves into rhyming quatrains, sometimes with a strong beat at the end of every line, sometimes with strong and weak endings alternating. The metre of the two 'Summons' poems is a development of this in which the weak lines end with the same nonce-word refrain throughout the poem and the strong–weak pattern has become invariable, producing the effect of a seven-syllable line with a caesura after the fourth syllable and a single-syllable refrain after the seventh. In *Zhao hun* the refrain is (in modern pronunciation) *xie*, in *Da zhao* it is *zhi*.

> *Zhao hun*   tum tum tum tum : tum tum tum xie
> *Da zhao*   tum tum tum tum : tum tum tum zhi

The songs of *Jiu ge* are in a metre unlike anything found in *Shi jing*. Each line of the songs contains a refrain-word, but instead of being at the end of the line, it comes in the middle. The refrain-word used in these songs is *xi*. It is occasionally encountered in *Shi jing*, but its invariable use inside the line is first found in *Chu ci*. Its significance is probably melismatic and it should perhaps be thought of as representing a musical rather than a purely metrical development. The lines of *Jiu ge* vary considerably in length, though all are fairly short. The shortest line has two syllables on either side of the *xi*:

> tum tum xi tum tum

but three before and two after is common:

> tum tum tum xi tum tum

and three on each side of the *xi* is also found in some poems:

tum tum tum xi tum tum tum

The use of this metre became widespread during the early reigns of the Han dynasty, when most songs, whether religious or secular, were written in it – a fact sometimes obscured by the contemporary tendency to save labour by omitting the *xi*, leaving its presence to be understood.

The Category B poems, on the other hand, are almost wholly written in long, flowing lines suitable for recitation, differing, therefore, from the Category A metres in much the same way that Greek epic metre differed from lyric ones. Because *Li sao* is the earliest example of it, it is often spoken of as the 'Sao style'. It looks as if it might have been deliberately created by putting two Song-style lines together and welding them into a single long line. There is every reason to believe that Qu Yuan himself may have been its inventor.

Di Gao Yang zhi miao-yi xi: zhen huang kao yue Bo Yong
tum tum tum ti tum tum xi: tum tum tum ti tum tum

The opening line of *Li sao* with its ten stressed and two unstressed syllables divided in two by the refrain-word *xi* could easily be resolved into two short Song-style lines:

Di Gao Yang *xi* miao-yi
Zhen huang kao *xi* Bo Yong

It was, I believe, the reverse of this process which produced the lengthened Sao-style line. The lyrical measures of Category A make an occasional appearance in these B poems when a brief contrast is required – for example, in the *luan* or 'envoi' at the end of some of the *Jiu zhang* poems. In one solitary example, the beautiful 'Orange Tree' poem, the heptasyllabic 'Summons' measure is used throughout.

The other indication that Category B represents a later secular literature and Category A the oral religious tradition that it developed from is the use the *Li sao* poet makes of themes and even verbal formulae that are found in *Jiu ge* and *Tian wen* – for example, the poet's allegorical wooing of the water goddess Fu Fei in *Li sao*, *ll*.217–28, which parallels, both verbally and thematically, the shaman's quest of the river goddess in the third of the *Jiu ge* songs. No doubt the *Jiu ge* song is a somewhat late and rather literary example of its type – it may, indeed, have been worked on by the *Li sao* poet himself, as Wang Yi affirms – but the derivative nature of the *Li sao* passage is unmistakable.

Shamanism and Chu Poetry

Curiously enough, the Chinese secular poet's most fruitful borrowing from the shaman, the spirit journey or 'flight', is something we hear little about in accounts, whether ancient or modern, of Chinese shamans, though it is often the first thing we are told about shamans in other parts of the world. When the Nišan shamaness in sixteenth-century Manchuria[7] was engaged by bereaved parents to bring a dead boy back to life, she flew off, attended by her helper spirits, to haggle with the rulers of the underworld for possession of the dead boy's soul, rather as Orpheus had to for the soul of Eurydice. The Chinese shamans in the 'Summons' poems have a good deal to say about the underworld and various other unpleasant places in which the errant soul may be straying, but they do not, as far as I can make out, actually go off themselves in quest of it; they seem content merely to shout at it from a safe distance: 'Come back, come back! It is much nicer here, where we are!' The shamans patronized by Emperor Wu in the second century B.C. seem, like modern mediums, to have specialized in producing spirit voices and, rather exceptionally, in causing the spirits to materialize, but we hear nothing about their going off personally to fetch them.

Centuries later, in Bo Juyi's famous poem 'The Ballad of Everlasting Regret', the magician employed by another Chinese emperor to make contact with his dead favourite does in fact undertake very extensive spirit journeys in his search for her, eventually locating her in a palace on one of the Islands of the Blessed which float in mid-air above the waters of the Eastern Ocean; but Bo Juyi evidently regarded him as some sort of Taoist. In *Jiu ge* the shamans simulate river journeys in quest of the river goddess (hardly 'spirit journeys', these, since the worship of river deities often entailed real outings in real boats: see p. 106), and in a hymn addressed to one of the celestial deities the shaman hints at assignations with the god among the constellations and journeys made in his company. But the overall picture – though it is very hard to be sure of this – seems to be of shamans firmly planted on the ground, calling on their gods, like the priests of Baal, to come down amongst them.

Spirit journeys made apparently for fun rather than for any practical purpose are attributed by Qu Yuan's contemporary, the Taoist philosopher Zhuang Zi, not to shamans but to hermits living

7. See Margaret Nowak and Stephen Durrant, *The Tale of the Nišan Shamaness: A Manchu Folk Epic*, University of Washington Press, 1977.

in the mountains who made themselves 'pure as virgins' by learning to subsist on a diet of dew. The more grandiose sort of aerial travel, in dragon chariot attended by minor deities and assorted mythical birds and beasts, is attributed in legend not to shamans but to god-kings like the Yellow Ancestor.

The problem is partly one of terminology. 'Shamanism' is a word invented by nineteenth-century anthropologists from the Tungusic word *shaman*. Modern anthropologists have exercised their proprietorial right to define it in various ways, generally rather narrowly, but in popular usage it has come to apply to a rather wide range of religious beliefs and practices for which old-fashioned terms like 'animism' and 'sorcery' are felt to be inadequate or unsuitably patronizing. Before considering its use in a Chinese context, let me attempt to list what I believe to be the characteristics most commonly attributed to its practitioners.

(1) A shaman is an expert in spirit-matters who knows the world of spirits at first hand and can use this knowledge to give professional advice and assistance to his (or her) fellow men.

(2) Shamans often receive their vocation during, or as a result of, an illness – what is sometimes called the *maladie initiatique*.

(3) Shamans are able, while in a state of trance or ecstasy, to project their souls on journeys into the world of spirits.

(4) Shamans often receive guidance from a long-dead Shaman Ancestor who in some cases is thought to have been the First Shaman or the inventor of shaman techniques: ecstasy, healing, etc.

(5) Drumming and dancing are the almost invariable accompaniment of the shaman's self-induced ecstasy.

The now common practice I have followed in using the word 'shaman' as a substitute for the Chinese word *wu* (Japanese *miko*, which is written with the same character) is, I believe, fully justified; but it can occasionally become a source of confusion. This is due to the fact, already mentioned in the first section of this Introduction, that the status of *wu* early underwent a profound change for the worse. Under the Shang kings *wu*, like the great churchmen of medieval and Tudor England, often held important offices of state. An early text insists on the intellectual and moral excellence required in those wishing to fit themselves for this profession. The Shaman Ancestor Wu Xian, consulted by Qu Yuan in the *Li sao* and referred to in the contemporary 'Commination of Chu' as 'the great and glorious god Wu Xian', is named in one ancient source as the inventor of divination and in another as a divine healer. He was also credited with the authorship of an early work on astronomy.

Evidently the ancient Chinese shaman was a master of many arts and a repository of many kinds of lore. In the course of centuries, however, as the *wu*'s status sank and more and more of what had once been *wu* accomplishments were taken over by other specialists, the term '*wu*' came to have a far more limited connotation. In making a study of Chinese shamanism it is easy to forget that the dwindling functions of the *wu* are not necessarily indicative of the atrophy of shamanism itself but of a growing specialization taking place within it. The fairy men or Perfecti of Zhuang Zi and the *fang-shi* or wizards who flew through the air, scouring the universe in search of an emperor's lost favourite, were, we may be sure, performing what, in an earlier age, had been part of the stock-in-trade of the *wu*. A later age, unable to see any connection between the illiterate witch-doctors who ministered to the needs of credulous villagers and the majestic beings who in days gone by had charioted across the firmament attended by troops of subservient gods and spirits, attributed the exercise of such supernatural potency to legendary kings or mythological heroes.

In fact, many aspects of shamanism which in the case of other cultures we learn about from the fieldwork of anthropologists are to be found paralleled in Chinese mythology. For example, when the anthropologist Andreas Lommel[8] informs us that he was told by an Australian shaman that he visited the world of spirits 'to learn new dances from them', we are at once reminded of Qi's visits to heaven from which he brought back the Nine Songs and the Shao dances that were danced to them. The Chinese myth to which this story belongs turns out to be connected with shamanism at almost every point. Qi's father, Yu, was born as a result of a Caesarean section performed on his dead father, Gun, who was thereupon revived by shamans (see 'Heavenly Questions', *ll*.73–6, p. 129) and turned into a bear. Yu himself assumed a bear's shape from time to time. During the Han dynasty exorcists dressed in bear skins were a regular feature of New Year celebrations at the imperial court. Yu, like several other heroes of antiquity, appears to have been lame. A hopping dance called the 'Yu Walk' or the 'Yu Steps' was performed by shamans and sorcerers in historical times. Qi's mother, the goddess of Tu-shan mountain, who turned into stone when she caught sight of Yu in his bear shape, was believed to have

8. In *Die Unambal, ein Stamm in Nordwest-Australien: Ergebnisse der Frobenius Expedition 1938–9*, Hamburg, 1952.

invented the Southern style of singing which was used by Chu shamans in their invocations. And so on.

An interesting example of specialization depriving the *wu* of his functions and consequently narrowing the connotation of the term concerns the shaman's art of healing. In primitive societies all illness is believed to be psychic in origin, and the shaman, with his specialized knowledge of the spirit world, is the only healer. (The belief is not confined to primitive societies, of course – readers of the *Tale of Genji* will recall that the sophisticated courtiers in that novel almost always attributed their illnesses to possession and resorted to the priest or exorcist for their cure – but the shaman's monopoly of healing probably is.) Now, in China the shamans must, at a very early date, have enhanced their spiritual therapy with knowledge of a pharmacological kind. According to an ancient tradition, medicine and divination were invented by two Shaman Ancestors: medicine by Wu Peng and divination by Wu Xian.[9] The character for 'Peng' represents the sound made by a drum and would anciently have had a pronunciation something like *boom*. Wu Peng is therefore Shaman Boom. No doubt his ministrations included drumming and dancing to induce the state of trance in which he would be able to deal in whatever way was appropriate with the soul of the sick person he was treating. However, in the 'Book of Seas and Mountains', a text which some scholars believe to have been compiled by Chu shamans, we find this same Shaman Boom in the company of five other shamans on the top of Kun-lun, the World Mountain, with a life-restoring herb in his hand;[10] and there are other early references to shamans collecting and dispensing medicinal herbs. The words for 'healing' and 'divination' were once both written with characters which included the symbol for *wu* or 'shaman'. The 'divination' character is still written in this way,[11] but in the character for 'healing' the 'shaman' element was early replaced by the symbol for a bottle. This change in the script symbolized a change in medical practice. The science of medicine, including diagnosis by sphygmoscopy and the use of herbal

9. In *Li sao*, ll.279–300, Wu Xian makes an appearance to confirm the divination already made for the poet by the shaman Ling Fen.

10. The text of the 'Book of Seas and Mountains' appears to consist of the collected explanations of illustrations on a long-lost *mappa mundi*; hence everything, including long-past events, is frozen in a perpetual present: 'Here is XYZ being killed' and so forth.

11. Not the modern word for 'divination', I hasten to add, which has a quite different etymology. The 'divination' written with the *wu* symbol refers specifically to divination made with twigs or stalks – the kind associated with the *Yi jing* and, incidentally, the kind resorted to by Qu Yuan in the *Li sao* – and is no longer in current use in the colloquial language.

remedies, was already, by the first century A.D. and perhaps much earlier, a specialization from which *wu* were excluded and which educated people were more and more coming to prefer to the services of the drumming and dancing *wu*, who would now be called in only when all else had failed, and without any very strong expectation of success. The sceptic Wang Chong, writing in the first century, tells a story of a man with a sick son calling in a *wu* because he could not – or thought he could not – afford the services of a 'really good doctor'. The boy dies, and Wang Chong assumes that we shall think the man a fool for preferring a *wu* to the skilled physician who was in fact available.

In ancient China one of the shaman's most important contributions to human welfare was rain-making. He[12] did this by means of dancing and incantations; but if dancing and incantations failed, he might be exposed naked in the sun, in the hope that his sufferings would move the gods to pity, or, in extreme cases, he might be burned alive. The importance of his rain-making function is clearly demonstrated in the character *ling*, which is made up of the symbols for *wu* and 'rain'. The word *ling* must originally have been used to denote the shaman's spiritual power, with particular reference to his power to make rain, but it came in time to mean any sort of supernatural power, whether of the shaman, of the gods and spirits, or even of inanimate objects like talismans and herbs if they were believed to be preternaturally potent. Wang Yi tells us that the word *ling* could be used in the Chu dialect, by metonymy, to mean the shamans themselves, i.e. as a substitute for the word *wu*. In fact we find it being used in *Chu ci* in no less than four different ways: (1) of the supernatural powers of shamans or gods; (2) of the shamans themselves; (3) of the gods themselves; and (4) in combination with other words to make proper names, in which case it probably has the sense of 'divine' or 'holy'. In *Li sao* the poet gives such names to himself, to his king and to the Shaman Ancestor who divines for him the course he should take in his aerial travels.

Rain-making may have been the original purpose of the Chinese shaman's 'flight'. In order to manipulate natural forces like wind and rain, it would have been necessary to win mastery over the nature gods who controlled them. The majestic aerial progress

12. Or she. One ancient source does in fact maintain that the word *wu* was confined to female shamans and another word, *xi*, used for the males; but in practice *xi* is never found and *wu* seems to have been used impartially for male and female alike. Frequent use of the term *nü wu* ('female *wu*') in texts dating from the Han period suggests that by that time *wu* by itself was taken to mean a male shaman unless otherwise specified.

through the heavens with gods and spirits in attendance as described in *Li sao* and other poems may have been the way in which this mastery was obtained. The idea that it could be undertaken in order to acquire magical or spiritual power, not for the purpose of rain-making but as an end in itself, may have been a later development. In *Li sao* the spirit journey is an allegory and the idea of rain-making must in any case have been far from the poet's mind; nevertheless, lingering traces of a rain-making ritual are unintentionally preserved in it. The poet's cortège includes clouds, rainbows and the gods of rain, wind and thunder, all of which a rain-making shaman would need to have at his command, and his chariot is drawn by flying dragons, which in Chinese tradition have always been associated with clouds and rain.

The idea that a ritual journey, usually a ritual circuit, could be a means of acquiring or affirming power proved an extraordinarily persistent one, recurring in different forms in art, literature, even in political theory. Along with it there developed the idea of a symmetrical, mandala-like cosmos whose various parts were presided over by various powers. These powers could be induced to give either their submission or their support to the traveller who approached them with the correct ritual. A complete and successful circuit of the cosmos would therefore make him a lord of the universe, able to command any of its powers at will. The astrologers of Mo Zi's day, a little before the time of Qu Yuan, regarded God himself as a sort of super-shaman, perpetually engaged in just such a power-sustaining circuit:

> God kills the green dragon of the east on *jia* and *yi* days, the red dragon of the south on *bing* and *ding* days, the white dragon of the west on *geng* and *xin* days, and the black dragon of the north on *ren* and *gui* days.[13]

A mandala-like cosmos presided over not by coloured dragons but by coloured *di* or sky gods, each with his attendant theriomorphic guardian, is hinted at in the 'Far-off Journey', a somewhat later poem than *Li sao*, whose protagonist is evidently a mystic and whose object appears to be the attainment of spiritual enlightenment rather than of magic power.

The theriomorphic guardians appear in representations of the cosmos on bronze mirror-backs dating from the first century B.C., surrounded in at least one instance by a circular inscription of

---

13. *Mo Zi*, Ch. 47: 'Gui yi'. The days referred to belong to the ancient ten-day week. The two middle days, *wù* and *ji*, were presumably God's days of rest.

doggerel verses about the Taoist fairy men who live on dew and ride above the clouds on flying dragons.

The period of imperial unification was propitious to cosmological theories, particularly to the fashionable new Five Elements theory, which soon attained the status of an official orthodoxy. The four sky gods became five (one for the centre)[14] and emperors were urged by their advisers to extend their suzerainty into the world of spirits by making a ritual circuit of the empire and sacrificing in turn on each of the Five Holy Mountains situated in the northern, southern, eastern, western and central portions of their domains. The circuit was to begin at Tai-shan in the east, the holiest mountain of them all. Only two emperors, the first Qin emperor and the Han emperor Wu, attempted this ritual progress, and neither of them completed it; but the mere fact that it was undertaken at all shows the extent to which these ideas, deriving from a now somewhat discredited shamanism, continued to haunt men's minds.

The mandala-cosmos of the mirror-backs and the later Chu poems is not to be found in *Li sao*. The aerial journey in *Li sao* certainly has many of the characteristics of a magic-making progress, but the cosmos in which it takes place is not defined. Even the route taken is uncertain. We are vaguely given to understand that it is westward, like the journey of the sun; but the itinerary could in no way be described as a circuit. The airborne *Li sao* poet employs gods as his lackeys, orders the sun to stand still, and in general behaves as if he were a master of the universe. In that respect he resembles the cloud-commanding shamans of my hypothesis or the triumphant mystic of the 'Far-off Journey'. In two other respects, however, his journey is very unlike a power-affirming rite. (1) The main purpose of it appears to be erotic: the poet complains (*l.*216) that he has no woman, and a substantial section of *Li sao* is thereafter devoted to the quest for some goddess or legendary princess who shall become his 'mate'; (2) in spite of his masterful behaviour with minor deities, everything undertaken on this journey, including the quest for a 'fair lady', proves a failure; it ends in sadness, frustration and despair.

It would be possible, as I have suggested elsewhere, to explain the sexual imagery of *Li sao* which turns kings into mistresses or paramours and courtiers into sexual rivals as a product of the

---

14. Gods of the Five Directions (north, south, east, west and centre) appear, however, to be worshipped by shamans in other parts of the world where – as far as I know – no Five Elements theory exists: 'The Californian Yokut appealed to the gods who ruled the sacred four directions and the vital centre.' (See 'Stones, Bones and Skin', p. 41, in *Arts Canada* 1973/4.)

allegorical interpretation of *Shi jing* – and the influence of *Shi jing* can never be discounted. But when we compare this 'quest' part of the *Li sao* journey with the 'goddess' poems of the 'Nine Songs', the conclusion is inescapable that the combination of erotic pursuit and lachrymose despair which so exactly suits the mood of his poem was taken over by Qu Yuan from contemporary shamanism.

In the 'Nine Songs' the shamans and shamanesses appear to be actually wooing the deities they invoke, but the wooing seems invariably to end in sadness and frustration. The male shaman of the third hymn pursues the elusive river goddess in a boat shaped like a flying dragon, sighing and groaning for love of her, like any troubadour. His 'tears run down over cheek and chin'; he is 'choked with longing'. When it becomes apparent that he is not going to find her, he leaves his girdle for her in one of the river's inlets as a token of his love, just as Qu Yuan in the *Li sao* (*ll.*221-24) unfastens his girdle to send as an earnest of good faith to the river goddess whom *he* is pursuing. The mountain goddess of the ninth song, addressed by the questing shaman with a title, *Ling xiu*, which is used by the *Li sao* poet of his mistress/king, inspires the same longing, and proves equally elusive – though in a later poem (not in *Chu ci*) attributed to the Chu poet Song Yu she shows less reticence, appearing to the King of Chu in a dream and offering him the 'services of pillow and mat'.

The chiding lamentations which are so characteristic of Chu poetry and which, in the verses of its less inspired practitioners, can become so monotonous may derive, then, from the complaints of the shaman lover whose goddess was forever eluding him. When allegory is abandoned, as in the *Jiu zhang* poems, the lamentations turn into straightforward political complaint: 'I was loyal; I was pure; yet I was rejected. The world is evil; my prince is benighted; the times are out of joint.' As a fully developed genre, these plaints, as we might term them, seem at the farthest possible remove from the 'lewd rites' and indecent posturings of the village shaman, and the poets themselves would no doubt have repudiated with horror any idea that they might be connected. Yet their progenitor is undoubtedly *Li sao*; and behind *Li sao* is the larmoyant eroticism of the 'Nine Songs'; and the 'Nine Songs', Wang Yi plausibly assures us, are literary, much-prettified imitations of cruder rustic prototypes.

The origin of this lachrymose element in Chinese shamanism can only be guessed at. Various possibilities suggest themselves:

(1) It was the conventional way in which a god or goddess was supposed to be wooed. The European courtly lover, who did in fact elevate his lady to the status of a goddess, attempted to win

her in the same way, with tears and groans and insistence on the physical and mental suffering which deprivation of her person was causing him.

(2) It was the shaman's way of explaining to his audience why his goddess had failed to materialize. She was shy; she was in hiding; or she was faithless and had broken her tryst.

(3) It was a sort of *post coitum tristitia* experienced by the shaman after the blissful but all too brief union with his deity.

(4) It was the expression of a more generalized sense of anticlimax and dejection which a shaman would experience on returning from an ecstatic trance-state to ordinary consciousness.

The last explanation would certainly have been the one most congenial to the manic-depressive allegorist of *Li sao*, who used this shaman-sadness as a symbol of his own alienation. A consequence of his doing so is that Chinese romantics have turned to the ancient spirit-world of shamanism for their imagery ever since.

Plaint-poetry continued to be written for some centuries after the death of Qu Yuan, but its tone of slightly subversive disgruntlement made it wholly unsuitable for use as court poetry. Emperors and imperial princes wanted to be praised and flattered, not told that they were blinded or misled. The brilliant courtier-poet Si-ma Xiang-ru (d.118 B.C.) was quick to see that the triumphant celestial journeyings of *Li sao* and the 'Far-off Journey' could easily be adapted to represent the apotheosis of his imperial patron.

> When the year turns its back on autumn and edges into winter
> The Son of Heaven goes forth to hunt the driven game.
> In chariot of ivory drawn by six jade-scaled dragons,
> Fluttering with rainbow flags, with cloud banner outspread . . .

This is how, in his great *fu*, or verse-essay, on the Imperial Hunting Park, he begins his description of the chase. His readers would understand that the 'jade-scaled dragons' were a mere figure of speech. (The emperor would, of course, be riding in a horse-drawn chariot.) At the same time it is clear that he uses this language not as mere hyperbole, but in order to identify the imperial huntsman with the shamans and god-kings of old whose airborne chariots really were drawn by flying dragons. His intention becomes even clearer as he warms up to the actual business of the hunt:

> Next, with aspiring steps, aloft he soars,
> Treads the wind's startling blast,
> Cleaves through the whirlwind's shock,
> Rides in the empty void

Companion of the gods:
Tramples the ancient crane,
Confounds the jungle fowl,
Spurns peacocks underfoot,
Affrights the golden pheasant,
Grasps at the rainbow bird . . .

Clearly, as a description of what took place on the contemporary Chinese equivalent of a grouse-moor this is positively misleading. But Si-ma Xiang-ru is no longer describing an earthly hunt; once he gets carried away, his thoughts are literally 'in the clouds'.

Zhang Heng, in his 'Fu on the Royal Hunt', written some two centuries later, describes the emperor's cortège in the following terms:

Then, the phoenix having presented a lucky day,
The Master of Horse made ready horses and carriage,
Chi You rides at the head of the procession,
And the Rain God with sprinklings clears the road ahead.
The mountain spirits form a protective guard;
The Guardians of the Quarters make up the royal train.
Xi He holds the reins, and with slow paces drives to
westward . . .

Chi You and Xi He are both mythical beings. Zhang Heng has abandoned all pretence here of writing about a real-life procession. His 'description' could have come straight out of *Li sao*, to which, indeed, it is partly indebted.

These two kinds of poetry then, the imperial epiphanies of the successful courtier-poet and the unsuccessful or banished courtier's complaints, can be said to have developed out of different elements of *Li sao*; but it is only in *Li sao* that we find them successfully combined. In this, as in other respects, Qu Yuan was not only China's first poet, but an incomparably greater poet than his successors; and his greatness is in no way diminished if we conclude that *Li sao* is the only work that can with certainty be attributed to him, since no other work in this genre approaches *Li sao* in originality and power.

Qu Yuan

The earliest reference to Qu Yuan in any text occurs in a lament for him written by the young statesman Jia Yi in 176 B.C., more than a century after his death. Jia Yi had advised the Han emperor Wen Di on ways of curbing the excessive power of the imperial princes, and the hostility of the latter had led to the 'upstart from Luo-yang' being dismissed from the emperor's service and sent off to be a tutor to the young prince of Changsha. To Jia Yi Changsha was the Deep South, a miasmic area from which he could not hope to return alive. It was also the area to which Qu Yuan had been banished, and where he had finally drowned himself in despair. Struck by what he saw as the similarity of their fates, Jia Yi was inspired to write this lament as an offering to the earlier poet's shade. The lament refers to Qu Yuan's nobility of soul and to his meeting with slander and rejection and drowning himself in the River Mi-luo, and includes a quotation from the concluding section of *Li sao*.

Until the appearance of Si-ma Qian's biography of Qu Yuan some eighty years later, that was the extent of what most people seem to have known about Qu Yuan: he was an honest minister of King Huai of Chu; he was banished from court because of some scandal or intrigue; he wrote the *Li sao* to protest against the injustice of his dismissal; and, having written the *Li sao*, he committed suicide by throwing himself into the Mi-luo, a tributary of the River Xiang.

Si-ma Qian's biography of Qu Yuan is far more circumstantial but, as an historical document, of very uncertain value. One of his aims in compiling his great 'History' was to encapsulate and preserve for posterity all that was best of Chinese culture, and it was no doubt for that reason that his biographies of great poets like Qu Yuan include very generous samples of their works. Qu Yuan's biography includes all seventy lines of 'Embracing Sand' (the fifth of the *Jiu zhang* poems), that of Jia Yi, which makes a pair with it, includes the complete texts of two quite substantial *fu*, while the verse included in his biography of Si-ma Xiang-ru must amount to several hundred lines. It is possible that he may have regarded these biographies primarily as a background or framework for the poems. At all events, the biography of Qu Yuan reads like a not very successful patchwork of contradictory and in some cases obviously unhistorical sources.

One of these sources is the 'Introduction to *Li sao*', which Liu An, Prince of Huai-nan, was commissioned to write by the Han emperor Wu Di (see p. 29). The 'Introduction' is a lost work, but a paragraph of it is preserved in quotation in a 'Preface to *Li sao*' by the first-century historian Ban Gu, and this same paragraph is found in the biography. Probably rather more of the 'Introduction' than that single paragraph has been included, but how much is a matter of conjecture.

Another source is the story with dialogue which, under the title of 'The Fisherman', appears as an independent work in the *Chu ci* anthology (see pp. 206–7). Si-ma Qian has incorporated it almost verbatim into the narrative with no indication that he is quoting from another text. 'The Fisherman' is fairly obviously a Taoist parable of the kind frequently encountered in the pages of *Zhuang zi* and almost certainly fictitious.

The third source is unidentifiable. It would appear to have been a sort of historical-romance-with-a-moral in which Qu Yuan was the hero and Zhang Yi and a Chu courtier referred to as 'the Lord High Administrator' were the villains. Parts of it strongly resemble the third-century B.C. 'Diplomacy of the Warring Kingdoms'.[15] A fine disregard for chronology and the logistics of travel seem to place it firmly on the farther side of the boundary which separates history from fiction. One incident from it appears twice elsewhere in the 'History': once in the biography of Zhang Yi and once in the 'Annals of the Royal House of Chu'. Another incident is attributed to Qu Yuan in the biography but to another person when it reappears in the 'Annals'. Si-ma Qian presumably made use of this source because there was nothing else available. His dissatisfaction with it is evident from the not very successful attempt he made at editing it so as to fit in with his other materials and with what he believed to be the facts. This unknown source would seem to have had the following peculiarities:

(1) It referred to its hero not as 'Qu Yuan' but as 'Qu Ping'.

(2) It dated the composition of *Li sao* not after but many years *before* Qu Yuan's banishment.

(3) It made no reference to any other work of Qu Yuan's besides *Li sao*.

Qu Yuan was one of Si-ma Qian's heroes. In the fashionable jargon of our time it could even be said that he 'identified' with Qu Yuan. Si-ma Qian had spoken out honourably in defence of a defeated general and paid a horrible price for his outspokenness, and Qu Yuan, like him, was an honest man whose honesty had brought him suffering: in his case calumny, banishment and despair. There are no less than three references to Qu Yuan in Si-ma Qian's autobiographical preface to the 'History' besides a highly personal tribute to him in the epilogue to Qu Yuan's and Jia Yi's biographies.

When I first read *Li sao*, the 'Heavenly Questions', the 'Summons of the Soul' and the 'Lament for Ying', I grieved for the noble

15. See J. I. Crump, *Chan-kuo ts'e*, in the Oxford Library of East Asian Literatures, Oxford, 1970.

spirit revealed in them. Later, when I visited Changsha and saw
the spot where Qu Yuan drowned himself, I wept to think what
manner of man he was. Then I read Jia Yi's 'Lament' and
marvelled, with him, that a man of Qu Yuan's genius, who, if he
had been willing to try his fortune elsewhere, would have been
received into any of the other kingdoms with open arms, should
have chosen such an end . . .

Twice – once in the autobiographical preface and once in his Letter
to Jen An – Si-ma Qian speaks of Qu Yuan writing the *Li sao* 'in
his banishment'; yet a cryptic statement in the autobiographical
preface seems to imply that he accepted his unknown source's
assertion that Qu Yuan's banishment occurred after King Huai's
death, i.e. in the third year of King Qing Xiang of Chu:

> When King Huai died in a strange land
> Zi Lan put the blame on Qu Yuan.

His 'solution' appears to have been to edit the text in such a way
that it would imply that Qu Yuan had been banished twice: once
under King Huai, in a half-hearted way which amounted to little
more than secondment, and once with the full rigours of exile under
King Qing Xiang. In fact his editing only added inconsistency and
confusion to a text which scholars have continued to argue about
inconclusively ever since.

   In the translation which follows I have put all those parts of the
biography which I believe to have come from the text of Liu An's
'Introduction to *Li sao*' and also that part of it which is taken from
'The Fisherman' in italics. I have tried to distinguish, in the
footnotes, between what is known and what is only my own
conjecture.

   *Qu Yuan's original name[16] was 'Ping'. He belonged to a
collateral branch of the royal house of Chu[17] and served in the
office of zuo-tu under King Huai.[18] He was a man of wide
learning with a good memory for what he had learned, skilled in
statecraft and well able to express himself in speech and writing.
At court he participated in the debates on affairs of state which
took place in the king's presence before they became the subject
of decrees; when out of court he was charged with the reception
of state visitors, speaking on behalf of his own king in exchanges*

16. i.e. the name he was given at birth. In ancient China adult males were
normally referred to by a second name given them at puberty.
17. i.e. he belonged to the Mi clan. The Qu, Zhao and Jing families who
supplied most of the Chu statesmen and generals of the Warring States
period were all three of them branches of this clan.
18. Reigned 328–299 B.C.

with the representatives of other states. The king held his services in high esteem.

Now the Lord High Administrator,[19] who was Qu Ping's equal in rank and office and his rival for the king's favour, secretly envied him for his ability. Once [when King Huai had commanded Qu Yuan to draft a law],[20] the Lord High Administrator saw a draft that Qu Ping was working on and tried to steal it from him; and because Qu Ping would not let him have it, he slandered him to the king, saying that it was common knowledge that whenever the king asked Qu Ping to draft a decree, he always went around afterwards boasting that only he could do it. The king was angry and became estranged towards Qu Ping.

Qu Ping was grieved that the king should be so undiscerning, that false witness could so easily darken counsel, private meanness injure the public good and the just man be left without a place. Full of these sad and gloomy thoughts he composed the *Li sao*.

[*'Li sao' means 'Encountering Sorrow'. Heaven is the origin from which we all come; our parents are the stock from which we grow. When men are desperate they turn towards their beginnings. That is why, when a man is in great trouble or extreme weariness, he invokes heaven and why, when he is in great vexation of spirit, he invokes his parents.*][21]

Qu Ping was a man of undeviating rectitude who had exhausted loyalty and knowledge alike in the service of his king, only to have this slanderer standing between him and the man he served. No wonder he should be in despair. Faithful, yet disbelieved, loyal, yet calumniated, how could he help feeling wronged? It was Qu Ping's sense of wrong that inspired him to write the *Li sao*.

The Songs of the States[22] *are sensual without being licentious; the*

19. *Shang-guan dai-fu*: evidently the title of a high-ranking official, otherwise unknown, but titles similar to this were common in the courts of the late Warring States period. Qu Yuan's own title, according to 'The Fisherman', was *San-lü dai-fu* ('Lord of the Three Wards').

20. This is obviously an interpolation, either by Si-ma Qian or by some later editor. In no other place does the 'unknown source' refer to 'Qu Yuan'. The interpolation in any case makes nonsense of the text. If the king had ordered Qu Yuan personally to draft the law, there would have been no point in the Lord High Administrator stealing it. Whoever made the interpolation may have been inspired to do so by *Jiu zhang* VII, *ll*.1–5 (q.v.); or perhaps he thought (mistakenly) that it was necessary to anticipate the Lord High Administrator's charge: 'Whenever the king asked . . .'.

21. I believe that the italicized passage inside square brackets comes from the 'Introduction to *Li sao*' by Liu An. Whatever point is being made here is not developed and what follows it is a *non sequitur*.

22. The first of the four major sections into which the 'Book of Songs' is divided. Many of the 160 poems in it are love-songs. The 'Lesser Ya' is the

Lesser Ya poems are plaintive without being seditious. Li sao may be said to combine both virtues. Ranging from Di Ku in high antiquity through Tang and Wu down to the time of Duke Huan of Qi, it uses these historical parallels in order to satirize contemporary affairs. The exaltation of true morality and the principles of good government are all to be found in this poem. The poet's style is concise, his wording subtle, his mind pure, his actions noble. He can write of small things in a way that suggests great ones, or use simple themes to express complex ideas. Because his mind was pure, his subjects breathe a natural sweetness. Because his actions were noble, he preferred death to compliance. He withdrew himself from the muck and mire. He sloughed off the impurities of life to soar away out of reach of the dust and turmoil. Refusing to accept the foulness of this world, he emerged shining and unspotted from its mud. Such a mind may, without hyperbole, be said to rival the sun and moon in brightness.[23]

Some time after Qu Ping's dismissal, Qin wished to attack Qi.[24] Qi was an ally of Chu, and King Hui of Qin, feeling uneasy about this alliance, commissioned Zhang Yi to leave Qin with costly presents with which he was to pretend to pledge his services to Chu. He was then to tell the King of Chu that Qin had a bitter enmity against Chu's ally Qi, and that if Chu were to break off relations with Qi, Qin would be willing to present Chu with six hundred li of the Shang-wu territory.

King Huai's greed caused him to believe Zhang Yi, and relations with Qi were promptly severed. But when an ambassador was sent to Qin to receive the promised territory, Zhang Yi claimed that he had said 'six li' and knew nothing about 'six *hundred* li'. The Chu ambassador left in a rage and returned to report the matter to the King of Chu.

King Huai was furious. He raised a large army and invaded Qin. Qin levied forces, attacked the Chu army and heavily defeated it at Dan-zhe,[25] taking 80,000 heads and capturing the Chu general Qu Gai. They then went on to annex the Han-zhong

name of the second section. The song referred to on p. 24 which the 'gentleman' who had fought in the Southland campaigns composed 'to express his grief' is one of the Lesser Ya poems.
23. The passage in italics beginning 'The Songs of the States' is quoted by Ban Gu as part of the 'Introduction to Li sao' by Liu An.
24. In 313 B.C. Other dates will be found in the Chronological Table on p. 346. The place-names mentioned in the passage which follows will be found in the map on p. 350.
25. This seems to be the battle of Dan-yang, 312 B.C. The 'Dan-zhe' of this text is probably due to scribal error.

territory. King Huai thereupon carried out a mobilization of the country's entire military strength and penetrated deeply into Qin territory. A battle was fought at Lan-tian.

At this point Wei seized the opportunity to invade Chu and advanced as far as Deng, and the Chu army returned from Qin in alarm. Qi, smarting under her late rebuff, refused to help, and Chu found herself in great difficulties.

Next year Qin offered to give back part of the Han-zhong territory and make peace with Chu; but the king of Chu said that it was not the land he wanted: he would prefer to get hold of Zhang Yi and have his revenge on him. When Zhang Yi heard this he said, 'If the sacrifice of a single person can save the Han-zhong territory for Qin, I am willing to go to Chu.'

On his arrival in Chu, Zhang Yi heavily bribed the influential minister Jin Shang, and by insinuating speeches managed to obtain the support of the King's favourite concubine, Zheng Xiu, so that, at her insistence, King Huai was eventually persuaded to release him.

Qu Ping, who was still out of favour and held no office at court, was at this time on an embassy in Qi. Hearing of these events, he returned and expostulated with King Huai for not having killed Zhang Yi. The king now regretted his mistake, but it was already too late to catch him.

Some time after this, an alliance of other states launched an attack on Chu and heavily defeated her, killing the Chu general, Tang Mei. King Zhao of Qin, who was allied to Chu by marriage, asked for a conference with King Huai. King Huai was prepared to go, but Qu Ping advised him not to because Qin was 'a country of wolves and tigers and not to be trusted'. However, one of King Huai's younger sons, Zi Lan, urged the King to go, on the grounds that to break off good relations with Qin would be senseless.

King Huai did in the end decide to go; but when he had got as far as the Wu-guan pass, his retreat was cut off by a Qin ambush and he was forcibly detained and told that his release could be guaranteed only in return for certain territorial concessions. He angrily refused to concede anything and escaped to Zhao. But Zhao refused him asylum and deported him back to Qin, where he eventually died. His body was sent back to Chu for interment, and his eldest son, King Qing Xiang, ascended the throne and made his younger brother, Zi Lan, Prime Minister.

The people of Chu blamed Zi Lan for having persuaded King

Huai to go on his fatal mission to Qin. Qu Ping, too, resented Zi
Lan . . .²⁶

[*Although in exile, his concern for his country's welfare and his
affection for King Huai remained undiminished and he never stopped
hoping for a recall. If only King Huai would come to his senses and
the people mend their ways, both king and country might yet prosper.
Again and again he returned to this theme in his poem. But it was of
no avail. There was no recall, and in the end . . .*]²⁷

Thus we see that King Huai ended his days without ever
coming to his senses. It seems that all princes, whether wise or
foolish, good or bad, want loyal men to govern for them and
wise men to advise them. Yet, notwithstanding, states fall and
noble families are ruined in endless succession, and generation
after generation goes by without the appearance of a sage king or
a truly well-governed state. This is because those who are taken
for loyal are not really loyal and those taken for wise not really
wise. Because King Huai could not tell who among his ministers
was really loyal, he was deceived by Zheng Xiu and tricked by
Zhang Yi. He rejected Qu Ping and trusted the Lord High
Administrator and the Prime Minister Zi Lan, with the
consequence that his armies were vanquished and his possessions
diminished. He lost six commanderies and died a stranger in
Qin, a laughing-stock to the world. This was the fatal result of
not being able to judge men's characters. The 'Book of Changes'
says,

> Not to drink when well is pure
> Fills my heart with sorrow sore:
> Draw therefrom, if king be wise,
> You shall share his blessings too.

If the king is not wise, what blessings can there be then?²⁸

---

26. The 'unknown source' appears to break off at this point. Presumably it
contained some reference to disparaging remarks made by Qu Yuan about Zi
Lan which eventually came to the ears of the latter, and to Qu Yuan's
subsequent banishment and death.
27. Here the text of what I take to be another extract from Liu An's
'Introduction to *Li sao*' ('his poem' obviously refers to *Li sao*) breaks off.
Presumably, what followed was a short passage referring to Qu Yuan's
despair and suicide.
28. This passage, beginning 'Thus we see . . .', I take to be the moralizing
conclusion of the 'unknown source', which would have ended at this point.
The three sentences which follow were, I believe, adapted and transposed by
Si-ma Qian from the passage that originally came after 'Qu Ping, too,
resented Zi Lan . . .'.

The Prime Minister Zi Lan was furious when he heard this. In the end he suborned the Lord High Administrator to speak ill of Qu Yuan[29] to King Qing Xiang. The King was angry and banished him.

Qu Yuan[30] came to the banks of the Jiang, where he wandered by the water's edge, his hair hanging down his back in disarray, singing as he went, a dejected expression on his emaciated features. A fisherman caught sight of him.

'Are not you the Lord of the Three Wards?' said the fisherman. 'What has brought you to this pass?'

'Because all the world is muddy and I alone am clear,' said Qu Yuan, 'and because all men are drunk and I alone am sober, I have been sent into exile.'

'The Wise Man is not chained to material circumstances,' said the fisherman, 'but can move as the world moves. If the world is muddy, why not help them to stir up the mud and beat up the waves? And if all men are drunk, why not sup their dregs and swill their lees? Why get yourself exiled because of your deep thoughts and your fine aspirations?'

Qu Yuan replied, 'I have heard it said: "He who has just washed his hair should brush his hat; and he who has just bathed, should shake his clothes." How can you expect anyone to submit his spotless purity to the dirt of others? I would rather cast myself into the ever-flowing waters and be buried in the bowels of fishes than hide my shining light in a murky world . . .'[31]

Then he composed the poem called 'Embracing Sand'. The words are as follows:[32]

Then, clasping a stone to his bosom, he threw himself into the River Mi-luo and perished.

After Qu Yuan's death Chu produced other writers, like Song Yu, Tang Le and Jing Cuo, all of them accomplished poets who became famous by writing *fu*. All based themselves on Qu Yuan's free, flowing style, but none dared imitate his outspoken satire.

From this time onwards Chu declined with ever-increasing

29. Si-ma Qian's editing is responsible for this 'Qu Yuan'. The 'unknown source' of which this is an adaptation or abridgement always refers to him as 'Qu Ping'.

30. From here onwards, with only a few very minor variations, is the text of 'The Fisherman' (see pp. 206–7).

31. Si-ma Qian omits the final paragraph of 'The Fisherman', thereby leaving the last word with Qu Yuan.

32. Si-ma Qian here gives the complete text of *Huai sha* (see p. 170 *et seq.*) with only a few very insignificant variants.

rapidity and within half a century was completely overwhelmed by Qin.

Quite apart from its more obviously fictional aspects (who was at hand in that remote wilderness to witness the encounter with the fisherman? How, if the poet drowned himself on its completion, were the words of 'Embracing Sand' preserved?), the second, 'Qu Yuan', half of the biography ill accords with the notion that Qu Yuan, as Si-ma Qian himself elsewhere asserts, was the author of 'A Lament for Ying', in which (p. 165, *l.*46) the poet distinctly states that he has already spent some nine years in exile: the wording of the biography allows us to suppose weeks or even months to have elapsed between the poet's sentence of banishment and his fatal leap into the river, but certainly not years.

As for the 'Qu Ping' half of the biography, the overriding impression one is left with after reading it is that its author – i.e. the anonymous author of the 'unknown source' – was determined to find some means or other of keeping his hero around long after the historical Qu Yuan had departed from the scene. The historical Qu Yuan, we may be sure, did not long survive his disgrace. We may suppose that he died some time in the middle years of King Huai's reign, say about 315 B.C., before the series of defeats and disasters which culminated in King Huai's death in Qin in 296 B.C.

But to say that Qu Yuan was an able, honest courtier who fell out of favour, wrote the *Li sao* and drowned himself – that, after all, is the sum of what most Han informants seem able to tell us about him – is hardly a story at all. How much more interesting to let him live on, so that he could witness the dreadful price that King Huai had to pay for not heeding his repeated admonitions to the 'Fair One' to mend his ways! The distraught courtier who drowned himself when he fell from favour now becomes a prescient statesman who foresaw the ruin of both king and country and, having lived to witness, with anguish, what he had foreseen, rang down the curtain on this great historical tragedy with his own calculated self-destruction.

Chinese and Japanese works of reference continue to give 343 B.C. as the date of Qu Yuan's birth, and scholars continue to construct elaborate chronologies of his life; but the belief that Qu Yuan's birth-date is calculable rests on a misinterpretation of the second line of *Li sao*, and the elaborate chronologies depend on the dubious premise that some or all of the *Jiu zhang* poems are by Qu Yuan himself and on a circular process whereby the 'facts' of the biography are interpreted in the light of the *Jiu zhang* poems and the 'facts' of the *Jiu zhang* poems are interpreted in the light of the biography.

In fact no one has, or is ever likely to have, the foggiest idea either when Qu Yuan was born or when he died. I hazard the guess – and it is no more than that – that he died in the middle years of King Huai's reign for the reason given by the eighteenth-century scholar Wang Mou-hong:

> Nothing could be a source of greater grief to the loyal servant of a king than that his master should die a prisoner in a foreign country, yet in all of Qu Yuan's writings there is not a single reference to this happening . . . only protests about the harsh way in which he was silenced and denied access to his king and complaints about his banishment and isolation. In so far as he touches on matters of a political nature, it is only to give warning that when the hand which steers the ship of state loosens its grip, disaster is sure sooner or later to ensue. He nowhere states that the disaster has already happened. It is clear from this that Qu Yuan did not live to see King Huai's ambushing and detention in Qin, and that by the time King Qing Xiang came to the throne he had already been dead for several years.

If we cannot safely use the poems of *Jiu zhang* as biographical material, the same cannot be said of *Li sao*, which has unvaryingly, from the very start, been associated with the name of Qu Yuan. To what extent can the aristocratic statesman and diplomat of Si-ma Qian's biography be identified with the learned astronomer of *Li sao* who either himself wrote or was certainly familiar with the 'Heavenly Questions', who embellished his strictures on political immorality and the purblindness of kings with a profound knowledge of the history and genealogies of men and gods, and who, if he was not a shaman himself, was fully acquainted with the preoccupations and practices of shamanism? As a matter of fact, the combination of these two sets of qualities in a single person is by no means as improbable as it might seem. Consider the following passage taken from the entries for the year 541 B.C. in an ancient chronicle:[33]

> Hearing of the Marquess of Jin's illness, the Earl of Zheng sent Zi Chan on an official visit to Jin to inquire after him. Shu Xiang, speaking as the Marquess's representative, said that the diviner, when consulted about the Marquess's illness, had told them that it was being caused by Shi Chen and Tai Tai, but that none of the Marquess's learned clerks had ever heard of these gods. 'Perhaps *you* could tell us who they are?' he asked Zi Chan.

33. *Zuo zhuan*, first year of Duke Zhao.

'Yes,' said Zi Chan. 'In the ancient time the high lord Gao Xin had two sons, E Bo and Shi Chen, who dwelt in the wood of Kuang-lin. They could not get on together and were constantly running to take up arms and falling on each other with shield and spear. The Lord God [i.e. Gao Xin] was displeased. He banished E Bo to the hill of Shang to be the warden of the Great Fire constellation. Afterwards the Shang people came to dwell in that land; that is why the Great Fire is the constellation corresponding to Song, who are the present-day successors of the Shang.[34] Shi Chen he banished to the land of Xia to be warden of the Shen constellation [the three 'belt' stars of Orion]. The Tang people inherited that land and continued to hold it both under the Xia kings and under the Shang. In this latter age[35] it has belonged to the descendants of your lord's ancestor, Yu of Tang. When King Wu's queen, Jiang Yi, was near her time, the Lord God appeared to her in a dream, saying, "The child you bear shall be called 'Yu' and shall be given the land of Tang, which is under the sign of Shen; and he shall be fruitful and have many heirs." When the child was born he had a mark in his hand like the character "yu"; and so "Yu" became his name. Afterwards, when his elder brother King Cheng extinguished the line of the old ruling house of Tang, he gave the land of Tang to Yu, as had been foretold. And Tang later became known as Jin, so Shen is the constellation which corresponds to Jin. So the Shi Chen mentioned by the diviner must be the god of that constellation.

'As for the other god: in ancient times the high lord Jin Tian had a descendant called Mei who inherited the office of Master of the Waters; and this Mei had two sons, Yun Ge and Tai Tai. Tai Tai inherited his father's office. He cleared the channels of the Fen and Tao rivers and dyked the Great Marsh, so that the plain of Tai-yuan became habitable. The Lord God was pleased and made him Lord of the River Fen. The little states of Chen, Si, Hu and Huang used to maintain his sacrifices; but when Jin gained dominion over the valley of the Fen and extinguished their ruling houses, there was no one to maintain them. The Tai

---

34. To Chinese astrologers each section of the night sky corresponded to an area of the known world, and unusual astronomical events (planetary conjunctions, the appearance of comets, etc.) in a particular part of the sky were thought to portend a terrestrial event in the corresponding area of the earth's surface. The much-misunderstood story of the Star of Bethlehem no doubt rests on a similar belief. The Wise Men, it will be recalled, went first to the court of Judaea, the land indicated by their 'star', to make inquiries. They did not 'follow' the star except in a metaphorical sense.
35. i.e. under the Zhou dynasty. King Wu was the first Zhou king.

Tai mentioned by the diviner must therefore be the god of the River Fen.'

Having identified the names mentioned by the diviner as the names of two local deities, Zi Chan goes on to express disbelief in the view that the Marquess's illness could have been due to their influence. River gods, he says, cause calamities like floods, droughts, and pestilences, and star gods, like the other celestial deities, are responsible for inclement and unseasonable weather. He goes on to suggest, as tactfully as he can, that the Marquess's illness is more likely due to the fact that four of his wives are ladies of the same surname as himself. His illness had been caused by breaking the taboo against marrying endogamously. When all this was in due course relayed by Shu Xiang to the Marquess, the latter observed that Zi Chan was 'a very learned gentleman'.

This Zi Chan, who knew more about the names and genealogies of the gods of Jin than the learned clerks of Jin did themselves, was a statesman famous for his wisdom both in his own day and long after it. Confucius in the 'Analects' praises him for his eloquence, and the *Zuo zhuan* chronicler writes admiringly of his good government. He held high office under the Earl of Zheng, eventually becoming Chief Minister of that state. Like the Qu Yuan of the biography, he was a high-ranking nobleman and kinsman of the ruler whom he served; like Qu Yuan, he frequently represented his country abroad (it was as a diplomat that he was most famous); and like Qu Yuan, he was a law-maker, author of the first published code of laws in any Chinese state – to the great disgust of aristocratic contemporaries like Shu Xiang, who believed that familiarity with the law would encourage the common people to become insubordinate.

Zi Chan lived some two centuries before Qu Yuan's time, but I do not think the comparison of the two men is for that reason far-fetched. One of the few things that *can* be deduced about Qu Yuan is that he must have been a very old-fashioned kind of nobleman-official, very *ancien régime*. He had, in fact, more in common with Zi Chan than with the political parvenus of his own day, the new men who wrote books about economics and statecraft and the art of war, who went around questioning everything and subverting the old order. The 'political' parts of *Li sao* are a regular litany of complaint against newfangledness, against those who set aside the old, tried patterns and 'carve after their own fancy'.

> I take my fashion from the good men of old:
> A garb unlike that which the rude world cares for:
> Though it may not accord with present-day manners,
> I will follow the pattern that Peng Xian has left.

During the Sino-Japanese war of 1937–45 it became the fashion to represent Qu Yuan as the great Patriot Poet, even as the People's Poet. An article by the great liberal scholar Wen Yi-duo was actually published under the second of those titles. It ended with these words:

> Although Qu Yuan did not write about the life of the people or voice their sufferings, he may truthfully be said to have acted as the leader of a people's revolution and to have struck a blow to avenge them. Qu Yuan is the only person in the whole of Chinese history who is fully entitled to be called 'the People's Poet'.

Guo Mo-ruo's play *Qu Yuan*, written during ten days in 1942 and compared by his enthusiastic friends with *Hamlet* and *King Lear*, accords his subject a similar treatment. Under the People's Republic this view of Qu Yuan became *de rigueur*. A little book for high-school students published in 1957 opens with the words, 'Qu Yuan is the first great patriotic poet in the history of our country's literature.' An inevitable consequence of this view has been a reluctance to question Qu Yuan's authorship of any of the works traditionally attributed to him – as if the rejection of even the most improbable of these attributions would in some way diminish his stature – and a revulsion from the highly sceptical attitude which many scholars formerly entertained towards the biography.

In fact these modern attempts to 'reclaim' an ancient poet for our own time are, I believe, anachronisms. The idea of Qu Yuan as a great patriot rests on a misunderstanding of the biography. By preferring self-immolation to the pursuit of a career in some other state Qu Yuan was not displaying the sort of loyalty we should associate with an intelligence officer who chooses to blow his brains out rather than defect to a foreign power: loyalty of that kind implies an idea of nationalism totally unheard of in Qu Yuan's day. Rather, he was demonstrating the chivalrous, aristocratic kind of personal loyalty which Zi Chan would very well have understood but which in the thoroughly 'liberated' world of the fourth century B.C. was remarkably old-fashioned.

As for the 'People's Poet', that notion stems from the fact that Qu Yuan is the nominal hero of a popular festival, the Double Fifth or Dragon Boat festival, which is celebrated in South China in the early summer with boat-races and the eating of a kind of glutinous rice-cake called *zong-zi*. In fact, as Wen Yi-duo himself was the first to admit, the Double Fifth festival is much older than Qu Yuan and was not associated with him until centuries after his death. The Swedish anthropologist Gøran Aijmer has very plausibly suggested that it was originally a fertility festival associated with the planting-out of the rice. The dragons, i.e. the Nagas of the river, not Qu Yuan, were the original recipients of the offerings, and the boats with their dragon-headed prows represented the beneficent powers who, it was hoped, would bestow fertility on the paddy-fields.

It was Confucian literati who were responsible in this, as in so many other cases, for foisting one of their own heroes on to a popular local cult, just as the Christian priesthood in Europe succeeded – nominally at any rate – in capturing the old pagan festivals for their own religion.

During the Han dynasty the fertilizing water god worshipped in the festival of the Double Fifth was identified throughout the south-eastern part of China not with Qu Yuan but with Wu Zi-xu, another Chu statesman whose honest admonitions were rejected and who, like Qu Yuan, ended up in the river. In the 'History of the Later Han Dynasty' we read of one Cao Xu, a skilled musician and shaman who, on the fifth day of the fifth month of the year Han-an (A.D. 142), was drowned while rowing out on the Shang-yu river towards the incoming bore 'to meet the god with dancing'. Wang Chong, writing in the first century, enables us to identify this god:

> The history-books say that when King Fu Cha of Wu killed Wu Zi-xu, he boiled him in a cauldron, put his body in a wineskin, and threw it into the river. But Zi Xu's hate was so powerful that it drove the waters before it and made the rushing tidal bore in which people are drowned. Today in the Gui-ji area there are temples to Zi Xu at Dan-tu on the Yangtze and at Qian-tang on the River Zhejiang, erected there to mollify his hatred and assuage the violence of the tide ... The Zhejiang river, the Shan-yin river and the Shang-yu river all have this tidal bore.

The story of Wu Zi-xu may already have been popular in Qu Yuan's day since it appears at some length in the (probably) contemporary *Zuo zhuan*. It is the subject of a long *chantefable*[36] found among the manuscripts brought back from Dun-huang by Sir Aurel Stein in 1907 dating from perhaps the eighth or ninth century, i.e. at least a thousand years later.

Of these two Confucian martyrs, Qu Yuan and Wu Zi-xu, Wu Zi-xu was decidedly the more popular figure. This was because he had an interesting story, whereas Qu Yuan had hardly any story at all. It was centuries before Qu Yuan finally supplanted him as the presiding spirit of the Dragon Boat festival throughout the whole of Southern China.

36. A kind of ballad-story very popular in medieval China in which prose narrative was interspersed with passages of verse which the storyteller was intended to sing. *Aucassin et Nicolette* is a notable example of this genre in medieval European literature.

But to call the author of *Li sao* a popular poet on the ground that his name is – somewhat factitiously – associated with a popular festival is rather like saying that belief in Christianity must necessarily go with a taste for mince-pies. The *zong-zi* eater's Qu Yuan has no more – or less – to do with the *Li sao* poet than our jolly furred and booted Santa Claus with the saintly Bishop of Myra.

The Confucian cult of Qu Yuan is another matter. In it a whole class – that of the office-holding man of letters – found a heroic symbol of itself, one that would serve to shore up a bureaucrat's flagging self-esteem in times of rejection, unemployment and adversity. To speak out for what one believed to be the right policy, even if one was alone in believing it and when the cost of doing so was demotion, disgrace or even death – that was the scholar-official's idea of honour. It was, in a way, a curiously literary one, because it meant that he looked no longer towards his contemporaries but towards a literate posterity to judge him. Qu Yuan first gave expression to this heroic ideal and we see it again and again being developed in the later poems of this anthology. The following lines may not have been written by the great Master himself, but they echo what he more than once stated in the *Li sao*:

> The world is muddy-witted; none can know me; the heart of man cannot be told.
>
> I know that death cannot be avoided, therefore I will not grudge its coming.
>
> To noble men I here plainly declare that I will be numbered with such as you.

Li sao *'On Encountering Trouble'*

The key to this extraordinary poem is in its first and last lines. In the opening line of the poem the poet tells us that he is a nobleman, descended from the gods; in the closing lines he cries out despairingly that there is no one 'worthy to work with in making good government' and that he intends to abandon the corrupt world which is incapable of understanding him and join the company of the holy dead.

Armed with this knowledge, we are able to understand that the inconstant 'Fair One' who rejects him is the weak-minded, vacillating king who rejected his policies, and that his unsuccessful quest for a suitable 'mate' among the goddesses and legendary princesses who inhabit the spirit world which he journeys through after his rejection is an allegorical survey of the political alternatives: employment in one or other of the neighbouring states. His conclusion is that all are equally bad and that his only real alternative is death.

A good deal has already been said in the General Introduction about the shamanistic elements in this poem. We can only guess at the nature of the recitals which Chu shamans may be supposed to have given recounting the aerial journeys or 'flights' they made into the land of spirits, but by studying *Li sao* and the 'Nine Songs' we can fairly easily deduce that they must have been dramatic ('Here I am, suddenly, in this House of Spring', *Li sao, l.217*) and that they must have employed various formulaic devices for conveying the passage of time. (It has always been held, and by other peoples besides the Chinese, that time in the spirit world passes more quickly than our earthly time.) One of these formulae occurs twice in *Li sao*:

> I started out in the morning on my way from Cang-wu;
> By evening I had arrived at the Hanging Garden.

(ll.185–6)

> I set off at morning from the Ford of Heaven;
> At evening I came to the world's western end.

(ll.345–6)

In the 'Nine Songs' we find the shaman using exactly the same formula as he cruises along the riverside looking for his goddess:

In the morning I race by the bank of the river;
At evening I halt at this north island.

                                    ('The Goddess of the Xiang', *ll.*29–30)

The dreamlike changes and shifts of focus in *Li sao* are a product
not of textual corruption, as has sometimes been suggested, but of
this shamanistic convention.

The most remarkable thing about this very remarkable poem is
that we can see a genius at work in it actually in the process of
inventing a completely new sort of poetry out of an old oral
tradition. Qu Yuan's despairing cry signals, paradoxically – or
perhaps not so paradoxically – the birth of literature.

1 Scion of the high lord Gao Yang,
   Bo Yong was my father's name.
   When She Ti pointed to the first month of the year,
   On the day *geng-yin* I passed from the womb.
   My father, seeing the aspect of my nativity,
   Took omens to give me an auspicious name.
   The name he gave me was True Exemplar;
   The title he gave me was Divine Balance.

9 Having from birth this inward beauty,
   I added to it fair outward adornment:
   I dressed in selinea and shady angelica,
   And twined autumn orchids to make a garland.
   Swiftly I sped as in fearful pursuit,
   Afraid Time would race on and leave me behind.
   In the morning I gathered the angelica on the mountains;
   In the evening I plucked the sedges of the islets.

17 The days and months hurried on, never delaying;
   Springs and autumns sped by in endless alternation:
   And I thought how the trees and flowers were fading and falling,
   And feared that my Fairest's beauty would fade too.
   'Gather the flower of youth and cast out the impure!
   Why will you not change the error of your ways?
   I have harnessed brave coursers for you to gallop forth with:
   Come, let me go before and show you the way!

'The three kings of old were most pure and perfect:
Then indeed fragrant flowers had their proper place.
They brought together pepper and cinnamon;
All the most-prized blossoms were woven in their garlands.
Glorious and great were those two, Yao and Shun,
Because they had kept their feet on the right path.
And how great was the folly of Jie and Zhòu,
Who hastened by crooked paths, and so came to grief.

'The fools enjoy their careless pleasure,
But their way is dark and leads to danger.
I have no fear for the peril of my own person,
But only lest the chariot of my lord should be dashed.
I hurried about your chariot in attendance,
Leading you in the tracks of the kings of old.'
But the Fragrant One refused to examine my true feelings:
He lent ear instead to slander, and raged against me.

How well I know that loyalty brings disaster;
Yet I will endure: I cannot give it up.
I called on the ninefold heaven to be my witness,
And all for the sake of the Fair One, and no other.
There once was a time when he spoke with me in frankness;
But then he repented and was of another mind.
I do not care, on my own count, about this divorcement,
But it grieves me to find the Fair One so inconstant.

I had tended many an acre of orchids,
And planted a hundred rods of melilotus;
I had raised sweet lichens and the cart-halting flower,
And asarums mingled with fragrant angelica,
And hoped that when leaf and stem were in their full prime,
When the time had come, I could reap a fine harvest.
Though famine should pinch me, it is small matter;
But I grieve that all my blossoms should waste in rank weeds.

All others press forward in greed and gluttony,
No surfeit satiating their demands:
Forgiving themselves, but harshly judging others;
Each fretting his heart away in envy and malice.

Madly they rush in the covetous chase,
But not after that which *my* heart sets store by.
For old age comes creeping and soon will be upon me,
And I fear I shall not leave behind an enduring name.

65   In the mornings I drank the dew that fell from the magnolia;
At evening ate the petals that dropped from chrysanthemums.
If only my mind can be truly beautiful,
It matters nothing that I often faint for famine.
I pulled up roots to bind the valerian
And thread the castor plant's fallen clusters with;
I trimmed sprays of cassia for plaiting melilotus,
And knotted the lithe, light trails of ivy.

73   I take my fashion from the good men of old:
A garb unlike that which the rude world cares for;
Though it may not accord with present-day manners,
I will follow the pattern that Peng Xian has left.
Heaving a long sigh, I brush away my tears,
Sad that man's life should be so beset with hardship.
Though goodness and beauty were my bit and bridle,
I was slandered in the morning and cast off that same evening.

81   Yet, though cast off, I would wear my orchid girdle;
I would pluck some angelicas to add to its beauty;
For this it is that my heart takes most delight in,
And though I died nine times, I should not regret it.
What I regret is the Fair One's waywardness,
That never once stops to ask what is in men's minds.
All your ladies were jealous of my delicate beauty;
In their spiteful chattering they said I was a wanton.

89   Truly this generation are cunning artificers,
From square and compass turn their eyes and change the true
     measurement,
Disregard the ruled line to follow their crooked fancies;
To emulate in flattery is their only rule.
But I am sick and sad at heart and stand irresolute:
I alone am at a loss in this generation.
Yet I would rather quickly die and meet dissolution
Before I ever would consent to ape *their* behaviour.

Eagles do not flock like birds of lesser species;
So it has ever been since the olden time.
How can the round and square ever fit together?
How can different ways of life ever be reconciled?
Yet humbling one's spirit and curbing one's pride,
Bearing blame humbly and enduring insults,
But keeping pure and spotless and dying in righteousness:
Such conduct was greatly prized by the wise men of old.

Repenting, therefore, that I had not conned the way more
      closely,
I halted, intending to turn back again –
To turn about my chariot and retrace my road
Before I had advanced too far along the path of folly.
I walked my horses through the marsh's orchid-covered margin;
I galloped to the hill of pepper-trees and rested there.
I could not go in to him for fear of meeting trouble,
And so, retired, I would once more fashion my former raiment.

I made a coat of lotus and water-chestnut leaves,
And gathered lotus petals to make myself a skirt.
I will no longer care that no one understands me,
As long as I can keep the sweet fragrance of my mind.
Higher still the hat now that towered on my head,
And longer the girdle that dangled from my waist.
Fragrant and foul mingle in confusion,
But my inner brightness has remained undimmed.

Suddenly I turned back and let my eyes wander.
I resolved to go and visit all the world's quarters.
My garland's crowded blossoms, mixed in fair confusion,
Wafted the sweetness of their fragrance far and wide.
All men have something in their lives that gives them pleasure:
With me the love of beauty is my constant joy.
I could not change this, even if my body were dismembered;
For how could dismemberment ever hurt my mind?

My Nü Xu was fearful and clung to me imploringly,
Lifting her voice up in expostulation:
'Gun in his stubbornness took no thought for his life
And perished, as result, on the moor of Feather Mountain.

Why be so lofty, with your passion for purity?
Why must you alone have such delicate adornment?
Thorns, king-grass, curly-ear hold the place of power:
But you must needs stand apart and not speak them fair.

137   'You cannot go from door to door convincing everybody;
No one can say, "See, look into my mind!"
Others band together and like to have companions:
Why must you be so aloof? Why not heed my counsel?'
But I look to the wise men of old for my guidance.
So sighing, with a full heart, I bore her upbraidings
And crossing the Yuan and Xiang, I journeyed southwards
Till I came to where Chong Hua was and made my plaint to him.

145   'Singing the Nine Songs and dancing the Nine Changes,
Qi of Xia made revelry and knew no restraint,
Taking no thought for the troubles that would follow:
And so his five sons fell out, brother against brother.
Yi loved idle roaming and hunting to distraction,
And took delight in shooting at the mighty foxes.
But foolish dissipation has seldom a good end:
And Han Zhuo covetously took his master's wife.

153   'Zhuo's son, Jiao, put on his strong armour
And wreaked his wild will without any restraint.
The days passed in pleasure; far he forgot himself,
Till his head came tumbling down from his shoulders.
Jie of Xia all his days was a king most unnatural,
And so he came finally to meet with calamity.
Zhòu cut up and salted the bodies of his ministers;
And so the days were numbered of the House of Yin.

161   'Tang of Shang and Yu of Xia were reverent and respectful;
The House of Zhou chose the true way without error,
Raising up the virtuous and able men to government,
Following the straight line without fear or favour.
High God in Heaven knows no partiality;
He looks for the virtuous and makes them his ministers.
For only the wise and good can ever flourish
If it is given them to possess the earth.

69 'I have looked back into the past and forward to later ages,
Examining the outcomes of men's different designs.
Where is the unrighteous man who could be trusted?
Where is the wicked man whose service could be used?
Though I stand at the pit's mouth and death yawns before me,
I still feel no regret at the course I have chosen.
Straightening the handle, regardless of the socket's shape:
For that crime the good men of old were hacked in pieces.'

77 Many a heavy sigh I heaved in my despair,
Grieving that I was born in such an unlucky time.
I plucked soft lotus petals to wipe my welling tears
That fell down in rivers and wet my coat front.
I knelt on my outspread skirts and poured my plaint out,
And the righteousness within me was clearly manifest.
I yoked a team of jade dragons to a phoenix-figured car
And waited for the wind to come, to soar up on my journey.

85 I started out in the morning on my way from Cang-wu;
By evening I had arrived at the Hanging Garden.
I wanted to stay a while in those fairy precincts,
But the swift-moving sun was dipping to the west.
I ordered Xi He to stay the sun-steeds' gallop,
To stand over Yan-zi mountain and not go in;
For the road was so far and so distant was my journey,
And I wanted to go up and down, seeking my heart's desire.

93 I watered my dragon steeds at the Pool of Heaven,
And tied their reins up to the Fu-sang tree.
I broke a sprig of the Ruo tree to strike the sun with:
First I would roam a little for my enjoyment.
I sent Wang Shu ahead to ride before me;
The Wind God went behind as my outrider;
The Bird of Heaven gave notice of my comings;
The Thunder God warned me when all was not ready.

101 I caused my phoenixes to mount on their pinions
And fly ever onward by night and by day.
The whirlwinds gathered and came out to meet me,
Leading clouds and rainbows, to give me welcome.

In wild confusion, now joined and now parted,
Upwards and downwards rushed the glittering train.
I asked Heaven's porter to open up for me;
But he leant across Heaven's gate and eyed me churlishly.

209 The day was getting dark and drawing to its close.
Knotting orchids, I waited in indecision.
The muddy, impure world, so undiscriminating,
Seeks always to hide beauty, out of jealousy.
I decided when morning came to cross the White Water,
And climbed the peak of Lang-feng, and there tied up my steeds.
Then I looked about me and suddenly burst out weeping,
Because on that high hill there was no fair lady.

217 'Here I am, suddenly, in this House of Spring.
I have broken off a jasper branch to add to my girdle.
Before the jasper flowers have shed their bright petals,
I shall look for a maiden below to give it to.'
So I made Feng Long ride off on a cloud
To seek out the dwelling-place of the lady Fu Fei.
I took off my girdle as a pledge of my suit to her,
And ordered Lame Beauty to be the go-between.

225 Many were the hurried meetings and partings:
All wills and caprices, she was hard to woo.
In the evenings she went to lodge in the Qiong-shi mountain;
In the mornings she washed her hair in the Wei-pan stream.
With proud disdain she guarded her beauty,
Passing each day in idle, wanton pleasures.
Though fair she may be, she lacks all seemliness:
Come! I'll have none of her; let us search elsewhere!

233 I looked all around over the earth's four quarters,
Circling the heavens till at last I alighted.
I gazed on a jade tower's glittering splendour
And spied the lovely daughter of the Lord of Song.
I sent off the magpie to pay my court to her,
But the magpie told me that my suit had gone amiss.
The magpie flew off with noisy chatterings.
I hate him for an idle, knavish fellow.

41 My mind was irresolute and havering;
I wanted to go, and yet I could not.
Already the phoenix had taken his present,
And I feared that Gao Xin would get there before me.
I wanted to go far away, but had nowhere to go to:
Where could I wander to look for amusement?
Before they were married to Prince Shao Kang,
Lord Yu's two daughters were there for the wooing.

49 But my pleader was weak and my matchmaker stupid,
And I feared that this suit, too, would not be successful.
For the world is impure and envious of the able,
Eager to hide men's good and make much of their ill.
Deep in the palace, unapproachable,
The wise king slumbers and will not be awakened.
That the thoughts in my breast should all go unuttered –
How can I endure this until I end my days?

57 I searched for the holy plant and twigs of bamboo,
And ordered Ling Fen to make divination for me.
He said, 'Beauty is always bound to find its mate:
Who that was truly fair was ever without lovers?
Think of the vastness of the wide world:
Here is not the only place where you can find your lady.
Go farther afield,' he said, 'and do not be faint-hearted.
What woman seeking handsome mate could ever refuse you?

65 'What place on earth does not boast some fragrant flower?
Why need you always cleave to your old home?
The world today is blinded with its own folly:
You cannot make people see the virtue inside you.
Most people's loathings and likings are different,
Only these men here are not as others are;
For they wear mugwort and cram their waistbands with it,
But the lovely valley orchid they deem unfit to wear.

73 'Since beauty of flower, then, and of shrub escapes them,
What chance has a rarest jewel of gaining recognition?
They gather up muck to stuff their perfume bags with;

The spicy pepper-plant they say has got no scent at all.'
I wanted to follow Ling Fen's auspicious oracle,
But I faltered and could not make my mind up.
I heard that Wu Xian was descending in the evening,
So I lay in wait with offerings of peppered rice-balls.

281 The spirits came like a dense cloud descending,
And the host of Doubting Mountain came crowding to meet him.
His godhead was manifested by a blaze of radiance,
And he addressed me in these auspicious words:
'To and fro in the earth you must everywhere wander,
Seeking one whose thoughts are of your own measure.
Tang and Yu sought sincerely for the right helpers;
So Yi Yin and Gao Yao worked well with their princes.

289 'As long as your soul within is beautiful,
What need have you of a matchmaker?
Yue laboured as a builder, pounding earth at Fu-yan,
Yet Wu Ding employed him without a second thought.
Lü Wang wielded the butcher's knife at Zhao-ge,
But King Wen met him and raised him up on high.
Ning Qi sang as he fed his ox at evening;
Duke Huan of Qi heard him and took him as his minister.

297 'Gather the flower of youth before it is too late,
While the good season is still not yet over.
Beware lest the shrike sound his note before the equinox,
Causing all the flowers to lose their fine fragrance.'
How splendid the glitter of my jasper girdle!
But the crowd make a dark screen, masking its beauty.
And I fear that my enemies, who never can be trusted,
Will break it out of spiteful jealousy.

305 The age is disordered in a tumult of changing:
How can I tarry much longer among them?
Orchid and iris have lost all their fragrance;
Flag and melilotus have changed into straw.
Why have all the fragrant flowers of days gone by
Now all transformed themselves into worthless mugwort?
What other reason can there be for this
But that they all have no more care for beauty?

43 I thought that orchid was one to be trusted,
But he proved a sham, bent only on pleasing his masters.
He overcame his goodness and conformed to evil counsels:
He no more deserves to rank with fragrant flowers.
Pepper is all wagging tongue and lives only for slander;
And even stinking dogwood seeks to fill a perfume bag.
Since they only seek advancement and labour for position,
What fragrance have they deserving our respect?

51 Since, then, the world's way is to drift the way the tide runs,
Who can stay the same and not change with all the rest?
Seeing the behaviour of orchid and pepper-flower,
What can be expected of cart-halt and selinea?
They have cast off their beauty and come to this:
Only my garland is left to treasure.
Its penetrating perfume does not easily desert it,
And even to this day its fragrance has not faded.

59 I will follow my natural bent and please myself;
I will go off wandering to look for a lady.
While my adornment is in its pristine beauty
I will travel around looking both high and low.
Since Ling Fen had given me a favourable oracle,
I picked an auspicious day to start my journey on.
I broke a branch of jasper to take for my meat,
And ground fine jasper meal for my journey's provisions.

67 'Harness winged dragons to be my coursers;
Let my chariot be of fine work of jade and ivory!
How can I live with men whose hearts are strangers to me?
I am going a far journey to be away from them.'
I took the way that led towards the Kun-lun mountain:
A long, long road with many a turning in it.
The cloud-embroidered banner flapped its great shade above us;
And the jingling jade yoke-bells tinkled merrily.

75 I set off at morning from the Ford of Heaven;
At evening I came to the world's western end.
Phoenixes followed me, bearing up my pennants,
Soaring high aloft with majestic wing-beats.
'See, I have come to the Desert of Moving Sands!'

Warily I drove along the banks of the Red Water,
Then, beckoning the water-dragons to make a bridge for me,
I summoned the God of the West to take me over.

353 So long the road had been and full of difficulties,
I sent word to my escort to take another route,
To wheel around leftwards, skirting Bu-zhou Mountain:
On the shore of the Western Sea we would reassemble.
When we had mustered there, all thousand chariots,
Jade hub to jade hub we galloped on abreast.
My eight dragon steeds flew on with writhing undulations;
My cloud-embroidered banners flapped on the wind.

361 In vain I tried to curb them, to slacken the swift pace:
The spirits soared high up, far into the distance.
We played the Nine Songs and danced the Shao Dances,
Borrowing the time to make a holiday.
But when I had ascended the splendour of the heavens,
I suddenly caught a glimpse below of my old home.
My groom's heart was heavy and the horses for longing
Arched their heads back and refused to go on.

LUAN

369 Enough! There are no true men in the state: no one understands
     me.
Why should I cleave to the city of my birth?
Since none is worthy to work with in making good government,
I shall go and join Peng Xian in the place where he abides.

Notes

*l.*1 *the high lord Gao Yang*: 'high lord' is a translation of the Chinese
word *di*. When the peoples inhabiting what we now call China were
still living in a tribal state, *di* was the name of the god, usually a sky
god, from whom a tribe derived its origin. In a typical origin-myth, e.g.
that of the Shang people, the *di* ('God') miraculously impregnates a
virgin ('Mother of the People') who gives birth to the *zu* ('First
Ancestor') of the tribe. As horizons widened to accommodate a larger

world than the tribe, it became evident that there must be more than one *di*. The *di* were now thought of sometimes as a number of sky gods subordinate to one all-encompassing Top God, or 'Heaven', sometimes as earthly ancestors. Later the word was occasionally somewhat loosely applied to historical or even to living persons. After its arrogation by Qin Shi-huang in the third century B.C. as part of the imperial title, it came to be used exclusively in the sense of 'emperor'. To Qu Yuan, as to other members of the ancient Chinese aristocracy, *di* were the legendary forefathers from whom one traced one's ancestry: divine beings who had once lived heroic lives on earth and who were now 'up there', though at the same time they were in some mysterious way also present in the places where they had been buried. Gao Yang, also known as Zhuan Xu, was one of a pair of *di* (the other one being Gao Xin, also known as Di Ku) from whom nearly all the princely houses of Qu Yuan's day believed themselves to be descended. Two of the three dynasties which successively held sway over the North China Plain during the two millennia before his time, the Shang and the Zhou, traced their ancestry from Gao Xin. The Xia, the most ancient of the three, were supposed to have been descendants of Gao Yang. Gao Yang was also the god-ancestor of the princely houses of Qin, Qi, Zhao and Chu. In recognition of the cultural affinity of these two groups, genealogists gave them a common ancestor in the person of Huang Di, the 'Yellow Ancestor' or 'Yellow Emperor'. According to this rather late and sophisticated view, Gao Yang and Gao Xin were both grandsons of Huang Di, and all Chinese, irrespective of their lineage, were 'children of the Yellow Emperor'. Qu Yuan could trace his ancestry back to Gao Yang because the Qu lineage to which he belonged was a collateral branch of the Chu royal clan.

l.3 She Ti pointed to the first month of the year: She Ti was the name of a Chinese constellation made up of two groups of three stars to left and right of the bright star Arcturus in Boötes. They were thought of as continuing the line of the Plough's handle, and were used by ancient Chinese astronomers as indicators which marked the beginning of spring, i.e. the beginning of a calendar year starting approximately one and a half months before the vernal equinox. Just how they were thought to do this is nowhere stated, but it seems probable that the ancient astronomers must have observed the late winter sky at a fixed time each night until they saw the Plough's handle pointing vertically downwards with the She Ti stars of Boötes directly underneath, over a point on the north-east horizon which they called *yin*: i.e. two-thirds of the way between North and East if you start at North and move round the compass in a clockwise (NESW) direction. In very ancient times, when the Chinese were making their first calendars, the sun on New Year's Day rose in the right ascension of Arcturus; so the appearance of the She Ti stars at *yin* on the night before was a good indication that the New Year was about to begin. That is why the eastern quarter of the sky (NE–SE) was called by Chinese astronomers 'the Palace of Spring' and why the ancient Xia calendar was said to 'start from *yin*'. For '*first month of the year*' in *l.*3 Qu Yuan uses a very unusual term employed only by astronomers: *meng zou*, which means literally 'big niche' or 'big notch'. It might refer to the configuration of the stars as they appeared at this time of night, or possibly to a notch on some primitive astronomical instrument. At all events, *l.*3 tells us that the poet was well versed in the astronomical lore of his day. It also tells us that he was able to reinforce the confident belief in his superiority over other men, frequently expressed elsewhere in this poem, with the knowledge that he was born, like Bao Yu's elder sister in 'The Story of the Stone', on the most auspicious day of the whole year.

Rather confusingly, the She Ti stars were also used as markers in another, completely different, connection. The planet Jupiter completes its revolution round the sun in approximately twelve (actually 11·86) years. This 'great year' of Jupiter, in which every month lasts twelve of our earthly months, was thought to begin when the 'Year Star', as Jupiter was called, was in the 'She Ti position', which marks the beginning of our earthly year. A cycle of twelve signs (see note on *l.*4), of which the *yin* mentioned above was one, was already in use in the naming of days and in the clockwise, i.e. NESW, designation of twelve compass-points – based, presumably, on the movement of the gnomon's shadow and the apparent diurnal movement of the sun; but the natural desire to correlate all these duodenary cycles – days, months and years – and use the same set of signs for each was at first frustrated by the fact that Jupiter, like the other heavenly bodies, appears to move round the night sky in an anti-clockwise, i.e. NWSE, direction. The ancient calendar-makers' solution was to invent a shadow Jupiter, or Counter-Jupiter, which made its way through the constellations at the same rate as the actual Jupiter but in contramotion. The 'She Ti position' therefore came to be used as a way of designating the first year of the duodenary Jupiter-cycle when the Counter-Jupiter was in *yin*. The earliest recorded instance of this usage occurs in a text of the third century B.C., but by Wang Yi's time it had come to be almost the only way in which the expression was used. Wang Yi's quite mistaken assumption that the She Ti position of *l.*3 refers not to the beginning of the year but to the beginning of the duodenary Jupiter-cycle has misled many scholars into fruitless attempts at calculating the date of Qu Yuan's birth. The best commentary on this line is a passage in the chapter on calendar-making in Si-ma Qian's 'History' in which the historian refers to a time in remote antiquity when the world had fallen into disorder and the star-clerks in charge of the calendar were no longer doing their job: 'Some time after this the

Miao broke out into new rebellions and these two offices fell into disuse, with the result that *meng zou* was lost [i.e. no one any longer knew when the year was supposed to begin], She Ti ceased to function as an indicator, and the whole calendar was thrown into disorder.'

l.4 the day geng-yin: the ancient Chinese had a week of ten days, each with a name of its own, whose meaning, if it ever had one, is now unknown. The ten names are:

> 1. *jia* 2. *yi* 3. *bing* 4. *ding* 5. *wù*
> 6. *ji* 7. *geng* 8. *xin* 9. *ren* 10. *gui*

These ten were combined with the twelve signs of the duodenary cycle referred to in the previous note (which could also be thought of as houses of the moon, compass-points or two-hour divisions of the celestial equator) to make up a total of sixty pairs. The names of the twelve, with principal directions and modern animal equivalents, are:

1.	*zi* (NORTH: rat)	7.	*wù* (SOUTH: horse)
2.	*chou* (ox)	8.	*wei* (sheep)
3.	*yin* (tiger)	9.	*shen* (monkey)
4.	*mao* (EAST: hare)	10.	*you* (WEST: cock)
5.	*chen* (dragon)	11.	*xu* (dog)
6.	*si* (snake)	12.	*hai* (pig)

The first sign of the cycle of ten was combined with the first sign of the cycle of twelve, the second with the second, and so on until the cycle of ten was exhausted, after which the cycle of ten recommenced, its first sign being combined with the eleventh sign of the duodenary cycle, and so on. In the sexagenary cycle beginning with *jia-zi* and ending with *gui-hai* which is produced by combining the two cycles until both are simultaneously exhausted, *geng-yin* is the twenty-seventh pair. The sixty pairs came subsequently to be used for naming years as well (hence the modern habit of referring to the 'Year of the Snake', etc.), but in Qu Yuan's time they were used exclusively as day-names. Since the New Year was thought to 'begin in *yin*', as I have explained in the note on *l.3*, to have been born on New Year's Day when the day itself was a *yin* day was no doubt exceptionally remarkable and auspicious; but there is reason to believe that of the five *yin* days in the cycle – *bing-yin* (No. 3), *wù-yin* (No. 15), *geng-yin* (No. 27), *ren-yin* (No. 39) and *jia-yin* (No. 51) – *geng-yin* had some special significance for the people of Chu. The fire god Zhu Rong, descendant of the sky god Gao Yang and First Ancestor of the group of lineages to which the Chu aristocracy belonged, becomes, in the euhemerized account of him we find in Si-ma Qian's 'History', an historical personage who was appointed to the office of Master of Fire on a *geng-yin* day. I think we can deduce from the evident importance of this gratuitous particular that the first *geng-yin* day of the year must have been the fire god's feast-day. It was on a *geng-yin* day that the 'good' Chu king Zhao Wang, whose death had been prophesied, died in 489 B.C. Clearly it was quite the best day in the year either to be born or to die on.

*ll.*7–8 *True Exemplar, Divine Balance*: these are pseudonyms, not real names. Si-ma Qian's biography states that Ping ('level') was Qu Yuan's original name and Yuan ('plain') his courtesy name or 'style' – the name a boy was given when he reached puberty and by which he was ever afterwards known to his peers. The usual explanation is that 'True Exemplar' and 'Divine Balance' are word-plays on Qu Yuan's real names. Both the real and the pretended names might have been chosen in reference to the 'correct', 'balanced' state of the heavens at the time of the poet's nativity. 'Divine Balance' in the Chinese text is 'Ling Jun', a name similar to that of the shaman Ling Fen in *Li sao*, *l.*258, and to the form of address used for the king in *l.*44 and for a mountain goddess in the 'Nine Songs'.

*ll.*11–12 *I dressed in selinea and shady angelica*: the allegorical use of flower-names in this poem is not consistent. Here the flowers with which the poet adorns himself represent the various accomplishments which he acquired in the course of his education. As well as history, genealogy and astronomy, these would no doubt have included medicine, or herb-lore. The use of flower-names to symbolize accomplishments seems doubly appropriate if the gathering and processing of herbs was one of them.

*l.*20 *my Fairest's beauty would fade too*: in ancient China the word *mei-ren* (literally 'beautiful person') was sexually ambiguous, though it later came to be used only of women. In this poem Qu Yuan constantly uses sexual relations as a metaphor for other sorts of relationship. There is little doubt that the *mei-ren* here and elsewhere in this poem symbolizes the king, but what is the intended meaning of the imagery? Is the poet imagining himself as a handsome, flower-decked youth and his king as a beautiful maiden whom he seeks to woo? His pursuit, later in the poem, of various goddesses and legendary women symbolizing (presumably) rulers of neighbouring states seems to favour such an interpretation. But when we next encounter the king/*mei-ren* in *l.*85, we learn that the *mei-ren*'s women were jealous of the poet's beauty. So is the poet representing himself as a woman and the king as a man? In that case, what of the above-mentioned Quest of Fair Women which forms the central part of the poem? A third possibility, sometimes discussed, though not, as far as I am aware, in print, is that the relationship here imagined is a homosexual one: flower-decked male poet in pursuit of beautiful male lover. Since Chinese pronouns, both ancient and modern, make no distinction of gender, the text is non-committal. Unfortunately it is impossible to reproduce this ambiguity in translation.

l.25 The three kings of old: Wang Yi thought this meant the founding
kings of the three dynasties which successively held sway over the
North China Plain during the millennium and a half before Qu Yuan's
day: Yu the Great, founder of the Xia dynasty, Tang the Successful,
founder of the Shang dynasty, and King Wu, founder of the Zhou
dynasty. Modern scholars are mostly of the opinion that Qu Yuan is
referring here to three former kings of Chu; but, with the exception of
the 'Heavenly Questions', the poet's forays into ancient history seem
elsewhere to be of an ecumenical kind, avoiding the local and particular
and concentrating on the remoter antiquity which was the common
heritage of Northerners and Southerners alike. For this reason I think
Wang Yi's explanation is to be preferred. It seems to be borne out by a
passage in one of the *Jiu zhang* poems ('The Outpouring of Sad
Thoughts', *l.*33).

l.29 Yao and Shun: two 'sage-kings' constantly referred to by Qu Yuan
and his contemporaries as symbols of a Golden Age in high
antiquity when rulers ruled by good example alone and won the
allegiance of distant tribes not by military conquest but by cultural
magnetism. Confucius calls Yao 'sublime' ('Analects' VIII, 19) and
praises Shun for his masterly inaction: he merely had to sit with his face
to the south and the world was transformed by the benign power of his
virtue. Yao was the son of Gao Xin and Shun was a descendant of Gao
Yang. Shun's other name was Chong Hua. He was buried in Southern
Chu, where he was presumably worshipped. (His wives became river
goddesses and were the object of an important local cult.) Shun served
in Yao's court, along with the ancestors of most of the royal and
princely houses of ancient China. Yao chose him as his successor,
marrying his daughters to him (like the kings in the story-books) and
voluntarily abdicating in his favour. The Golden Age of Yao and Shun
portrayed in the legends is probably a garbled recollection of a time
when a confederacy of two groups of tribes, a Gao Xin group and a Gao
Yang group, were led by elected high kings chosen alternately from one
or other of the two groups.

l.31 Jie and Zhòu: Jie was the last king of the Xia and Zhòu the last
king of the Shang dynasty. I have given him an accent to
distinguish him from the name (written in Chinese with a different
character) of the dynasty which supplanted him. Both kings were
represented as monsters of iniquity. The stories about them are
probably mostly legendary, but Zhòu was certainly an historical
person. Large numbers of inscriptions dating from his reign are found
among the oracle bones excavated at Anyang. Wu Wang, who
overthrew him and founded the Zhou dynasty, was the chieftain of a
tributary border state and therefore a vassal of the Shang king. It
required a good deal of propaganda to persuade the conquered Shang

people that he was qualified to assume the mantle of the long line of priest-kings he had overthrown. It was necessary to show that because of Zhòu's monstrous tyrannies the dynasty had forfeited the mandate to govern bestowed on it by Heaven. The stories about Jie are also part of this propaganda – a fabricated historical precedent for a dynasty's forfeiture of its mandate through the wickedness of a single ruler. This is the sort of 'history' we encounter in the chronicle plays of Shakespeare. However, some of the barbarities attributed to Zhòu, like his cutting out of Bi Gan's heart (see note on *l.*159) and his dismemberment of various vassals, may in fact be historical. To judge from the archaeological remains, not only Zhòu but all of the Shang kings practised ritual slaughter on an almost Aztec scale.

*l.*39 *the Fragrant One*: the Chinese word *quan*, literally a kind of iris or flowering rush, is used here by the poet in addressing his king. We find it again in one of the 'Nine Songs' ('The Lesser Master of Fate', *l.*24), where the worshipper uses it in addressing a god.

*l.*44 *the Fair One*: the Chinese *Ling Xiu*, here used of the poet's king, is found in the 'Nine Songs' applied to a mountain goddess. *Ling* means 'divine', 'godlike' or 'magical'. In *l.*8 it was an element in one of the names given to Qu Yuan by his father. We find it again in *l.*258 as the first element in the name of a shaman. As a substantive, *ling* could be used to mean either the gods themselves or the power or brightness they radiate (as in *l.*283). In his commentary on the 'Nine Songs' Wang Yi tells us that in Chu the people also used *ling* in the sense of 'shaman'; but since the shamans he is talking about had been possessed by a god, we cannot be sure exactly what he meant by that assertion. *Xiu* meaning a beautiful or fine person is a usage that seems peculiar to these poems. Cf. *ll.*73 and 176, where 'the former *xiu*' is used to mean 'the good men of old'. The usual meaning of *xiu* is 'adorn' or 'embellish'. The good men of old were presumably, like the poet, *adorned* metaphorically with the flowers which symbolize hard-won accomplishments. The goddesses in the 'Nine Songs' would have been literally adorned with feathers, flowers and jewels. The king – if *Ling Xiu* here does indeed, like the fragrant iris of *l.*39, refer to the poet's king – is presumably being thought of as a god (or perhaps a goddess).

In the Chinese text there is an extra line between *ll.*44 and 45 which I have omitted. It is the only line in the poem which does not belong to a couplet and cannot have been in Wang Yi's text, since it lacks a comment by him here but is explained when it reappears later in the anthology (*Jiu zhang*, 'The Outpouring of Sad Thoughts', *ll.*14–15).

*l.*76 *Peng Xian*: Peng Xian reappears in the very last line of the poem:
'Since none is worthy to work with in making good government/ I shall go and join Peng Xian in the place where he abides.' Wang Yi says

that Peng Xian was the name of an upright minister at the court of one of the Shang kings, who drowned himself when his good advice was not taken. In Wang Yi's view the talk of following Peng Xian's example is Qu Yuan's way of saying that he is going to drown himself, as he subsequently did, in the River Mi-luo. This seems to have been the view of Liu Xiang nearly two centuries earlier. In one of his poems ('Leaving the World', p. 286, *l.*42) he speaks of 'Shi Yan floating among the eyots' and 'Peng Xian on his watery wanderings'. Shi Yan was the Music Master or Court Musician of King Zhòu of Shang. He was supposed to have drowned himself in the River Pu and his spirit is supposed to have been heard playing ghostly music by Duke Ling of Wei when he was camping by the side of this river some time in the fifth century B.C. By mentioning Shi Yan and Peng Xian together, Liu Xiang seems to be implying that both, like Qu Yuan, were loyal servants who drowned themselves in despair when their advice was rejected by their royal masters. However, a number of modern scholars are of the opinion that Peng Xian is not one name but two: Shaman Peng (Wu Peng) and Shaman Xian (Wu Xian). Wu Xian in fact makes an appearance later on in this poem (*l.*279). He, or his eponym, was one of the principal advisers of the seventh Shang king, Tai Wu, and oracle bone inscriptions show that he was sacrificed to in later reigns with almost the same honours as those paid to royal ancestors. The name of the 'great and glorious god Wu Xian' is several times invoked in the 'Commination of Chu' dating from Qu Yuan's lifetime (see note on *l.*279). There are references to 'Shaman Peng' and 'Shaman Xian' in several ancient texts: for example, in the 'Book of Seas and Mountains' Wu Xian and Wu Peng are two of the names in a list of ten holy shamans said to climb up and down a magic mountain in the midst of the Great Wilderness of the West in quest of herbs. To judge from a line in the 'Anti-*Li sao*' of Liu Xiang's contemporary Yang Xiong (53 B.C.–A.D. 18), the whole text of which is included in Yang Xiong's biography in the 'History of the Former Han Dynasty', Yang Xiong may also have held the view that 'Peng Xian' here and in *l.*372 is two people rather than one. When, in the 'Anti-*Li sao*', he speaks of Qu Yuan 'rejecting what You Ran prized and choosing what Peng Xian bequeathed', it is quite certain that 'You Ran' refers to two people, Xu You and Lao Ran. It therefore seems extremely likely that he is employing a similar sort of shorthand in 'Peng Xian': i.e. just as by 'You Ran' he intends you to understand 'Xu You and Lao Ran', so by 'Peng Xian' he intends you to understand 'Wu Peng and Wu Xian'. A somewhat similar example of 'Peng Xian' paralleling a contraction of two names occurs in *Jiu zhang* ('The Outpouring of Sad Thoughts', *ll.*33–4). The uncertainty about Peng Xian is therefore a very ancient one. Conceivably Peng Xian, like Xi He and Zhong Li, was one of the Great Inventors (see note on *l.*189) whose followers took their founder's name as their own (like the Greek followers of Asklepios) but later divided it between them as the various branches of their profession became more specialized. The third-century B.C. encyclopedia *Lü-shi chun-qiu* names Shaman Peng as the inventor of medicine and Shaman Xian as the inventor of divination. Another source names both as 'divine healers'; yet another says that Shaman Peng invented dancing. Drumming, dancing, the collection and preparation of medicinal herbs and divination were all shaman skills to begin with; so perhaps there was a First Shaman called Peng Xian who was equally competent in them all. That Qu Yuan should have identified him with a shaman who lived at the court of one of the Shang kings and drowned himself in protest when his loyal advice was rejected is by no means impossible. At all events it seems more natural to read 'Peng Xian' here and in *l.*372 as a single name, like all the other bisyllabic names in which this poem abounds, than to treat it as a contraction of two. The idea that 'following Peng Xian' meant not going off to live with shamans but joining the spirit of Peng Xian by throwing oneself in the river is a comparatively ancient one and was certainly not invented by Wang Yi. It is implied by the anonymous author of the last of the *Jiu zhang* poems: 'Riding the great waves, drifting with the wind/I would go to rest where Peng Xian dwells' ('Grieving at the Eddying Wind', *ll.*69–70).

*l.*129 *Nü Xu*: no earlier authority than Wang Yi can be found for the tradition that this was the name of Qu Yuan's sister, though a reference to it by one of his contemporaries suggests that it was already established in his time and not one that he invented. By the fourth century Chinese tourists were being shown Nü Xu's house and the washing-block on which she had done her laundry, and a prefecture was said to have been given its name in her honour. In fact, it is not even certain that 'Nü Xu' here is a proper name. 'Nü' is the ordinary word for 'daughter', 'girl' or 'maiden'. Its occasional use as the first element in a woman's name (e.g. 'Nü Qi' and 'Nü Wa' in 'Heavenly Questions', *ll.*83–90 and 97–8) may be compared with the 'maid' of 'Maid Marion'. 'Xu' itself first appears (in the 'Book of Changes') as a common noun meaning 'secondary wife', 'concubine' or 'bridesmaid', but is found in use as a proper name in the early second century B.C. The Founder of the Han dynasty's ferocious empress, Lü Hou, had a younger sister called Xu. (One imagines that it was a rather vulgar sort of name, like 'Sissy' or 'Sonny'.) A Chu shamaness called Nü Xu was patronized by one of Emperor Wu's sons, the Prince of Guang-ling, in the first century B.C., but whether it was her real name or one she had found in *Li sao* and was using as her professional name, like the fancy names mediums sometimes give themselves today, we have no means of knowing. It could be that *nü-xu* here is simply a collective common noun ('my maidens') paralleling the Fair One's envious 'ladies' in *l.*87, but I have preferred to understand it as a proper name. Probably it is a fanciful made-up name like so many others in this poem. Whether it represents the poet's wife, concubine, sister or friend it is quite impossible to say.

*l.*131 *Gun*: according to legend there was a great flood in the time of the high king Yao (see note on *l.*29) and Gun, the son of Gao Yang (see note on *l.*1), was given the task of dealing with it. His chosen methods – building dykes and infilling – were unsuccessful and he was put to death as a punishment, his body being exposed on Feather Mountain, where it lay for three years without rotting. At the end of that time it was cut open, releasing his son, Yu the Great, who was alive inside his belly. Gun thereupon turned into a bear (some say a water monster) and dived off a cliff into the water below. Yu the Great was more successful in dealing with the flood. In fact, he did not only drain the flood; the whole Chinese landscape is supposed to have been his creation. The story of Gun is dealt with at some length in the 'Heavenly Questions'.

*ll.*143–4 *crossing the Yuan and Xiang ... till I came to where Chong Hua was*: Chong Hua was the name of the high king Shun (see note on *l.*29). The place 'where he was' is Doubting Mountain (*Jiu-yi shan*: literally 'the Mountain of Nine Doubts'), where Shun was buried. Shun is supposed to have died while campaigning against the Miao tribes in what was then the Deep South, near the source of the River Xiang in South Hunan. (For the rivers Yuan and Xiang and Doubting Mountain, see map on p. 351.) Shun's two queens, the daughters of the high king Yao, were supposed to have wandered southwards along the banks of the Xiang looking for him. They turned into river goddesses (two of the 'Nine Songs' are addressed to them) and their tears are supposed to have turned into the markings on a certain sort of bamboo which grows in that area. Though not himself an ancestor of the kings of Chu, Shun was, like them, a descendant of Gao Yang. That, and the fact that he was buried in Chu and was the consort of the local river goddesses, must have made him an object of special veneration by the Chu people. In the sixth century B.C., according to the 'Sayings of the States' (*Guo yu*, Ch. 17), King Ling of Chu – a bad king – built a sort of ziggurat for himself, in imitation of Doubting Mountain, on the flatlands north of Lake Dong-ting (see map, p. 351) and surrounded it with a stone-lined water-course in imitation of the River Xiang 'so that he could make himself like the high lord Shun'.

*ll.*145–56 *Singing the Nine Songs, etc.*: Qi, the son of Yu the Great (see note on *l.*131), wrested the kingship from the chieftain to whom his father, following the custom of his predecessors, had entrusted it, thereby bringing the Golden Age to an end and instituting hereditary monarchy. The line of kings of which his father was retrospectively reckoned to have been the founder was called the Xia dynasty. Qi was believed to have visited heaven and been entertained by God and to have brought back the Nine Songs and the Nine Shao Dances. (The 'Nine Changes' was, I believe, the music to which the Shao dances were danced.) There must have been strong resistance from the Gao Xin group of chieftains to the monopoly of the high kingship by a lineage belonging to the Gao Yang group, since it was a representative of the former, Lord Yi (the 'Yi' of *l*.149), who took advantage of the quarrelling among Qi's five sons after their father's death to seize power for himself in the Central Plain. In Chinese mythology Lord Yi was the Mighty Archer whose arrows brought down nine of the suns when all ten came out together and burned up the earth. The eponymous chieftain was presumably an historicized avatar of the toxophiliac sun hero. Lord Yi's wife and his henchman Han Zhuo ('Zhuo' for short in *l*.153) plotted against him. They waylaid and killed him on his return from the hunt, cooked his body and served his flesh up to his son. When the son refused to eat it, they killed him too. Jiao the Strong Man (*l*.153) was one of the two sons of Han Zhuo and Lord Yi's treacherous wife. He was slain by the young Xia prince Shao Kang (see note on *l*.247), whose father he had killed, when Shao Kang had grown up and came out of hiding to avenge his father, overthrow the usurpers and claim his patrimony. After this long interregnum kingship returned to the House of Xia and remained with it until the reign of Jie (*l*.157), whose wickedness brought the dynasty to an end.

l.159 *Zhòu cut up and salted the bodies of his ministers*: for Zhòu, last king of the Shang dynasty, see note on *l*.31. Legend names three of his vassals who came to this grisly end: the Lord of Gui, with whom Zhòu was displeased because his daughter had proved a refractory bed-fellow, and the Lords of Mei and E, who protested too outspokenly against his tyranny. The first two Zhòu is said to have had cut up and pickled and to have distributed pickled portions of among his nobles *pour encourager les autres*; the third he had made into a stew which was offered up in the ancestral temple.

l.186 *the Hanging Garden*: a terrestrial paradise on the mythical mountain of Kun-lun. Kun-lun was thought of as being shaped like a ziggurat, rising up in terraces of diminishing size. The Hanging Garden was a terrace half-way up the mountain. Kun-lun is described in ancient cosmographical writings as God's footstool on earth and the gateway to heaven. After his ascent of Kun-lun, Qu Yuan's journey is mainly an aerial one. As the highest mountain in the world, Kun-lun was naturally a suitable place for the ancient space-traveller to take off from.

*l.*189 *I ordered Xi He to stay the sun-steeds' gallop*: in Chinese as in Greek
        mythology, the sun was *driven* across the sky, but the charioteer
was, originally at any rate, not a male god but a woman. According to
some ancient sources, Xi He gave birth to the sun – or rather suns, for
there were ten of them, one for each day of the week. They roosted in
the branches of the Fu-sang tree, a giant tree at the eastern edge of the
world, corresponding to the Ruo tree at the world's western end whose
leaves give off the red glow that we see in the sunset sky. Xi He bathed
them in the Gulf of Brightness before driving one of them on its
day-long journey across the sky. From the *Canon of Yao*, an ancient
text purporting to record transactions at the court of the high king Yao,
we learn that the calendar-makers whose job it was to observe the
risings and settings of the sun throughout the year were named after
her. As there were six of them, they had to share her name between
them: Big, Middle and Little Xi and Big, Middle and Little He. *Yan-zi*
(*l.*190) belongs, like Kun-lun, to mythical cosmography rather than to
real geography. It was one of the mountains behind which the setting
sun was supposed to go down into the Vale of Murk. For the Gulf of
Brightness and the Vale of Murk, see 'Heavenly Questions', *ll.*15–16.

*ll.*193–208 *I watered my dragon steeds at the Pool of Heaven, etc.*: the
              Pool of Heaven (Xian-chi) is the name of a constellation
corresponding very roughly to our Auriga. Poets and shamans often
speak of the constellations as if they actually were the things that their
names suggest. In the hymn to the Lesser Master of Fate in the 'Nine
Songs' the shaman sings of washing his hair with the god in the Pool of
Heaven, and in the hymn which follows a shaman impersonating the
Sun God ladles wine with the Dipper and shoots at the Wolf of Heaven
(another constellation) with his bow and arrow. *Ll.*193–208 make a sort
of interlude in which the poet appears to imitate the sun's journey
through the constellations, since we find him, by *l.*213, once more in
the region of Kun-lun more or less where he started. Wang Shu (*l.*197)
was, according to the second-century B.C. *Huai nan zi*, the lady driver
of the moon (the lunar counterpart of Xi He). The Wind God (*l.*198:
Fei Lian in the Chinese text) is usually represented as a winged deer:
the *fei* part of his name means 'flying'. The aerial journey made like a
royal progress across the heavens with gods and spirits in attendance
seems at one time to have been a regular feature of Chinese shamanism.
The third-century B.C. philosopher Han Fei-zi describes a progress
made 'in the olden time' by the Yellow Ancestor which reads
remarkably like the celestial journey in this poem. He 'assembled the
spirits on the summit of Mt Tai, riding in an ivory chariot drawn by six
dragons, with the Fire God at his side, Chi You in front, the Wind God
sweeping the dust, the Rain God sprinkling the road ahead, tigers and

wolves as vanguard, spirits and gods bringing up the rear, jumping snakes writhing over the ground below and flying phoenixes making a canopy overhead ...' The purpose of such processions was no doubt the acquisition or affirmation of power over the world of spirits. They were aped by the imperial tours of emperors like Qin Shi-huang and Han Wu-di to holy mountains and other sacred places in order to assert their spiritual overlordship over the land of which they were already the territorial proprietors.

ll.213–14 the White Water ... Lang-feng: the White Water was one of the different-coloured rivers flowing out of the magic mountain of Kun-lun. *Huai nan zi* says that those who drank from it became immortal. Some claimed that it turned farther on in its course into the river that we know as the Yellow River. (In the 'Nine Songs' the god of the Yellow River climbs up Kun-lun to survey his domain.) Lang-feng was one of Kun-lun's terraces. One authority identifies it with the Hanging Garden (see note on *l.*186).

l.217 Here I am, suddenly, in this House of Spring: the House of Spring was the home of the Green God of the East; it was also one of the four equatorial palaces of ancient Chinese astronomy. The abrupt movement in the course of a line or two from one end of the world to the other which is a feature of this second half of the poem has prompted some scholars to suppose displacements in the text but was probably characteristic of all shamanistic accounts of spirit-journeying. A similar switch occurs in the hymn to the River Earl in the 'Nine Songs', where in two lines the scene changes from the mouth of the Yellow River to the summit of Kun-lun.

ll.221–2 So I made Feng Long ... the lady Fu Fei: commentators are divided over the identity of Feng Long: some say that this was the name of the Thunder God (cf. *l.*200), others that he was the Master of Clouds. Wang Yi thought that this was the god worshipped in the second of the 'Nine Songs' ('The Lord within the Clouds'). Perhaps 'Thunder God' and 'Master of Clouds' were simply different titles for the same deity, since thunder is associated with stormclouds and the Thunder God's main function was to slit the clouds open with his lightnings and release the rain. The 'Ping' of 'Heavenly Questions', *ll.*81–2, is probably yet another name for him. 'Rain God', 'Cloud God' and 'Thunder God', in other words, though turned into three separate deities by the lexicographers, were all, I believe, different aspects of the same god and the 'confusions' between them in which ancient texts abound are not really confusions at all. Fu Fei was a water goddess, the guardian of the River Luo. The 'Heavenly Questions' refers to a legend (now lost) about Lord Yi, the Mighty Archer, shooting the River Earl (the god of the Yellow River) and carrying off the Luo goddess to be his wife. Since the River Luo is a tributary of the Yellow River, it would be natural to think of its goddess as the Yellow River god's consort. Qiong-shi (*l.*227) was traditionally the home of Lord Yi. In the passage which follows, the goddess's vacillations between Qiong-shi and Wei-pan are, I think, meant to imply that she is carrying on simultaneously with both Lord Yi and the River Earl. Those who see the poet's unsuccessful wooing of three legendary ladies in this section of the poem as an allegory of the rejected statesman's search for a better government to work under (cf. *l.*371) have made various attempts, none of them in the least convincing, to identify Fu Fei and the other ladies with contemporary Chinese rulers. The name 'Lame Beauty' (*l.*224) is unknown outside this poem. *Jian Xiu*, the Chinese of which 'Lame Beauty' is meant to be a translation, contains the same second element as *Ling Xiu* ('the Fair One') which is explained in the note on *l.*44. Fu Fei, according to Wang Yi, was the daughter of Fu Xi, who played an important part in the creation myths of several of the peoples inhabiting China in ancient times. He and his sister Nü Wa, like Deucalion and Pyrrha in the Greek legend, were thought to have peopled the earth after a great flood. Both Fu Xi and Nü Wa were serpents from the waist down. According to one ancient source, Nü Wa founded the institution of marriage and was the first go-between. Conceivably she is the matchmaker used here and 'Lame Beauty' is a 'kenning' for her invented by the poet. With a serpent's tail instead of legs she could certainly be thought of as 'lame'.

*l.*236 *the lovely daughter of the Lord of Song*: this is Jian Di, the First Ancestress from whom the kings of the Shang dynasty were descended. She was shut up in a tower like Danaë, but became pregnant by swallowing an egg brought to her by a swallow sent by 'Heaven'. Later versions of the story make her one of the consorts of Di Ku (*al.* 'Gao Xin': *l.*244). The First Ancestress of the Zhou kings was also a consort of Gao Xin and was also a virgin when she conceived the Zhou Ancestor. Miraculous conception in her case took place when she stepped in a giant footprint (presumably God's). It seems probable that Gao Xin and Gao Yang (see note on *l.*1) were originally the sky gods of their respective peoples. Gao Xin is not mentioned in the earliest version of the legend because to the people who told it 'Heaven' was in fact Gao Xin. For them Gao Xin was not an earthly king cuckolded by a bird 'sent from God' but God himself, who sent the bird. Qu Yuan must have been familiar with a version of the legend representing an intermediate stage in its evolution from myth into pseudo-history. In this version Gao Xin is now a human king (like Shao Kang below), yet it is still he who sends the swallow which impregnated his wife (a sort of ancient Chinese version of A.I.H.). In Qu Yuan's account the bird has become a phoenix (*l.*243). He naturally chooses a bird as messenger in presenting himself as Gao Xin's rival for the lady's hand; unfortunately the bird he chose proved an unreliable one.

ll.247–8 Prince Shao Kang ... Lord Yu's two daughters: when the Strong Man Jiao (see note on *ll.*145–56) killed Prince Xiang (one of the five quarrelling sons of Qi mentioned in *l.*148), Xiang's wife, who was pregnant at the time, escaped to her own people and gave birth to Shao Kang. Shao Kang obtained employment as a cook with the Lord of Yu, who subsequently gave him his two daughters in marriage and enfeoffed him with lands.

l.258 Ling Fen: for this kind of name, see notes on *ll.*7–8 and *l.*44.
Perhaps this is the same person as the Wu Fen ('Shaman Fen') mentioned in the 'Book of Seas and Mountains' as one of the Ten Shamans who live on a holy mountain in the West. For the equation '*ling* equals *wu*', see note on *l.*44. Chopped-up pieces of bamboo were a recognized substitute for the milfoil stalks normally used in the kind of divination associated with the 'Book of Changes' (*Yi jing*).

l.279 Wu Xian: see note on *l.*76, 'Peng Xian'. Wu Xian was the greatest of all the Shaman Ancestors (shamans worshipped after their death and taken by living shamans as their 'guides'). According to some, he was the First Shaman, who invented all the techniques of shamanism; in other sources he appears as the inventor of divination or of medicine – two of the most important of those techniques. Qu Yuan was perhaps, as I have suggested elsewhere, a sort of shaman himself. Being still not quite certain what he should do after listening to the expert advice offered him by Ling Fen, it is natural that he should turn to the great patron and founder of the profession to have his doubts resolved. The rice-balls of *l.*280 are often mentioned as appropriate offerings for mountain spirits in the 'Book of Seas and Mountains'. Like the blood-drinking ghosts in the *Odyssey*, Wu Xian will feel constrained to speak in return for the food. Chinese spirits always operated on a *quid pro quo* basis.

l.282 the host of Doubting Mountain: the host of Doubting Mountain (where Shun was buried: see note on *ll.*143–4) appears in an almost identical line in one of the 'Nine Songs' – a hymn addressed to the goddess of the River Xiang ('The Lady of the Xiang', *ll.*33–4). As Shun was the Xiang goddess's husband and Doubting Mountain quite near the source of her river, their appearance in that context is natural and to be expected; here it seems unaccountable and has in fact never been satisfactorily explained. The fact that this line is the only one in a poem of ninety-three couplets which does not rhyme with the other line in the couplet makes it extremely likely that it is either misplaced or corrupt.

ll.287–8   *Tang and Yu . . . Yi Yin and Gao Yao*: Yi Yin was the Chief
　　　　　Minister of Tang the Successful, the founder of the Shang
dynasty (cf. note on *l*.25). As a baby he was found inside the hollow
mulberry tree his mother had turned into when fleeing from a flood. He
became a cook in the Lord of You-xin's kitchen. Tang the Successful
fell in love with his cooking when visiting the Lord of You-xin and
arranged for him to be sent in the train of You-xin's daughter when he
married her. Gao Yao was first the colleague and then the minister of
Yu the Great, the founder of the Xia dynasty. As Shun's Minister of
Justice he was famous for his judgements and for his suppression of
crime. Though completely colourless – not a single story is told about
him – he is mentioned with curious frequency in ancient sources,
probably because he was the First Ancestor of several noble clans. A
section of the ancient 'History Classic' or 'Book of Documents' is
named after him.

ll.291–2   *Yue . . . Wu Ding*: Wu Ding, the seventeenth Shang king,
　　　　　dreamed of the man best qualified to help him with the
government of his empire and afterwards painted a likeness of the man
he had seen in his dream so that he could have a search made for him
throughout his dominions. He was eventually discovered in a gang of
convicts ramming earth at a place called Fu-yan. Ramming earth
between wooden shutters with a sort of spiked beetle was for centuries
the standard Chinese way of making walls. Buildings were constructed
of wooden frames supported on a stone base with outer walls of *terre
pisée* made in the way described. Yue, as the convict who became a
king's counsellor was called, is generally referred to as 'Fu Yue' after
the name of the place where he was 'discovered'. Some Chinese scholars
claim that Fu Yue is the 'Dream Father' who appears in some of the
oracle bone inscriptions of Wu Ding's reign.

l.293   *Lü Wang wielded the butcher's knife at Zhao-ge*: Lü Wang, chief
　　　　　adviser of King Wen, father of the King Wu who overthrew the
last Shang king and established the Zhou dynasty (see notes on *ll*.25
and 31), was, according to one tradition, a butcher when King Wen
first 'discovered' him. Another tradition has it that he was a fisherman.
After King Wen's death and the conquest of Shang by his son, Lü
Wang was enfeoffed as the first Duke of Qi and his descendants
continued to be Dukes of Qi until the fourth century B.C., when they
were supplanted by a rival family.

ll.295–6   *Ning Qi . . . Duke Huan of Qi*: Duke Huan of Qi, the
　　　　　fifteenth Duke, who inherited the duchy of Qi in the eleventh
generation after Lü Wang, was the first of the Great Hegemons who led
the confederacy of Zhou states in the days of the royal house's decline

and the most powerful and progressive ruler of his day. Like many other successful autocrats, he preferred men of humble origin as his chief advisers. One of them, Ning Qi, was a travelling merchant when he first came to the Duke's attention. Wu Xian offers all these examples of men who were 'discovered' by powerful and virtuous rulers as a means of encouraging the rejected poet: let him look around elsewhere; some enlightened ruler is sure sooner or later to recognize his talents and give him the employment he deserves.

*l.*313 *I thought that orchid was one to be trusted*: the 'orchid' here and the 'pepper' of *l.*317 ('*lan*' and '*jiao*' in Chinese) are, according to a well-established Han tradition, the names of real people: King Huai of Chu's younger son (Wang Yi says his younger brother), Prince Lan, and a nobleman called Lord Jiao, who were Qu Yuan's principal enemies at court. Although lack of evidence makes it quite impossible to either prove or disprove the existence of two such people, it is clear that all the 'good' and 'bad' plants of this passage (*ll.*307–24) are used allegorically to represent persons, not as symbols of virtues or accomplishments like the herbs and flowers in the opening lines of the poem.

*l.*345 *the Ford of Heaven*: this is the name of a constellation (cf. the Pool of Heaven in *l.*193). The poet appears to be airborne once more. The Chinese thought of the Milky Way as a celestial river. The Ford of Heaven was their name for the stars in Sagittarius which span its narrowest part.

*ll.*349–50 *Moving Sands ... Red Water*: the Red Water was one of the coloured rivers flowing out of Kun-lun (see note on *ll.*213–14). The Moving Sands (literally, 'Flowing Sands') may be based on travellers' tales of the Central Asian deserts, but, like the Red Water, belong to the wonderland of shamanistic cosmography rather than to any real geography.

*l.*355 *Bu-zhou Mountain*: somewhere 'west of Kun-lun'. Bu-zhou Mountain was the north-western of the eight pillars which once supported the sky. According to legend, Gao Yang contended with a demon called Gong Gong for mastery of the world and in the course of the struggle Gong Gong butted against this pillar and broke it, thereby causing the earth to tilt up and the sky to tilt down on the north-west side. This is the reason why Chinese rivers mostly flow in an easterly or south-easterly direction. It is also, presumably, the reason – though the version of the legend which has come down to us omits to say so – why the constellations revolve. The shock which dislodged the sky from its supporting pillars must have caused it to spin, and it has been doing so ever since. *Bu-zhou* means literally 'not fit', 'not correspond'. The original intention of the legend must have been to explain why the centre of the sky is not, as it ought to be, straight overhead. At one time it *was*, we are told: when the sky was firmly propped up on its eight pillars. At that time the fixed stars would have stood still and the whole universe have been perfectly symmetrical.

*l.*363 *the Nine Songs*: not the 'Nine Songs' of this anthology, of course, but the Nine Songs brought back from heaven by Qi (see note on *ll.*145–56). The *Shao* was the dance, or dances, that went with them. Confucius heard the music for the Shao dances when he was visiting a neighbouring state and was so overcome that he scarcely noticed what he was eating for weeks afterwards. 'I never realized that music could be so perfect,' he told his disciples.

*l.*369 *Luan*: many of the Chu poems have an epilogue, coda or envoi called a '*luan*', sometimes in a different metre from the rest of the poem. The usual meaning of *luan* is 'disorder' or 'confusion', but it appears to have been used in a technical sense in ancient Chinese music. Confucius speaks approvingly of the tremendous volume of sound produced by the court musicians under the direction of a new Music Master when rendering 'the *luan* of "The Ospreys"'. 'The Ospreys' is the first song in the 'Book of Songs', an epithalamium in several stanzas. 'The *luan* of "The Ospreys"' presumably means the musical accompaniment of its final stanza, the words of which do in fact call for 'welcoming the bride with bells and drums'. These musical finales were no doubt played *tutti* and *fortissimo*, producing a 'confusion' of sound. Hence the term. As to whether we should infer from its use in these poems that they were intended for musical performance, I think there can be little doubt that at least some of them *were* so performed; but I suspect that the poets who wrote them simply borrowed the term from music and had nothing specifically musical in mind.

Jiu ge   *'Nine Songs'*

The first thing to be observed about the 'Nine Songs' is that there are eleven of them: nine addressed to various gods and goddesses, a tenth to the spirits of warriors killed in battle, and a short concluding hymn or recessional at the end.

The 'Nine Songs' can best be described as religious drama; but though it is obvious from the most cursory reading of them that they were written for performance, the absence of stage directions indicating who at any given point was supposed to be singing, or what they were doing while they sang, makes it impossible to be sure *how* they were performed. In some cases we cannot even be sure whether what we are reading is monologue or dialogue or dialogue with choric interruptions. Everyone who interprets the songs has to begin by making his own reconstruction; and because the uncertainties are so numerous, there are almost as many reconstructions as there are interpreters.

The words themselves provide us with some clues. It appears that the actors or dancers in these dramas were gorgeously dressed shamans; that musical accompaniment was provided by an orchestra of lithophones, musical bells, drums, and various kinds of wind and string instruments; that – to judge from one or two references to a 'hall' – the performance took place indoors. In several of the songs a shaman appears in the first half to be invoking or searching for some god or goddess, and in the second half to be complaining because the god or goddess either failed to turn up or left after too short a visit; in others it is the god or goddess him- or herself who appears to be addressing us.

Wang Yi thought that the 'Nine Songs' were written by Qu Yuan during his exile:

> In the old days the people of Chu who lived in the area around the old southern capital and the lands lying between the rivers Yuan and Xiang were a superstitious folk much addicted to a kind of religious rite in which they entertained various gods with singing, drumming and dancing. After his banishment, when Qu Yuan was living in hiding in this area, he would sometimes emerge to seek distraction from the burden of grief and care which oppressed him by observing the villagers at these rustic festivals, singing and dancing to delight the gods. Though the words they used were vulgar and uncouth, they inspired him to write these 'Nine Songs', partly to do honour to the gods, but partly also to give allegorical expression to his private griefs and wrongs . . .

Although his treatment of the 'Nine Songs' as allegory led him into many absurdities and has long been discredited, Wang Yi's view that they represent a literary improvement on an earlier, much cruder, oral tradition is in principle quite a sensible one; however, it is one that he probably arrived at for the wrong reasons. Wang Yi did not believe what seems obvious to us: that the 'Nine Songs' were written for performance at some court – one which expected to obtain the same high level of aesthetic satisfaction from shamanistic performances that European courts did in a later age from the masses and motets composed for them by celebrated musicians.

This was because in his day the sort of erotic relationship between god and worshipper which the 'Nine Songs' takes for granted *was* only to be found in the shamanism of the villages and would have been quite unthinkable in the stately religious rituals of the imperial court. The combination of great poetry with what, to him, was a vulgar, popular form of religion *had* to be explained in the sort of way he proposed.

Wang Yi was not the first person to believe that the 'Nine Songs' were written by Qu Yuan. A century earlier Liu Xiang must evidently have shared this belief, since they account for eleven of the twenty-five *pian* which he attributed to Qu Yuan in his 'Catalogue'. The attribution was probably felt to be justified by the references to the 'Nine Songs' in *Li sao*:

> We played the Nine Songs and danced the Shao Dances,
> Borrowing the time to make a holiday.

> *(ll.363–4)*

But the 'Nine Songs' of that passage are, of course, the legendary Nine Songs of Qi already referred to earlier in the poem:

> Singing the Nine Songs and dancing the Nine Changes,
> Qi of Xia made revelry and knew no restraint.

> *(ll.145–6)*

Qu Yuan was certainly familiar with 'questing' songs like III and IV, the theme of which inspired the central part of his allegory; it is even possible that he may have written or arranged one or two such songs himself; but it is most unlikely that he was the author or editor of the whole of the 'Nine Songs'.

Si-ma Qian, who lived half a century earlier than Liu Xiang and who may quite likely have seen the 'Nine Songs' performed, appears to have been unaware that they were in any way connected with Qu Yuan. Tai Yi, the 'Great Unity', chief of the gods to whom the 'Nine Songs' are dedicated, is first mentioned as an object of religious worship in the reign of Si-ma Qian's employer, the Han emperor Wu Di. Wu Di was a keen patron of shamans and had a weakness for lavish ritual, particularly for night-time rituals involving massed choirs and troops of dancers in which songs and dances specially composed for him by the poets and musicians of his court were performed by the light of thousands of flickering torches. He was introduced to the worship of Tai Yi by his favourite shamans. Tai Yi was 'their' god – the god whom they would undertake to summon into his presence. He was attended, they told him, by various lesser gods, one of them the Master of Fate (Si Ming), to whom Songs V and VI of the 'Nine Songs' are dedicated. Song V does in fact speak of the Master of Fate

'conducting the *di* [presumably Tai Yi] to the height of heaven'. A
hymn to 'Heaven and Earth' dating from Wu Di's reign – one of a
set used in the great Suburban Sacrifice which the emperor himself
performed outside his capital – mentions Tai Yi and the 'Nine
Songs' almost in the same breath:

> A thousand youths and maidens dance in lines of eight to give
> pleasure to Tai Yi;
> The 'Nine Songs' finally conclude, with delightful symphony of
> pipes and zithers and all the instruments.

Of the five other gods referred to by name in the 'Nine Songs' only
two, the Master of Fate and the Xiang Goddess, are known from
other sources to have been worshipped in the Warring States
kingdom of Chu. Two of the remaining three, Dong Jun, Lord of
the East (i.e. the sun), and Yun-zhong Jun, the Lord within the
Clouds, are unknown except for a reference in Si-ma Qian's 'History'
which tells us that shamans from Jin (i.e. Shanxi) were installed in
the capital by the Founder of the Han dynasty charged with the
responsibility of maintaining the cults of – among others – these
two gods. The implication would seem to be that these were, at any
rate until the beginning of the Han dynasty, thought of as
characteristically Northern cults.

It might be thought that the obvious conclusion to draw from all
this is that the 'Nine Songs' were written or compiled for Wu Di
and date from no earlier than his reign. In the 1940s some Chinese
scholars did in fact advocate this view. The great objection to it is
that all the songs, with the exception of I, X and XI, show obvious
traces of Chu dialect or contain linguistic features similar to ones
that we find in *Li sao*. In content the 'Nine Songs' are as eclectic as
a Baroque suite including dance-tunes from half a dozen different
countries, but from their outward form it is clear that they can only
have been written by a Chu poet.

For a number of reasons I believe this to have been a poet (or
poets) at the Chu court in Shou-chun (241–223 B.C.). For one thing,
the choice of Dong Huang ('Lord of the Eastern Sky') as the high
god to whom the first of the series is addressed would be
inexplicable in any other circumstances. During the latter part of
the Warring States period the old term '*di*', which had originally
been reserved for the sky god, was beginning to be used of human
rulers. In 288 B.C. the King of Qin proposed to the other most
powerful ruler of the day, King Min of Qi, that they should call
each other '*Di* of the West' and '*Di* of the East'. The idea was
dropped after a brief trial period, but similar proposals were made
from time to time in the following decades, and after the final

unification of China by Qin in 221 B.C. *di* was adopted as part of the imperial title. During these final decades of the Warring States period the feeling that the word *di* had lost some of its divinity led to another word, *huang*, being occasionally used in its stead to mean 'God' or 'Heaven'. We find this characteristically late Warring States usage several times in *Li sao*. In *Li sao*, *l*.352, we even find Dong Huang's western counterpart Xi Huang, God of the West – one of the regional viceroys of 'High God in Heaven'. The worship of Dong Huang as a sort of national Top God suggests not only a late Warring States date, but specifically a date when Chu was in fact an eastern power, either during the period when the Chu court had its capital at Chen (278–241 B.C.) or, more probably, during the period when its capital was even farther east at Shou-chun (241–223 B.C.).

No one has ever succeeded in producing a very convincing explanation of the title 'Dong Huang Tai Yi', which is found nowhere else outside the 'Nine Songs'. It is my belief that Liu An, who became Prince of Huai-nan some sixty years after the extinction of the Warring States kingdom of Chu and who had his provincial capital at the former Chu capital of Shou-chun, revived and perhaps re-edited the 'Nine Songs' and introduced them to the imperial court, where they were used, perhaps after further editing, in Wu Di's Tai Yi spectaculars. It was then, I suggest, that 'Tai Yi' was added to the title of the first song. Before that it was simply 'Dong Huang': an Eastern sky god for an Eastern king.

Various more or less plausible theories have been propounded to explain why the 'Nine Songs' song-cycle contains not nine but eleven songs. One commonly held view is that Songs I and XI were intended as a sort of prologue and epilogue to the series and so 'do not count'. Song XI is certainly very short and differs from the others in referring only to the ritual itself and not being addressed to any particular god or group of spirits. It is easy to think of it as an appendage or coda outside the series and therefore not to be counted as a separate song. But this is altogether untrue of Song I, which not only has the name of a god for its title but contains specific references to him in the text as 'God on High' and 'Lord'.

Another theory which has enjoyed a certain vogue among Chinese scholars but which was first advanced, I believe, by Liu Yong-ji is that the 'Hymn to the Fallen' (No. X) is really the 'Summons of the Soul' attributed to Qu Yuan in Si-ma Qian's biography, and does not belong here at all. Arthur Waley also believed that it was 'appended later' (see p. 15 of his *The Nine Songs: A Study of Shamanism in Ancient China*, 1955), but not for this bizarre reason. None of those who believe that Song X is an intruder have ever attempted to explain how or why it became attached; and as regards

the notion that it is really a 'summons' poem, several examples of
such poems do exist, including two in this anthology, but the
'Hymn to the Fallen' does not in the least resemble any of them.

The most plausible theory to my mind is that of the Japanese
scholar Aoki Masaru, who held that the 'Nine Songs' song-cycle was
designed for twice-yearly performance, once in spring and once in
autumn, and that the two most popular gods, the Xiang Goddess
and the Master of Fate, have a version for each season. On each
occasion, therefore, only nine songs would in fact have been
performed:

> *Spring*   I II III V   VII VIII IX X XI
> *Autumn*   I II IV VI VII VIII IX X XI

I find Aoki's theory convincing for a number of reasons. Song
XI, the finale which follows the 'Hymn to the Fallen', is called *Li
hun*, 'Honouring the Souls (of the dead)'. This seems to indicate
that the whole cycle may be a sort of requiem for those who died in
war. According to the ancient books of ritual, spring and autumn
were the two seasons when the most important sacrifices to the
souls of the dead were made. In Song XI it is explicitly stated that
the cycle is to be performed at these two seasons:

> Orchids in spring and chrysanthemums in autumn:
> So it shall go on until the end of time.

and both IV and VI contain seasonal references which would have
been gratuitously inappropriate if the songs in question had been
sung at any other time than the season specified:

> Gently the wind of autumn whispers;
> On the waves of the Dong-ting lake the leaves are falling.
>
> (Song IV, *ll.*3–4)

> The autumn orchid and the deer-parsley
> Grow in a carpet below the hall
>
> (Song VI, *ll.*1–2)

According to one of Wu Di's shaman advisers, spring and
autumn were also the seasons in which the most important sacrifices
had to be made to Tai Yi. The 'Nine Songs' would therefore have
lent themselves very easily to his worship. In the Suburban Sacrifice
his place of worship was on the south-east side towards the sunrise,
so it was no great problem to identify him with Dong Huang, High
God of that lesser, eastern Chu which King Xiang and his
successors ruled over for the half-century following 278 B.C., when
the old Central Yangtze capital of Ying and the vast area of lake
and river country which surrounded it became a south-eastern
province of Qin.

Although the 'Hymn to the Fallen' is not the 'Soul Summons' of Si-ma Qian's biography, it is possible to think of the whole 'Nine Songs' as a sort of extended summons, though it is the gods and not the souls of men who are summoned in it. If we accept Jiang Liang-fu's theory that the *Jiu ge*, *Jiu bian* and *Jiu zhao* of the Qi legend are simply the names for different aspects of the same liturgy – *Jiu ge* for the words, *Jiu bian* for the music and *Jiu zhao* for the dances – then it becomes more than probable that the Nine Songs of Qi were shaman-songs in which various gods were invoked, each with a different kind of music; for *zhao* means 'beckon' or 'summon' and no doubt referred to the gestures with which the dancers entreated the gods to descend.

But, as I have suggested elsewhere, the 'nine' of the Qi legend may be an empty number and *Jiu bian* mean no more than several different modes or several different types of music (the *bian* with which *Jiu bian* is written actually means 'discriminate' rather than 'change'); whereas to the Chu poet who composed the 'Nine Songs' it must have seemed crucial that the liturgy should consist of nine distinct parts, no more, no less.

There are still many questions about these songs that remain unanswered and it is always possible that the whole reconstruction here offered may be mistaken. Fortunately their beauty remains unaffected by our understanding of how they were performed or when they were written and continues to be an inspiration to Chinese poets and painters as it has been throughout the ages.

'The Great Unity, God of the Eastern Sky' (Dong huang tai yi)

Tai Yi, to his worshippers, seems originally to have been simply one of the names of God. The cult of God as Tai Yi so enthusiastically espoused by the emperor Wu Di in the second century B.C. might be compared to a local cult of the Virgin in Catholic Europe, or to the worship of the Pythian as distinct from the Delian Apollo in Ancient Greece. Tai Yi had his dwelling-place in the sky. An essay on astronomy in the book *Huai nan zi*, a collection of treatises written by philosophers at Liu An's court in Shou-chun during the reign of Wu Di, places it among the circumpolar constellations:

> The Tai Wei constellation is where Tai Yi holds his court; the Purple Palace is his private residence; the constellation Xuan Yuan is where his Imperial Consort lives; the Pool of Heaven is

his fish-pond; the Heavenly Gap is the gateway through which the other gods go in and out . . .

Later Tai Yi was himself identified as a star, probably one of the central stars in Draco. He continued to be so regarded by astronomers long after his religious cult had been forgotten, just as Jupiter continues to give his name to one of our planets although we no longer make sacrifices to his godhead.

The cult of Tai Yi is sometimes said, on rather flimsy evidence, to have originated in the eastern state of Qi (Shandong) and it is just possible that the eastern kingdom of Chu (as it was in the last decades of its existence) may have adopted the cult from Qi and given the title 'Dong Huang' to this new god. I prefer to think that the High God worshipped by this late Chu court was a Dong Huang who had nothing to do with Tai Yi and that 'Tai Yi' was added to the title of this first song a century later when the 'Nine Songs' were adopted by Wu Di for his Tai Yi sacrifices.

Tai Yi is occasionally mentioned by Warring States philosophers as the undifferentiated 'Oneness' out of which all things were produced, but there is no evidence that anyone ever worshipped him as a god before the beginning of the Han dynasty.

1   On a lucky day with an auspicious name
    Reverently we come to delight the Lord on High.
    We grasp the long sword's haft of jade,
    And our girdle pendants clash and chime.
5   From the god's jewelled mat with treasures laden
    Take up the fragrant flower-offerings,
    The meats cooked in melilotus, served on orchid mats,
    And libations of cinnamon wine and pepper sauces!
    Flourish the drumsticks, beat the drums!
10   The singing begins softly to a slow, solemn measure:
    Then, as pipes and zithers join in, the sound grows shriller.
    Now the priestesses come, splendid in their gorgeous apparel,
    And the hall is filled with a penetrating fragrance.
    The five notes mingle in a rich harmony;
15   And the god is merry and takes his pleasure.

II *'The Lord within the Clouds'* (Yun-zhong jun)

This god would be wholly unknown to us but for an entry in the monograph on sacrifices in Si-ma Qian's 'History', where he is mentioned along with Dong Jun (the Sun God) as one of the gods worshipped by shamans from Jin (i.e. Shanxi) who were installed for this purpose in the imperial capital of Changan by the Founder of the Han dynasty. Wang Yi tells us that Yun-zhong Jun was the Cloud God and identifies him with Feng Long, whom the questing poet in *Li sao* sends to the river goddess Fu Fei as his messenger:

So I made Feng Long ride off on a cloud
To seek out the dwelling-place of the lady Fu Fei.

(*ll.*221–2)

However, this is probably only a guess.

The great *Chu ci* scholar Jiang Liang-fu thinks that *all* the songs from II to IX – not just III–IV and V–VI – make up pairs. Yun-zhong Jun, he says, is the moon and makes a pair with Dong Jun, the sun, whose hymn has somehow got out of place and ought really to come next to Yun-zhong Jun's in the series. I very much doubt whether this is so. Apart from the fact that there is not a shred of evidence to support such a view, the comparison of Yun-zhong Jun's brightness with 'that of the sun and moon' (in *l.*6) seems very odd if he (or she) *is* the moon.

I cannot help thinking that the 'Yun-zhong' of the god's title is in some way connected with the Yun-zhong Mountain in Shanxi. From ancient times the name 'Yun-zhong' was given to various places in N. Shanxi and at one time a huge area extending from N. Shanxi across the Great Wall as far as Central Suiyuan was all known as 'Yun-zhong'. Ji-zhou in *l.*11 of the hymn was the old name for the area north of the Yellow River corresponding to present-day Shanxi and Hebei. The Yun-zhong Mountain was presumably so called because its head was 'in the clouds'. Perhaps the god worshipped by the shamans from Shanxi was both the god of Yun-zhong Mountain *and* a rain-bringer, so that Wang Yi, to that extent, was right.

We have bathed in orchid water and washed our hair with
     perfumes,
And dressed ourselves like flowers in embroidered clothing.
The god has halted, swaying, above us,
Shining with a persistent radiance.

5   He is going to rest in the House of Life.
    His brightness is like that of the sun and moon.
    In his dragon chariot, dressed in imperial splendour,
    Now he flies off to wander round the sky.

    The god had just descended in bright majesty,
10 When off in a whirl he soared again, far into the clouds.
    He looks down on Ji-zhou and the lands beyond it;
    There is no place in the world that he does not pass over.
    Thinking of that lord makes me sigh
    And afflicts my heart with a grievous longing.

III 'The Goddess of the Xiang' (Xiang jun)

Si-ma Qian's 'Annals of the First Qin Emperor', which make up the
sixth section of his great History, has the following entry under the
emperor's twenty-eighth year (219 B.C.):

> Travelling in a south-westerly direction, he crossed over the
> River Huai intending to visit, Heng-shan. At Nan-jun he took
> boat and was sailing down the river to the Xiang Jun shrine when
> a great wind arose and nearly prevented his getting to land. The
> emperor inquired of his wise men who Xiang Jun (the god of the
> shrine) was. They replied, 'According to our information, Xiang
> Jun are the daughters of Yao and wives of Shun who are buried
> in this place.' At this the First Emperor was greatly enraged. He
> set three thousand convicts to work to cut down the trees of
> Xiang-shan and paint the mountain red. He then left Nan-jun
> and returned to Xian-yang (his capital in Shaanxi) by way of the
> Wu-guan pass.

Nan-jun, the 'Southern Commandery', was the name given by Qin
to the central and southern parts of the former kingdom of Chu
after their annexation of them in 278 B.C. Here what is meant by
'Nan-jun' is the administrative capital of the commandery, the old
Chu capital of Ying near present-day Jiangling on the central
Yangtze – the city of Qu Yuan's King Huai. Xiang-shan, where the
goddess had her shrine, was the name of an island, more usually
known as 'Jun-shan' (the 'Mountain of the Goddess') or 'Dong-ting-
shan', in the north-east corner of Lake Dong-ting. Heng-shan was
the southernmost of the Five Sacred Mountains of China. Before
visiting Heng-Shan, presumably to make offerings on it, the First

Emperor had already ascended, and offered sacrifices on, Tai-shan in Shandong, the most holy mountain of the five. Evidently it was a ritual progress that was interrupted by the inhospitable behaviour of these patron goddesses of his old enemy. Some nine years later, in the last year of his reign, we find him on another progress visiting Doubting Mountain (Jiu-yi-shan), near the source of the Xiang, where Shun was buried – a journey which, it may be recalled, Qu Yuan makes in the *Li sao*:

> . . . crossing the Yuan and Xiang, I journeyed southwards
> Till I came to where Chong Hua [i.e. Shun] was and made my plaint to him.

(*ll*.142–3)

Presumably the emperor must some time previous to this have issued an imperial pardon to the offending goddesses. Shun was supposed to be their husband and could hardly be expected to receive favourably a visitor who was treating his wives like convicts. (The red paint with which the mountain shrine was covered on the emperor's orders in 219 B.C. was meant to symbolize the red of convict dress.)

In the account of the Qin emperor's unfortunate experience which I have translated above I have used plurals ('daughters', 'wives') where the Chinese is non-committal, because in all versions of the legend it was *two* daughters that the high lord Yao gave in marriage to Shun. In ancient legends royal brides usually come in pairs. (Compare, for example, the two daughters of the Lord of Yu in *Li sao*, *l*.248.) Aristocratic society in ancient China was exogamous and princesses travelled into another country to marry, like the goose-girl princess in the fairy-tale. The bridesmaids who accompanied them were their sisters or cousins, who, as a matter of course, became the concubines or secondary wives of the groom. The two princesses who are constantly turning up in Chinese legend were the minimum that could be offered a young prince in marriage.

It has generally been assumed that Song III is addressed to the elder and Song IV to the younger of the two sisters. Arthur Waley in his *Nine Songs: A Study of Shamanism in Ancient China* suggested that there was originally only one Xiang goddess and that these two songs are different versions of a hymn addressed to the same goddess. In other words, the identification of Xiang Jun with Shun's two queens was part of that euhemerizing tendency one observes constantly at work in Chinese sources which turns mythology into pseudo-history.

I believe that Songs III and IV *are* essentially two versions of the same hymn. I also believe, as I have said elsewhere, that they were designed for alternate use in different seasons. But the idea that Xiang Jun was not one but a pair of goddesses seems to be a very

ancient one. The 'Book of Seas and Mountains' calls the goddesses
of Dong-ting 'the two children of God' with no euhemerizing
references to Yao or Shun, and this same expression, 'Child of
God', is used by the shaman in referring to the goddess in Song
IV. Perhaps both songs were originally written for an
undifferentiated 'Xiang Jun' and it only later became accepted that
the goddess of the spring sacrifice was the elder sister and the
goddess of the autumn sacrifice was the younger one. At all events I
do not believe, as Wang Yi seems to have done and as some
scholars still do, that the Xiang Jun of this song is a male deity and
the Xiang Fu-ren of Song IV his consort, though I accept that a
case can be made for this, as indeed it can for several other
interpretations quite different from my own.

According to my interpretation, the words in both of these songs
are sung throughout *in propria persona* by a male shaman who is
pretending to be out in a boat looking for the goddess among her
island haunts. I do not think he is impersonating Shun, though that
is a possibility. I think Shun is his rival and the probable cause of
his failure to reach the goddess. His boating and other activities
would have been mimed, but doubtless these songs had prototypes
which were sung by shamans who went out in real boats on real
water. That shamans did approach the water deities in this
sometimes hazardous manner can be seen from the story of Cao Xu
cited above (p. 65). Qu Yuan himself must have witnessed such
spectacles and been deeply impressed by them, for they provided
him with the central theme of his allegory in *Li sao*.

In spite of the many uncertainties and ambiguities in the text,
these two songs, III and IV, are – in the original Chinese at any
rate – the most hauntingly beautiful part of the whole series. The
shaman's love-song as he pursues, through rivers, lakes and wooded
islands, a brooding presence which he senses and sometimes believes
he can hear, but never, or only in faint, fleeting glimpses, ever sees,
evokes for us, with an extraordinary vividness, an ancient, forgotten
time in which men loved, even more than they feared, the
mysterious world of nature that surrounded them.

1   The goddess comes not, she holds back shyly.
    Who keeps her delaying within the island,
    Lady of the lovely eyes and the winning smile?
    Skimming the water in my cassia boat,
5   I bid the Yuan and Xiang still their waves
    And the Great River make its stream flow softly.

I look for the goddess, but she does not come yet.
Of whom does she think as she plays her reed-pipes?

North I go, drawn by my flying dragon,
Steering my course to the Dong-ting lake:
My sail is of fig-leaves, melilotus my rigging,
An iris my flag-pole, my banner of orchids.
Gazing at the distant Cen-yang mooring,
I waft my magic across the Great River.

I waft my magic, but it does not reach her.
The lady is sad, and sighs for me;
And *my* tears run down over cheek and chin:
I am choked with longing for my lady.

My cassia oars and orchid sweep
Chip all in vain at ice and snow.
I am gathering wild figs in the water!
I am looking for lotuses in the tree-tops!
The wooing is useless if hearts are divided;
The love that is not deep is quickly broken.

The stream runs fast through the stony shallows,
And my flying dragon wings swiftly above it.
The pain is more lasting if loving is faithless:
She broke her tryst; she told me she had not time.

In the morning I race by the bank of the river;
At evening I halt at this north island.
The birds are roosting on the roof-top;
The water laps at the foot of the hall.
I throw my thumb-ring into the river.
I leave my girdle-gem in the bay of the Li.
Pollia I've plucked in the scent-laden islet
To give to the lady in the depths below.
Time once gone cannot be recovered:
I wish I could play here a little longer.

IV 'The Lady of the Xiang' (Xiang fu-ren)

1   The Child of God, descending the northern bank,
Turns on me her eyes that are dark with longing.
Gently the wind of autumn whispers;
On the waves of the Dong-ting lake the leaves are falling.

5   Over the white sedge I gaze out wildly;
For a tryst is made to meet my love this evening.
But why should the birds gather in the duckweed?
And what are the nets doing in the tree-tops?

The Yuan has its angelicas, the Li has its orchids:
10   And I think of my lady, but dare not tell it,
As with trembling heart I gaze on the distance
Over the swiftly moving waters.

What are the deer doing in the courtyard?
Or the water-dragons outside the waters?
15   In the morning I drive my steeds by the river;
In the evening I cross to the western shore.
I can hear my beloved calling to me:
I will ride aloft and race beside her.
I will build her a house within the water
20   Roofed all over with lotus leaves;

With walls of iris, of purple shells the chamber;
Perfumed pepper shall make the hall.
With beams of cassia, orchid rafters,
Lily-tree lintel, a bower of peonies,
25   With woven fig-leaves for the hangings
And melilotus to make a screen;
Weights of white jade to hold the mats with,
Stone-orchids strewn to make the floor sweet:
A room of lotus thatched with the white flag
30   Shall all be bound up with stalks of asarum.

A thousand sweet flowers shall fill the courtyard,
And rarest perfumes shall fill the gates.
In hosts from their home on Doubting Mountain
Like clouds in number the spirits come thronging.

I'll throw my thumb-ring into the river,
Leave my girdle-gem in the bay of the Li.
Sweet pollia I've plucked in the little islet
To send to my far-away Beloved.
Oh, rarely, rarely the time is given!
I wish I could play here a little longer.

v 'The Greater Master of Fate' (Da si ming)

Si Ming was the God of Fate, the bestower of life and death. He decided how long a man's life should be, and hence whether or not an illness should be a fatal one. The manipulation of *yin* and *yang* on whose balance a man's life depends was his special concern. Shamans and physicians had to employ this balancing of *yin* and *yang* in the treatment of their patients; though, as Bian Que, the Chinese Aesculapius, says in Si-ma Qian's biography of him, 'Even the Si Ming can do nothing for you if the sickness has got into your bones.'

In a dream conversation with a skull he had come across the day before, the Warring States philosopher Zhuang Zi speaks of asking the Si Ming to give it a body again and bring it back to life – to the great disgust of the skull, who thought it was better off dead.

Early Han sources tell us that Si Ming was a popular god, worshipped in private households. (Later he became identified with the Kitchen God who was sent up to heaven each year having previously had his lips smeared with honey so that he would give a good report of his household.) A source dating from the second century A.D. speaks of wooden figures of Si Ming about a foot high being kept in little shrines in the house or carried around in a box by the householder when he was on his travels. The painted wooden dolls representing bearded males in costume of the Warring States period which have been found in tombs near Changsha may conceivably be images of this god.

In all extant sources Si Ming is spoken of as a single deity, yet here we have two songs, one addressed to the 'Greater' or 'Senior' and one to the 'Lesser' or 'Junior' Si Ming. As well as being a god,

Si Ming, like Tai Yi, was a star, the fourth in a constellation of six stars called Wen Chang corresponding to six of the outer stars of Ursa Major. A very late tradition which maintained that there were *two* stars in Wen Chang called Si Ming can, I think, be discounted as a rather obvious fabrication designed to explain this text. So, I believe, can Guo Mo-ruo's claim to have found a Greater Master of Fate in the inscription on a ritual bronze vessel dating from the sixth century B.C. The 'Da-si-ming' of that inscription is almost certainly the title of an official at the Zhou court and not the name of a god.

One possibility which as far as I know has not so far been discussed is suggested by the fact that in Si-ma Qian's account of the shaman-cults established under imperial patronage at the beginning of the Han dynasty Si Ming is the only god who appears in two lists: that of the shamans from Jin and that of the shamans from Chu. Although Songs V and VI are both written in the Chu dialect, it occurs to me that they may represent two different aspects of the god corresponding to the different ways in which he was envisaged in these two different cults, rather as the one god Apollo appears in the *Homeric Hymns* both as the Delian and as the Pythian Apollo. At all events, I think it is fairly clear that there is the same seasonal distinction between V and VI as between III and IV, even though the precise significance of the 'Greater' and 'Lesser' of their titles can only be guessed at. They could of course simply refer to the fact that Song VI is shorter than Song V.

1   Open wide the door of heaven!
    On a black cloud I ride in splendour,
    Bidding the whirlwind drive before me,
    Causing the rainstorm to lay the dust.

5   In sweeping circles my lord is descending:
    'Let me follow you over the Kong-sang mountain!
    See, the teeming peoples of the Nine Lands:
    The span of their lives is in your hand!'

    Flying aloft, he soars serenely,
10 Riding the pure vapour, guiding *yin* and *yang*.
    Speedily, lord, I will go with you,
    Conducting High God to the height of heaven.

My cloud-coat hangs in billowing folds;
My jade girdle-pendants dangle low:
15   A *yin* and a *yang*, a *yin* and a *yang*:
None of the common folk know what I am doing.

I have plucked the glistening flower of the Holy Hemp
To give to one who lives far away.
Old age already has crept upon me:
20   I am no longer near him, fast growing a stranger.

He drives his dragon chariot with thunder of wheels;
High up he rides, careering heavenwards.
But I stand where I am, twisting a spray of cassia:
The longing for him pains my heart.

25   It pains my heart, but what can I do?
If we only could stay as we were, unchanging!
But all man's life is fated;
Its meeting and partings not his to arrange.

VI '*The Lesser Master of Fate*' (Shao si ming)

The autumn orchid and the deer-parsley
Grow in a carpet below the hall;
The leaves of green and the pure white flowers
Assail me with their wafted fragrance.

The autumn orchids bloom luxuriant,
With leaves of green and purple stems.
All the hall is filled with lovely women,
But his eyes swiftly sought me out from the rest.

Without a word he came in to me, without a word he left me:
He rode off on the whirlwind with cloud-banners flying.
No sorrow is greater than the parting of the living;
No happiness is greater than making new friendships.

Wearing a lotus coat with melilotus girdle,
Quickly he came and as quickly departed.
15 At night he will lodge in the High God's precincts.
'Whom are you waiting for at the cloud's edge?'

I will wash my hair with you in the Pool of Heaven;
You shall dry your hair on the Bank of Sunlight.
I watch for the Fair One, but he does not come.
20 Wildly I shout my song into the wind.

With peacock canopy and kingfisher banner,
He mounts the ninefold heaven and grasps the Broom Star;
He brandishes his long sword, protecting young and old:
'You only, Fragrant One, are worthy to be judge over men.'

VII 'The Lord of the East' (Dong jun)

This Lord of the East is, as the words of the song make abundantly clear, the sun. To us the idea that the sun should be an archer is unsurprising. In the *Iliad* and the *Homeric Hymns* the Greek sun god is 'far-shooting' (*hekēbolos* or *hekatēbolos*): a fit epithet for the god who killed the she-dragon of Pytho and the children of Niobe with his arrows. But the archer god of this Chinese hymn is, in fact, not at all like the Xi He of Chinese myth, the mother of the suns who bathed them in the eastern ocean and drove one of them across the sky every day, more like a nanny than a fierce huntsman. If anything he resembles Lord Yi, the Mighty Archer, who *shot down* the suns. In former times several of China's northern neighbours used to believe that they were descended from divine archers who were in some way or other related to the sun. The North Korean Dong Ming ('Eastern Brightness'), who, like the ancestor of the Shang people, was born from a celestial egg, was one of them.

In Si-ma Qian's account of shaman-cults at the beginning of the Han dynasty the cult of Dong Jun, Lord of the East, was the responsibility of shamans from Jin, a part of China anciently much subject to Northern influences. (Horseback riding and the 'barbarian dress' – i.e. trousers – which went with it were introduced to China through this area.) The Sun God of this hymn is, I believe, a Sun God with Northern attributes.

With a faint flush I start to come out of the east,
Shining down on my threshold, Fu-sang.
As I urge my horses slowly forwards,
The night sky brightens, and day has come.

I ride a dragon car and chariot on the thunder,
With cloud-banners fluttering upon the wind.
I heave a long sigh as I start the ascent,
Reluctant to leave, and looking back longingly;
For the beauty and the music are so enchanting,
The beholder, delighted, forgets that he must go.

Tighten the zither's strings and smite them in unison!
Strike the bells until the bell-stand rocks!
Let the flutes sound! Blow the pan-pipes!
See the priestesses, how skilled and lovely,
Whirling and dipping like birds in flight,
Unfolding the words in time to the dancing,
Pitch and beat all in perfect accord!
The spirits, descending, darken the sun.

In my cloud-coat and my skirt of the rainbow,
Grasping my bow I soar high up in the sky.
I aim my long arrow and shoot the Wolf of Heaven;
I seize the Dipper to ladle cinnamon wine.
Then holding my reins, I plunge down to my setting,
On my gloomy night journey back to the east.

VIII 'The River Earl' (He bo)

He Bo, the god of the Yellow River, is the only one among the
'Nine Songs' deities about whom very much is known. Sacrifices to
him, in some cases human sacrifices, are mentioned in oracle bone
inscriptions dating from the Shang era, and in some places the
custom of giving the river god an annual 'bride' seems to have
persisted until well into the Warring States period. The unfortunate
virgin chosen for this honour was dressed in wedding finery and
laid on a sort of couch on which she floated, like Ophelia, until she
drowned. A Confucian official is said to have put a stop to the

custom in one area by throwing the shamans themselves into the river to inquire whether the god was satisfied with the virgin they had chosen for him. The ferocity of this river, which within living memory was still from time to time causing devastating floods, meant that it required constant propitiation. Even in the Han dynasty, when human sacrifice was associated only with barbarians or with a barbarous and best-forgotten past, it was thought necessary to throw in an occasional live horse along with the jade discs and other offerings which were his customary tribute.

In the early fifth century B.C. a king of Chu refused to sacrifice to He Bo, when his diviners told him that his illness was being caused by this god, on the grounds that the Yellow River was not in his territory and therefore not in a position to be offended by him. The chronicler commends the king for the correctness of his attitude, but the king died nevertheless. This story is sometimes thought to make it seem peculiar that Chu shamans should be found worshipping He Bo in the fourth or third century B.C., but if anything I should have thought quite the opposite conclusion was indicated. If He Bo's influence was already so far-reaching in the early fifth century, the likelihood is that he was being worshipped on a regular basis in Chu by the end of that century.

At the beginning of the Han dynasty the imperial cult of He Bo was maintained by shamans devoted exclusively to his worship installed not in the capital but at a riverside shrine in Shaanxi.

1   I wander with you by the Nine Mouths of the river
    When the storm wind rises and lashes up the waves.
    I ride a water chariot with a canopy of lotus;
    Two dragons draw it, between two water-serpents.

5   I climb the Kun-lun mountain and look over the four quarters,
    And my heart leaps up in me, beating wildly.
    Though the day will soon end, I forget to go in my pleasure:
    Longingly I look back to that distant shore.
    Of fish-scales his palace is, with a dragon-scale hall;
10   Purple cowrie gate-towers; rooms of pearl.
    And what does the god do, down there in the water?

    Riding a white turtle, he chases the spotted fishes.
    Let me play with you among the river's islets,
    While the swollen waters come rushing on their way!

Eastward you journey, with hands stately folded,
Bearing your fair bride to the southern harbour.
The waves come racing up to meet me,
And shoals of fishes are my bridal train.

IX 'The Mountain Spirit' (Shan gui)

The unidentified subject of this poem is usually taken to be a goddess. Waley seems to be alone among modern interpreters in taking it to be a male god, but even he admits uncertainty: ' . . . if it were possible in English to be non-committal about genders, I would have left the question open in my translation'. It has been plausibly suggested that the mountain goddess intended is the Lady of Gao-tang, goddess of Shaman Mountain (Wu-shan) above the Yangtze gorges near the eastern border of Sichuan – the same who offers herself to the King of Chu in the beautiful *Gao-tang fu* erroneously attributed to Song Yu. The Lady of Gao-tang was a fertility goddess. Her physical manifestation was in 'the clouds of morning and the rain of evening': hence 'clouds and rain' is one of the Chinese euphemisms for sexual intercourse. The Chinese scholar Yuan Ke in his notes on the 'Book of Seas and Mountains' suggests that Wu-shan (Shaman Mountain), Ling-shan (Holy Mountain) and Yun-yu-zhi-shan (Cloud and Rain Mountain) were three different names for one and the same mountain. Ling-shan, according to the 'Book of Seas and Mountains', was the mountain on which ten great shamans (including Wu Xian and Wu Peng) climbed up and down in search of magic herbs. The clouds and rain and sad gibbon cries for which Wu-shan is celebrated are all mentioned in this poem.

There seems to be someone in the fold of the mountain
In a coat of fig-leaves with a rabbit-floss girdle,
With eyes that hold laughter and a smile of pearly brightness:
'Lady, your allurements show that you desire me.'

Driving tawny leopards, leading the striped lynxes;
A car of lily-magnolia with banner of woven cassia;
Her cloak of stone-orchids, her belt of asarum:
She gathers sweet scents to give to one she loves.

'I am in the dense bamboo grove, which never sees the sunlight,
10 So steep and hard the way was, therefore I am late.'
Solitary she stands, upon the mountain's summit:
The clouds' dense masses begin below her.

From a place of gloomy shadow, dark even in the daytime,
When the east wind blows up, the goddess sends down her
        showers.
15 Dallying with the Fair One, I forget about returning.
What flowers can I deck myself with, so late in the year?

I shall pluck the thrice-flowering herb among the mountains,
Where the arrowroot spreads creeping over the piled-up boulders.
Sorrowing for my lady, I forget that I must go.
20 My lady thinks of me, but she has no time to come.

The lady of the mountains is fragrant with pollia;
She drinks from the rocky spring and shelters beneath the pine
        trees.
My lady thinks of me, but she holds back, uncertain.

The thunder rumbles; rain darkens the sky:
25 The monkeys chatter; apes scream in the night:
The wind soughs sadly and the trees rustle.
I think of my lady and stand alone in sadness.

x 'Hymn to the Fallen' (Guo shang)

Guo means state, country or kingdom; *shang* is one who dies
prematurely, who is cut off in his youth or prime. The *guo shang*
are those who die fighting in the service of their country.

Readers worried by the fact that the 'Nine Songs' are more than
nine in number have frequently suggested that this 'Hymn to the
Fallen' does not belong to the series and has become attached to it
by accident or error. Some modern Chinese scholars go even
further, identifying it with the 'Summons of the Soul' which Si-ma
Qian's biography attributes to Qu Yuan. The trouble with this last
theory is that the 'Hymn to the Fallen' lacks the 'Come back! Come
back!' refrain that all soul summonses appear to have had. Its tone
in fact is not invocatory at all but commemorative. Song XI, which

follows, is entitled *Li hun*, literally 'performing rites for the souls':
i.e. honouring the dead. I suspect that the souls being honoured in
it are those of the dead warriors of Song X and that the whole
song-cycle was originally intended for twice-yearly performance as a
sort of requiem for those who died far from home on foreign
battlefields. Far from being out of place in the 'Nine Songs', I believe
that Songs X and XI represent that climax of the ceremonies for
which the entire cycle was put together. But whatever one believes
about the relation of *Guo shang* to the other songs in the series, it
need not affect one's enjoyment of what is surely one of the most
beautiful laments for fallen soldiers in any language.

Grasping our great shields and wearing our hide armour,
Wheel-hub to wheel-hub locked, we battle hand to hand.

Our banners darken the sky; the enemy teem like clouds:
Through the hail of arrows the warriors press forward.

They dash on our lines; they trample our ranks down.
The left horse has fallen, the right one is wounded.

The wheels are embedded, the foursome entangled:
Seize the jade drumstick and beat the sounding drum!
The time is against us: the gods are angry.
Now all lie dead, left on the field of battle.

They went out never more to return:
Far, far away they lie, on the level plain,
Their long swords at their belts, clasping their Qin bows,
Head from body sundered: but their hearts could not be
    vanquished.

Both truly brave and also truly noble;
Strong to the last, they could not be dishonoured.
Their bodies may have died, but their souls are living:
Heroes among the shades their valiant souls will be.

XI 'Honouring the Dead' (Li hun)

The rites are accomplished to the beating of the drums;
The flower-wand is passed on to succeeding dancers.
Lovely maidens sing their song, slow and solemnly.
Orchids in spring and chrysanthemums in autumn:
So it shall go on until the end of time.

Notes

II 'The Lord within the Clouds'

*l.*5 *the House of Life*: literally 'Palace of Longevity' (*shou gong*) – a
      chapel specially constructed for the reception of spirits conjured up
in shamanistic séances. We hear of one being built by Wu Di in
118 B.C. at his Gan-quan Palace some fifty kilometres north of Changan
for the reception of Tai Yi and other familiars of the shamaness from
Shang-jun who had successfully predicted his recovery from a serious
illness. Shang-jun was a Northern commandery which shared a
common boundary with the Yun-zhong commandery in Suiyuan. It is
quite possible that this song may have undergone editing for use in Wu
Di's services.

III 'The Goddess of the Xiang'

*l.*9 *my flying dragon*: I take it that a dragon boat, i.e. a boat which, like
      a Viking ship, had a carved dragon on its prow, is meant both here
and in *l.*26. The shaman is not pretending to be drawn by a dragon
chariot like the one used by the *Li sao* poet on his journeys through the
air. Boats of this kind survive to the present day in places where the
Dragon Boat festival is still celebrated.

*ll.*33–4 *my thumb-ring ... my girdle-gem*: the thumb-ring, usually
         made of jade, was worn as a protection by archers. It marks
the shaman as a male. (It appears to be the rule that male gods are
invoked by female shamans and female gods by male ones.) The 'Book
of Songs' contains many instances of men giving their jade ornaments to
women as love-pledges. Noblemen in the Zhou era wore a cluster of
dangling jade ornaments below the waist which tinkled as they walked.
A possible origin of this custom is suggested by the account of a
fourteenth-century Chinese traveller who tells us that the nobles and
rich men of Siam wore tiny bells implanted in their foreskins which
made a similar attenuated tinkling sound when they moved around.

IV 'The Lady of the Xiang'

*ll.*33–4 *In hosts from their home on Doubting Mountain*: Li sao,
*ll.*281–2, where Qu Yuan describes the throng of spirits
heralding the arrival of the Shaman Ancestor Wu Xian, reads like a
paraphrase of these lines. Except for the small adjustment necessitated
by the difference of metre, the Chinese text of *Li sao*, *l.*282, is in fact
identical with *l.*33 of this song. Doubting Mountain was the
burial-place of Shun (Chong Hua), the goddess's husband. The
continuity in these lines is a little hard to discern. I suppose their
meaning is that now the imaginary palace in the water has been
completed, the arrival of a throng of attendant spirits indicates that the
goddess is about to come and occupy it, and so the shaman proceeds (in
*ll.*35–6) to throw his offerings into the water. At this same juncture in
the *Li sao* passage, presumably, Qu Yuan made his rice-ball offering to
Wu Xian.

The phrase which I have translated in *Li sao* as 'the host of Doubting
Mountain' and here as 'in hosts from Doubting Mountain' is in Chinese
Jiu-yi bin. The word *bin*, 'multitudinous(ly)', is written with a
composite character made up of the character *bin*, 'guest' (used for its
sound), and the character for 'silk' (possibly because of the
multitudinous fibres of silk floss). However, the same phrase *Jiu-yi bin*
appears in one of the nineteen 'Hymns for Use in the Suburban
Sacrifice' dating from the reign of Wu Di (late second century B.C.)
with the simple character for 'guest' instead of the one for
'multitudinous' as the third word:

> *Jiu-yi bin* : *Kui Long wu*
> *Shen an zuo* : *xiang ji shi*

The meaning of these lines is very obscure. One early commentator
thought that *Jiu-yi* had to be understood as referring metonymously to
Shun and that *bin* had to be understood verbally:

> (He of) Doubting Mountain comes as our guest: Kui and Dragon
> dance
>
> The spirits settle in their places: floating hither in a blessed hour.

It looks as if *Jiu-yi bin* may have been a very ancient ritual expression
the original meaning of which had been forgotten. A possible clue to
what it might have meant is to be found in the ancient 'Canon of Yao' in
the 'Book of History', where we read that the High Lord 'sent down his
two daughters to the land north of the River Gui to be wives to Shun'.
The word for 'wives' in this context is the archaic *pin*, a composite
character written with the characters *bin*, 'guest' (for its sound), and
'woman'. I suspect that *Jiu-yi bin* meaning 'the consorts of Doubting
Mountain' was an ancient epithet of the Xiang goddesses and that the
whole of *l.* 33 (and *Li sao*, *l.*282) *Jiu-yi bin* . . . *bing ying* may have

survived from some ancient shaman hymn. Its original meaning would
have been 'the consorts of Doubting Mountain both come to meet me';
but it clearly meant something quite different to the person who wrote
this poem.

*ll.*35–6 *I'll throw my thumb-ring ... girdle-gem*: instead of
      'thumb-ring' and 'girdle-gem' in these two lines, the Chinese
text has two characters meaning 'sleeve' and 'shift'. However, the
character for 'sleeve' is a composite one in which the more important
element is the one found in 'thumb-ring'. In view of the near identity of
*ll.*35–40 of this poem with *ll.*33–8 of the preceding poem, I have
assumed, as Waley does, that the 'sleeve' and 'shift' of this song are due
to textual corruption.

v 'The Greater Master of Fate'

*l.*6 *the Kong-sang mountain*: the name Kong-sang, 'Hollow Mulberry',
      and its variant Qiong-sang, 'Blasted Mulberry', make several
appearances in Chinese mythology. Tang the Successful's famous
minister Yi Yin was supposed to have been found when a baby inside
the hollow mulberry tree his mother turned into while escaping from a
flood (see 'Heavenly Questions', *ll.*121–6 and note), but the
place-name probably existed long before this etymology was invented to
explain it. In fact there seem to have been several places of this name.
The *di* Shao Hao and the *di* Zhuan Xu (*al.* Gao Yang: see *Li sao*, *l.*1)
were both associated with places called Kong-sang which, like the place
where Yi Yin was born, are thought to have been somewhere in Henan;
but the 'Book of Seas and Mountains' has a Kong-sang mountain 'on
which neither tree nor herb grows and which is covered with snow both
winter and summer alike' which appears to have been somewhere in
northern Shanxi. The flood demon Gong Gong was associated with a
Kong-sang; so was Xuan Ming or Xuan Wu, the 'Dark One', Guardian
of the North, who in Chinese iconography is represented as a tortoise
or turtle with a snake coiled round his middle. Presumably Xuan
Ming's Kong-sang was the snow-covered northern mountain of that
name. Chinese cosmologists of the third century B.C. confused matters
by identifying Zhuan Xu with the God of the North and making Xuan
Ming his attendant spirit. Zhuan Xu, Xuan Ming and Kong-sang are all
three lumped together in the last of Liu Xiang's 'Nine Laments'
(*ll.*41–4, p. 301): 'I rode in the high wind's face, hither and thither;/ I
wandered, gazing, all over the North./ There I came to Zhuan Xu and
laid my plaint before him,/ And examined Xuan Ming on Kong-sang
mountain.' Wang Yi, in explaining this passage, tells us that Xuan
Ming had control over the winter darkness and over punishment and

slaughter. (In China executions were supposed to be carried out only in autumn and winter, when the destructive emanations released by them could do no harm to the processes of growth in plants and animals.) The scholar Wen Yi-duo, on the strength of Si Ming's association with Kong-sang in this hymn, suggested that Xuan Ming and Si Ming (these 'mings' are written with different characters and are in no way connected) were the same god, but this is no more than a learned guess. If the ancient Chinese did in fact identify these two gods, they kept very quiet about it.

*l.*12 *Conducting High God to the height of heaven*: for 'height of heaven' the Chinese text has *jiu gang*, 'the Nine Hills', with variants. Wang Yi, followed by most later commentators, says that *jiu gang* means the principal mountains in each of the Nine Lands of the earth, but the expression is otherwise unknown. Wen Yi-duo, on the evidence of a very late source, said that Jiu-gang was the name of a mountain near the Chu capital sacred to Zhuan Xu/Gao Yang. I believe that *jiu gang* and its two variants represent miscopyings of the various ways in which the expression *jiu he*, 'the highest heaven', was written. This expression is found (1) in *Huai nan zi*'s account of the extraterritorial travels of the magician Lu Ao; (2) in 'Heaven's Gate', the eleventh of the 'Hymns for Use in the Suburban Sacrifice'; and (3) in a posthumous essay by the Han poet Si-ma Xiang-ru – all three of them works dating from the reign of the Han emperor Wu Di.

VI 'The Lesser Master of Fate'

The Chinese text of this hymn contains four lines which I believe to be interpolations and have omitted from my translation: two between *ll.*4 and 5 and two between *ll.*16 and 17. The latter are the same as *ll.*1–2 of Song VIII and are so obviously out of place in this song that there has long been a consensus that they are interpolated. The pair of lines I have omitted between *ll.*4 and 5 may conceivably be a fragment of a lost stanza but certainly do not make sense in the text as it stands at present.

VII 'The Lord of the East'

*l.*2 *my threshold, Fu-sang*: for the Fu-sang tree, the giant mulberry tree at the edge of the Eastern Ocean in whose branches the sun rests before beginning his daily journey across the sky, see *Li sao*, *l.* 194 and note to *l.*189. In the middle ages the name 'Fu-sang' was sometimes given to Japan, the 'Land of the Rising Sun'.

*l.*21 *the Wolf of Heaven*: this is the star Sirius, part of Canis Major, the Dog.

X *'Hymn to the Fallen'*

*l.*1 *wearing our hide armour*: the Chinese word used here means
    specifically 'rhinoceros hide'. The rhinoceros-hide armour of Chu is
more than once mentioned in contemporary sources. The Confucian
philosopher Xun Zi, a Northerner who for a short period ending in
238 B.C. was a local magistrate in eastern Chu, refers to it in the
fifteenth chapter of his *Works*, a discussion of arms and warfare:

> The soldiers of Chu were equipped with armour made of sharkskin
> and rhinoceros hide as hard as metal or stone, and with pikes of
> Nanyang steel that could sting a man like a wasp or a scorpion. They
> were so light and mobile that they seemed to move about like the
> wind. Yet at Chui-sha the Chu army was all but destroyed and its
> commander Tang Mie [this is the 'Tang Mei' of the Si-ma Qian
> biography: see p. 57] was killed. Zhuang Jiao led a rising in the
> capital and the country split up into several parts. This was not
> because they lacked strong armour and sharp weapons but because
> they did not know how to use them.

Tian wen *'Heavenly Questions'*

The sky revolves; the earth stands still; the sun and moon
contend for dominion over the sky. Who controls all this? Who
makes the rules? Who, while himself remaining at rest, sets all
this in motion? Or is it some mechanism which never stops, or
their own spontaneous movement which keeps them perpetually
revolving? Do the clouds make the rain or does the rain make
the clouds? Who does the compressing and the releasing? Who,
while himself remaining at rest, by his voluptuous imagining
causes this fertilizing discharge? The wind rises up in the north;
it veers now to the east, now to the west or wanders about on
high. Whose breathing is this? Or who, while himself remaining
at rest, sets it going with the movements of his hand?

This questionnaire from the fourteenth chapter of *Zhuang zi* is
interrupted, somewhat impatiently, by the shaman Wu Xian, who
proceeds to provide the anonymous questioner with what, to most
readers, must seem a wholly irrelevant answer.

Tian wen, a much longer questionnaire (172 questions), also
begins with questions about the sky but soon progresses from

cosmological, astronomical and meteorological subjects to questions about the earth and its marvels and thence to questions about the affairs of men: the legendary heroes of antiquity and the kings and princes of a more recent past.

I have translated the title of this long poem as 'Heavenly Questions' because that seems to me the natural way in which the words *Tian wen* should be understood; but the fact that only a small fraction of the total number of questions are about celestial matters has from the earliest times been accounted a difficulty – an obstacle on the very threshold of this very difficult poem.

Wang Yi, or rather the source from which he copied his preface, attempted to resolve the difficulty by understanding '*Tian wen*' not as 'Questions *About* Heaven' but as 'Questions *Directed At* Heaven'. This interpretation of the words is so forced and unnatural that it required a good deal of explaining. 'Why "*Tian wen*"?' he asks. 'Why isn't it called "*Wen tian*" ("Questioning Heaven")? Because Heaven is too exalted to be questioned, that's why.' (In other words, God is too exalted to be subjected to the normal rules of grammar.) He goes on to give an ingenious but highly improbable reconstruction of the circumstances in which the 'Heavenly Questions' were written. After his banishment, he says, Qu Yuan wandered about in great distress of mind through mountains, marshes and plains, lifting up his eyes and *crying out to heaven* as he went. Sometimes, exhausted by his wanderings, he would sink down to rest under the walls of the ancestral temples of former kings and ministers of Chu. Looking up and observing the pictures with which the walls were covered – pictures representing the mysteries of heaven and earth and the acts of the men of old, both wise and wicked – he would write these questions on the walls 'to ease his mind'. (Wang Yi is a great believer in the therapeutic value of creative writing.) After his death the people of Chu felt sorry for him, so they copied down and collected together what he had written. That is why the questions often appear to be in the wrong order.

Few people nowadays believe that the 'Heavenly Questions' started off as graffiti on temple walls, though the notion was revived in this century in a curiously altered shape by the German scholar Conrady, who suggested that the questions were based on inscriptions on walls corresponding to the captions which accompany the bas-reliefs on the walls of the Wu-liang shrine in Shandong. Qu Yuan, according to Conrady's odd theory, copied down these explanatory inscriptions and turned them from statements into questions by supplying the appropriate interrogatory words.

Neither the idea that a literary work should have started off as a collection of graffiti nor the idea that it should have had a pictorial basis is intrinsically improbable. The poems of the anonymous medieval recluse whom we refer to as 'Cold Mountain' are said to have been copied from walls and trees, and the text of the ancient 'Book of Seas and Mountains' was undoubtedly written to explain a pictorial map or maps which are now lost. The fact is, though, that *Tian wen*, in spite of its rugged, antique style, is far too abstract and intellectual to have been related to a picture-series: its juxtapositions seem often to depend on an association of ideas or an ethical comparison which no graphic illustration could depict. Students of Gothic sculpture may take exception to such an assertion, but the Chinese art of bas-relief at no time reached a Gothic level of sophistication – certainly not in the fourth century B.C.

Tian wen is difficult for a number of reasons. One of them is that the text is out of order – not because it was copied from graffiti and never properly arranged, but because the planed slips of bamboo on which it was written got shuffled up. The ancient *pian* or bamboo books were remarkably durable in one respect, in that the slips themselves and their black-lacquer characters could survive for centuries and centuries unimpaired; their weakness was in the binding-strings which held the slips together. According to a tradition cited by Si-ma Qian, Confucius made such frequent use of his copy of the 'Book of Changes' that the leather thong binding it broke no less than three times. The story may be apocryphal but illustrates the well-known fact that bamboo books were liable to come apart in this way. And of course once the binding-string had gone, the chances of one or two slips getting out of order were very great. In the case of *Tian wen*, which has displaced passages all the way through and a really hopelessly shuffled-up text in the concluding section, it looks as if the ancestor of our present text was a unique copy of a very old bamboo book whose binding-strings had long since rotted away and whose slips therefore required sorting out. I believe that the person who did this job must have been left with a number of slips which he could not place and that he simply put them all together in no sort of order at the end. It is also possible that a fair number of slips from the end section of the book may have got lost. Although the historical questions are evidently supposed to be arranged in chronological order, one consequence of this is that nothing can be deduced about the date of composition by determining what is the most recent event referred to in the surviving text.

Another difficulty is that many of the legends referred to in the 'Heavenly Questions' are now unknown. The story of the pre-dynastic Shang chieftain Hai, or Wang Hai, and his brothers is referred to glancingly and in a very garbled way in one or two ancient sources, but it is only since the decipherment of the oracle bone inscriptions from Anyang during the present century that it has been possible to identify the names and events in *ll*.109–20 as belonging to this forgotten legend. It is clear that in *Tian wen* we have a remarkably rich source-book of Chinese mythology, untainted by the euhemerism, systematizing and rationalizations which mythology underwent in so many Chinese texts; but our uncertainty as to whether or not an obscure passage is in the right context, added to our realization that the story it refers to may in any case be lost, tantalizingly reduces the use we are able to make of its treasures.

However, much of the obscurity of *Tian wen* is a deliberate creation of the person who first composed the questions. He shows a fondness for kennings, acronyms and other concealments which at times makes his questions look like riddles. In order that the text should not be impenetrably obscure, I have sometimes supplied a word which is not in the original (e.g. 'moon' in *ll*.17–18). The Chinese is a good deal more baffling than my translation.

This brings us to the hardest question of all: what are the 'Heavenly Questions' for?

Questionnaires, it seems to me, can be divided into two main categories: those in which the questioner doesn't know the answers and those in which he does. The former may be speculative, like the questions in the passage from *Zhuang zi* cited above or those found in some of the Vedic hymns; or inquisitorial, like the questions we have to answer when we are filling in an Income Tax return or an application for a visa. The latter may be for amusement, like the poetic riddles of the third-century B.C. philosopher Xun Zi or, in European literature, the Latin riddles of Symphosius or the Old English riddles of the *Exeter Book*; or they may be contests of wit or learning, like the one between Odin and the giant Vafthruthir in the Icelandic *Edda*; or they may be designed to test the knowledge or fitness of a candidate who wishes to enter a religious or professional or any other kind of qualified or exclusive group or to acquire some sort of certification of his knowledge: such are all kinds of examinations, catechisms and the sets of questions asked in various kinds of initiatory ceremony.

Tian wen is curiously enough not easy to assign to either of these two main categories. Sometimes we feel that the questioner knows the answer to what he is asking, e.g. in *ll*.91–2, in which the second question contains in it the answer to the first; at other times we feel that he does *not* know, as in the unanswerable opening question about the creation of the world.

Of the 'speculative questions', as we may call those questions to which the questioner neither knows nor expects to be given an answer, I believe a rather larger number than is generally supposed may be concerned with moral issues. The old-fashioned morality, in China as in other parts of the world, assumed that prosperity was an indication of moral worth, and failure and misfortune, whether of the individual in his own lifetime or of his posterity, was a sign of moral obliquity. Like the author of the 'Book of Job', the questioner in *Tian wen* is familiar with this sort of morality but has found it wanting. Surveying the whole world from its beginning until recent times, he observes that, although there is a general tendency for the virtuous to prosper and the wicked to come to bad ends, there is a good deal of unfairness and ambiguity about these dispensations.

The dispensing authority is, of course, Heaven. In the 'Nine Songs' we met a Master of Fate who has charge over men's destinies; but the Master of Fate acts only as the agent and minister of Heaven. It was Heaven which conferred on royal dynasties their mandate to rule the earth and which withdrew the mandate when they misbehaved, Heaven, ultimately, which determined the fates of individuals, lineages and states.

Here, then, is an explanation of the title of this poem which does not oblige us to resort to bad grammar or improbable reconstructions. The 'Heavenly Questions' are questions about the parts and motions of Heaven, about the world which it helped to produce, and about the various destinies which it dispenses to mortal men.

There is one aspect of this text about which everyone is agreed: the antiquity of its style. *Tian wen* is written in an archaic language to be found nowhere else in the Chu anthology with the exception of one or two short passages of *Li sao*. It is my belief that its somewhat odd combination of archaic riddles with questions of a speculative or philosophic nature may be due to the fact that it started as an ancient, priestly riddle-text (a sort of catechism to be used for mnemonic purposes) which was rewritten and greatly enlarged by a secular poet; and since Si-ma Qian unhesitatingly ascribes *Tian wen* to Qu Yuan and the *Li sao* is undoubtedly related to *Tian wen* in one way or another (the same stories, the same attitudes, even, once or twice, the same phrases, are found in both), I have assumed that Qu Yuan was this adapter. The tradition that Qu Yuan was inspired to write these questions by looking at pictures on temple walls has at least this much substance in it: that it seems to recognize the fact that this was not a wholly original work by the great poet but an ancient one having priestly, i.e. shamanistic, associations which he took over and improved.

Who passed down the story of the far-off, ancient beginning of things? How can we be sure what it was like before the sky above and the earth below had taken shape? Since none could penetrate that murk when darkness and light were yet undivided, how do we know about the chaos of insubstantial forms?

What manner of things are the darkness and light? How did Yin and Yang come together, and how could they originate and transform all things that are by their commingling?

Whose compass measured out the ninefold heavens? Whose work was this, and how did he accomplish it? Where were the circling cords fastened, and where was the sky's pole fixed? Where did the Eight Pillars meet the sky, and why were they too short for it in the south-east?

Where do the nine fields of heaven extend to and where do they join each other? The ins and outs of their edges must be very many: who knows their number?

How does heaven coordinate its motions? Where are the Twelve Houses divided? How do the sun and the moon hold to their courses and the fixed stars keep their places?

Setting out from the Gulf of Brightness and going to rest in the Vale of Murk, from the dawn until the time of darkness, how many miles is the journey?

What is the peculiar virtue of the moon, the Brightness of the Night, which causes it to grow once more after its death? Of what advantage is it to keep a toad in its belly?

How did the Mother Star get her nine children without a union? Where is Lord Bluster, the Wind Star, and where does the warm wind live?

What is it whose closing causes the dark and whose opening causes the light? Where does the Bright God hide before the Horn proclaims the dawning of the day?

23 If Gun was not fit to allay the flood, why was he given this
charge? All said, 'Never fear! Try him out and see if he can
do it.' When the bird-turtles linked together, how did Gun
follow their sign? And if he accomplished the work according
to his will, why did the high lord punish him? Long he lay
cast off on Feather Mountain: why for three whole years did
he not rot? When Lord Gun brought forth Yu from his
belly, how was he transformed? Yu inherited the same
tradition and carried on the work of his father. If he
continued the work already begun, in what way was his plan
a different one? How did he fill the flood waters up where
they were most deep? How did he set bounds to the Nine
Lands? What did the winged dragon trace on the ground?
Where did the seas and rivers flow?

33 What did Gun plan and what did Yu accomplish? Why,
when the Wicked One was enraged, did the earth sink down
towards the south-east? Why are the lands of the earth dry
and the river valleys wet? They flow eastwards without ever
getting exhausted: who knows the cause of this? What are
the distances from east to west and from south to north?
From north to south the earth is longer and narrower. What
is the difference between its length and breadth? Where is
Kun-lun with its Hanging Garden? How many miles high are
its ninefold walls? Who goes through the gates in its four
sides? When the north-east one opens, what wind is it that
passes through? What land does the sun not shine on and
how does the Torch Dragon light it? Why are the Ruo
flowers bright before Xi He is stirring? What place is warm
in winter? What place is cold in summer? Where is the stone
forest? What beast can talk? Where are the hornless dragons
which carry bears on their backs for sport? Where is the
great serpent with nine heads and where is the Shu Hu?
Where is it that people do not age? Where do giants live?
Where is the nine-branched weed? Where is the flower of the
Great Hemp? How does the snake that can swallow an
elephant digest its bones? Where is the Black Water that
dyes the feet, and where is the Mountain of Three Perils?

The folk there put death off for many years: what is the limit of their age? Where does the man-fish live? Where is the Monster Bird?

When Yi shot down the suns, why did the ravens shed their feathers?

Yu laboured with all his might. He came down and looked on the earth below. How did he get that maid of Tu-shan and lie with her in Tai-sang? The lady became his mate and her body had issue. How came they to have appetite for the same dish when they sated their hunger with the morning food of love?

Qi supplanted Yi and made himself lord, but later met with mishap. How did Qi fall into trouble, and how did he succeed in warding it off? All gave him their allegiance and did no harm to his person. How is it that Yi lost lordship and Yu's seed was continued? Qi was many times the guest of God in heaven and brought back the Nine Changes and the Nine Songs. Why, if he was so good a son, did he kill his mother, and why were his lands divided up after his death?

God sent down Lord Yi to overcome the calamities of the people below. Why then did he shoot the River Lord and take to wife that Lady of the Luo? With his trusty bow and good thumb-ring he shot the Great Swine. Why, when he offered the fat of its flesh cooked as a sacrifice, was the Lord God displeased? Zhuo took the Black Fox to wife, and that Dark Woman plotted with him. How was Yi's body boiled, and how did they conspire to have him eaten?

On that westward journey from Zu to Qiong-shi how did Yi cross the heights? And when Gun turned into a brown bear, how did the shamans bring him back to life? Both sowed the black millet, and the rushlands became a place of husbandry. Why, if each made the same sowing, did Gun alone reap a harvest of infamy?

77   What is the halo of white light doing in this hall? Where did
      Yi get that goodly herb, and why could he not keep it? The
      heaven-made pattern embraces all, and when the *yang*-spirit
      leaves, death ensues. Why did the great birds cry? How did
      they lose their substance?

81   When Ping summons up the rain, how does he raise it?
      When those different parts were assembled and joined on to
      a deer, how were they fitted into shape?

83   When the Great Turtle walks along with an island on his
      back, how does he keep it steady? When the Strong Man
      made the boat move over dry land, how did he lift it? When
      Jiao was in Hu, what did he want with his sister-in-law?
      How did Shao Kang go hunting with his dogs and bring his
      head tumbling down? Nü Qi sewed Jiao's lower garment for
      him, and he lodged with her in her house. How did her head
      fall from her body and she herself meet the end that was
      meant for him? When the Strong Man prepared his warriors
      for battle, with what did he strengthen them? When he
      overturned the boat of the Lord of Zhen-xun, by what means
      did he take it?

91   What did Jie get when he attacked Meng-shan? How did Mo
      Xi bewitch him, and how did Tang kill him?

93   If Shun had a wife in his house, how could he be a bachelor?
      How could Yao's two daughters be married to him if he did
      not tell his family?

95   Who built the ten-storeyed tower of jade? Who foresaw it all
      in the beginning, when the first signs appeared?

      By what law was Nü Wa raised up to become high lord? By
      what means did she fashion the different creatures?

99   Shun served his brother, but his brother still did him evil.
      Why, when he behaved worse than a brute beast to Shun,
      did Shun's brother come to no harm?

101   Fleeing from Gu Gong, they possessed Wu and stayed in

Nan-yue. Who would have thought to find the two princes in that place?

From a bird-shaped vessel embellished with jade the high lord was feasted. How did he receive counsel for Jie of Xia's overthrow, so that at the last he destroyed him? The high lord came down and looked about, and there he met Yi Zhi. How did he bring about Jie's chastisement, so that the people were mightily rejoiced?

When Jian Di was in the tower, how did Ku favour her? When the swallow brought his gift, why was the maiden glad?

Hai inherited Ji's prowess. His father was a goodly man. Why did he end by losing his oxen and sheep in You-yi? How did he win her heart by dancing with shield and plumes, and how did she of the smooth sides and lovely skin become his paramour? What did You-yi's herdsmen say when they found them? When they struck the bed, he had already left the chamber: how did he meet his fate? Heng, too, inherited Ji's prowess. How did he get back those oxherds and oxen? How did he go about there dispensing gifts, but not return empty-handed? Dark Wei followed in his brothers' footsteps and the Lord of You-yi was stirred against him. Why, when the birds flocked together, did she forsake her own son and give herself to him? The Dark Man lay with her adulterously and destroyed his elder brother. Why, after such falsehood and treachery, was it given to his posterity to flourish?

Tang the Successful travelled to the east and came to You-xin. How did he come to ask for that bondsman and win a goodly queen? From the tree by the water's edge they got that little child. Why did they so hate him that they sent him away with the lady of You-xin? Tang came out of Chong-quan: for what crime was he shut up there? Who provoked him to march with impatient heart against his lord king?

On the morning of the first day we took our oath. How did we all arrive on time? When the grey geese came flocking together, at whose summons did they gather? When Zhòu's body was beheaded and mutilated, why was Shu Dan unhappy? When on his own he planned to make the dominion of Zhou secure, why did King Fa sigh? For what kingly virtue did Heaven bestow Yin's empire on him, and for what sin was it taken from him so soon after he had achieved it? How were the princes able to make rebellion when all the weapons of war had been handed in? And how did Shu Dan lead his armies to smite them on both their flanks?

135   Lord Zhao did much travelling. What did it profit him to meet that white rhinoceros when he went to the South Land?

137   King Mu was a breeder of horses. For what reason did he roam about? What was he looking for when he made his circuit of the earth?

139   When the witches were tied up together, what was it that was crying in the market-place? Whom was You of Zhou punishing when he got that Bao Si?

141   Huan of Qi nine times assembled the vassals, yet in the end his body was destroyed. Heaven in its dispensations veers first to one side and then to the other. Why did it first favour him and then afterwards punish him?

143   Who was it that led King Zhòu into folly? Why did he hate his ministers and let flatterers and backbiters serve him? How had Bi Gan offended that he should be suppressed, and how had Lei Kai found favour to be given a fief? Mei Bo was sliced and salted, but Ji Zi feigned madness. Why is it that wise men whose virtue is the same yet act in different ways?

149   King Millet was his firstborn: why did the high lord treat him so cruelly? When he was left out on the ice, how did the birds keep him warm? Drawing his bow to the full and grasping the arrow, how did he become a war-leader? After giving the high lord so great a shock, how did he come to have a glorious future?

Lord Chang abandoned his own title and consented to be a shepherd of the marches for King Zhòu. Why then did he remove his altars from Qi and claim heaven's mandate to supplant Yin?

When Tai packed up his possessions and moved to Qi, how did he get the people to follow him? Yin had a woman of guile: what protests did he hear?

When Zhòu bestowed that flesh on him, the Lord of the West declared it to heaven. Why did Zhòu invite God's chastisement, so that the dominion of Yin could not be saved?

When Wang the Counsellor was in the market, how did Chang know him? When he struck with his knife and the sound rang out, why was the king pleased?

When Wu set out to kill Yin, why was he grieved? He went into battle carrying his father's corpse: why was he in such a hurry?

Why did Bo Lin hang himself? When heaven was moved by his death to afflict the earth, who was so afraid?

When High God in heaven confers His mandate, how does He give notice of it? When He has bestowed dominion over the world on one, why does He take it away and give it to another?

At first Tang made Zhi his servant, but afterwards he made him his counsellor. How did Zhi end by becoming Tang's minister, and after his death share in the sacrifices of the royal ancestors?

He the Valiant was the grandson of Meng. When he was young he was an outcast. How did he make strong his might, so that he could spread his authority abroad?

What happened when Peng Keng offered the pheasant's broth to the high lord? After enjoying so long a life, why did he still have regrets?

173   When the lords of the centre ruled together, why was the lord king angry? Wasps and ants have a mean fate: how could their power be enduring?

175   When the maiden warned the brothers not to pick ferns, how did the deer come to their aid? When they came north to the whirling water, why were they glad to be in that place?

177   The elder brother had a hunting-dog. Why did the younger brother desire it? The elder bestowed a hundred chariots on him, yet he ended by losing all his substance.

179   Towards evening there was thunder and lightning. Why was the lady sad? The high lord did not reveal his majesty. What was he seeking?

181   What was the king's sorrow when he lay in hiding and lived in caves? What did we say when he awoke to the error of his ways? When Jing was glorious in war, how came we to be the leaders? But when Guang of Wu seized power, why were we so long defeated?

185   Round the village they went and through the altars until they came to the holy mounds. How came Zi Wen to be the fruit of such wantonness?

186   . . . Du Ao did not reign for long. How is it that though he murdered his lord and seized kingship for himself, yet the fame of his loyalty spread throughout the world?

Notes

*ll.*5–6 *How did Yin and Yang come together*: from the composition of the characters with which they are written, the earliest meaning of these words would seem to have been 'shady' and 'sunny'; hence the somewhat confusing fact that the south side of mountains and the north side of eastward-flowing rivers are both called 'yang', these being, in the northern hemisphere, the sides which face the sun. Later they came to be thought of in an abstract sense as two principles or forces, each equally important in the process of creation, which in the advanced thought of Qu Yuan's day was conceived of as a spontaneous, natural process: viz. the emergence of these two forces from a primordial, undifferentiated One, their polarization of formless matter into a Yang heaven and a Yin earth, and their engendering, by an infinite number of interactions and combinations, of the Ten Thousand Things – the myriad forms of organic life which inhabit the earth.

*ll.*7–10 *the ninefold heavens*: in the world-view of the ancient Chinese, the earth was square and comparatively flat, whilst the sky was round and suspended over it like an inverted bowl. The sky was 'ninefold' in a double sense. It was divided, like the earth, into nine regions or 'fields' (see note on *ll.*11–12 below); it was also ninefold in the sense that it was made up of nine layers, like a very heavy plywood. It is in the latter sense that 'ninefold' is intended here. Chinese philosophers associated 'nine' with 'heaven' because the sky is Yang and nine is a perfect Yang number. Thus in the *Yi jing*, or 'Book of Changes', the unbroken Yang lines are called 'nines' and the hexagram consisting entirely of 'nines' was said to symbolize the sky or 'heaven'. However, the idea of a 'ninefold heaven' is probably much more ancient than the numerological theories of the philosophers. God's heavenly palace could be reached only by penetrating a whole series of gates, each one an opening through a separate layer of the sky. In the 'Summons of the Soul', *ll.*42–3, the nine successive gateways through which the soul must pass in order to enter heaven are said to be guarded by man-eating tigers and leopards. Earthly kings and princes made themselves awesome and inaccessible in the same way, by interposing layer upon layer of walls and gateways between themselves and those who came to visit them. 'How should I not think anxiously of my lord? / But nine gates, gate within gate, divide me from him. / Fierce, snarling dogs run out from them and bark, / And they bar me against him and will not let me through' complains the poet in the 'Nine Changes' (IV, *ll.*13–16). The multiple barriers of heaven are a concept of worldwide distribution, and references to them are to be found in the architecture, religious traditions and rituals of many peoples. In some parts of the world they were represented by the rungs of a ladder which the shaman himself ascended in his trance. Many features of the mythological heaven are merely reflections of their human counterparts, but this particular concept probably antedates the construction of earthly palaces.

the circling cords . . . the sky's pole . . . the Eight Pillars: the Eight Pillars were eight mountains situated at the eight points of the compass around the edges of the earth (see diagram). They feature in a cosmological myth designed to explain (1) why the Celestial Pole around which the sky appears to revolve is not at the zenith immediately overhead but north of it, and (2) why the earth (i.e. China) inclines downwards towards the south-east, causing the major rivers to

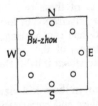

flow in an easterly direction: in a word, why the cosmos, instead of being perfect and symmetrical as you would expect it to be, is askew. The myth, which is invoked here in connection with the northward tilting of the Celestial Pole, is referred to again in *ll*.33–5 in connection with the downward tilting of the earth. A version of it is preserved in *Huai nan zi* (second century B.C.): 'Long, long ago Gong Gong contended with Zhuan Xu for mastery of the world. Enraged by his defeat, he butted against the Bu-zhou Mountain, breaking the supporting pillar, snapping the cords, and causing the sky to tilt downwards towards the north-west. That is why the sun, moon and stars revolve from east to west, and why the earth is lower on its south-east side, so that water and silt drain away from it in a south-easterly direction.' Bu-zhou Mountain was the north-western of the Eight Pillars. The 'perfect' cosmos, as it existed before Gong Gong's assault on it, would have been a motionless firmament, supported at the centre by a Celestial Pole, rising vertically from the middle of the earth to the zenith above, and at the edges by the Eight Pillars, to which, as an additional reinforcement, cords from the top of the Celestial Pole were fastened, like guy-ropes sustaining a mast. Apart from breaking the Pillar, the shock of Gong Gong's assault snapped the cords and dislodged the sky from its eight supports, causing the Celestial Pole to heel over towards the north, the sky to start spinning in an east–west direction (which it has continued to do ever since), and the earth to tilt downwards on the south-east side. Qu Yuan's evident unhappiness about the dynamics of this myth must have been shared by many others to judge from the attempts at improving on it made in later versions.

*ll.*11–12 *the nine fields of heaven*: the nine fields of the sky (it is to these, not the layers of *ll.*7–8, that the ancient Chinese were generally referring when they spoke of 'the nine heavens') are best thought of in relation to the Nine Lands into which the earth was thought to have been divided by the demiurge Yu (see *ll.*23–32). Yu invented drainage and irrigation, which turn the landscape, wherever it is a comparatively flat one, into a grid. The simplest grid having a square as its centre is made by the right-angled intersection of two pairs of parallel lines inside a larger square, and this is how Yu is supposed to have divided the earth. The nine fields of the sky represent a somewhat

arbitrary attempt to give the earthly pattern a celestial counterpart.
This was apparently done for astrological reasons: celestial events in a
particular field – a planetary conjunction, the appearance of a nova, etc.
– could be said to portend events in the corresponding earthly area. For
astronomical – i.e. calendrical – purposes the sky was divided in other
ways, the most important being the quintuple division into a central
circumpolar area and four quadrants, the Palaces of Spring, Summer,
Autumn and Winter. Times and seasons were marked by the
culminations of twenty-eight equatorial constellations, the *xiu*, which
girdled the heavens like our zodiac, except that they were associated not
with the Ecliptic but with the Celestial Equator. *Huai nan zi* not only
gives us the names of each of the nine fields but also tells us which of the
xiu were associated with each field. The correlations it gives seem at
first sight rather surprising. For example, we associate Scorpio with
winter, whereas *Huai nan zi* associates the corresponding Chinese
constellations with the eastern field and with spring. This is because the
stars we can see in the evening sky are the ones that will be overhead at
midday in three months' time. Armed with this knowledge, Chinese
astrologers could look at the night sky and make predictions about
things that would happen in a particular area of the earth in the day-
time – which is when things usually happen. The 'ins and outs' are those
caused by the contours of the constellations, which, like our
constellations, are often interlocked. Unlike the Meridian and the other
imaginary Great Circles with which astronomers divide the sky, the
boundaries between one heavenly field and another must be full of
indentations. If we could see them, they would look rather like the
sutures of a skull. This notion may have derived from the fact that
primitive astronomical instruments had indentations in which certain
stars of a constellation had to fit in order to give a position for other
sightings. See note on *Li sao, l.*3.

*ll.*13–14 *the Twelve Houses*: the Twelve Houses were the twelve
stations of the imaginary Counter-Jupiter planet (see note on
*Li sao, l.*3). It was by means of this imaginary planet that the
twelve-year (actually 11·86-year) cycle of Jupiter was correlated with
the twelve cyclical characters and with the twelve lunations of the year.
The solar, lunar and sidereal years are all different but eventually 'come

together' (approximately) inside larger cycles, just as, in the ancient Chinese calendar, the cycles of ten and twelve eventually 'came together' at the end of each sexagenary cycle. Qu Yuan is asking, in effect, what mysterious, complicated mechanism coordinates the movements of the sun, moon and planets with those of the fixed stars.

*ll.*17–18   *a toad in its belly*: the characters *gu-tu* appear to mean 'backward-looking hare' and have been so understood by most interpreters of this passage. Certainly there *was* a tradition – though I think it was rather a late one – that the dark shadows on the moon's surface represent a hare perpetually engaged in the pounding of magic herbs; yet most early sources, pictorial ones included, suggest that the moon's sole inhabitant was a toad. The scholar Wen Yi-duo (1899–1946), in a lengthy note on this passage, adduced what seem to me convincing reasons for believing that the characters *gu-tu* are used here as an alternative way of writing one of the words for 'toad'. Chang E, wife of the fox-hunting Lord Yi referred to in *Li sao*, *ll.*149 *et seq.*, is supposed to have stolen the herb of immortality from her husband and fled with it to the moon, where she turned into a toad. The advantage to the moon, which 'dies' every month (many Zhou inscriptions actually refer to the 'death' of the moon in recording the date), of harbouring a creature which possesses the secret of immortality must be obvious.

*ll.*21–2   *the Bright God ... the Horn*: the Bright God is the sun. The Horn is the name of a constellation consisting of α Virginis, i.e. Spica, and one much fainter star. It was the first of the twenty-eight *xiu* which divided the Celestial Equator. Its two stars were also called the Gate of Heaven. These questions are thought to refer to the heliacal rising of this constellation in the first month of spring, i.e. the beginning of the year.

*ll.*23–32   *Gun was not fit to allay the flood*: Gun's failure to control the flood-waters and his consequent punishment by exposure on Feather Mountain are cited in *Li sao*, *l.*131 (see note, *loc. cit.*), as an awful example of the danger of clinging too persistently to a discredited theory. The story of Gun and Yu, the unsuccessful father and the successful son, appears to have existed in a number of different versions. It seems to symbolize the transition from one mode of subsistence to another among peoples inhabiting the flood plains of the Yellow River and its tributaries in ancient times. Gun represents a more primitive society whose small-scale reclamation of areas rising somewhat above the level of the surrounding marshes may have been eked out with floating 'gardens' of brushwood and soil like those made by some riverine peoples in our own day. (One version of the myth maintains that Gun was punished for stealing magic soil from God with which to 'fill up the waters'.) Yu represents a society able to organize itself on the the much vaster scale required for constructing networks of ditches and canals capable of eliminating the marshes altogether. The seemingly miraculous transformation of the landscape which drainage brings about is reflected in the myth's portrayal of Yu as a demiurge responsible for every feature of China's geography. In fact the 'Nine Lands' into which he is supposed to have divided the inhabited earth (see note on *ll*. 11–12) are simply the basic drainage grid on a very large scale. The Chinese term means literally 'nine islands', viz., lands surrounded or intersected by water-channels. (The word for 'island' used in this expression has a riverine rather than maritime connotation.) Qu Yuan's opening question refers to the text of the ancient 'Book of History' (*Shu jing*), with which most educated men in his time would be familiar. In the section of it called *Yao dian* the high lord sits in council and asks his assembled chieftains what he should do about the flood: 'On every hand the waters spread havoc; they encircle the hills; they rise up level with their summits; they threaten the sky; the people below cry out. Is there any one who can control them?' The assembly unanimously recommend Gun, and the high lord, despite some misgivings, appoints Gun to control the flood. 'For nine years he laboured,' says the text, 'but he did not succeed.' But not all texts make Gun out to have been a failure. The story about his stealing God's magic soil, for instance, seems to imply that he was punished not for failure but for succeeding all too well. Qu Yuan probably knew several versions of the story and was puzzled by their inconsistency.

When Lord Gun brought forth Yu from his belly: three years after his death on Feather Mountain Gun's belly was cut open and his son Yu came out. His body turned into a yellow dragon – some accounts said a turtle or a bear – which dived into a nearby lake.

l.56 *When Yi shot down the suns*: at one time the ten suns of Fu-sang (see note on *Li sao*, *l*.189) came out together and dried up the earth. Lord Yi, the Mighty Archer, was commanded by God to shoot them down. The ravens are the ravens of the suns. (A raven was said to inhabit the sun just as a toad or hare was said to inhabit the moon.) Perhaps their feathers were meteorites.

ll.57–60 *How did he get that maid of Tu-shan*: Yu's labours involved him in perpetual journeying and left little time over for domesticity. The mother of his only son, Qi, is said to have been a mountain nymph, the Lady of Tu-shan, whom he met on his travels. Visiting her some time later, when she was pregnant, Yu was unwise enough to let her see him when he had changed himself (as he sometimes did, apparently) into a bear. This gave the lady so great a shock that she turned into stone. Yu called out anxiously to the petrified mother to give him his son, whereupon the stone burst open revealing the infant Qi inside. (The name Qi means 'open'.)

ll.61–6 Qi supplanted Yi: this is not Yi the Mighty Archer but Yi
          (written with another character) the son of Gao Yao, to whom
Yu is supposed to have passed on the high kingship at the time of his
death. The people preferred Yu's own son, Qi, however, and so
kingship became hereditary. As to whether this came about by violent
or peaceful means, existing sources are divided, and it is not very clear
from the text which version of the story Qu Yuan was familiar with.
Whichever it was, I think he must have found Qi a morally confusing
character. He was a rebel (against his father's chosen successor, Yi) and
a matricide (his birth having caused the destruction of his stone
mother), yet he was favoured by Heaven ('many times the guest of
God'). On the other hand, if he was Heaven's favourite, and therefore,
presumably, 'good', how is one to explain the calamities which followed
his demise?

Why were his lands divided up: this refers to the quarrelling that broke
out among Qi's sons (see *Li sao, ll.*145–8), which Lord Yi, the Mighty
Archer, took advantage of by usurping the high kingship and seizing
part of his lands.

ll.67–72 that Lady of the Luo: goddess of the Luo river, the lady Fu
           Fei of *Li sao, l.*222. Lord Yi shot the River Earl, god of the
Yellow River, and took his consort, the goddess of his tributary the
Luo, to be his own wife. The Great Swine was the son of another of
Lord Yi's wives-by-capture, the beautiful Black Fox, by a former
husband. The story of Han Zhuo ('Zhuo') is also referred to in *Li sao*
(see *ll.*152 *et seq.* and note). Lord Yi seems originally to have been a
culture-hero of the Di Ku/Gao Xin people (see note on *Li sao, l.*1) and
the tasks he was sent down into the world to perform were all beneficial
– shooting down superfluous suns, killing monsters, etc. In the
legendary history of the House of Xia, however, he appears as a wicked
usurper. That is because the legend represents the struggle between the
Gao Yang (Xia) people and the Gao Xin (Yi) people for mastery of the
North China Plain. Not surprisingly, Qu Yuan finds the inconsistency
in the surviving legends about Lord Yi confusing, and his questions
reflect his difficulty in reaching a moral judgement about this morally
ambiguous hero.

ll.73–6 how did Yi cross the heights?: the name Yi does not appear in the
          Chinese text and the extreme obscurity of this and the
following passages has given rise to very widely varying interpretations.
I do not, however, think that the fact that the questions appear to range
from Lord Yi to Gun and back again presents any real difficulty. Both
are morally ambiguous characters in that both appear as benefactors in
one set of myths and evildoers in another. For Lord Yi's journey from
Zu (or Ju) to Qiong-shi, see note on *Li sao, ll.*221–2.

*ll.*77–80 *What is the halo of white light*: I have followed the modern
scholar Jiang Liang-fu's interpretation of this passage in
taking the subject of the first question to be Lord Yi's wife who stole
the herb of immortality from him and fled with it to the moon, and the
subject of the second to be the ravens of the suns which Lord Yi shot
down (cf. *l.*56). The Chinese text is very obscure, however, and it is by
no means certain that Yi and his wife are the subjects of these
questions. Jiang Liang-fu understands *wei ci tang*, the words I have
translated as 'doing in this hall', in a quite different sense which
seems to me to place a very great strain on their meaning. Wang Yi
evidently understood them in the sense I have translated and
presumably used them as the basis of his interesting hypothesis about
the circumstances in which the 'Heavenly Questions' came to be
written. I think myself it is extremely likely that they are the product of
textual corruption, but the whole passage is so obscure that there seems
no point in trying to emend them.

*ll.*81–2 *When Ping summons up the rain*: Ping, Ping Yi or Feng Yi was
the name of the Rain God. Qu Yuan knows that the water
precipitated from the clouds must have come from the earth, but how
does it get up there? The subject of the second question is Fei Lian, the
Wind God, who is usually represented as a flying deer with a horned
bird's head and the tail of a snake.

*ll.*83–90 *the Great Turtle*: the Islands of the Blest in the Eastern Sea
were said to be supported on the backs of giant turtles. The
turtles carrying islands on their backs put Qu Yuan in mind of Han
Zhuo's son Jiao, the Strong Man, carrying a boat on his back over the
dry land. The circumstances of this heroic feat are no longer known,
but the story was a well-known one in antiquity. Someone in the
'Analects'. refers to it in a conversation with Confucius: 'Yi was a
mighty archer and Ao [an alternative form of Jiao's name] shook the
boat; yet both of them came to a bad end.' The full story of how the Xia
prince Shao Kang overthrew the sons of Han Zhuo and regained his
patrimony is also lost, though there are cryptic references to it in 'Zuo's
Chronicles' and the 'Bamboo Annals'. The Han commentator Wang Yi
appears to be better informed about it but may be only guessing. He
says that Nü Qi was Jiao's sister-in-law; Jiao was having an adulterous
affair with her, and when Shao Kang, using a hunting expedition as an
excuse for being under arms, stole into Jiao's room to kill him, he cut
off Nü Qi's head by mistake. The Lord of Zhen-xun was one of the Xia
princes whom Jiao had overthrown.

*ll.*91–2 *What did Jie get*: Jie was the wicked last king of Xia (*Li sao*,
*l.*31) and Mo Xi his queen. She came to him as the spoils of
war when he conquered Meng-shan, and his infatuation with her led to

his overthrow by Tang the Successful, founder of the Shang dynasty. The text of this section of 'Heavenly Questions' is in considerable confusion. *Ll.*91–2 seem to belong with *ll.*103–6, which are also about Tang and Jie.

*ll.*93–4 *If Shun had a wife in his house*: this and the question about Shun and his brother in *ll.*99–100 look as if they ought to come together. Both questions seem out of place in terms of traditional chronology, which puts Yao and Shun before Yu. The story of Shun's persecution by his parents and his wicked brother Xiang was still a popular one with unsophisticated audiences in the ninth century A.D. (see 'The Story of Shun' in Arthur Waley's *Ballads and Stories from Tun-huang*). Like King David, Shun started life as a poor country boy. The sage-king Yao was so impressed by the meekness with which he bore his sufferings that he gave him his two daughters in marriage and later entrusted him with the government of the whole empire. In the text of the 'Book of History' which we read today Shun is described as a 'bachelor' by the courtiers who first recommend him to Yao's attention, but there is nothing in the existing text which lends any point to this question. Perhaps the text that Qu Yuan was familiar with was a somewhat different one.

*ll.*95–6 *Who built the ten-storeyed tower of jade?*: the subject of this question is an unbroken mystery.

*ll.*97–8 *By what law was Nü Wa raised up*: readers of 'The Story of the Stone' will remember Nü Wa as the goddess who repaired the broken sky in the novel's opening chapter. A late arrival in the Chinese pantheon, she was given a place among the sage-kings and early 'emperors' somewhat before that of the Yellow Ancestor. (In the pseudo-history of what was called 'high antiquity' the latest arrivals were made to antedate their predecessors because there was nowhere else to put them.) Mythology makes her the wife or sister of Fu Xi and the pair of them are represented iconographically as human above and serpentine below, with their lower serpent-halves intertwined. Generally they are shown holding carpenter's tools in their hands, or sometimes they the sun and moon. Evidently they were a personification of the male and female principles, the Yin and Yang, by which all other things were created. Sometimes (as in this question) Nü Wa alone was said to be the creator. The second-century lexicographer Xu Shen refers to this alternative tradition.

*ll.*99–100 *Shun served his brother*: presumably these lines belong with *ll.*93–4 above. Shun's brother was Xiang, 'Elephant'. Elephants were still found in parts of China until well into the Shang period. There was an ancient tradition that Shun tamed the elephant and that he used tame elephants in his campaigns against the southern tribesmen. The stories of his patience with his savage brother and of his finally conquering him by kindness may represent a dim folk memory of a remote age when elephants still existed in China in a wild state and were induced by human skill and patience to work for men. By the Warring States period Xiang had become fully anthropomorphized and the point of the story had been forgotten. (Mencius tells us that Xiang was enfeoffed in the Land of Trunk without betraying any awareness that he is repeating a joke.) The natural meaning of the Chinese text of the first sentence of this passage would be 'Shun tamed his brother', but I think Qu Yuan is merely repeating the words of an ancient tradition without understanding what they literally meant.

*ll.*101–2 *Fleeing from Gu Gong*: Gu Gong is the 'Old Duke' Tan Fu, great-grandfather of King Wu of Zhou, who overthrew the last Shang king and founded the Zhou dynasty. Gu Gong's two elder sons realized that their younger brother was destined to be the father of a sage-king and tactfully removed themselves from the scene so that he could inherit the dukedom after their father's death. The two brothers are said to have fled south and to have become kings of the semi-barbarous kingdom of Wu in Jiangsu. This question, like several other parts of the text of the 'Heavenly Questions', is hopelessly out of place. It ought to come somewhere after *ll.*149–52, which are about the Corn God, King Millet, First Ancestor of the Zhou royal house, and *ll.*155–6, which are about Gu Gong's removal with all his people to the land around the Qi mountain in order to escape pressure from neighbouring tribes.

*ll.*103–6 *From a bird-shaped vessel embellished with jade*: we are now back with the last Xia king, Jie, and his conqueror, Tang the Successful (cf. *ll.*91–2). The 'high lord' here is Tang. Yi Zhi, more often referred to as 'Yi Yin' or 'Steward Yi', was Tang's famous counsellor, an historical person, evidently, as he is referred to sometimes in the oracle bone inscriptions. Yi Yin first found favour with Tang through his excellence as a cook.

*ll.*107–8 *When Jian Di was in the tower*: Jian Di was the First Ancestress of the Shang people. See note on *Li sao*, *l.*236, for her story. Ku is Di Ku or Gao Xin, who sent the swallow with the egg which made Jian Di pregnant.

*ll.*109–20 *Hai inherited Ji's prowess*: this is a passage of extraordinary interest to ancient historians and students of Chinese mythology. The names in it are those of pre-dynastic ancestors of the Shang kings whose existence has been confirmed in recent times with the decipherment of the oracle bone inscriptions. The story of the three brothers Hai, Heng and Wei (the last-mentioned is more usually referred to as Tai-jia Wei) can be only partially reconstructed from garbled and fragmentary references in several ancient texts. Hai, according to one source, was the First Herdsman. (It is interesting, in this connection, to note the scale and importance of animal sacrifice in Shang ritual and the use of the symbol for 'sheep' in the characters for 'good', 'beautiful', etc. in the Chinese script, which the Shang, presumably, invented.) Hai committed adultery with the wife of Mian Chen, Lord of You-yi, where he was pasturing his flocks and herds, and was killed by Mian Chen in revenge. The details of the story as it is referred to in this passage are unknown. The Dark Man is Tai-jia Wei, whose name Wei means 'dark' or 'faint'. The first Shang king, Tang, traced his ancestry in direct line of descent from Tai-jia Wei. Fraternal succession remained normal throughout the entire Shang dynastic period and in some places survived even longer.

*ll.*121–6 *Tang the Successful ... came to You-xin*: Yi Yin, famous minister of the first Shang king, Tang (see note on *ll.*103–6 above), was found as a baby in the hollow mulberry tree which his pregnant mother had turned into when fleeing from a flood. He became the Lord of You-xin's cook. Tang fell in love with his cooking when visiting You-xin and arranged for him to be sent in the train of the Lord of You-xin's daughter when he married her. Jie's capricious imprisonment of Tang at a place called Cong-quan and equally capricious decision to release him are mentioned in several sources. No crime was alleged to justify the imprisonment. Tang's victorious campaign against the wicked Jie is said to have been divinely inspired.

*ll.*127–34 *On the morning of the first day we took our oath*: the questions in this section of the poem concern another victorious campaign to overthrow a dynasty, that of King Wu of Zhou against the tyrant Zhòu, last king of the Shang dynasty which Tang established. King Wu's name was Fa (Wu was not really his name but a descriptive title meaning 'warlike'). His younger brother Dan ('Shu Dan'), known in history as the 'Duke of Zhou', was regent during the minority of King Wu's infant son. Yin is another name for the Shang dynasty. Palaeographers sometimes reserve this name for the last two centuries of the dynasty, or as a means of designating the last Shang capital, which was near present-day Anyang in southern Henan. The question in the first part of this section concerns the great battle of Mu-ye, in which King Wu ('King Fa') and his allies defeated the army of the Shang king Zhòu; those in the latter part concern the unsuccessful rebellion of two of King Wu's brothers acting in league with the Shang prince Wu Geng during the Duke of Zhou's regency after his brother's death. The question about Heaven bestowing the empire only to take it away again a short time afterwards is a reference to King Wu's death not long after the conquest of Shang, when his heir was still a child.

ll.135–6 *Lord Zhao did much travelling*: Zhao, fourth of the Zhou
            kings, was drowned on an expedition against the people of
Chu. When in the seventh century B.C. an army of confederate Zhou
states was asked by a delegation from the King of Chu what reason it
could possibly have for invading his territory, the rather feeble pretext
given was that King Zhao had failed to return from his southward
expedition (which took place some three centuries earlier) and they had
'come to investigate'.

ll.137–8 *King Mu was a breeder of horses*: King Mu was the fifth of the
            Zhou kings, the son of King Zhao. He was a great traveller.
A fictitious account of his journey to the far west called *Mu, Son of
Heaven* was discovered in the third century A.D. in the tomb of a
fourth-century B.C. king of Liang. The names of his horses and of their
driver, Bo Le, who is supposed to have had a preternatural flair for
assessing equine capabilities, make frequent appearances in the poems
of Qu Yuan and his imitators, who saw in them a parable of the wise
king who is able to choose the right statesmen for harnessing to the
chariot of state.

ll.139–40 *When the witches were tied up together*: Xuan, the eleventh of
            the Zhou kings (*reg.* 827–781 B.C.), heard a prophecy that a
mulberry bow and a bamboo quiver would destroy the kingdom of
Zhou. A man and his wife caught selling these objects were tied up and
exposed in the market-place. At this time a waiting-maid at the palace
had given miraculous birth to a fatherless child (she was impregnated
by a terrifying flood of dragon-sperm which someone had imprudently
let out of a chest) which she then abandoned. The couple, escaping
from their bonds, heard its cries and fled with it to the land of Bao. The
abandoned infant grew up to become King You's queen Bao Si, whose
follies hastened the downfall of Western Zhou. The only thing which
ever made Queen Bao Si smile, it is said, was the expression of angry
surprise on the faces of the King's vassals when they turned out with
their armies in response to the kindling of the warning beacons which
the King had caused to be lit for her amusement. Unfortunately, like
the boy in the fable who cried 'wolf', King You found that his joke was
an expensive one, for when his barbarian enemies really did come
marching down over the hills and he lit the beacon fires to summon his
vassals, no one would turn out to protect him. The answer to the second
question is the Lord of Bao. It was in order to avert a punitive
expedition that the men of Bao sent the beautiful Bao Si to the court of
King You.

ll.141–2 *Huan of Qi nine times assembled the vassals*: with the fall of
            King You's capital to the barbarians in 771 B.C., the period
known as Western Zhou came to an end. The Zhou kings who ruled

from their eastern capital of Luoyang during the centuries which
followed had none of the power and authority of their predecessors, and
the lands of their feudatories became virtually autonomous states.
Anarchy was averted by the emergence of the Hegemons, powerful
feudatories who, acting nominally as deputies or protectors of the Zhou
kings, organized the other states into a confederacy, bound by solemn
and frequently renewed covenants to observe certain conventions and
to act together under the Hegemons' leadership against common
enemies. The Age of the Hegemons is more often referred to as the
Spring and Autumn period, after the name of the chronicle on which
we mainly rely for its history. It lasted for approximately two centuries,
after which it was succeeded by the anarchic Warring States period.
Duke Huan of Qi (*reg.* 685–643 B.C.) was the first of the Great
Hegemons. He was the most powerful and respected ruler of his day (his
bronze knife-coins were China's first real currency), yet when he died
his sons started quarrelling before his corpse was cold and he lay
untended until the worms from his neglected body came wriggling
across the threshold of his bedchamber. To Qu Yuan and his Warring
States contemporaries Duke Huan was an ambivalent figure – a
defender of the Zhou monarchy and the old-fashioned virtues it
represented, and yet at the same time a usurper. According to more
old-fashioned notions of morality, Heaven rewards the good and
punishes the wicked; so if a man is fortunate he must be good, and if he
is unfortunate he must be bad. To Qu Yuan, as to the author of the
'Book of Job', Heaven's dispensations are inscrutable and moral
judgements consequently more problematical.

*ll.*143–8 *Who was it that led King Zhòu into folly?*: the Shang king Zhòu
            is said to have been led astray by his vicious wife Da Ji.
Throughout their history Chinese males have shown a curiously
persistent tendency to attribute the consequences of their own political
folly to the baneful influence of some *femme fatale*. Mo Xi, the consort
of the last Xia king (*ll.*91–2), Zhòu's wife Da Ji, Bao Si, the unsmiling
queen of You Wang, last king of Western Zhou ... the list could be
continued into our own day. Bi Gan was Zhòu's uncle, a minister at his
court and renowned for his great wisdom. Zhòu had his heart cut out in
order to find out if it was true, as was commonly stated, that a sage's
heart had an extra chamber in it that ordinary people's had not got. Lei
Kai, another minister at Zhòu's court, won lands and a title for himself
by his obsequious flatteries. Already in *Li sao* (*l.*159) Qu Yuan refers to
Zhòu's distribution among his feudatories, as a means of terrorizing
them into submission, of pickled portions of those who had had the
temerity to criticize him. Ji Zi, a Shang prince who, along with Mei Bo,
had protested against his tyrannies, escaped this grisly fate by
pretending to be mad. He was released from imprisonment by Zhòu's

conqueror, King Wu, and treated by him with great respect. According to ancient tradition, he ended his days in Korea and is buried in Pyongyang, the North Korean capital.

ll.149–52 King Millet was his firstborn: the corn god King Millet was the First Ancestor of the Zhou people. His mother, Jiang Yuan, conceived him by stepping in a giant footprint left by God. As a fatherless child, he was exposed shortly after his birth (his name Qi means 'the castaway' or 'the abandoned one'), but, as in the case of other heroic infants, all attempts at getting rid of him were frustrated: 'They laid him in a narrow lane / But the sheep and oxen stood over him and protected him / They laid him in a wood / But the woodcutters found him and brought him back / They laid him on the cold ice / But the birds came and covered him with their wings' (*Shi jing 245*). In the 'modernized' version of the myth which Qu Yuan appears to be referring to here, Di Ku, or Gao Xin, instead of being the name of God, has become Jiang Yuan's earthly husband, the high lord Gao Xin (cf. *ll.107–8*, where Di Ku is the husband of the Shang ancestress Jian Di). In this version it was Di Ku, presumably, who exposed King Millet: hence the question 'Why did the high lord treat him so cruelly?'. The custom of killing the firstborn was noted by the ancient Chinese among certain neighbouring tribes. They explained it by saying that the womenfolk among these peoples were unchaste, and that it was only in this way that fathers could make sure that the first son they reared would be their own. The point of the last two questions in this passage is obscure.

ll.153–4 Lord Chang abandoned his own title: Chang was the name of King Wen of Zhou, father of King Wu, who founded the Zhou dynasty. His home was under Mount Qi in what is now the province of Shaanxi. The Zhou were originally an independent people on the western marches of the Shang empire. As they became more powerful, the Shang kings sought to control them by making them 'guardians' or 'shepherds' of the western marches. Why, the question seems to be asking, did the Zhou chieftains consent to abandon their status of independent kinglets and become the Shang king's vassals if they were not prepared to serve their new masters loyally?

ll.155–6 When Tai packed up his possessions and moved to Qi: 'Tai', short for 'Tai Wang' ('King Tai') is the 'Gu Gong' of *ll.101–2*, the grandfather of King Wen, who was the subject of the passage preceding this one. 'Gu Gong' and 'Tai Wang' are both titles. His actual name was Tan Fu. By rights these two passages about him (*ll.101–2* and 155–6) ought to come between *ll.149–52* (about the First Ancestor of the Zhou kings, King Millet) and *ll.153–4* (about Tai Wang's grandson King Wen). The Zhou people's migration to the Plain of Zhou underneath Mount Qi under the leadership of their chieftain Tan Fu ('King Tai') is celebrated in *Shi-jing*: see pp. 248 *et seq*. in the section 'Dynastic Legends' of Arthur Waley's *Book of Songs*. Yin's (i.e Shang's) 'woman of guile' is Da Ji, subject of the first question in *ll.*143–8.

King Millet (*al.* Qi)

Tan Fu (*al.* Gu Gong, Tai Wang, Tai)

Tai Bo   Yu Zhong   Ji Li (*al.* Wang Ji)

Chang (*al.* Bo Chang, Wen Wang, King Wen)

Fa (*al.* King Fa, Wu Wang, King Wu)

*ll.*157–8   *When Zhòu bestowed that flesh on him*: this was the pickled flesh of the unfortunate Mei Bo (see *ll.*143–8: 'Mei Bo was sliced and salted'). The Lord of the West is King Wen, whose unconcealed distress at receiving this 'present' caused the tyrant Zhòu to imprison him for a time at Jiu-li. He is supposed to have written the *Yi jing* ('Book of Changes') during his imprisonment.

*ll.*159–60   *When Wang the Counsellor was in the market*: Lü Wang ('Wang the Counsellor'), the famous minister of King Wen ('Chang'), once worked as a butcher. In *Li sao*, *ll.*293–4, the shaman Wu Xian cites this example of the talent-spotting King Wen's 'discovery' of Lü Wang at his butcher's stall in the market in support of his view that a person with Qu Yuan's qualifications is sure to find suitable employment. Lü Wang is supposed to have been an old man when he was 'discovered' but to have survived King Wen by many years. He was one of the commanders of King Wu's forces at the battle of Mu-ye, which is the subject of the following questions.

*ll.*161–2   *When Wu set out to kill Yin*: the Han historian Si-ma Qian twice tells us that it was the wooden 'spirit tablet' of his dead father that King Wu carried into battle, but that is because he was trying to make sense of two irreconcilable traditions. The first time he asserts it, in his 'Annals of the Royal House of Zhou', he says that these events took place in King Wu's eleventh year, i.e. eleven years after King Wen's death; the second time, in the 'Biography of Bo Yi', he says that Bo Yi and his brother travelled to the Zhou court intending to offer their services to King Wen, but were shocked to find that King Wen had just died and that his son was preparing to lead an army against the Shang king. What shocked them was not merely that the new Zhou ruler was planning to lead an armed insurrection against his overlord, but that he was planning to do it *before his father was in his grave*. I suspect that in the original version of the story which Qu Yuan is here referring to it was a dead body, as in El Cid's last battle, which led the troops to victory.

*ll.*163–4 *Why did Bo Lin hang himself?*: no one has ever satisfactorily explained this passage. The name Bo Lin is unknown. The characters with which it is written are probably corrupt, but the various attempts that have been made at emending them are unconvincing.

*ll.*167–8 *At first Tang made Zhi his servant*: this passage seems to have strayed from its proper place. A series of questions abut Tang the Successful, the founder of the Shang dynasty, occurs in *ll.*121–6, and the story of Tang's first meeting with his cook-counsellor Yi Yin is referred to in *ll.*103–6. The Shang kings' inclusion of Yi Yin in the sacrifices they offered to their own ancestors has been verified by oracle bone inscriptions found on the site of their ancient capital.

*ll.*169–70 *He the Valiant*: He Lü, scourge of the Chu armies, was King of Wu from 514 to 496 B.C. He Lü's father was the eldest of three brothers, each of whom reigned in turn after the death of their father, Shou Meng. The third brother was succeeded by his son Wang Liao. He Lü thought that the succession should by rights have gone to him and eventually had Wang Liao assassinated, becoming king in his place. Wu, a little kingdom founded by Chinese settlers (cf. *ll.*101–2 and note) in what is now southern Jiangsu probably some time in the Shang period (the type of fraternal succession exemplified in the generation before He Lü was customary throughout most of the Shang dynasty), was undeveloped and still semi-barbarous until well into the sixth century B.C. Thanks partly to the efforts of foreign advisers who had come as political refugees from Chu and partly to the development of superior weaponry, it enjoyed a brief period of importance in the late sixth and early fifth centuries, culminating in He Lü's successful invasion of Chu and his son Fu Cha's intervention in the affairs of the northern states. Wu was annexed by the even more 'barbarian' settler-state of Yue (north Zhejiang) in 472 B.C. Yue was itself annexed by Chu in 333 B.C., probably when Qu Yuan was a youth. The text of this whole final section of the 'Heavenly Questions' (from *ll.*169–70 to the end) is in a state of great confusion. Presumably the whole final section was originally devoted exclusively to Chu history. The rise of Wu, Chu's humiliation – referred to again in *ll.*181–4 – at the hands of this new and powerful neighbour, and Wu's extinction, almost overnight, as a political entity just as she seemed at the very height of her power would have appeared as one of the most memorable and remarkable episodes in Chu history to a Chu citizen of Qu Yuan's day for whom Wu was a mere province of the Chu kingdom.

ll.171–2 What happened when Peng Keng offered the pheasant's broth:
Peng Keng is presumably Peng Zu, the Chinese Methuselah, to whose enormous longevity there are numerous references in ancient Chinese texts, e.g. the 'Analects', in which Confucius says that 'not even Old Peng' could have excelled him in his love of the ancients and his faithfulness to their teachings. Peng Zu was supposed to have been one of the six sons of Lu Zhong, son of the Fire God, Zhu Rong, through whom the kings of Chu traced their ancestry to Gao Yang. (Qu Yuan was born on Zhu Rong's feast-day: see note on *Li sao, l.*4.) He was the third of Lu Zhong's sons. It was from the youngest, Ji Lian, that the Mi lineage, to which the Chu kings belonged, was descended. These ancient genealogies were treated with the greatest seriousness. In the mid sixth century B.C. a king of Chu seriously suggested laying claim to some territory which had for centuries belonged to another state on the grounds that it had once been inhabited by his ancestor's uncle, Kun Wu, i.e. Lu Zhong's eldest son. In the original, probably much longer, version of 'Heavenly Questions' this question about Old Peng would have come near the beginning of the final section on Chu history – certainly before the previous section about He Lü.

ll.173–4 When the lords of the centre ruled together: the Chinese text of this passage is so obscure that Jiang Liang-fu, the greatest modern *Chu ci* specialist, declined to comment on it. One plausible explanation sometimes offered is that it refers to an episode in Zhou history when the unpopular king Li (*reg.* 878–842 B.C.) was driven by rebellion from his capital and there was for some years (according to one tradition) a regency of the Dukes of Zhou and Shao. After his death King Li's outraged ghost sent calamities to plague the usurpers. I have no great confidence that this is the subject of these lines, but have translated them as if it were.

ll.175–6 When the maiden warned the brothers: this question is hopelessly out of place. The brothers Bo Yi and Shu Qi (see note on *ll.*161–2) were princes of Gu-zhu who travelled to King Wen's court having been told that he was a sage, only to find that King Wen was dead and his son, King Wu, was plotting rebellion against his overlord, the Shang king. King Wu listened politely to their remonstrations but refused to abandon his expedition, and the two brothers, rather than 'eat the corn of Zhou', retired to Shou-yang Mountain, where they lived on ferns. A woman suggested that even the wild herbs of the mountain were 'corn of Zhou', and the over-scrupulous brothers would have starved to death but for the miraculous appearance of a white doe which suckled them. All versions of this very popular story are agreed that they did eventually starve to death, so the diet of deer-milk can have been only a temporary alleviation. The question about the whirling water must refer to some episode in a version of the legend which has been lost.

*ll.*177–8 *The elder brother had a hunting-dog*: this question is said to refer to Duke Jing of Qin and his younger brother, Hou Zi-chen, who fled to the neighbouring state of Jin in 541 B.C. with a force of 1,000 chariots. 'Substance' presumably refers to his lands in Qin. If this explanation is correct, this question, like the last one, would appear to be out of place.

*ll.*179–80 *Towards evening there was thunder and lightning*: the subject of this question is unknown. All attempts so far made at explaining it are no more than wild guesses and none is in the least convincing.

*ll.*181–4 *What was the king's sorrow*: the subject of this passage appears to be the same as that of *ll.*169–70 – the wars of Chu and Wu. 'Jing' was another name for Chu. 'Guang' was King He Lü's name. Chu led a successful campaign against Wu in the sixth year of He Lü's uncle Yu Mei (538 B.C.), but He Lü's generalship put an end to Chu's run of victories. In 506 B.C. his armies entered Ying, the Chu capital, and desecrated the tomb of King Ping in revenge for the wrongs done by that monarch to the Chu émigré Zi Xu, who was Wu's principal adviser. King Zhao of Chu had to flee into the marshes with his sister and a single retainer and for several months lived like a hunted animal. This appears to be what the first question is about; but there are many other theories.

*l.*185 *Round the village they went*: Zi Wen, famous Chief Minister of King Cheng of Chu (*reg.* 671–626 B.C.) was born as a result of a 'union in the fields'. He was exposed in the marshes, but was miraculously suckled by a tigress. This question must originally have come nearer the beginning of the Chu section.

*ll.*186–7 ... *Du Ao did not reign for long*: the first line of the Chinese text of this passage is corrupt. Du Ao became King of Chu in 676 B.C. He was assassinated five years later by his younger brother, Xiong Yun, more generally known in history as King Cheng of Chu (see note on preceding question). After murdering his brother, Cheng proved, at any rate in the first part of his reign, an exemplary king. The question may refer to this, but the meaning of it is by no means clear.

Jiu zhang *'Nine Pieces'*

In this group of poems we return to the metre and to some extent the themes of *Li sao*. Once more we encounter the honest, loyal courtier, traduced by his peers and rejected by his king, strenuously protesting his innocence, pouring scorn on a corrupt society, and affirming his willingness to die, if necessary, for his convictions. They differ from *Li sao*, though, in two important respects: the journeys undertaken in them, which are not shamanistic excursions by flying chariot into the world of gods and spirits but real journeys through identifiable places, and the slightly self-pitying tone of their lamentations – a feature of 'Sao-style' poetry which provoked the great twelfth-century philosopher Zhu Xi to describe some of its later exponents as 'people who moan and groan when they are not in pain'.

Wang Yi thought that all the poems in this section were written by Qu Yuan during his banishment in Jiang-nan (the area of lakes and rivers to the south of the old Chu capital of Ying) and that their collective title, *Jiu zhang*, meant 'Nine Declarations', understanding the word *zhang* in the rather unusual sense of 'illuminate' or 'publish'; but even if we make the highly questionable assumption that they are indeed all by Qu Yuan, the words of the poems themselves give the lie to Wang Yi's assertion that they were first conceived of as a poem-cycle or written at one time or in one place. Already in the twelfth century Zhu Xi was observing that the *Jiu zhang* poems 'must have been collected in one volume by some later person', and nowadays *all* scholars, whatever other ideas they may entertain about these poems, share his opinion in this.

One of the first things to strike anyone reading the Chinese text of these poems is that whereas five of them, II–V and VIII, have proper titles of their own, the rest have to be referred to, in lieu of title, by the first two or three words of their opening lines. Of the five which have titles, four (II–V) also have a *luan* or 'envoi'. In No. III it is, like the *luan* of *Li sao*, in the same metre as the rest of the poem,* but in the other four it is in what we might call the '7-plus' metre which is found elsewhere in *Chu ci* in the two 'Summons' poems and in parts of *Tian wen*:

---

*There is, however, some doubt about the text of this poem. See p. 163.

tum tum tum tum: tum tum tum ti

This same metre is used throughout in the charming poem about the orange tree (No. VIII), a poem in every way so different from the other eight that it is hard to see how it came to be included in the same collection.

The earliest mention of the collective title *Jiu zhang* occurs in the sixth of the 'Nine Laments' by Liu Xiang (77–6 B.C.): 'Sadly I sang the *Li sao* to give vent to my feelings/ But I could not get to the end of *Jiu zhang*/ For the long sobs rose in my throat and choked me . . .'. A century earlier, in his biography of Qu Yuan, Si-ma Qian seems to know nothing of a series called *Jiu zhang*, though he mentions one of the poems in it by its title (No. III: *Ai Ying*) and gives not only the title but the whole text of another of them (No. V: *Huai sha*). Yet another of the individual poem-titles (No. II: *She jiang*) is referred to in the 'Summons of the Soul', which was almost certainly composed by a poet at one of the Eastern Chu courts in Chen or Shou-chun. It is mentioned there as one of the 'latest songs' which were sung by girl musicians at a very lively party. Liu Xiang's contemporary Yang Xiong (53 B.C.– A.D. 18), an admirer of Qu Yuan's poetry who nevertheless had reservations about his character and wrote imitations of his poems in which he corrected what he believed to be his erroneous attitudes and beliefs, also makes no mention of the collective title *Jiu zhang*, but is said by his biographer to have written a series based on 'the five poems beginning with *Xi song*', i.e. *Jiu zhang* I–V, a group in which are to be found (1) four of the five poems with titles, (2) all the four poems with a *luan*, (3) all the poems containing personal accounts of travel, and (4) the only two *Jiu zhang* poems ascribed to Qu Yuan by Si-ma Qian in his biography.

This set of circumstances has led some modern Chinese scholars to reach the following conclusions:

(1) that the person who first edited these poems into a series and gave them their collective title was Liu Xiang, and

(2) that only I–V, or alternatively II–V and VIII, were written by Qu Yuan, the rest being the work of unidentifiable later poets.

I am somewhat dubious about both of these conclusions. Liu Xiang certainly had a good deal to do with the Chu anthology, but, as I have said elsewhere (p. 33), I think another Liu, the Prince of Huai-nan, is much likelier to have been the first editor of *Jiu zhang*, some eighty years before him. And the view that some half of these poems were written by the author of *Li sao* does not stand up very well to a careful analysis of the text. All the *Jiu zhang* poems except III, V and VIII 'quote' *Li sao*, that is, they incorporate lines borrowed from the longer poem, slightly modified in some cases to fit their new contexts; and when we compare the language of *Li sao* – its vocabulary and grammar – with that of the *Jiu zhang* poems, we find that in *all* of the latter there are striking differences of usage. My own feeling is that though the poems of *Jiu zhang* may be by different hands, *all* were produced by poets of a generation later than Qu Yuan's.

The Japanese scholar Kominami Ichirō ingeniously suggests, if I understand him aright, that II–V represent instalments in a sort of saga portraying the wanderings of Qu Yuan in different parts of Chu. No. II shows the poet travelling westwards to the upper reaches of the River Yuan; III is a journey from the Chu capital of Ying along the Yangtze downstream to the east; IV places the poet far to the north in Han-zhong (the north-west tip of Hubei); only V seems to be set in the southlands where Qu Yuan is traditionally supposed to have wandered as a banished man and finally taken his own life.

Clearly, most of the *Jiu zhang* poems are *about* Qu Yuan even if they are not *by* him, and it seems extremely likely that some at least of them were intended for recitation, perhaps with some sort of musical accompaniment. The whole genre of Sao-style poetry must have had its pre-literary origins in the recitations of shamans, and the dramatic monologue, with Qu Yuan as its almost invariable subject, had a very long life in this type of literature. Even Liu Xiang was writing this sort of thing a couple of centuries later, though probably with little or no hope of performance. The attempt to throw light on the origins of these poems by dividing them into two classes, however, seems to break down on closer analysis. They are too miscellaneous for such simple categorization.

Take the five titled poems for a start. At first sight II–V seem to have much in common and very little to do with VIII; yet III is probably not about Qu Yuan at all (as I shall show elsewhere) and has a quite different sort of *luan*, whereas II, IV, V and VIII have the '7-plus' metre in common, which could be taken as an indication that II, IV, V and VIII but not III are by the same poet. And again, of the four titleless poems, VII and IX are very different both from each other and from the other two. Neither VII nor IX contains first-person pronouns (a solitary example at the end of IX is probably corrupt), the subject of VII is referred to throughout as 'the Loyal Servant' – an expression which occurs in none of the other poems – and IX bears striking stylistic resemblances to parts of *Jiu bian*. On top of all this it must be added that some of these poems seem to contain fragments of other poems in them or indeed to be made up entirely of fragments, so that the collection as a whole represents a total of more than nine poems.

Much the commonest use of the word *zhang* in ancient Chinese was to denote a section of something: a paragraph of prose or a stanza of a poem or song. Whoever first edited the miscellaneous collection of early Sao-style poetry which we now call *Jiu zhang* was for some reason anxious to reduce his rather unmanageable material to nine sections, no more, no less. He may have had performance in mind: a set of nine musical variations to which a series of nine poems might be recited; or he may simply have wanted a title with 'nine' in it, like *Jiu bian* and *Jiu ge*. Paradoxically *Jiu bian* and *Jiu ge* both contain *more* than nine sections; but their titles were ancient ones, culled from Chinese mythology. Probably he knew that some at any rate of these poems were meant to be recited and thought of nine as a good 'performing' number.

In the *Jiu zhang* poems the strange, enchanted world of *Li sao* has largely vanished. The loss is partly offset by a new awareness of the grandeur and wildness of nature; but the lachrymose, self-pitying strain which keeps creeping in can hardly be reckoned a gain. In later imitations of this poetry, where it has become conventional, it is a deadly bore.

1 'Grieving I Make My Plaint'
(Xi song)

Stylistically this poem seems closer to *Li sao* than any of the other *Jiu zhang* poems. Like *Li sao* it consists entirely, from beginning to end, of rhymed couplets, and it has the same combination of somewhat rugged metre with pedantically correct rhyme. However, I rather doubt whether Qu Yuan was the author of this poem – even whether he is its intended subject. Apart from the reasons already given (differences of vocabulary and the presence of 'quoted' lines), it seems rather unlikely that the high-ranking kinsman of King Huai would, even in his more dejected moments, describe himself as 'forgetful of lowly rank and poverty' (l.26); and *Xi song* ends not, like *Li sao*, with an outburst of suicidal despair, but with the poet's quietly expressed wish that he may be allowed to get away with his modest savings to live in peace in some far-away retreat.

Qu Yuan monologues were not the only progeny spawned by *Li sao*. The rejected courtier's – or would-be courtier's – complaint early established itself as a separate genre. The poems written in this genre bear a strong resemblance to the complaints of European troubadours, the principal difference being that they are addressed not to a disdainful lady but to an unappreciative prince. This particular poem could be described as a verse epistle, and a more accurate comparison would perhaps be with one of those letters written by mythological ladies to their menfolk in Ovid's *Heroides*. The convention that the whole poem is a sort of extended farewell note written on the point either of departure or of death appears not only here (*ll*.85–6) but also in No. IV (*ll*.11–12) and No. VII (*ll*.75–6).

1 Grieving I make my plaint, to give my sorrows rein,
To vent my wrath and tell my pent-up thoughts.
If what I say is not in honesty,
I call on Heaven above to testify;
I bid the Five Lords to come and judge between us;
I summon the Six to appear with me in witness;
The spirits of mountain and river I'll cause to support my suit;
And Gao Yao shall hear my words and judge whether they are
 true.

9 I served my prince with all of my devotion,
Yet I was cast out from the rest like an unwanted wen.
I forgot to fawn and simper; I turned my back on the crowd,
Awaiting my prince in his wisdom to know the true from the
 false;
For my words and my deeds followed one in the steps of the
 other,
And that which I felt and that which I showed, between them
 there was no change.
Who better can judge a man than the prince he serves?
For to test him he has not far to seek for proofs.

17 My loyalty put my prince first and my own life after;
And because of this, I earned the crowd's enmity.
I thought of my prince alone, and of no other;
And that, too, was a thing that the mob abhorred.
But I see that to serve with all one's heart, careless of all things
 else,
Is a way that holds little promise that a man may be secure;

And a reckless devotion to a prince, with no thought for any
    other,
Is a road whereby he may easily court disaster.

There is no one who in his thoughts has been more loyal to his
    prince:
Forgetful of lowly rank and poverty.
In serving my prince with an undivided heart
My mind was obsessed; I knew not the door to his favours.
What crime was my loyalty, that it should be thus punished?
Sure, this was not the return that in my heart I looked for.
I walked not with the rest, and when I fell
My fall gave cause to the crowd for merriment.

I was charged with many crimes; I met with many a slander;
Caught in a mesh that I knew not how to untie.
My feelings were stifled and could not find expression,
For they screened me from my lord, that I might not explain
    myself.
Heavy with sorrow, I waited irresolutely;
But none cared to examine what lay within my heart.
I could not collect my disordered words to present him;
I wished to set forth my mind, but there was no way.

If I left and retired into silence, then no one could ever know;
And if I went in and shouted, still no one would hear my cries.
I stood for a long time waiting, sore perplexed by the quandary,
And my mind was vexed and troubled with many sorrows.

Once I dreamt that I climbed up to the heavens,
But when my soul had reached half-way, it could go no farther.
I summoned the God of Plague to interpret it for me:
He said, 'Your ambition aspires, but will find no helpers;
And in the end you face peril alone, cut off from other men.
You may think of none but your prince, but you should not rely
    on him.'

It is true that 'many tongues can make metal molten':
Pure metal was I at first, and yet I have come to this pass.
'He that was burnt by broth will afterwards blow on pickles':

Why then should I not alter my high intent?
I have cast down the ladder, but still I would mount to heaven:
My plight is the same as it was that time in my dream.

57   The crowd are frightened and turn their hearts against me;
How can I make companions of such as these?
Our end is the same, but the paths we tread are different.
How can I look to such as these to guide me?
Shen Sheng of Jin was a son most filial;
Yet his father gave ear to slander and loved him not.
Stiff-necked in all his ways and recking nothing,
Gun's work, because of this, had no prosperous conclusion.

65   I once heard it said that he who acts loyally wins hatred for his
             pains,
And at that time I lightly said that the saying was a false one.
But 'he who has nine times broken his arm may set up as a
             physician';
And now at last I know that what I was told is true.
The crossbow was set and waiting overhead,
And the bird-nets spread out ready down below,
And all was set, and the traps laid out to gratify my lord,
So that even if I wished to escape, there was no way to turn.

73   If I thought to tarry where I was and asked that I might stay,
I feared that a heavier fate might fall and he find more faults in
             me.
If I thought to fly up high and settle far off elsewhere,
My lord would, feigning, ask me, 'Where will you go?'
I might seek to pursue a crooked path and leave the straight road
             behind,
But my will was too strong and would not allow me to.
My back and my breast are split like a tally and my heart, torn
             between them, aches,
And my mind is gloomed and perplexed in a skein of care.

81   I have pounded magnolia and mixed it with orchids,
And ground up pepper flowers to make my provender;
I have sown gracillary and planted chrysanthemums
To serve when the spring days come as savours for my food.

And because I fear that my true intent will not be believed,
I have rehearsed all here to make myself understood.
I wish only to speed away and remove myself far off,
To cherish these my delights in a private place.

II *'Crossing the River'* (She jiang)

This poem appears to have been edited together out of a number of different fragments: *ll.*1–12, *ll.*15–38, *ll.*39–48 and the '7-plus' *luan*, *ll.*49–54. The subject of the central part, *ll.*15–38, is a journey westwards, first by chariot and then later by boat, from E-zhu, near Wuhan on the Central Yangtze, to the upper reaches of the Yuan. The title 'Crossing the River' (i.e. the Yangtze) is hard to make sense of in the light of this itinerary, since the entire journey takes place south of the river and nowhere involves crossing it. The isolated couplet 13–14 looks like an editorial attempt to provide the poem with a river-crossing before the journey from E-zhu begins, but makes matters worse with mention of the River Xiang, since the route described in the poem at no point comes within fifty miles of it. I suspect that 15–38 was originally part of a very long poem written in the form of a monologue describing Qu Yuan's wanderings and that this section of it was called 'Crossing the River' because the preceding section had dealt with the poet's wanderings *north* of the Yangtze. No. IV ('The Outpouring of Sad Thoughts') does in fact place the poet in Han-bei and may contain part of this 'northern' section.

The juxtaposition of seemingly disconnected fragments gives an intriguingly 'modern' feeling to this poem which is presumably unintentional. I suspect that the intention of the editor who first put these different parts together was to prepare the instalment of Qu Yuan's wanderings (*ll.*15–38) for performance as a dramatic monologue. In *ll.*1–12, I suggest, a fantastically dressed performer got up to represent Qu Yuan introduces himself to the audience before launching into his recitation. The '7-plus' *luan* may conceivably have been specially written by this editor.

When I was young I loved this rare apparel;
And now I am old in years, the passion has not abated:
At my belt a long sword swinging,
On my head a 'cleave-cloud' hat up-towering,

5   Round my neck moon-bright jewels, and a precious jade at my
        girdle.
    But the world was muddy-witted and could not understand me,
    And so I rode high and would not look back on it.
    With a team of azure dragons, white serpents in the traces,
    I rode with Chong Hua in the Garden of Jasper,
10   Climbed up Kun-lun and ate of the flower of jade,
    And won long life, lasting as heaven and earth;
    And the sun and moon were not more bright than I.

*

13   I was sad that the southern tribesmen could not understand me,
    For at dawn I had to cross the Jiang and the Xiang.

*

15   Climbing the height at E-zhu I looked back:
    Ah! the last breath of autumn and winter's chill!
    I walked my horses along the mountain side;
    I drove my chariot towards Fang-lin;
    Then, boarding a barge, I sailed up the River Yuan.
20   The oars of Wu dipped in time and beat the billowing water.
    The boat went slowly, making little headway:
    Held by the whirling water she stuck fast.
    That morning we put off from Wang-zhu;
    The night we spent at Chen-yang.
25   – If only my heart is straight and true,
    What matters it how remote my abode? –
    When we entered Xu-pu, I halted uncertainly,
    Too distraught to think where I was going.
    Amid the deep woods there, in the twilight gloom,
30   Are the haunts where monkeys live.
    The mountains' awful height screens the noonday sun,
    And below it is dark and dim with perpetual rain;
    Sleet and snow fall there unendingly,
    And the heavy clouds begin where the roof-tops end.

*

Alas, that my life should be so devoid of pleasure!
That I should live here, alone and obscure, among the
    mountains!
But I cannot change my heart and follow the vulgar crowd,
And so I must face bitter sorrow and a hopeless end as my lot.

*

Jie Yu shaved his head;
Sang Hu naked ran;
So a loyal man is not certain to be used,
Nor a wise man certain to be employed.
Wu Zi-xu met a bad end;
Bi Gan was cut up and made into pickles.
In former times it was always like this;
Why should I complain of the men of today?
I shall make my path straight, with no fear of the rest;
For my days are sure to end in dark confusion.

LUAN

The phoenix and the phoenix's mate are daily more and more
    remote,
And swallows, sparrows, crows and pies nest in the chambers
    and the high halls.
The daphne and lily-magnolia die in the wild wood's tangle;
Stinking weeds find a position: fragrant flowers may not come
    near.
For the Dark and Light have changed places: the times are out
    of joint.
With true heart long I pondered; then suddenly I set forth.

III 'A Lament for Ying' (Ai Ying)

Chinese interpretations of this poem vary greatly. The opening lines
appear to refer to a national disaster of some kind. More
specifically, *ll.*39–40 (though their meaning has been disputed) seem

to imply that the city of Ying, capital of the great kingdom of Chu, has been destroyed. Yet the main body of the poem reads like an account, not of the panic-stricken exodus of refugees from a city about to fall into enemy hands, but of the poet's own rather leisurely journey into exile – an exile which, *ll*.49–60 seem to suggest, was occasioned by his having forfeited the favour of his king. The two principal questions which interpreters of this poem have endeavoured to answer are (1) what was the public disaster which the opening lines of the poem appear to be referring to? and (2) in what way was it connected with the poet's fall from favour and consequent journey into exile?

An answer often given to the first question is that it was the sack of Ying by the Qin general Bo Qi in 278 B.C. In that campaign the entire metropolitan area of Chu was lost to Qin and the Chu court was forced to move to a new capital in Chen, some 250 miles to the north-east of the old one. On that occasion the inhabitants of Ying did indeed 'move to the east' (*l*.4). In the words of a contemporary, 'the people of Chu quaked with fear, fled to their eastern areas and dared not so much as turn their faces to the west'. (See J. I. Crump, *Chan-kuo ts'e*, p. 117.)

The objections that have been made to this view are (1) that it is incompatible with the information given in Si-ma Qian's biography of Qu Yuan, according to which Qu Yuan was exiled at the beginning of King Xiang's reign, whereas Bo Qi's capture of Ying took place some twenty years later, and (2) that the Chu capital in 278 B.C. was not the old Ying of King Huai's day near present-day Jiangling on the Yangtze, but a new Ying or 'Yan-ying' some 180 miles to the north of it on the River Han; and whatever else is obscure about this poem, it is clear that the journey it describes is eastwards down the Yangtze, starting out from the old capital near Jiangling.

Another view is that the opening lines refer to the troubles which followed a series of defeats sustained by the Chu armies in 301 and 300 B.C., when the whole country fell for a while into anarchy and there was a popular rising in the capital headed by the veteran general Zhuang Jiao. However, though the scale of this débâcle was such as to merit awed reference in the writings of at least three contemporaries (Xun Zi, Han Fei-zi and the 'Book of Lord Shang'), there is no evidence that it was the occasion of an eastward exodus from Ying. Moreover, in terms of the biography, the date of this earlier disaster is no more suitable than that of the later one. The biography implies that Qu Yuan was banished in King Xiang's reign some time after the death of King Huai in Qin, i.e. at least four years after Zhuang Jiao's rebellion in 300.

As an attempt to solve the problem of dates, it has sometimes been suggested that the poet was indeed, as the biography states, banished in the early part of King Xiang's reign, but that it was the news of Ying's sack and destruction by Bo Qi years later that inspired him to write this poem. It is true, of course, that the poem was written long after the river journey which occupies its central part (cf. *l*.46: 'Yet now I have been here nine years without returning'), but it is surely impossible to believe that *ll*.1–4 refer to events occurring years later than the poet's own exodus in *l*.5. And in any case, even if the 'nine years' is not to be taken literally, it can hardly be thought of as referring to a period of nearly two decades.

Yet another, rather drastic, way of dealing with these difficulties has been simply to dismiss them: to deny that the opening lines refer to the exodus of refugees from a fallen city or that *ll*.39–40 refer to the destruction of Ying's gates and palaces. The objection to this, apart from the fact that it involves putting a very strained interpretation on the text, is that it seems to overlook the real meaning of the poem's title. *Ai Ying* implies not merely a nostalgic recollection of Ying but a lament for its destruction or fall.

One possible key to a solution lies in the fact that *ll*.51–60 are all to be found duplicated in the 'Nine Changes': *ll*.51–2 = *NC* X, 47–8, *ll*.53–6 = *NC* IX, 9–12 and *ll*.57–60 = *NC* X, 5–8. This makes it seem not impossible that the whole last section, from *l*.49 to the end, is either a fragment which originally had nothing to do with this poem and got stuck on to the end of it in error, or else a new ending for it which somebody deliberately spatchcocked together. Probably the poem is not about Qu Yuan and his banishment at all but merely, as its title suggests, a lament for the lost city of Ying, when it was destroyed by Bo Qi's armies in 278 B.C. The date when it was written must therefore have been within a year or so of 269 B.C.

The fourth objection, already mentioned above, that the Chu capital between 300 and 278 B.C. was at Yan (*al.* 'Yan-du' or 'Yan-ying'), is not a very convincing one. It may have been a secondary capital, but I doubt very much whether it was the permanent seat of government throughout that period. In 283 B.C. the Chu annals (*ap.* Si-ma Qian's 'History') speak of the kings of Qin and Chu meeting for discussions 'at Yan', and in the Qin annalist's account of Bo Qi's campaign of 279–278 B.C. Yan is said to have been taken in the twenty-eighth year of King Zhao of Qin (279 B.C.), whereas Ying was not taken until the following year: 'In the twenty-ninth year the *da-liang-zao* Bo Qi attacked Chu and took Ying . . . The King of Chu fled.' And even if Yan ('Yan-ying') was in fact the seat of government from 300 to 279 B.C., the court would have had to

move back to the old Ying when Yan was captured, so that it would in
any case have been the old Ying that King Xiang and his court fled
to the east from in 278 B.C.

1   High Heaven is not constant in its dispensations:
    See how the country is moved to unrest and error!
    The people are scattered and men cut off from their fellows.
    In the middle of spring the move to the east began.
    I left my old home and set off for distant places,
    And following the waters of the Jiang and Xia, I travelled into
        exile.
    I passed through the Gate of Chu with a heavy heart:
    On the day *jia*, in the morning, my journey began.

9   As I set out from Ying and left my old ward in the city,
    An endless turmoil started in my mind.
    And as the oars slowly swept in time,
    'O my Ying, I shall never look on you again!'
    I gazed on the high catalpa trees and heaved a heavy sigh,
    And the tears in torrents, like winter's sleet, came down.
    We passed the head of the Xia; and once, when we drifted
        westwards,
    I looked back for the Dragon Gate, but I could not see it.

17 My mind was drawn with yearning and my heart was grieved.
    So far! I knew not whither my way was leading,
    But followed the wind and waves, drifting on aimlessly,
    A traveller on an endless journey, with no hope of return.
    As we rode on the Wave God's surging swell,
    Oh, when, I thought, will this aimless wandering cease?
    My heart was caught in a mesh that I could not disentangle;
    My thoughts were lost in a maze there was no way out of.

25 I let my boat float on, following the current downstream,
    South up to the Dong-ting lake, and then north again to the
        River.
    I had left behind the home where I dwelt so long,
    And now, at random drifting, I travelled towards the east.
    But my soul within me longed to be returning:

Ah! when for one moment of the day have I not longed to go
    back?
I turned my back on Xia-pu, and my thoughts went speeding
    westwards,
And I grieved that the Old City grew daily farther from me.

I climbed a steep islet's height and looked into the distance,
Thinking to ease the sorrow in my heart:
But only grief came for the rich, blest River Kingdom,
For its cherished ways, now lost beyond recall.
I may not traverse the surging waves to return there,
Or cross south over the watery waste to reach it.
To think that its palace walls should be mounds of rubble,
And its two East Gates a wilderness of weeds!

It is now a long time since my heart has known happiness;
Grief comes following sorrow and sorrow following grief.
I think how long and hard the road to Ying is,
And the River and the Xia how hard for me to cross.
Sometimes it seems but a night or two since I left it;
Yet now I have been here nine years without returning.
I am overcast with a sadness which cannot find expression;
I am tied to one spot and my mouth is full of gall.

*

When your favour was courted with outward show of charm,
You were too weak; you had no will of your own.
But when, with deep loyalty, I tried to go in before you,
Jealousy cut me off and blocked my way to you.

Though Yao and Shun excelled in noble actions,
So that their glory reaches to the skies,
The crowd of backbiters were envious of their fame
And gave them a false name, saying they were not kind.

You hate the deep and studious search for beauty,
But love a base knave's braggart blusterings;
And so the crowd press forward and each day advance in your
    favours,
And true beauty is forced far off, and retires to distant places.

LUAN

61   Long my eyes rove, upon the distance gazing.
  I long but once to return; but when will that time be?
  The birds fly home to their old haunts where they came from;
  And the fox when he dies turns his head towards his earth.
  That I was cast off and banished was truly for no crime.
  By day and night I never can forget.

IV 'The Outpouring of Sad Thoughts' (Chou si)

The poetic convention whereby the relationship between a man and a woman could be made to symbolize the quite different relationship between a courtier and his prince was already an ancient one when these poems were written. For the Chu poets it was reinforced by religious convention as well. In the shamanistic religion of Chu the worshipper approached his god as a lover; so kings, who are earthly gods, were naturally approached in the same way and with the same endearments ('the Fair One', 'the Fragrant One', etc.). In none of this group of poems is the analogy of king-mistress/courtier-lover so fully worked out or so vividly expressed as it is here. Much of this poem reads like a passionate love-letter, and only the occasional line reminds us that this is an exile's poem addressed by a banished courtier to his fickle king.

Traditionally the exiled courtier of this poem is supposed to be Qu Yuan, but there is nothing in the text which identifies him and nothing in Si-ma Qian's biography of Qu Yuan to suggest that the poet was at any time an exile in the Han-bei region ('north of the Han'). Even the more fanciful of Qu Yuan's modern 'biographers' find their imaginations strained somewhat in attempting to fit the itinerary of this poem into their reconstructions.

Chou si not only has a *luan* (in '7-plus' metre) at the end, but also two other sections (ll.41–4 and ll.45–50) whose headings seem to have some sort of musical significance. This seems to confirm that some at least of these poems were written or subsequently edited for performance.

1   My heart is clouded over with melancholy thoughts.
  Long and alone I sigh, but the pain grows only greater.
  My thoughts are ravelled in a skein that cannot be disentangled;
  And when it comes to the night, the time drags endlessly.

Woe's me, how the autumn wind sets all the world a-scurrying!
See how from every point swirling and rushing it goes!
Often I think of my lord, so easily stirred to anger,
And it pains my heart with a grievous and bitter sorrow.

I would like to rise up and fly to him unbidden,
But seeing how others have fared, I restrain myself,
And instead I have set out my secret thoughts and put them into
    verse,
And offer them up to lay before the Fair One.

Once, my lord, you had made a tryst with me;
You said, 'The dusk shall be our meeting-time.'
But when you had gone half-way, you turned back again,
And instead of keeping tryst, you were of another mind.

You vaunted your comeliness before me;
You showed me all your fine array;
But the words you told me, you were not true to.
Why, then, should you vent your anger on me?

I wanted to wait on his leisure and explain myself to him,
But my heart quaked fearfully and I did not dare.
Sad and troubled, I thought to go in to him;
But my heart was sore afflicted, and I held my peace for fear.

And when I unlocked these thoughts of mine and put them into
    words,
The Fragrant One feigned deafness and would not listen to them.
My words were direct, without fawning or flattery,
And so, sure enough, the courtier crowd found me a stumbling-
    block.

That which I first set forth is there to see, plain and clear:
How can it be that today you suddenly cannot remember?
The words I offered you were a bitter medicine,
But only because I would have you shine with a brighter beauty.

I hoped that the Three and the Five would be your exemplars;
I pointed to Peng Xian as the pattern of what *I* would be.
There is no goal that cannot be attained by striving,
And, once attained, ours a fair fame that will not soon perish.

37 For goodness is not a thing to be got from outside us,
    And fame not a thing we can fabricate from nothing.
    Who without works has ever been rewarded?
    Who without fruits ever reaped a harvest fair?

SHAO GE

41 I unlocked my thoughts to set before the Fair One,
    But neither night nor day would he show any discernment.
    He vaunted his comeliness before me,
    Disdained my words, and would not hear them.

CHANG

45 There is a bird from the South Country
    Come to settle north of the Han;
    Most fair and rare and beautiful,
    Forlorn he sits in this foreign land,
    Alone and cut off from the rest of the flock,
    With no one by to find him a mate.

51 The way is so far, that each day I remember less;
    And I wish to make my plaint, but I cannot, for none will hear.
    I gaze on the northern hills and my tears come falling,
    Look down on the flowing waters and heave a dolorous sigh.

5   I long for the early summer to bring me shorter nights:
    What dreary years the darkness now seems to me!
    Though the road to Ying is a far, far distant journey,
    Many a time each night my soul goes speeding there.
    And because it does not know the twists and turns of the way
        there,
    It takes the moon and stars as guides to lead it southwards,
    Thinking to fly straight there; but still it can never reach it
    And flies distractedly, weaving this way and that.

Why should my soul be so true and constant?
The hearts of other men are not the same as my heart.
My advocate was weak and my matchmaker unable;
And so my lord still does not know the nature of my suit.

LUAN

In the long shallows the current races, flowing to meet the deeps
of the River;
There, with wild glances, I wander southwards, thinking to ease
my heart a little.
But the sheer cliffs rising frowning and awful forbid my hopes of
returning homewards.
Then, resolution with a rush returning, my steps unbidden lead
me onwards.
Uncertain, faltering and fearful, I halt and take my lodging at
Bei-gu.
Sorrow and rage confuse my looks: I long to speed south with
the flowing waters.
The sad sighs rack my soul; my spirit far is yearning.
Distant the road, obscure the place, and no one to make my suit
to!

I tell my thoughts in song, thinking to ease my sorrow;
But my melancholy finds no course; to whom can these words be
uttered?

v *'Embracing Sand'* (Huai sha)

This is the poem which Si-ma Qian quotes in full in his biography
of Qu Yuan. 'Then,' he adds, after he has finished quoting it,
'clasping a stone to his bosom, he threw himself into the River
Mi-luo and perished.'

The title *Huai sha* is generally thought to mean 'Embracing
Sand', i.e. filling the bosom of one's robe with sand as a practical
preliminary to drowning oneself. Japanese suicides are said to have
once filled their sleeves with sand or gravel for the same purpose.
Why Si-ma Qian substituted a stone for sand in the brief narrative
he wrote after the poem is a mystery. Perhaps he was influenced by

the reference to this alternative form of ballast in what is now the last poem in this series, *Bei hui feng*: 'What good did it do to clasp a great stone and drown?' (IX, *l.*108), although in fact it is to another drowned worthy and not to Qu Yuan that the poet is there referring. The eighteenth-century *Chu ci* specialist Jiang Ji thought that the '*sha*' of this title was an acronym for Changsha, the nearest town of any size to the place where Qu Yuan is supposed to have drowned himself, and that *Huai sha* means not 'Embracing Sand' but 'Thinking Longingly of Changsha'. Some modern scholars go along with this ingenious but implausible interpretation, perhaps for the interesting new possibilities it opens up in the field of pseudo-biography, but it has little to recommend it. The whole poem reads like a greatly expanded restatement of the closing lines of *Li sao*, in which the poet despairs of finding anyone to join with in 'making government' and resolves to end it all in the river. This was the sense in which Si-ma Qian understood the title of this poem and remains the most obvious way of understanding it today.

1 In the teeming late summer
When flowers and trees burgeon,
My heart with endless sorrow laden,
Forth I went to the southern land.

5 Eyes strain unseeing into the hazy gloom
Where a great quiet and stillness reign.
Disquieted and tormented,
I have met sorrow and long been afflicted.

9 I soothed my feelings, sought my purposes,
Bowed to my wrongs and still restrained myself.
Let others trim square to fit the round:
I shall not cast the true measure away.

13 To change his first intent and alter his course
Is a thing the noble man disdains.
I made my marking clear; I set my mind on the ink-line;
My former path I did not change.

17 Inwardly sound and of honest substance,
In this the great man excels so richly.
But when Chui the Cunning is not carving,
Who can tell how true a line he cuts?

When dark brocade is placed in the dark,
The dim-eyed will say that it has no pattern.
And when Li Lou peers to discern minutest things,
The purblind think that he must be sightless.

White is changed to black;
The high cast down and the low made high;
The phoenix languishes in a cage,
While hens and ducks can gambol free.

Jewels and stones are mixed together,
And in the same measure meted.
The courtier crowd are low and vulgar fellows;
They cannot understand the things I prize.

Great was the weight I carried, heavy the burdens I bore;
But I sank and stuck fast in the mire and could not get across.
A jewel I wore in my bosom, a gem I clasped in my hand;
But, helpless, I knew no way whereby I could make them seen.

The dogs of the village bark in chorus;
They bark when they do not comprehend.
Genius they condemn and talent they suspect –
Stupid and boorish that their manner is!

Art and nature perfected lay within me hidden;
But the crowd did not know of the rare gifts that were mine.
Unused materials I had in rich store;
Yet no one knew the things that I possessed.

I multiplied kindness, redoubled righteousness;
Care and probity I had in plenty.
But it was not my lot to meet such as Chong Hua;
So who could understand my behaviour?

It has always been so – this failure of happy meeting;
Though I do not know what can be the reason.
Tang and Yu lived a great while ago –
Too remote for me to long for!

53   I must curb my rebelling pride and check my anger,
    Restrain my heart, and force myself to bow.
    I have met sorrow, but still will be unswerving;
    I wish my resolution to be an example.

57   Along my road I will go, and in the north halt my journey.
    But the day is dusky and turns towards the evening.
    I will unlock my sorrow and ease my grief,
    And end it all in the Great End.

LUAN

61   The mighty waters of the Yuan and Xiang with surging swell go
      rolling on their way;
    The road is long, through places dark and drear, a way far and
      forlorn.
    The nature I cherish in my bosom, the feelings I embrace, there are
      none to judge.
    For when Bo Le is dead and gone, how can the wonder-horse go
      coursing?

65   The lives of all men on the earth have each their ordained lot.
    Let my heart be calm and my mind at ease: why should I be afraid?
    Yet still, in mounting sorrow and anguish, long I lament and sigh.
    For the world is muddy-witted; none can know me; the heart of
      man cannot be told.
    I know that death cannot be avoided, therefore I will not grudge its
      coming.

70   To noble men I here plainly declare that I will be numbered with
      such as you.

VI 'Thinking of a Fair One' (Si mei ren)

Like No. III (*Ai Ying*), this poem looks very much as if it has been
constructed from two large fragments, each of which originally
belonged to a different poem. *L*.31 appears to be the beginning of
one of these poems. Its similarity to the opening of the preceding
poem, *Huai sha*, is, I believe, no accident. I suspect that *Huai sha*
and *ll*.31–67 of this poem were originally two sections of a long

dramatic monologue depicting the wanderings and death of Qu Yuan. VI, *ll.*31–67, came first, with the poet setting out in springtime on his journey to the south. In *Huai sha*, which, I believe, followed it, the season is high summer and the poet, already in the south, is beginning to make preparations for his death. The first section of this poem, *ll.*1–30, seems to be unconnected with what follows. Its grafting on to the Spring Journey poem, unless it is simply due to editorial error, may have been made with separate performance in view: an attempt to provide this instalment of the saga with an interesting prologue, rather like the twelve-line passage at the beginning of No. II.

Thinking of a Fair One,
I brush back my tears and long stand gazing.
Sundered from friends to plead for me, for the road is blocked,
I can frame no message to send to him,
And my burning wrongs, in tumult,
Are choked within and cannot find an outlet.
Until the dawn I pour out my inner heart;
But my will is thwarted and cannot reach its object.

I thought to trust my words to the floating clouds to carry,
But when I met Feng Long, he would not take them.
I thought to send a message by the homing birds;
But they flew so fast and high that I could not reach them.
Blessed indeed was Gao Xin
To meet the swallow that carried his gift for him.
If I could I would compromise and follow the current fashion;
But I am ashamed to abase my mind and change from what I
    was.

I will pass through the years alone and encounter sorrows;
But my high-mettled heart I will never change.
How can I tamely yield, and end my days in quietness?
How can I bring myself to change?
I know that my former road holds no hope of advancement;
But I will not alter my course.
My chariot has overturned and my horses have fallen;
Yet still, alone, I cleave to this path, different from all the rest.

25 I harness the wonder horse, Qi Ji, and prepare to ride once
 more;
Cao Fu holds the reins and drives for me;
But he falters and dawdles and will not gallop forward:
I shall stay a while and wait till the right time comes.
I point to the western folds of Bo-zhong:
The golden sunset shall be our trysting time.

*

31 When springtime opens and brings forth the year,
And the bright sun tarries longer in the sky,
I shall unloose my heart's desire and yield to happiness,
And, following the River and the Xia, find solace for my sorrow.

35 I have culled wild parsley in the woodland thickets,
And gathered everlastings on the long island;
But alas! it was not my lot to be born in the olden time:
With whom can I enjoy these flowers that I have gathered?

39 I have plucked knotgrass and herbs of various hue,
And gathered all ready to twine a garland girdle.
A girdle I weave of rich and rare profusion;
But in the end it will fade and be rejected . . .

43 I shall stay here a while and seek easement of my sadness
By contemplating the South Men's strange behaviour.
When they are happy they conceal their gladness,
But are always quick in choler, always impatient . . .

47 Sweet odours and rich savours mingle in wild abundance:
The flower and the fragrance come from within my breast;
Their ravishing sweetness reaches far and wide,
Suffusing my frame within and wafting outside me.
If my spirit and substance keep their integrity,
Though I dwell unseen and obscure, my fame can yet be bright.

53 I thought to make the dwarf fig plead my cause for me,
But I feared to climb up into his branches.
I thought to use the lotus as my matchmaker,
But I feared to lift my skirts up and wet my feet.

To climb up high I do not please;
To go down low I am not able.
Thus will my body never yield;
Thus do I halt in indecision.

I shall to the full pursue my former plan,
And never alter this course.
It is my lot to live in darkness . . .
[The day is growing dark and] draws towards its close:
I must go while the bright sun has not yet reached his setting.
Alone, forlorn, I pass on my southward journey,
With my thoughts all on Peng Xian bending.

VII *'Alas for the Days Gone By'* (Xi wang ri)

The extent to which this poem differs from all the preceding ones is
somewhat obscured in translation. English demands pronouns.
Classical Chinese could, to a large extent, dispense with them. In
our own classical languages, Latin and Greek, too, you can often
dispense with pronouns, but there the 'person' is made clear by
grammatical inflection: *amo, amas*. In Chinese there is no such
indicator. *Xi wang ri*, unlike the preceding poems, has no 'I's',
'you's' or 'he's'. Only two persons appear in it: one is called
'Prince', the other is called 'Loyal Servant' or simply 'Servant'. The
'I's' and 'me's' of my translation could just as well have been 'he's'
and 'him's'.

There can be little doubt that the 'Loyal Servant' of this poem is
Qu Yuan. What is particularly interesting is that this Qu Yuan,
unlike the Qu Yuans of the other poems, exactly resembles the one
in Si-ma Qian's 'anonymous source' (see p. 53 *et seq.*), even down to
the hero's early work as a legislator. The writer of this poem is familiar
with the fully developed legend of Qu Yuan as the Patriot Poet, whose
drowning in the Mi-luo was a heroic political gesture. Unlike No. V, in
which the reciter portrays the poet wandering through the southern
countryside contemplating his imminent death, this poem is more a
posthumous survey of his whole life, a verse autobiography which
concludes with its subject's actual death. No one should be deceived
by the convention, already observed in No. I, that this was all written
down 'for the record' shortly before the poet took his life (*ll.*75–6).

1   Alas for the days gone by! when I was trusted,
    And received the king's decrees to publish to the world;
    When I made our ancestors' achievements shine for posterity,
    And made plain whatever was doubtful in the laws.
5   The land was rich and strong and its laws stood firm,
    And all was left to the Loyal Servant, while each day my lord
       took his ease.
    The secret affairs of state I carried locked in my heart.
    In those days, even if I was wrong, my lord did not correct me.
    But though my heart was pure and free from blemish,
10   I met with slanderers who were jealous of me.
    My lord was full of anger towards his servant,
    Not waiting first to make sure whether the thing was so.
    For over my lord's wits these men had set a screen of darkness,
    Bemusing him with empty words and falsely deceiving him.
15   And he, without examining to sound out the truth of it,
    Removed me to a far-off place and did not think of me,
    But trusted the filthy words of my traducers,
    Puffed up his anger and found fault in me.
    How innocent was I, his Loyal Servant!
20   Yet I was slandered and charges made against me.
    I was ashamed of the honest daylight,
    And hid myself in the dark to escape from it.
    I will stand above the Yuan's or the Xiang's dark waters,
    And steel myself to plunge in the flowing stream.
25   I can bear to destroy my body and wipe out my name for ever,
    But it grieves me that my lord is blinded and cannot see the
       light.
    Having no measure to judge men by,
    He causes the fragrant herb to hide in the marsh's tangle.
    How can I express my feelings and show my faithfulness?
30   No, I will gladly die, and without repining.
    Since I am screened from my lord and thrust into obscurity,
    I, his Loyal Servant, am left with no other way to turn.
    I have heard it said that Bo-li Xi was a prisoner;
    And Yi Yin cooked in a kitchen;
35   Lü Wang was a butcher at Zhao-ge;
    And Ning Qi sang as he fed his ox.

If they had not met with their Tang and Wu, their Huan and
    Mu,
How would the world speak of them and know their names?
Wu trusted the slanderer's tongue and did not ponder,
So Zi Xu died; but afterwards he was sorry.
Jie Zi-tui was loyal; when he starved himself
Lord Wen remembered, and hastened after him.
He made Mount Jie a holy place and set bans about it
As requitement for his surpassing service.
When he thought of their former close companionship,
He put on white weeds and wept for him.
Some men are honest and die martyrs;
Some men are cheats and are never doubted.
You would not look carefully and act upon the truth,
But listened to the lies of slanderers.
Now fragrant and foul are so mixed together,
Who, though he laboured all night, could discern between them?
Why have the sweet flowers died so soon?
A light frost descended and mowed them all down.
You are so deaf to reason, so benighted,
That slanderers and flatterers daily wax in your favour.
From of old those envious of the good
Have called orchid and azalea unfit to wear at a girdle.
Jealous of true beauty's fragrance,
Mo Mu preens herself on her comeliness;
But if you have Xi Shi's lovely face,
The slanderer will get in and supplant you.
I wished to set forth my thoughts and explain my actions:
I little dreamed that this would be held a crime.
That I was unjustly treated is clear as daylight,
Plain as the stars above in their constellations.
To harness swift steeds and go out coursing
And, without bit or rein, try to keep oneself in the chariot;
Or on a raft to drift downstream with the current
And, without boat-sweep, try to keep afloat –
When you turn your back on all sanctions and let your sole heart
    rule,
In comparison it is just like this.

I would gladly die straight away and meet dissolution,
If I did not fear that a greater ill might follow.
75 With my words unsaid I could plunge into the waters,
But for thought of my blinded lord and his lack of
   understanding.

VIII *'In Praise of the Orange-Tree'* (Ju song)

The 'orange-tree' of this poem is the *citrus nobilis*, which was
traditionally supposed not to grow naturally anywhere north of the
River Yangtze. It is this 'steadfastness' which seems to have
recommended it to the poet for comparison with the virtuous young
man to whom this poem appears to be addressed. We can only guess
whether this is a graceful tribute from an older to a younger poet or, as
some have suggested, a poet's tribute to a young prince of whom great
things are expected. Some modern Chinese scholars have classified it as
an 'early work' of Qu Yuan. The fact that it is written throughout in
'7-plus' metre makes this extremely unlikely; but what one believes
about its authorship does not seem to me to affect in any way one's
enjoyment of this charming poem.

1 Fairest of all God's trees, the orange came and settled here,
   Commanded by him not to move, but only grow in the South
      Country.
   Deep-rooted, firm and hard to shift: showing in this its
      singleness of purpose;
   Its leaves of green and pure white blossoms delight the eye of the
      beholder,
5 And the thick branches and spines so sharp, and the fine round
      fruits,
   Green ones with yellow intermingling to make a pattern of
      gleaming brightness,
   Pure white beneath the rich-hued surface: a parable of virtuous
      living;
   Its lusty growth to the gardener's art respondent, producing
      beauty without blemish.

Oh, your young resolution has something different from the rest!
Alone and unmoving you stand: how can one not admire you?
Deep-rooted, hard to shift: truly you have no peer!
Alert to this world's ways you hold your ground, unyielding
    against the vulgar tide.
You have sealed your heart; you guard yourself with care; have
    never fallen into error;
Holding a nature free from bias, impartial even as Heaven and
    Earth are.
I would fade as you fade with the passing years and ever be your
    friend.
Pure and apart and free from sin, and strong in the order of your
    ways:
Though young in years, fit to be a teacher of men;
In your acts like Bo Yi: I set you up as my model.

IX *'Grieving at the Eddying Wind'* (Bei hui feng)

This remarkable poem was clearly inspired by *Li sao*, from which
several of its lines are borrowed, yet stylistically it is utterly
different. Like No. VII, it uses no personal pronouns. Its richly
decorative language (impossible to do justice to in translation) and
the tell-tale use of the courtier's humilific *qie* suggest a possible
connection with *Jiu bian*, of which these are both characteristic.
Even the opening line, the beginning of which supplies the poem
with its 'title', is strongly reminiscent of *Jiu bian*.

The rhapsodic wanderings of *Bei hui feng* are a dreamlike passage
through scenery that is half real and half unreal, resembling neither
the spirit-crowded shaman-flights of *Li sao* nor the sober road and
river itineraries of the other *Jiu zhang* poems. *Ll.*71–94 read like a
phantasmagoric description of life after death. The soul of the
drowned poet speeds from the watery gloom of the river-bed
through crashing waves and rainbow-tinted mists to the source of
the great river and thence to the summit of the World Mountain in
an exultant burst of freedom in which the very boundaries of
language itself seem to be broken.

It has always been recognized that one or two things were wrong
with the text of the concluding section, but in my view rather more
is wrong with it than is usually suggested. In my view, *ll.*95–108
are a fragment of another poem which begins, however, not at *l.*95

but at *l.*101 (compare No. VII, which has a very similar opening). I
would place *ll.*95–100 between *ll.*102 and 103. All of these lines –
95–108 – have the same rhyme, which happens to be the same
rhyme as is found in the quatrain 91–4. I suspect that *Bei hui feng*,
having lost some of its end slips, broke off at *l.*94, and that some
early editor, struck by the coincidence that the unplaced fragment
95–108 had the same rhyme as *ll.*91–4, stuck it on the end of this
poem under the impression that he had found the missing piece.

1   Grieving at the eddying wind that shakes the orchid blossoms,
    My heart is sorely troubled and within me sorrows;
    For delicate things are by nature prone to fall;
    And the faintest notes lead in the full orchestra.
    How noble were the thoughts conceived by Peng Xian;
    And his purpose so strong, and he ever mindful of it.
    Though a man change his heart ten thousand times, how can he
        conceal it?
    And who by deceiving can succeed for long?

9   Birds and beasts cry out, calling to the flock.
    When flowers crowd amidst dead haulms, no fragrance comes
        from them.
    Fish, by their thatch of scales are told apart;
    But the dragon hides in the dark his patterned brightness.
    Bitter and sweet herbs do not share the same field;
    Orchid and sweet flag bloom unseen in solitary sweetness.
    Only the good man's lasting beauty
    Preserves its aspect unchanged through succeeding ages.

17   Remote is the ideal that my thoughts aspire to:
    I would be as the clouds that wander above in freedom.
    But because there was that by which my high thoughts were
        shaken,
    I have written these songs to make my meaning clear.

21   The good man nurses his thoughts in isolation:
    So pollia and pepper I pluck for my lonely dwelling,
    And sigh upon choking sigh I heave
    As I lie alone in my secret place and brood.

The tears from my eyes and nose join in a sorry stream;
Sleepless I lie with my thoughts until the dawn;
All through the dreary watches of the long night
I try to suppress this grief, but it will not go.
Rising, I slowly wander forth,
Thinking the exercise might bring some solace;
But a heavy sigh breaks from my sorrowing breast,
And gasping sobs rise, uncontrollable.

I have twisted my longing thoughts to make a girdle;
I have woven my bitter sorrow to make a stomach band.
I broke a branch of the Ruo tree to shade me from the
      brightness;
I would go wherever the wandering wind might blow me.
The world grew misty; I could not see before me;
My heart was leaping like boiling water.
I clutched my belt and my coat-front to calm my spirits,
And sorrowing I set out on my way.

Swiftly the year is turning to decay,
And my time draws gradually nearer.
The marsh grasses dry up and break at the joints;
The fragrance has faded; plants are thin and sparse.
I rejoice that suffering has left my mind undaunted,
Proving that the words I said were not idly spoken.
But I would rather swiftly die and meet dissolution
Than have to endure this sorrow endlessly . . .

The orphan sobs and rubs his tears;
The exile goes out and no more returns . . .
Who can reflect on this and not feel sad? . . .
Glorifying the name of Peng Xian . . .

I climbed a rock's summit and looked into the distance:
Far, far the road stretched, silent and deserted,
Entering places where no answering echo came,
Where the straining senses could perceive nothing.

57 Sorrow sits dark on me; all joy is gone;
    My thoughts are filled with sadness that cannot be dispelled;
    My heart is tied with bands of care that will not be unloosed;
    My breath is twisted up and tied in a knot together.

61 Deep and dim the distance, without a limit;
    Vast, vacant verdancy, sans shape or form;
    Even the faintest sound evokes an echo;
    Even the simplest act becomes impossible.
    Far on, far on, farther than can be measured;
    Along, along, and all along never a bend.
    In deepest melancholy of unassuaged grief;
    Inconsolable, in sombrest gloom . . .

69 Riding the great waves, drifting with the wind,
    I would go to rest where Peng Xian dwells . . .

71 I mounted a high cliff's rocky walls
    And stood at the woman rainbow's highest point;
    Resting on the sky, speeding over the rainbow,
    On I rushed until I touched the heavens.
    I sipped cool drops of refreshing dew,
    And rinsed my mouth with fine flakes of hoar frost.
    I went in the Cave of the Winds to rest myself,
    But woke up with a start, gasping for breath.

79 I lighted upon Kun-lun and peered into the mists;
    I rested on Min Mountain and looked down on the River.
    I quailed as the leaping waters crashed among the boulders;
    I listened to the shattering roar of the waves:

83 Wild and tumultuous, without order,
    Vast and immense, knowing no bounds;
    Sometimes compressed and swollen without an outlet,
    Sometimes racing uncurbed, with nothing to check them;
    Undulating, now upwards and now downwards,
    Swirling and swaying, now left and now right;
    Flowing in currents, now forwards and now backwards,
    Dividing ebb and flow into equal periods.

I watched the fiery vapours cloud on cloud ascending;
I saw them where they condense in the dewy vapour of mist;
I grieved when the frost and snow fell down together;
I listened to the booming shock of the tidal waters . . .

*

I would borrow the daylight to travel back and forth,
Using a crooked switch of the yellow thorn for my horsewhip.
I sought out the places where Jie Zi-tui lived;
I saw the haunts where Bo Yi spent his exile.
My resolution was graven, I would not swerve from it;
My heart was attuned to the measure and would not leave it.

[. . .]

I grieve for the high hopes of days gone by,
And sorrow for those that are yet to come.
I shall float down the River and the Huai until I enter the ocean,
And follow Zi Xu for my enjoyment.
I shall gaze on the Yellow River's islands,
And mourn at the place of Shen Tu's noble end:
Repeatedly he rebuked his lord, but his lord would not listen:
But what good did it do to clasp a great stone and drown? . . .

Notes

1 'Grieving I Make My Plaint'

*ll.*5–8 *The Five Lords . . . the Six . . . Gao Yao*: the Five Lords are the
gods of the Five Directions: the Green God of the East, the Red
God of the South, the White God of the West, the Black God of the
North and the Yellow God of the Centre. In the Warring States period
they were sometimes identified with the tribal sky gods of an earlier
age, reduced, in the process of cultural assimilation, to the status of
pseudo-historical 'emperors'. Thus Qu Yuan's ancestor Gao Yang (see
*Li sao, l.*1), originally sole 'God' or 'Heaven' to the people who
worshipped him, was now often identified with the Black God of the
North. In this passage here the poet is calling on a hierarchy of gods,
starting at the top and working downwards. At the top is the supreme

deity, the 'Heaven' of *l*.4. The Gods of the Five Directions are his viceroys, each ruling over one section of his great empire. The Six (*l*.6) are celestial gods of still lower status: gods of the sun, moon, rain, wind, etc. (The identity of the Six varies from one account to another, but it is clear from the earliest reference of all that they were 'celestial' rather than 'terrestrial' deities.) Gao Yao makes frequent appearances in the *Yao dian* section of the ancient 'Book of History' as one of the counsellors of the sage-kings Shun and Yu. Yu wanted Gao Yao to be his successor, and when Gao Yao predeceased him, handed the succession to Gao Yao's son Yi (see Heavenly Questions', *ll*.61–6, note). Gao Yao was famous for his wise judgements and became a sort of patron saint of judges. That is why the poet calls on him here to judge between himself and his prince.

ll.61–4   *Shen Sheng of Jin . . . Gun's work*: Shen Sheng, eldest son of
            Duke Xian of Jin (*reg*. 676–651 B.C.), was falsely accused by his wicked stepmother Li Ji, but hanged himself in order to spare his father the distress that unmasking her wickedness would have caused him. Gun's obstinacy is referred to in much the same terms in *Li sao*, *l*.131. See also 'Heavenly Questions', *ll*.23–32 and note.

II 'Crossing the River'

ll.9–10   *I rode with Chong Hua . . . Kun-lun*: for Chong Hua, another
            name of the sage-king Shun who was buried in Doubting Mountain near the source of the River Xiang, see *Li sao*, *ll*.143–4. The Garden of Jasper and Kun-lun both belong to the fairyland of the West visited by Qu Yuan in his aerial travels in *Li sao* (see *Li sao*, *l*.185 *et seq*.) where Qu Yuan in his dragon chariot flies from the tomb of Chong Hua, to whom he had been 'making his plaint', to the Hanging Gardens of Kun-lun in a single day's journey.

ll.13–14   *I was sad . . . the Jiang and the Xiang*: this couplet rhymes
            with l.12 but obviously has nothing to do with it; nor does it seem to have much to do with what follows: a journey from E-zhu to the upper Yuan, first by chariot and then by boat, which would not, at any point, bring the traveller within fifty miles of the River Xiang. There are two possibilities: (1) 13–14 is a stray couplet which a careless editor tacked on to the end of 1–12 because of the rhyme; (2) that 'Xiang' is used here in the generic sense of 'river', which, according to the scholar Wen Yi-duo (1899–1946), it sometimes had in the usage of ancient Chu. In that case *l*.14 refers to the crossing of the Yangtze ('the Jiang') at E-zhu, after which the entire journey is, in fact, through country 'south of the Jiang'. The second possibility looks attractive, even if the evidence for this usage is somewhat tenuous; the trouble is that a journey into exile which began with the banished man crossing the

Yangtze at E-zhu and viewing with trepidation the prospect of meeting 'southern tribesmen' on the other side would almost certainly have started from the northern court at Chen; and this would have been an impossibility, because by the time the Chu court was established in Chen, most of the country through which the poet journeys in this poem was in enemy territory.

*ll.*15–28 *Climbing the height at E-zhu I looked back*: the journey
       described here appears to be an east—west one starting from somewhere on the Yangtze about midway between lakes Boyang and Dong-ting. There is still a Xupu in West Central Hunan. The Xupu in the text was probably not in quite the same place as the modern one but in the same area. E-zhu must be near the modern E-cheng downstream from Wuchang. 'E' is the starting-point of a number of trade-routes listed on a set of inscribed bronze tallies discovered at Shouxian, Anhui (the old Shou-chun), in 1957, which were bestowed by King Huai of Chu on a Chu nobleman referred to as the 'Prince of E' in 323 B.C. and in which the King granted immunity from tolls and other imposts to the Prince's boats and vehicles travelling along these routes. One of them, starting at E and ending in the upper Yuan, is in fact very similar to the journey described in this poem. Chen-yang must have been on or near the River Chen, a tributary of the Yuan nowadays sometimes called the Jin, and Wang-zhu was probably named after another small tributary of the Yuan.

*ll.*39–44 *Jie Yu ... Sang Hu ... Wu Zi-xu ... Bi Gan*: Jie Yu, the
       Madman of Chu, is chiefly famous for having mocked the sage Confucius:

> Chieh Yü, the madman of Ch'u, came past Master K'ung, singing as he went: 'Oh phoenix, phoenix / How dwindled is your power! / As to the past, reproof is idle, / But the future may yet be remedied. / Desist, desist! / Great in these days is the peril of those who hold office.' Master K'ung got down, desiring to speak with him; but the madman hastened his step and got away, so that Master K'ung did not succeed in speaking to him.
>
> (A. Waley, *The Analects of Confucius*, p. 219)

He is also referred to in *Zhuang zi* and other contemporary sources. According to some accounts he wore his hair loose and tattooed himself. The text here says he cut his hair off. Whichever it was, it would have looked equally barbarous to a contemporary Chinese, to whom – as indeed to all Chinese until their conquest by the Manchus in the seventeenth century – the only acceptable male way of wearing the hair was in a bun on top of the head.

  Sang Hu was another eccentric, also mentioned in *Zhuang zi*.

Wu Zi-xu, *al.* Wu Yuan, was a nobleman of Chu whose father and brother were both killed by the tyrannical King Ping. He escaped to Wu, became He Lü's chief adviser (see note on 'Heavenly Questions', *ll.*169–70) and desecrated King Ping's tomb in the Wu invasion of Chu in 506 B.C. He Lü's successor, Fu Cha, was irritated by Zi Xu's warnings against accepting the feigned submission of his neighbour, the King of Yue, and forced him to commit suicide, afterwards causing his body to be sewn up in a sack and thrown into the river. Like Qu Yuan's, his ghost continued to haunt the river after his death, and in the Han dynasty he was worshipped locally in Zhejiang as the god of the Qiantang bore.

Bi Gan, uncle of the wicked King Zhòu, the last ruler of the Shang dynasty, was another wise man whose remonstrations brought about his death. Zhòu's habit of cutting up and pickling the bodies of courtiers who disagreed with him and of distributing the pickled pieces among his vassals is referred to in *Li sao*, *l.*159, and again in 'Heavenly Questions', *ll.*143–8. The 'Heavenly Questions' refer to the vivisection of Bi Gan but not to his pickling; however, the pickling of the other courtiers is mentioned in the same passage, so perhaps we are meant to infer that Bi Gan's body was disposed of post-operationally in the same grisly manner. In *Li sao* Qu Yuan seems to envisage his own outspokenness leading to a similar fate: 'I could not change this, even if my body were dismembered' (*l.*127. Cf. also *Li Sao*, *ll.* 173–6).

III 'A Lament for Ying'

*ll.*15–16 *the head of the Xia . . . the Dragon Gate*: the Xia waterway left the Yangtze some way downstream to the south-east of Ying and ran in a more or less north-easterly direction roughly parallel to the Yangtze for a hundred miles or more to rejoin the main river near the modern Wuchang. The poet evidently took the longer route, passing by the mouth of the Xia on his left hand, continuing in a south-easterly direction down the mainstream of the Yangtze towards the north-east corner of Lake Dong-ting and thence proceeding in a north-easterly direction towards Xiakou (the 'Xia-pu' of *l.*31), where the mainstream of the Yangtze and the Xia waterway rejoined. The Dragon Gate (*l.*16) was presumably the water-gate of Ying. Some modern scholars have made heavy weather of 'drifted westwards' in *l.*15 on the grounds that this could not happen in a journey whose general direction was towards the east, but downstream from Jiangling the main channel of the Yangtze does in fact describe a sweeping southward arc in which it is for a time actually flowing in a south-westerly direction before winding round once more towards the east. At some point in that arc a voyager might well find himself drifting west and gazing northwards across the flatlands to see if he could glimpse the distant city.

*ll.*49 *et seq.* *When your favour was courted* . . .: up to this point there has been no indication that the poet's journey was occasioned by personal banishment rather than by public disaster. The fact that *ll.* 51–60 can all be identified elsewhere in *Jiu bian* suggests that the *whole* of this final section is a late editorial addition to the original poem.

*ll.*53–6 *Yao and Shun . . . were not kind*: because they did not bequeath the kingship to their sons, but surrendered it in their lifetimes to the ablest of their subjects.

IV 'The Outpouring of Sad Thoughts'

*ll.*33–4 *the Three and the Five*: there is no unanimity among modern scholars as to who the Three and the Five are meant to be; but the author of *Chou si* leans so heavily on *Li sao* for his inspiration elsewhere in this poem that it seems probable that 'the Three' was suggested by 'the three kings of old' in *Li sao*, *l.*25, in which case 'the Five' are presumably the Five Hegemons. *L.*34 is clearly modelled on *Li sao*, *l.*76: 'Though it may not accord with present-day manners, *I will follow the pattern that Peng Xian has left*'. The *Chou si* poet has brought the ideas of *Li sao*, *ll.*25–30, and *Li sao*, *ll.*73–6, together into one couplet. 'I proposed heroic ancient models for us both,' he is saying to his fickle king. 'You were to have been a second Yu or Tang or King Wu or, at the very least, one of the Silver Age rulers like Duke Huan; I for my part promised to be an honest, outspoken, but unflinchingly loyal adviser, like Peng Xian of old, who was prepared to drown himself if his wise counsels went unheeded.'

*l.*41 *Shao ge*: 'little song' or 'canzonet'. A satirical poem on the confusion and darkness of the age written by the contemporary philosopher Xun Zi contains a similar 'small song' two-thirds of the way through it. The use of this term and the '*Chang*' at the head of the following section (*l.*45 *et seq.*) is a clear indication that, in its present form at any rate, *Chou si* was intended for performance: the main part of the poem was to be recited, the *shao ge* and *chang* (and possibly also the *luan*) passages were to be sung. What the exact significance of these terms are in this context can only be guessed. Normally *chang* meant to take the part of the leading singer or soloist, in contrast to *he*, which meant to sing the refrain (as in our sea-shanties and other forms of alternating solo and choral singing). Probably the *shao ge* passage was originally intended to be sung in unison by a small group of people and the *chang* passage was for virtuoso solo singing. The 'lone bird' seems somehow to call for a solo rendering.

l.71 *I halt and take my lodging at Bei-gu*: this place-name is
      unidentifiable; however, *ll*.45–6 make it unequivocally clear that
the subject of this poem is an exile from Ying living in banishment at
Han-bei, near the north-west frontier of Chu. Presumably Bei-gu was
somewhere on the upper Han. In *ll*.57–60 the poet speaks of returning
southwards in his dreams. In the *luan* he appears to be indulging his
fancy of returning south by making an actual waking excursion
downstream. The river of *l*.67 is, of course, the Han. Bei-gu is
evidently as far along it as he gets.

v 'Embracing Sand'

l.19 *Chui the Cunning*: a legendary carpenter of supernatural skill. He
      and Li Lou (*l*.23), whose eyesight was so keen that he is said to
have been able to see a fine hair at a distance of 100 paces, are
frequently mentioned in other writings of the Warring States period.
Mencius, for example, observed that even someone with the skill of
Chui and with Li Lou's eyesight could not draw perfect squares and
circles without a set-square and compasses. They belong, with a
number of other preternaturally endowed worthies, to a remote
antiquity in which all the crafts and skills of a later age were first
invented.

ll.47–51 *Chong Hua . . . Tang and Yu*: wise kings able to appreciate a
         man of talent (like the poet) when they saw one and to give
him the employment he deserved.

l.64 *when Bo Le is dead and gone*: Bo Le was a legendary charioteer
       and horse-fancier. The wonder-horse Qi Ji, stumbling up a hill
with a cartload of salt behind him, looked up and whinnied when it saw
him, knowing that it would soon be released and put to proper use.

vi 'Thinking of a Fair One'

ll.9–14 *I thought to trust my words to the floating clouds*: in seeking to
        use Feng Long and the birds as his messengers, the poet is
evidently thinking of *Li sao*, *ll*.221–2, where Qu Yuan sends Feng
Long off on a cloud to look for the river goddess whom he hopes to
marry, and of *Li sao*, *ll*.235–44, where Qu Yuan sends a magpie to pay
court to the legendary princess Jian Di, but is beaten to it by Gao Xin's
phoenix.

l.26 *Cao Fu holds the reins*: Cao Fu was the driver of King Mu's
       marvellous horses when he made his great journey to the West.
See 'Heavenly Questions', *ll*.137–8 and note.

*l.*29 *I point to the western folds of Bo-zhong*: a mountain in what is now
Shaanxi: the source of the River Han. Even allowing for poetic
licence, if the poet can indicate the position of the setting sun by
pointing in the direction of Bo-zhong, he cannot be any farther south
than Han-bei, which was his location in No. IV. This seems to confirm
the impression, already alluded to in the introduction to this poem, that
the passage beginning at *l.*31 is the beginning of another poem
originally unconnected with what precedes it.

VII 'Alas for the Days Gone By'

*l.*33 *Bo-li Xi*: a minister of the Lord of Yu, taken captive by Duke
Xian of Jin when he conquered Yu in 664 B.C. Sent in the train of
a Jin princess being married to the Duke of Qin, he escaped, but was
seized by the inhabitants of a frontier town of Chu. Duke Mu of Qin
was so impressed by reports of his cleverness that he offered the men of
Chu five black rams' skins as ransom, and when he had bought him
back, immediately appointed him to be his counsellor.

*l.*34 *Yi Yin cooked in a kitchen*: another example of talent recognized in
humble places. For Yi Yin's promotion from cook to counsellor,
see note on 'Heavenly Questions', *ll.*103–6.

*l.*35 *Lü Wang was a butcher*; the humble origin of King Wu's famous
minister is referred to in *Li sao*, *l.*293, and again in 'Heavenly
Questions', *ll.*159–60.

*l.*36 *Ning Qi sang as he fed his ox*: see *Li Sao*, *ll.*295–6.

*l.*37 *their Tang and Wu, their Huan and Mu*: these are the
talent-spotting rulers by whom the four above-mentioned
examples were employed. Like the horse-fancier Cao Fu when he saw
the wonder-horse sweating between the shafts of a salt-cart, they were
able to discern outstanding ability in a humble guise. Tang is Tang the
Successful, founder of the Shang dynasty, who discovered Yi Yin. Wu
is King Wu of the Zhou dynasty, who had Lü Wang as his chief
counsellor. Lü Wang was in fact discovered by King Wu's father, King
Wen, and not by King Wu. Although the author of *Xi wang ri* makes a
great parade of learned examples, he is not so good an historian as Qu
Yuan. Huan and Mu are, of course, Duke Huan of Qi and Duke Mu of
Qin.

*ll.*39–40 *Wu trusted the slanderer's tongue . . . So Zi Xu died*: we now
have examples of the other kind of ruler, the kind who, far
from being able to discern talent hidden underneath a mean exterior,
fail to recognize it even when it has been tried and proven. 'Wu' means

Fu Cha, King of Wu, the son of King He Lü. Zi Xu's tragic death is mentioned in II, *l.*43. Rather confusingly his surname was Wu, but written with a different character from the 'Wu' of the kingdom which employed him. Wu Zi-xu's surname is a composite character made up of the symbols for 'man' and 'five'. It is perhaps connected in some way with the fact that his festival as a water god was – like Qu Yuan's – celebrated on the fifth day of the fifth month.

*ll.*41–4 *Jie Zi-tui was loyal*: Jie Zi-tui followed Chong Er (later to become the great hegemon Duke Wen of Jin) in his long wanderings as an exile, and once, when provisions were short, fed him on a piece of his own flesh. When Chong Er became duke and rewarded his faithful followers, he forgot Jie Zi-tui, who thereupon retired in a huff and hid himself in a mountain. Later, when Chong Er suddenly remembered him, Zi Tui refused to come down, and when they tried to smoke him out, he clung to a tree and was burned to death.

*l.*60 *Mo Mu*: a legendary woman of hideous aspect. By a strange coincidence the Ancient Greeks believed in a hideous she-goblin called Mormo. According to one tradition, Mo Mu was one of the wives of the Yellow Ancestor.

*l.*61 *Xi Shi*: Xi Shi was a village maiden of dazzling beauty who became a palace lady of Gou Jian, King of Yue, in the early fifth century B.C. and who was sent by him as a gift to his hated rival King Fu Cha of Wu, so that Fu Cha's infatuation and her extravagance might hasten Wu's destruction. Her name, like Helen of Troy's, became a synonym for the *femme fatale*, the woman whose beauty causes men to lose their reason and cities and kingdoms to be overthrown.

VIII 'In Praise of the Orange-Tree'

*l.*18 *In your acts like Bo Yi*: elder of the two brothers who were so pure that they starved to death rather than 'eat the corn of Zhou', whom they regarded as usurpers. See note on 'Heavenly Questions', *ll.*175–6.

IX 'Grieving at the Eddying Wind'

*ll.*48–52 *Than have to endure this sorrow endlessly*: this passage appears to be in a somewhat fragmentary state. Probably some lines are missing.

*l.*80 *I rested on Min Mountain*: supposed to be the source of the River Yangtze.

*ll.*97–8 *Jie Zi-tui ... Bo Yi*: see notes on 'In Praise of the Orange-Tree', *l.*18, and 'Alas for the Days Gone By', *ll.*41–4.

*l.*104 *And follow Zi Xu for my enjoyment*: Zi Xu, whose corpse was sewn
up in a sack and thrown into the river by the ungrateful king of
Wu (see notes on 'Crossing the River', *ll.*39–44, and 'Alas for the Days
Gone By', *ll.*39–40), was later divinized as a spirit controlling the tides
of the lower Yangtze. To the writer of this poem Qu Yuan is himself
well on the way to becoming a water god. Significantly, the festival
celebrating Qu Yuan's death was, like Zi Xu's festival, celebrated on
the fifth day of the fifth month of each year.

*l.*106 *Shen Tu's noble end*: Shen-tu Di was a contemporary of the
wicked Shang king Zhòu, according to one tradition. When his
remonstrances against Zhòu's folly were ignored, he drowned himself
in disgust, clasping a stone, or, alternatively, holding a stone on his
back, and jumping into the river. Peng Xian, Shen-tu Di, Wu Zi-xu
and Qu Yuan were all loyal but outspoken ministers whose advice was
rejected and who ended up in the river. Martyrology was an important
part of the Confucian tradition.

Yuan you   *'Far-off Journey'*

Yuan you could be described as a Taoist's answer to *Li sao*. Without
any of the political allegory or flower symbolism of *Li sao*, it
describes a celestial journey which ends not in despairing gloom but
in triumphant fulfilment. The journey is presented as the climax in
a successful course of training in mysticism and the poem is full of
references to yoga techniques and to the hagiology of Han Taoism.

The combination of Taoist mysticism with an enthusiasm for Chu
poetry is a hallmark of the little group of poets and philosophers
who, in the second half of the second century B.C., under the
patronage of Liu An, Prince of Huai-nan, produced not only the
Taoist 'Book of Huai-nan', but also the earliest edition of *Chu ci*
(see p. 33). Everything about *Yuan you* points to authorship by a
member of this group.

Besides its many borrowings from *Li sao* (not to mention *Zhuang
zi, Lao zi* and the odd line from *Jiu zhang* and the 'Nine Songs')
Yuan you has a good many lines, sometimes whole couplets, in
common with a long poem called 'The Mighty Man' (*Da ren fu*)
which the great Han court poet Si-ma Xiang-ru (179–118 B.C.)
presented to the emperor Wu. Indeed, so closely do these two
poems resemble each other that Guo Mo-ruo believed *Yuan you* to be

Si-ma Xiang-ru's own early draft of the other poem. Other scholars have suggested that *Da ren fu* was the original poem and that the author of *Yuan you*, who certainly showed no compunction in helping himself to lines from *Li sao*, made similar borrowings from *Da ren fu* as well. I myself used to subscribe to the second of these two views, but I now believe that both of them are mistaken.

As a court poet Si-ma Xiang-ru had in effect two separate careers. The first, when he was a young man, was in the company of poets like Zhuang Ji (see pp. 262–3) at the provincial court of Liu Wu, Prince of Liang. It was there that he wrote his famous *Zi-xu fu*, which Burton Watson in his *Chinese Rhyme-Prose* has translated as 'Sir Fantasy'. When the Prince of Liang died in 144 B.C., Si-ma Xiang-ru returned to his native Sichuan, where he ran off with an heiress and for a time, until reconciled with her millionaire father, made a living by running a small bistro. At the imperial court, where he had been briefly employed before joining the provincial court of Liang, he seems to have been totally forgotten, for when the young Emperor Wu, who succeeded in 140 B.C., was reading a copy of 'Sir Fantasy', he was heard to exclaim that he wished he 'had been born in the same age as the person who wrote this *fu*', and it was only the coincidence that his Master of Hounds, who happened to be standing by at the time, was a fellow-townsman of the poet's that opened up a second, more brilliant, career for Si-ma Xiang-ru as a resident poet and an adviser on south-west frontier affairs to the Han imperial court.

Si-ma Xiang-ru's first gift to his new patron was a revised version with a specially written supplement of the 'Sir Fantasy' *fu* which had first engaged the emperor's attention; but he soon observed that his imperial patron had other interests besides hunting-parks and palaces. Si-ma Xiang-ru's biographer, Si-ma Qian, gives the following account of the way in which his second great poetic offering came to be presented:

Xiang-ru, observing that the emperor had a liking for magic and mysticism, said, 'What I wrote about the Shang-lin Park [the supplement to "Sir Fantasy"] is not really so very wonderful. I can do much better than that. I once wrote a *fu* called "The Mighty Man" which I did not, however, finish. I should like to get it into shape and present it to Your Majesty.' Xiang-ru felt that the traditional picture of the Immortal, living in the mountains or the marshes, his body emaciated with fasting, was not at all a suitable model for mystically inclined royalty, and his 'Mighty Man' *fu* was written to suit the requirements of the latter.

It is my belief that the copy of *Yuan you* which Si-ma Xiang-ru no doubt had in his luggage was not, as Guo Mo-ruo thought, his own draft but a poem by someone else which he thought would lend itself very well to adaptation. The lean and hungry bits would have to go, so would the world-weariness, the boring bits of Taoist doctrine and the numerous lines copied from *Li sao* – a poem with which the emperor was probably by this time fairly familiar. The new poem would be purely celebratory: a triumphal imperial progress on a cosmic scale through a universe even more packed with forelock-tugging deities than the one described by the anonymous author of *Yuan you*. And instead of being written in the old-fashioned Sao-style metre of *Yuan you*, it would be in the much more varied *fu* metres which Si-ma Xiang-ru had himself invented or developed. All this gives the 'Mighty Man' a superficially original look; but *Yuan you*, in spite of its borrowed lines, is, in conception, the more original poem.

The heroes of the anonymous poet who wrote *Yuan you* are not great shamans like Wu Xian but Taoist Immortals like the Master of the Red Pine and Wang Qiao – names which are unheard of in the early Chu poems but are commonplace in the songs and poems of the Han era. Similarly, his symmetrical, mandala-like cosmos, so different from the confused, somewhat haphazard, picture of the spirit world we obtain from *Li sao*, is thoroughly typical of Han cosmology. The same mandala-like cosmos is portrayed on Han bronze mirror-backs; we even find echoes of *Yuan you* in the doggerel inscriptions round their rims.

Nowadays Chinese scholars either recognize *Yuan you* as an authentic part of the 'Works of Qu Yuan' and misinterpret it accordingly, or – far more often – dismiss it as a 'Han imitation' and refuse to discuss it altogether. This is a pity, because it is an interesting work, not least for the light it can throw on Han religious beliefs, about which we still have a great deal to learn.

Grieved by the parlous state of this world's ways,
I wanted to float up and away from it.
But my powers were too weak to give me support:
What could I ride on to bear me upwards?

Fallen on a time of foulness and impurity,
Alone with my misery, I had no one to confide in.
In the night-time I lay, wide-eyed, without sleeping;
My unquiet soul was active until the daylight.

9   I thought of the limitless vastness of the universe;
I wept for the long affliction of man's life.
Those that had gone before I should never see;
And those yet to come I should never know of.

13   Restless I paced, with my mind on distant things;
Despairing, frustrated, consumed with constant yearning.
My thoughts were wild and wandered distractedly;
My heart was melancholy and consumed with sadness.

17   My spirit darted forth and did not return to me,
And my body, left tenantless, grew withered and lifeless.
Then I looked into myself to strengthen my resolution,
And sought to learn from where the primal spirit issues.

21   In emptiness and silence I found serenity;
In tranquil inaction I gained true satisfaction.
I heard how once Red Pine had washed the world's dust off:
I would model myself on the pattern he had left me.

25   I honoured the wondrous powers of the Pure Ones,
And those of past ages who had become Immortals.
They departed in the flux of change and vanished from men's
    sight,
Leaving a famous name that endures after them.

29   I marvelled how Fu Yue lived on in a star;
I admired Han Zhong for attaining Oneness.
Their bodies grew dim and faded in the distance;
They left the crowded world behind and withdrew themselves.

33   In the ether's transformations they rose upwards,
With godlike swiftness miraculously moving.
Sometimes men see them, in remote, uncertain glimpses,
As their bright spirit forms dart across the sky.

37   Leaving the dust behind they shed their impurities,
Never to return again to their old homes.
Escaping all life's troubles they had no more need to fear them:
But no one in the world knows where they went to.

I came to be fearful of the passing of the seasons,
Of the Bright God's relentless journey to the west.
It grieved me to think that when the fine frost descended,
All my fragrant flowers would prematurely fade.
I wanted some time to roam in leisurely enjoyment:
I had gone through the length of years with nothing yet
    achieved.

With whom could I enjoy the fragrance that was left me?
Long I stood against the wind, unburdening my heart.
Gao Yang lived far from me in a distant time,
How could I . . .?

Spring and autumn hurried by, never delaying:
I could not go on staying in my old home for ever.
Xuan Yuan was too remote for me to aspire to;
But I could follow Wang Qiao for my delight.

I supped the Six Essences; drank the Night Dew;
Rinsed my mouth in the Sun Mist; savoured the Morning
    Brightness;
Conserving the pure elements of the divine;
Absorbing the subtle essence and rejecting the grosser parts.

Drifting in the wake of the gentle south wind,
I travelled to Nan-chao in a single journey.
There I saw Master Wang and made him salutation,
And asked about the balance made by unifying essence.

He said: 'The Way can only be received, it cannot be given.
        Small, it has no content; great, it has no bounds.
        Keep your soul from confusion, and it will come naturally.
        By unifying essence, strengthen the spirit; preserve it
            inside you in the midnight hour.
        Await it in emptiness, before even Inaction.
        All other things proceed from this: this is the Door of
            Power.'

69   Having heard this precious teaching, I departed,
And swiftly prepared to start off on my journey.
I met the Feathered Men on the Hill of Cinnabar;
I tarried in the ancient land of Immortality.

73   In the morning I washed my hair in the Gulf of Brightness;
In the evening I dried myself on the coast of heaven.
I sipped the subtle liquor of the Flying Spring,
And held in my bosom the flower-bright *wan-yan* jewel.

77   My jade-like countenance flushed with radiant colour;
Purified, my vital essence started to grow stronger;
My corporeal parts dissolved to a soft suppleness;
And my spirit grew lissom and eager for movement.

81   How fine was the fiery nature of the South Land!
How lovely the winter blooming of the cassia!
But the mountain was forlorn with no beasts upon it;
The moor was a lonely place with no man there.
I restrained my restless spirit and mounted the empyrean,
I clung to a floating cloud to ride aloft on.

87   I bade heaven's porter open his barrier,
And stand by his gate awaiting my arrival.
I summoned Feng Long; I made him ride ahead
And ask the way to the Palace of Mystery.

91   Passing through the Bright Walls I entered the House of God,
Visited the Week Star and gazed on the Pure City.
In the morning I set off from the Court of Heaven;
In the evening Wei-lü came in sight below.

95   I marshalled in order my ten thousand chariots
And moved slowly forwards in splendid procession.
Eight dragons drew my car, coiling and curvetting;
Over it a cloud-banner flapped upon the wind.

99   The standards we carried bore rainbow devices:
Five contrasting colours, dazzling to behold.
Splendidly the yoke-horses bowed and tossed their heads;
Proudly the trace-horses arched and curved themselves.

A din and bustle rose up confusedly
As our colourful, many-assorted train began to move.
I grasped the reins and, with my whip, I signalled the direction:
The first part of our journey should be to visit Gou Mang.

We crossed the eastern heaven, wheeling to the right hand.
I sent Fei Lian on ahead to clear the way for us.
The sky was just beginning to flush before the sunrise
As we forded the waters of the Pool of Heaven.

The Wind God meanwhile was riding on ahead,
Clearing the dust away to make it clean and cool;
Phoenixes sweeping overhead bore up my pennant.
Then we met Ru Shou in the western heaven.

I took hold of the Broom Star to use it as a banner;
I brandished the Dipper's Handle as my baton.
Up and down our long train went, plunging and soaring,
Drifting on the moving waves of the fleeting mist.

The daylight was fading and darkness was gathering
As I summoned Xuan Wu to serve in my train.
I made Wen Chang follow, too, to marshal the procession,
Disposing the gods in their places in my retinue.

Far the road stretched ahead, endlessly onwards:
We slowed down the pace as we crossed the height of heaven.
The Rain God went on my left hand to guide me;
The Thunder God went on my right hand as bodyguard.

I wanted to leave for good, to forget about returning:
My mind was exalted with a reckless sense of freedom;
A boundless satisfaction suffused my inner being:
I wanted to yield to this voluptuous contentment.

Traversing the blue sky, I was wandering freely,
When suddenly I glimpsed my old home below me.
My groom was homesick and my own heart downcast;
The trace-horses looked back and would not go forward.

135   I pictured my dear ones in imagination,
    And, with a heavy sigh, I brushed the tears away.
    Then slowly I drifted on, rising even higher,
    Suppressing these wilful thoughts, in control once more.

139   Pointing to the Fiery God, I made a straight line towards him:
    I wished to journey onwards to the world's southern shore.
    I gazed into the emptiness there, beyond the world's end;
    Then onwards still I floated, over that watery vastness.

143   But Zhu Rong stood in my way, warning me to turn back.
    I sent word by the phoenix to invite the lady Fu Fei.
    I made the Xiang goddesses play on their zithers,
    And I bade the Sea God dance with the River God.

147   They played the 'Pool of Heaven', then struck up 'To the
        Clouds',
    Then the two goddesses performed the Nine Shao Songs.
    They lined water monsters up to join them in the dance:
    How their bodies coiled and writhed in undulating motion!

151   Gracefully the woman-rainbow made circles round them;
    Phoenixes soared up and hovered overhead.
    The music swelled and swelled into infinity.
    After that I left them and resumed my wandering.

155   All keeping close in step, on and on we galloped,
    Till, at the world's other end, we came to the Gate of Coldness.
    There I raced the rushing wind to the Freezing Fountain;
    I followed Zhuan Xu over the piled-up ice.

159   I turned aside from my path to cross the realm of Xuan Ming;
    Bestriding the Dividers, I looked back behind me.
    I summoned Qian Lei to appear before me
    And caused him to go in front in the level way.

163   I toured the Four Outlands,
    Traversed the Six Regions,
    Up to the lightning's fissure,
    And down to the Great Abyss.

In the sheer depths below, the earth was invisible;
In the vastness above, the sky could not be seen.
When I looked, my startled eyes saw nothing;
When I listened, no sound met my amazed ear.
Transcending Inaction, I came to Purity,
And entered the neighbourhood of the Great Beginning.

Notes

*l.*23 Red Pine: the first historical references to the Ascetics or *fang-shi*
(literally 'formula-men': men with a method or formula – the
ingestion of drugs or herbs, breath-control, yoga exercises, dieting,
etc. – for prolonging life indefinitely and acquiring the ability to fly)
are found in the annals of the Qin First Emperor, who encountered
numbers of them in his imperial progresses through Shandong and
Hebei. The fata Morgana, occasionally observable from the Shandong
coast, were thought to be islands inhabited by the Immortals, the
successful *fang-shi* of a preceding age whose existence guaranteed the
efficacy of these 'methods'. It is in the same period when we begin to
hear the names of actual, historical *fang-shi* – some of them imperial
consultants, able to command the sort of subsidies that scientists
receive from governments today – that we also begin hearing of these
fictitious *fang-shi*, believed to have been born many centuries before,
who had turned themselves into Immortals and flown off to live
carefree lives in the Isles of the Blest or one of the terrestrial paradises.
The Master of the Red Pine was one of them. When Zhang Liang,
crafty adviser to the founder of the Han dynasty and companion of all
his campaigns, was an old man, he expressed a desire to 'lay aside the
affairs of the world and join the Master of the Red Pine in immortal
sport'. He then proceeded to cut out cereal foods from his diet and to
practise the breathing and other exercises that would lighten his body
and enable him to fly. The empress dowager was afraid that he would
starve himself to death, however, and persuaded him to desist.

*l.*25 *Pure Ones*: the Chinese word is *zhen-ren* – 'true men' or 'perfect
men'. The term is frequently used by Zhuang Zi. The *zhen-ren* of
old, he tells us, slept without dreaming and woke without a care. And
they were very deep breathers. The men of today breathe from their
chests, but the *zhen-ren* of old breathed from their heels.

*l.*29 *Fu Yue*: the convict labourer whom the Shang king Wu Ding saw
in a dream and raised to be his counsellor. See *Li sao*, *ll.*291–2
and note. Fu Yue's posthumous apotheosis as a star is referred to in the

sixth chapter of *Zhuang zi*: 'Fu Yue got it [i.e. the Tao] and became minister to Wu Ding, who extended his rule over the whole world, and at the end mounted up into the eastern sky, straddled the Ji and Wei constellations and took his place among the fixed stars.' Fu Yue's star was associated with the destinies of shamans.

*l.*30 *Han Zhong*: Han Zhong was an historical person twice mentioned in the annals of the Qin First Emperor, once under the year 215 B.C. and once under the year 212 B.C. He was one of the *fang-shi* whom the First Emperor sent off to look for the herb of immortality. Later, in an outburst of fury against all these cheating 'experts', the emperor singled Han Zhong out for special mention as one who had 'gone off and never reported back'. The anonymous author of *Yuan you* assumes that Han Zhong found what he was looking for and took it himself.

*l.*53 *Xuan Yuan*: one of the names of Huang Di, the 'Yellow Ancestor'. Han Taoists regarded the Yellow Ancestor as their founder. In the Han era Taoism itself was often referred to as 'the teachings of Huang and Lao': i.e. of the Yellow Ancestor and Lao Zi.

*l.*54 *Wang Qiao*: al. 'Wang Zi-qiao' or 'Zi Qiao'. The 'Master Wang' of *l.*61 refers to him, as well. One of the legendary Immortals, like Red Pine. According to Taoist hagiographers, he was the son of King Ling of Zhou (*reg.* 571–545 B.C.) who flew away on a great white bird and was never seen again. As far as I know, Wang Qiao is nowhere mentioned in any pre-Han work.

*ll.*55–6 *the Six Essences ... the Night Dew, etc.*: all these are invisible essences imbibed by the Taoist ascetic at different times of the day and night by means of different sorts of breathing exercises.

*l.*60 *I travelled to Nan-chao*: i.e. 'Chao-in-the-South' – perhaps Chao-xian in Anhui. The eighteenth-century commentator Jiang Ji says that in his day there was a Wang Qiao Cave in the mountains near Chao-xian. Chao-xian is about 100 miles south-east of Shou-chun, where the Prince of Huai-nan held court.

*l.*66 *By unifying essence, strengthen the spirit*: *qi*, the word I have translated as 'essence' in this passage, is a concept something akin to 'life force' except that it was said to be present not only in organic but also in inorganic substances like fire, air and water which have lifelike movement. 'Subtle spirits' and '*pneuma*' – the latter a Greek word having somewhat similar connotations – have been suggested by Joseph Needham as possible renderings of this term. (See *Science and Civilization in China*, II, 21–4.) In one of his rare incursions into mysticism the fourth-century B.C. Confucian philosopher Mencius speaks of a primal *qi* which is built up during the night but gets dissipated during the distractions of the day until, by constant wear, it loses the ability to renew itself. The opposite view, which we find here, that one's vital energy could escape at night unless concentrated ('unifying essence') into a single centre, was presumably based on the physical analogy of involuntary emissions of semen. Members of the fanatically ascetic Golden Lotus sect of Taoism founded in the twelfth century were so terrified of losing their precious semen during sleep that they endeavoured to give up sleeping altogether. (Involuntary emissions during waking hours could be dealt with by exerting pressure on the perineum and diverting the semen backwards into the bladder, a process which they fancifully referred to as 'turning the seed back to nourish the brain'.) Not only a man's semen but also his soul might escape from him during his sleep, with consequent loss of energy. The *Jiu zhang* poems contain several instances of the soul of a person suffering from great distress of mind leaving his body during the night and wandering distractedly about. The dreamlessness of the *zhen-ren* of old referred to by Zhuang Zi (see note on 'Pure Ones', *l.*25, above) was due to the fact that they were able to preserve their souls inside them 'in the midnight hour'.

*l.*71 *Feathered Men ... Hill of Cinnabar*: successful Taoist adepts who became Immortals were said to grow a fine covering of feathers on their bodies. Cinnabar, a natural sulphide of mercury, was from prehistoric times believed to have magical, life-giving properties. The vermilion made from it was applied to the bodies of the dead and to all sorts of holy objects. To the Chinese Taoists it was specially valued because of the comparative ease with which alchemists could bring about its spectacular transformation into quicksilver. Although the results were usually poisonous, it was for centuries regarded as an essential ingredient in the preparation of elixirs and life-prolonging drugs. *Dan*, the word for 'cinnabar', was in fact sometimes used to mean 'alchemy'. *Dan-qiu*, 'Hill of Cinnabar', is a made-up name: a hill of cinnabar is just the sort of place where you would expect Immortals to be found.

*ll.*89–90 *I summoned Feng Long ... Palace of Mystery*: in *Li sao*, *ll.*221–2, Qu Yuan sends Feng Long off on a cloud to look for the river goddess Fu Fei. The *Yuan you* poet has his eye on higher things. The Palace of Mystery is the Tai Wei constellation in which, according to *Huai nan zi*, the god Tai Yi holds his court (see p. 101). Hence in *l.*93 he speaks of setting out 'from the Court of Heaven'. From then on a heavenly progress begins, first from east (*l.*106) to west (*l.*114), and then from south (*ll.*139 *et seq.*) to north (*ll.*156 *et seq.*), after which the poet seems to leave not just the earth but the whole cosmos behind him and to enter on a different plane of being.

l.94 *Wei-lü*: according to the 'Autumn Floods' chapter of *Zhuang zi* (Ch. 17), this was the name of a great vortex in the Eastern Sea where the waters of the ocean drained away through a sort of gigantic plug-hole, without, however, any apparent diminution in their volume.

l.106 *Gou Mang*: tutelary spirit of the east. He appeared once to Duke Mu of Zheng (seventh century B.C.) in the form of a bird with the face of a man, 'dressed in white clothing, of serious, dignified mien'. Gou Mang means 'curly-sprout' (literally 'hook-sprout'), i.e. 'seedling', because the east was associated with the spring and with green, growing things. His theriomorphic avatar was the Green Dragon who presided over the Palace of Spring, the eastern quadrant of the astronomers' heaven.

l.107 *We crossed the eastern heaven*: the Chinese text actually has 'Tai Hao', the name of the god (*di*) of the eastern sky. Gou Mang was his attendant spirit. His name is used here as a metonymy for the region of the sky which was his domain.

l.108 *Fei Lian*: the Wind God, as he is called in *l*.111. Cf. *Li sao*, *l*.198.

l.114 *Ru Shou*: tutelary spirit of the west. In the seventh century B.C. he appeared to the ruler of the little state of Guo in a dream as a god with a human face, holding an axe in his hand, whose white hair and tiger's claws showed him to be the avatar of the White Tiger who presides over the Palace of Autumn, western counterpart of the Green Dragon of the East. The name Ru Shou means 'Abundant Harvest'.

l.120 *Xuan Wu*: the appearance of Xuan Wu here in the light of the 'Xuan Ming' in *l*.159 is rather puzzling. Normally Xuan Wu was thought of as the theriomorphic guardian of the Palace of Winter, defined in terms of the constellations which occupy the 'northern' quadrant of the sky. Iconographically he was represented as a turtle or tortoise with a snake coiled about his middle. Xuan Ming (*l*.159) was his anthropomorphic avatar, the tutelary spirit of the north and attendant spirit of the god Zhuan Xu. (Long before the cosmologists got hold of him he probably started off as a local river god or flood hero, rather like Gun.) I suspect that the *Yuan you* poet does not, in this context, intend us to remember Xuan Wu's association with the north. Simply his name 'Dark Warrior' and the fact that he is a star spirit make him sound like a good choice for a bodyguard to a man who is making a celestial journey in a time of gathering darkness.

l.121 *Wen Chang*: a cluster of stars in Ursa Major. The god of this constellation was a patron of officials. With his knowledge of protocol he would be well qualified to see that the attendant deities were arranged in correct order of precedence.

*l.*143 *Zhu Rong*: tutelary spirit of the south, corresponding to Gou Mang in the east and Ru Shou in the west. Zhu Rong was the attendant spirit of the Fiery God of the South, whom some identified with the ox-headed Shen Nong, the Divine Husbandman. Zhu Rong was the ancestor of the kings of Chu (see p. 18). One of his names was Zhong Li, whom one ancient text rather confusingly identified with 'Curly Sprout'. The tidy systems of latter-day cosmologists and antiquarians concealed, in China as they did in the West, many such confusions and inconsistencies.

*ll.*158–9 *Zhuan Xu ... Xuan Ming*: Zhuan Xu was the god of the north and Xuan Ming his attendant spirit.

*l.*161 *Qian Lei*: 'a creator-spirit; some say a water god', the early commentators tantalizingly inform us. Apart from the 'Mighty Man', I do not think any other source has ever referred to him.

Bu ju 'Divination'

Each of these two short pieces, 'Divination' and 'The Fisherman', which follows it without further introduction, is an anecdote about Qu Yuan of some incident supposed to have taken place during his banishment. Neither could conceivably have been written by the poet himself, to whom their authorship was, nevertheless, traditionally attributed. They were probably written long after his death and are almost certainly fictitious; yet it is quite possible that both may date from no later than the mid third century B.C., in which case they are the only pre-Han texts in which Qu Yuan is mentioned by name. One reason for thinking this is that both seem to imply greater knowledge of Qu Yuan's actual circumstances than is evinced by any Han authority. 'Divination' mentions the name of a Chu diviner and 'The Fisherman' gives Qu Yuan a title which is otherwise unknown. To this might be added that Si-ma Qian's incorporation of 'The Fisherman' into the text of his biography of Qu Yuan implies that he regarded it as a reliably early source.

Each of these pieces uses dialogue and each is a mixture of poetry and prose, though there is far more verse in the first one, 'Divination', than in the second. Beyond that the similarities end. 'Divination' was evidently written by someone very sympathetic to,

Qu Yuan's position, sharing his contempt for a corrupt and flattering court society and approving his lofty refusal to compromise; 'The Fisherman' takes the more practical view that it is better to bow with the wind than let it break you and seems to find something faintly ridiculous in Qu Yuan's heroic stance.

'The Fisherman' belongs to a certain class of Taoist parable (there is a similar story about Confucius and a fisherman in the thirty-first chapter of *Zhuang zi*) in which a simple countryman, an eccentric, a madman or even a very wicked person like Robber Zhi is shown to be much more sensible and perspicacious than some well-known paragon of conventional wisdom and virtue.

In the *Chu ci* collection compiled by Liu An and his courtiers these two pieces came before the 'Summons for a Recluse' written by or for the Prince of Huai-nan himself which is the last work in the collection. Probably they were taken from quite different sources and added as a sort of appendix to the 'Poems by Qu Yuan and Others' which made up the rest of the collection. Liu An's own 'Summons for a Recluse' was placed, with fitting modesty, as a second appendix at the very end.

Qu Yuan had already been in exile for three years without obtaining a recall. Though he had taxed his knowledge and strained his loyalty to the utmost, his worth had been obscured by the tongues of slander. His mind was in such a turmoil that he did not know which way to turn. And so he called on the Great Diviner, Zhan Yin of Zheng, and said:

'I have an uncertainty in my mind which I should like you to resolve for me.'

Zhan Yin accordingly set out his divining-stalks and dusted his turtle-shell.

'My lord,' he said, 'what are your instructions?'

'Is it better,' Qu Yuan asked him, 'to be painstakingly honest, simple-hearted and loyal, or to keep out of trouble by welcoming each change as it comes?

'Is it better to risk one's life by speaking truthfully and without concealment, or to save one's skin by following the whims of the wealthy and highly placed?

'Is it better to preserve one's integrity by means of a lofty detachment, or to wait on a king's mistress with flattery, fawning, and strained, smirking laughter?

'Is it better to be honest and incorruptible and to keep oneself pure, or to be accommodating and slippery, to be compliant as lard or leather?

'Is it better to have the aspiring spirit of a thousand *li* stallion, or to drift this way and that like a duck on water, saving oneself by rising and falling with the waves?

'Is it better to run neck and neck with the swiftest, or to follow in the footsteps of a broken hack?

'Is it better to match wing-tips with the flying swan, or to dispute for scraps with chicken and ducks?

'Of these alternatives, which is auspicious and which is ill-omened? which is to be avoided and which to be followed?

The world is turbulent and impure;
They call a cicada's wing heavy and a ton weight light;
The brazen bell is smashed and discarded; the earthen crock is
     thunderously sounded;
The slanderer struts proudly, the wise man lurks unknown.
Alas, I am silenced: who can know of my integrity?'

Zhan Yin threw aside the divining-stalks and excused himself.

'There are times,' he said, 'when a foot is too short; and there are times when an inch is too long. There are cases in which the instruments are of no avail, in which knowledge can give no enlightenment. There are things to which my calculations cannot attain, over which the divinity has no power. My lord, for one with your mind and with resolution such as yours the turtle and the divining-stalks are really unable to be of help.'

Note

divining-stalks ... *turtle-shell*: the kind of divination made by manipulating pieces of yarrow-stalk or bamboo (one which is associated with the *Yi jing* or 'Book of Changes') has already been encountered in *Li sao* (see *Li sao*, ll.257–8 and note). Another kind made use of the plastron – the flat belly-shell – of the freshwater turtle and the flat shoulder-bones of various animals. Heat was applied to nicks cut in one side of the shell or bone and omens

taken from the resulting cracks which appeared on the other side.
Huge numbers of these 'oracle shells' and 'oracle bones' inscribed
with the questions which were asked of the oracle have been
discovered by archaeologists in this century and the decipherment of
the previously unknown script in which the questions were written
has supplied us with almost all the knowledge we have about the
dynasty of Shang kings who ruled over the North China Plain in
the second millennium B.C.

Yu fu 'The Fisherman'

After Qu Yuan was banished, he wandered, sometimes along
the river's banks, sometimes along the marsh's edge, singing
as he went. His expression was dejected and his features
emaciated. A fisherman caught sight of him.

'Are not you the Lord of the Three Wards?' said the
fisherman. 'What has brought you to this pass?'

'Because all the world is muddy and I alone am clear,' said
Qu Yuan, 'and because all men are drunk and I alone am
sober, I have been sent into exile.'

'The Wise Man is not chained to material circumstances,'
said the fisherman, 'but can move as the world moves. If all
the world is muddy, why not help them to stir up the mud
and beat up the waves? And if all men are drunk, why not
sup their dregs and swill their lees? Why get yourself exiled
because of your deep thoughts and your fine aspirations?'

Qu Yuan replied, 'I have heard it said: "He who has just
washed his hair should brush his hat; and he who has just
bathed should shake his clothes." How can I submit my
spotless purity to the dirt of others? I would rather cast
myself into the waters of the river and be buried in the
bowels of fishes, than hide my shining light in the dark and
dust of the world.'

The fisherman, with a faint smile, struck his paddle in the water and made off. And as he went he sang:

'When the Cang-lang's waters are clear,
I can wash my hat-strings in them;
When the Cang-lang's waters are muddy,
I can wash my feet in them.'

With that he was gone, and did not speak again.

Notes

the Lord of the Three Wards: the traditional explanation of this title is that Qu Yuan was, *inter alia*, a sort of registrar or archivist with certain ritual or priestly functions of the three noble clans who were collateral branches of the royal house of Chu: the Zhaos, the Jings and the Qus. The 'three wards' were the districts in Ying, the Chu capital, where the members of these clans had their residences – and also, presumably, their family shrines.

When the Cang-lang's waters are clear: an identical version of this song appears in the *Book of Mencius* as 'the song sung by the child'. Tasselled hat-strings were a badge of official rank. The meaning of the song is that you should seek official employment in good times and retire gracefully when times are troubled.

Jiu bian 'Nine Changes'

Song Yu, to whom the authorship of these poems has always, with a few modern exceptions, been attributed, is the subject of a number of anecdotes, mostly of a humorous kind, none of them dating from any earlier than the first century B.C. He is also credited with the authorship of a number of *fu* found in the great 'Literary Anthology' compiled by Xiao Tong, Crown Prince of Liang, in the sixth century. These *fu* invariably begin with a dialogue between

Song Yu and King Xiang of Chu in the course of which the King
suggests some subject or other which he would like Song Yu to
make a poem about. The rest of the *fu* then consists of the poem
which Song Yu makes up at the king's request. These *fu* are no
more likely to have been written by Song Yu himself than
'Divination' or 'The Fisherman' to have been written by Qu Yuan.
As for the anecdotes, they are no more (or less) reliable than the
gossip about William Shakespeare recorded in Aubrey's *Brief Lives*.
Anecdotes and *fu* alike are agreed on three things which we may
tentatively regard as historical: (1) that he was a courtier of King
Xiang of Chu (*reg.* 298–263 B.C.); (2) that he was a gifted and
versatile poet; and (3) that he was a wit. Wang Yi, probably
following Liu Xiang (see p. 33 *et seq.*), tells us that Song Yu was also
the author of *Zhao hun* ('Summons of the Soul') which comes next
in this anthology. As I shall show elsewhere (p. 223), this may very
likely be so; but in the total absence of any verifiable historical facts
about him, the attribution of one or another work to his authorship
adds precious little to our understanding of the work. The catalogue
of books in the Han Imperial Library compiled by Liu Xiang and
his son lists the 'Collected Works of Song Yu in 16 *pian*' but does
not tell us of what the *pian* consisted.

Whoever it was who wrote these poems, he was a very fine poet
with a distinctive style of his own, quite unlike that of Qu Yuan,
whose *Li sao* they immediately followed in the original order of
pieces in the anthology (see p. 31). *Li sao* is full of allegorical
flowers, birds and trees, but its author, as he hurries from sage-king
to shaman ancestor pouring out his grievances, or rushes across the
firmament in his dragon-powered chariot attended by throngs of
spirits, has little time for contemplating the world of nature. It
would be hard to imagine him composing the magnificent threnody
to dying nature with which *Jiu bian* begins. In *Jiu bian* we
encounter, perhaps for the first time, a fully developed sense of
what the Japanese call *mono no aware*, the pathos of natural objects,
which was to be the theme of so much Chinese poetry throughout
the ages.

Like *Jiu zhang*, *Jiu bian* has the appearance of an originally
fragmentary text owing its present shape to editorial reconstruction.
Some parts of it may, in fact, not belong to it at all, which would
help to explain its very uneven quality. The sizeable portions of it
which are duplicated in *Jiu zhang* (see p. 163) must originally have
been unplaced fragments about whose provenance early editors came
to different conclusions.

The poems of *Jiu bian*, unlike those of *Jiu zhang*, have no
separate titles of their own. A consequence of this is that there is
great uncertainty about how the text should be divided. Some

editors divide it into nine sections, some into ten. Unlike the other Sao-style poems, the poems of *Jiu bian* for the most part consist not of rhyming couplets but of runs of the same rhyme. Following mainly the rhymes, the sense and my own intuition, I have arrived at eleven sections.

Whether Song Yu himself was responsible for the title *Jiu bian* is unknowable. I have translated it as 'Nine Changes' because, like 'Nine Songs', it was a ready-made title, borrowed from legend; and in the legend *Jiu bian* has the sense of musical changes or 'modes'. Song Yu might, of course, have meant something quite different by the title. The characters with which it is written suggest 'Nine Arguments' or 'Nine Disputes'. But I am inclined to think that it was not the poet's title but one that was imposed editorially to distinguish an originally untitled collection of Sao-style poems written by one of Qu Yuan's *epigoni* from other sections of the anthology.

I

Alas for the breath of autumn!
Wan and drear: flower and leaf fluttering fall and turn to decay;
Sad and lorn: as when on journey far one climbs a hill and looks
   down on the water to speed a returning friend;
Empty and vast: the skies are high and the air is cold;
Still and deep: the streams have drunk full and the waters are
   clear.
Heartsick and sighing sore: for the cold draws on and strikes
   into a man;
Distraught and disappointed: leaving the old and to new places
   turning;
Afflicted: the poor esquire has lost his office and his heart rebels;
Desolate: on his long journey he rests with never a friend;
Melancholy: he nurses a private sorrow.
The fluttering swallows leave on their homeward journey;
The forlorn cicada makes no sound;
The wild geese call as they travel southwards;
The partridge chatters with a mournful cry.

15 Alone he waits for the dawn to come, unsleeping,
Mourning with the cricket, the midnight traveller.
His time draws on apace: already half is gone;
Yet still he languishes, nothing accomplished.

II

Sad and in sore straits I dwell alone.
There is a Fair One, from my heart never sundered.
I have left home and country, and gone a traveller to distant
    places.
Far have I wandered: where will my journeying end?
5 But my lord would have none of it. What could I do?
Storing my resentment up, husbanding my anguish,
I was so sick at heart that I forgot to eat.
I longed but once to see him and give my thoughts expression,
But the heart of my lord was not the same as mine;
10 And though my chariot was harnessed, I had to turn back again:
It grieved me bitterly that I could not see him.
I leaned upon the chariot-board and heaved a heavy sigh,
And in a stream the tears ran down and wet the chariot-rail.
My high aspirations are cut off without hope;
15 I have fallen on dark, troubled times; I am lost and bewildered;
But though my private sorrow may be never-ending,
The heart that beats in me will always be loyal and true.

III

High Heaven divides the four seasons equally,
But I am grieved only by the chilly autumn.
The white dew has fallen on the hundred flowers;
The *tong* and catalpa trees will soon grow thin and bare.
5 Gone now is the radiance of the bright sun,
And come the dreary watches of the longer nights.

I have left behind my blossom-burgeoning prime:
Sere and withered, I am full of melancholy.
First autumn heralds with warning of white dew;
Then winter redoubles rigour with bitter frost.
High summer's fecund forces are gathered up,
Then trapped and buried away in winter's prison.
Leaves are sickly and lacking colour;
Stems are criss-crossed in confusion,
The boughs are thin and withered-looking;
The tapering twigs are sad to see.
Things creep in hue towards their coming end,
Their whole appearance wasted away and sick.
I think of the rich profusion soon to fall,
And grieve that I missed the time when I might have met my
    master.
Seizing the reins, I slowed down the pace of my horses,
Thinking to find some pleasure in idle wandering;
But my years move swiftly by and will soon be ended:
I fear that a good old age will not be for me.
I mourn that I was not born in a better time,
And have fallen on this mad and fearful age.
Slowly I pace or solitary stand,
While the cricket chirps here in the west hall.
My heart is afraid and sorely shaken;
I have so many sources of sorrow.
I look up to the bright moon and sigh,
And walk underneath the stars until daylight comes.

IV

I grieve for the orchid blossoms thickly spreading
That grow so gaily in the great courtyard.
Alas that these flowers should be without any fruits,
And, fluttering, bow to every wind and shower!
I had thought that my lord would only wear these orchids,
But he treated them no differently from any other flower.

I was sad that my matchless thoughts could find no way to him,
And resolved to leave my lord and fly off high.
My heart was grieved and sorely pained within me;
10   I longed but once to see him, so that all might be made clear.
How hard to be estranged when I had not offended!
My bosom was tormented with bitter anguish.
How should I not think anxiously of my lord?
But nine gates, gate within gate, divide me from him.
15   Fierce, snarling dogs run out from them and bark,
And they bar me against him and will not let me through.
High Heaven overflows; the autumn rains are with us,
And it seems that Earth will never be dry again.
I, only I, am deprived of nurturing moisture,
20   And look up at the floating clouds with a heavy sigh.

V

What wonderful craftsmen, this modern generation!
They abandon the inked string, preferring their own guidelines;
Fine steeds they reject when they would go out driving;
They prefer to take the road whipping a broken nag.
5   It is not that in this age there are no fine steeds;
Simply that there is no one skilful enough to drive them.
The fine steed sees that the man at the rein is a tyro,
So he kicks up his heels and takes himself far off.
Wild geese and ducks gobble millet and water-weed,
10   But the phoenix soars high up into the sky.

[If you take a square handle to use on a round chisel,
I am certain it will not fit and you will not make it go in.]

The common birds all have their perches to go to;
The phoenix hovers distractedly, having no place.

15   [I would willingly gag my mouth and say nothing,
Had I not once enjoyed rich favours from my lord.
Duke Tai was ninety years old before he was honoured,
Simply because, before that, he had never met his match.]

What of the fine steed? Where is he to turn?
What of the phoenix? Where is he to rest?
The old ways are altered, customs changed, the world decays:
The fancier of today extols a fine fat look.
The good steed lies hidden and will not show himself;
The phoenix flies high and will not come down and alight.
If even birds and beasts know how to maintain their virtue,
It need not be asked why the good man does not stay.
The steed, no longer coursing, is searching for a driver;
The phoenix has no appetite and forgets to eat.
My lord has banished me far off and will not examine my cause:
Even though I wish to be loyal, I have no means to show it.
I should like to keep silent and sunder all links with him;
But I dare not forget the great kindness he once showed me.
Alone with my grief, I suffer the more deeply;
And my choking anger knows no appeasement.

VI

Dew falls and the bitter frost follows to afflict me,
And my heart is distraught and will not be comforted.
Sleet and snow, thickly commingling, harder and harder come
    down,
And I know that the time is near when I must meet my end.
I wish that by some lucky chance I might be forgiven;
But I shall soon die, along with the moorland grasses.
I wish I could set off unbidden and fly straight to him,
But the road to him is blocked and impassable.
I wish I could follow the others' route and ride the easy way,
But that, too, is no good: I do not know how to do it.
And so I stop midway in perplexity,
Grieving and hesitant; unable to turn back.
And though dull and stupid by nature and poor in talents,
I restrain myself and learn to mourn in verses.
Orchid and iris are mixed with worthless mugwort:
Truly I am not skilled to imitate their fashion.

VII

I love the great spirit of Shen Bao-xu,
But fear this present age's unsteadfastness.
What wonderful craftsmen, this modern generation!
They efface the marked lines and carve after their own fancy.
5   I alone am staunch and will not follow them,
Wishing to take as my guidelines the pattern taught by the
    Sages.
To live in an impure world and be honoured
Is not a thing my heart delights in:
Rather than by unrighteous means be famous,
10 I would live poor and keep myself above them.
I can eat without greed and yet be full;
Dress without luxury and still be warm.
I love the spirit of that old poet:
I should like to take as my motto what he said of the 'bread of
    idleness'.
15 Full of impatient thoughts, with no end or beginning,
In this vast wilderness that has no limit –
I have no clothes and furs to protect me from winter's cold,
And I fear I shall shortly die and not live to see the warm
    spring.

VIII

When I think of the long nights of late autumn,
My heart is tormented and full of grief.
My springs and autumns are growing in number;
Sadly I lament my lot.
5   The seasons come and go, making up the year;
Light and dark alternate: I scarce can keep abreast.
The white sun reddens towards his setting;
The bright moon pines and wastes away.
All too soon the year will be ended,
10 And old age comes creeping on apace.

My heart is distraught; its passion increases:
I am disappointed; have nothing to hope for.
My breast is bitter with grief and anguish,
And sigh after long sigh I heave heavily.
Swiftly the years roll by, ever receding,
And old age finds me alone, without a place.
My affairs press upon me and urge me forward;
But I linger on here in uncertainty.

IX

How the floating clouds drift over everything!
See how they suddenly cover the bright moon!
My loyalty was shining bright; I longed to make it seen;
But the black clouds obscured it and it could not shine through.
I wanted the shining sun to come out in splendour,
But the clouds, dark and thick, came and hid his light.
I took no thought for myself, I wished only to be loyal;
But others with black, foul blots besmirched my name.
The noble actions of Yao and Shun
Shone with a glory that reached to the skies;
Yet the pernicious jealousy of others
Gave them a false report, calling them 'unkind'.
Even the sun and moon that shine with so bright a light
Are often dimmed and have flaws upon them.
Then how much more the affairs of an entire state
That are so many-sided and crookedly involved!

X

A lotus-petal coat is bright and gay to wear,
And yet too flimsy to be girded on.
He was too proud of his beauty and arrogantly boasted,
Rejecting the steadfast loyalty of his ministers.

5   He hated the beauty of the truly noble,
    But he loved a base fellow's blustering bravado.
    The crowd, all hustling forward, each day advanced in favour;
    But beauty left, and moved away to far distant places.
    When the farmer rests his plough and moves about in idleness,
10 I fear that field and meadow will be overgrown with weeds.
    When affairs of state are multiplied all for private ends,
    I fear that disaster is bound to follow.
    The world all agree as one and their eyes are dazzled:
    How blind the way in which they apportion praise and blame!
15 Today you deck yourselves and preen before the mirror:
    Tomorrow you may have to creep away and hide.
    I wanted to send my message by a shooting star,
    But he sped too fast and I could not catch up with him.
    Now the sky above is all veiled by these floating clouds,
20 And below is sombre gloom without any light.
    Because Yao and Shun had those they could trust with office,
    They were able to sleep sound and lead a life of ease.
    If, in the whole world, you had earned no man's spite,
    How could your heart have come by this fearful dread?
25 If you drove really noble steeds, rushing as swift as wind,
    Why would you need to use the coercing whip?
    Truly, moats and walls are not sufficient safeguard;
    Though you make your armour doubly thick, it is of no avail.
    Hoveringly I wait, but come to no conclusion;
30 I am plunged in blackest melancholy, constricted with sadness.
    My passage between heaven and earth seems almost over;
    Yet I have accomplished nothing; I am without achievements.
    Willingly I would sink from sight and never more be seen;
    Yet still I hanker to make my name known in the world.
35 So I wander restlessly, but never meet my goal;
    Wearing myself out – a fool for righteousness!
    Far and wide I roam, never coming to a stopping-place;
    Like a bird I swiftly soar, but never alight.
    The land has a good horse, but knows not how to drive him:
40 Why do they wildly search for one elsewhere?
    When Ning Qi sang beneath his cart,
    Duke Huan heard him and understood.

But now there is no Bo Le with his good eye for a horse,
Who could be found to judge his worth?
Often I weep as I brood on these things:
I see them most clearly, to my heart's pain.
With singleness of purpose, I tried to show my loyalty,
But the jealous came between us and screened me from his sight.

XI

Just grant me my worthless·body and let me go away,
To set my wandering spirit soaring amidst the clouds;
To ride the circling vapours of the primordial ether,
Racing the myriad hosts of spirits.
Bright rainbows darting swiftly in the traces,
I shall pass through the thick throngs of the powers of air:
On my left the Scarlet Bird, beating his wings,
On my right the Green Dragon, with undulating coils.
With rumblings the Lord of Thunder shall bring up the rear;
And the rushing Wind God shall lead the way:
Light coaches in the front, creaking as they go;
Waggons behind us, slowly trundling.
Cloud banners we shall bear, flapping on the wind;
A squadron of horsemen shall make a stately escort.
My plans are firmly fixed and cannot now be altered:
I will press forward, resolved to make them prosper.
Blessed with rich favours from the Lord of Heaven,
I shall return to see my lord free from all harm.

Notes

V

*ll.*11 *et seq. If you take a square handle*: *ll.*11–12 and 15–18 are, I
         believe, fragments which were inserted here in an
erroneous attempt at reconstruction. *L.*14 was tampered with in order
to make it rhyme with *l.*12. (An additional word was added after
'place'.) In the original text, I believe, *ll.*13–14 came immediately after
*ll.*9–10 and *l.*14 rhymed with *l.*10.

*l.*17 *Duke Tai*: this is Lü Wang, the butcher who was 'discovered' by
         King Wen of Zhou and made a counsellor. (Cf. *Li sao*, *l.*293, *Tian
well*, *ll.* 159–60, and *Jiu zhang* VII, *l.*35.) After the conquest of Shang,
Wen's son King Wu made Lü Wang Duke of Qi, where he was
posthumously referred to as 'Tai Gong' or 'the Grand Duke'. This
whole passage (*ll.*15–18) is, however, an interpolation.

VII

*l.*1 *Shen Bao-xu*: great rival of Zi Xu, the exiled Chu nobleman who
         became chief military adviser to the King of Wu. (See p. 186, note
on 'Crossing the River', *ll.*39–44.) When the army of Wu entered the
Chu capital Ying and Zi Xu desecrated the grave of King Ping, Shen
Bao-xu fled to Qin and, by weeping in the Qin court continuously for
seven days, induced the ruler of Qin to take action against Wu on Chu's
behalf.

*l.*14 *the 'bread of idleness'*: from the refrain of a poem in the *Book of
         Songs* (No. 112): 'That gentleman does not eat the bread of
idleness'. This poem becomes No. 259 in Waley's rearrangement. See
A. Waley, *The Book of Songs*, p. 286.

IX

*ll.*9–12 *The noble actions of Yao and Shun* ...: this is one of the
         passages duplicated in *Jiu zhang*. See 'A Lament for Ying',
*ll.*53–6 (p. 165) and note (p. 187).

X

*l.*41 *When Ning Qi sang beneath his cart*: the travelling merchant who
         became counsellor to the hegemon Duke Huan of Qi. See *Li sao*,
*ll.*295–6 and note.

*l.*43 *Bo Le*: see note on 'Embracing Sand', *l.*64 (p. 188).

XI

*ll.*7–8 *the Scarlet Bird ... the Green Dragon*: these are the
      theriomorphic guardians of the southern and eastern sky. See
notes on *Yuan you*, *ll.*107 and 143. The *Jiu bian* poet is evidently no
subscriber to the symmetrical, mandala-like view of the cosmos which
haunts the imagination of later writers. 'Green Dragon on the left,
White Tiger on the right' or 'dragon on the left, tiger on the right' was
to become a cliché in Han poetical accounts of aerial travel. Cf. *Xi shi*,
*ll.*11–12, on p. 240. ('Left' and 'right' for 'east' and 'west' because
traditional Chinese orientations assume a south-facing position.)

Zhao hun   *'Summons of the Soul'*

The *Yi li*, or 'Handbook of Ritual and Etiquette for Gentlemen',
gives careful directions for the procedure that had to be followed
when a Zhou nobleman had breathed his last:

> A soul-summoner must take a suit of court robes formerly worn
> by the deceased, and having first pinned the coat and skirt
> together, he is to lay it over his left shoulder with the collar
> tucked into his belt, and in this manner, setting a ladder against
> the east end of the front eaves of the house, is to mount up on
> to the ridge of the roof, and there, facing northwards and
> stretching out the clothing, to call out three times in a loud
> voice, 'Ho, *Such a One*! Come back!' Then he is to hand the
> clothing down from the front eaves to another below, who is to
> receive it into a box and carry it therein into the house, entering
> by way of the eastern steps. And this other one, going into the
> room where the deceased lies, is to lay the clothing down upon
> the corpse. The summoner, meanwhile, is to descend from the
> roof by the west end of the rear eaves.

The original intention of the ritual, no doubt, was to resuscitate the
dead man by catching his soul before it had gone too far away and

restoring it to his body. The Confucian ritualist who compiled the *Yi li* evidently did not expect this somewhat perfunctory soul-summoning to be successful; but in other places and at other times a very similar procedure has actually restored the apparently dead or nearly dead to life. In the second part of *The Golden Bough*, the volume on *Taboo*, James Frazer quotes a nineteenth-century anthropologist's account of an Australian Aborigine medicine-man in the Victoria area who went off in pursuit of the soul of a dying man and captured it just as it was about to disappear with the setting sun. He brought it back under his opposum rug, which he then laid on the dying man, thereby putting the soul back into him so that eventually he revived.

In China, as we have seen (p. 168), people's souls left them quite regularly in their dreams; but they could leave them in their waking hours as well, particularly as a result of shock or fear, with serious consequences if they could not fairly soon be got back into them. The poet Du Fu (712–770) in his poem 'The Road to Peng-ya' speaks of the kind friend who gave shelter to him and his wife and children after an appalling journey on foot, without food and in the rainy season, through rebel-infested countryside:

> Heating warm water to wash my tired feet;
> Cutting paper charms to summon my wandering soul.

In countries where the soul was not pursued and brought back forcibly by the shaman it had to be inveigled back by a combination of threats and blandishments. Frazer quotes two accounts of peoples living in parts of Asia not very remote from the ancient kingdom of Chu which illustrate this method, the first supplied by a French Catholic missionary in Burma in the late nineteenth century, the second by a British anthropologist in West China at the beginning of the twentieth:

> The Karens of Burma are perpetually anxious about their souls, lest these should go roving from their bodies, leaving the owners to die. When a man has reason to fear that his soul is about to take this fatal step, a ceremony is performed to retain or recall it, in which the whole family must take part. A meal is prepared consisting of a cock and a hen, a special kind of rice, and a bunch of bananas. Then the head of the family takes the bowl which is used to skim rice, and knocking with it thrice on the top of the house-ladder says: '*Prrroo*! Come back, soul, do not tarry outside! If it rains, you will be wet. If the sun shines you will be hot. The gnats will sting you, the leeches will bite you, the tigers will devour you, the thunder will crush you. *Prrroo*! Come back, soul! Here it will be well with you. You shall want

for nothing. Come and eat under shelter from the wind and the storm.' After that the family partakes of the meal, and the ceremony ends with everybody tying their right wrist with a string which has been charmed by a sorcerer. Similarly the Lolos, an aboriginal tribe of western China, believe that the soul leaves the body in chronic illness. In that case they read a sort of elaborate litany, calling on the soul by name and beseeching it to return from the hills, the vales, the rivers, the forests, the fields, or from wherever it may be straying. At the same time cups of water, wine and rice are set at the door for the refreshment of the weary wandering spirit. When the ceremony is over, they tie a red cord round the arm of the sick man to tether the soul, and this cord is worn by him until it drops off.

The two soul-summoning poems of *Chu ci* follow a remarkably similar pattern. First, threats: do not wander off; everywhere outside – east, north, south, west, above, below – is dangerous and horrible. Then blandishments: come back here, where everything is comfortable and delightful; here you will have a good time. The chief difference is one of scale. In both *Zhao hun* and *Da zhao* the soul being summoned appears to be that of a king, and the good things to which it is summoned are of a magnificence beyond the wildest imaginings of Karen or Lolo tribesmen. Chinese literary historians have sometimes seen in these shaman-inspired catalogues of royal luxury the origins of the descriptive *fu* which Han court poets like Si-ma Xiang-ru were to develop into dazzling celebrations of imperial real estate.

Although these two poems come together in modern editions, we know (p. 31) that in the original edition of *Chu ci* they were very far apart. *Zhao hun*, as may be seen from the following table, was the first of the works added by Liu Xiang to the early nucleus of *Chu ci* poems put together by Liu An, Prince of Huai-nan, in the second century B.C. *Da zhao* was not added to the collection until some two centuries later and was in fact, in the original order, the last work in the anthology before Wang Yi's own *Jiu si*. Si-ma Qian, who may however have been thinking of *Da zhao*, ascribes *Zhao hun* to Qu Yuan himself (see pp. 53–4), but it is evident that Liu An did not share this opinion because his proto-*Chu ci* does not include *Zhao hun*; and Liu Xiang, who must have been familiar with the 'Collected Works of Song Yu' because he lists them in his *Catalogue*, ascribes *Zhao hun* unhesitatingly to Song Yu. Wang Yi, while echoing Liu Xiang in this attribution, adds the extraordinary statement that Song Yu wrote it to summon back the soul of Qu Yuan, who was in exile at the time, and that his ulterior motive in

1 *Li sao*			
2 *Jiu bian*			
3 *Jiu ge*	works by Qu Yuan	Earliest *Chu ci*	
4 *Tian wen*	and his school	anthology	
5 *Jiu zhang*		edited by Liu An,	*Chu ci*
6 *Yuan you*		Prince of Huai-nan	anthology
			edited by
7 *Bu ju*	narratives		Liu Xiang
8 *Yu fu*	of Qu Yuan		
9 *Zhao yin shi*	by Liu An		
10 *Zhao hun*	by Song Yu		
11 *Jiu huai*	by Wang Bao		
12 *Qi jian*	by Dong-fang Shuo		
13 *Jiu tan*	by Liu Xiang		

writing it was to persuade King Huai [*sic*] to recall Qu Yuan from exile!

Zhao hun was quite obviously written for a king of Chu, certainly not for a private individual, much less a banished courtier; the question is, which king, and by whom? The text of *Zhao hun* as it has reached us today consists of four parts: (1) a few opening lines which could very easily have come from one of the *Jiu zhang* poems or from *Jiu bian* and which seem to have absolutely nothing to do with what follows; (2) a short dialogue in heaven, by way of prologue, in which, as far as one can make out from its fragmentary state, God instructs the Shaman Ancestor Wu Yang to go down to earth and help the man whose soul has left him; (3) the summons proper (some 115 lines); and (4) a *luan*, in which the poet recalls an expedition 'to the south' and an incident which occurred during a hunt there in which he and the king were briefly thrown together, and which ends with a cry of lamentation for the (presumably) lost territory of Jiang-nan.

Assuming that (1) is an unconnected fragment and that (2) and (4) do in fact belong to the main poem and are not late additions or interpolations, a key to the dating of *Zhao hun* would seem to lie in the *luan*:

In the new year, as spring began, we set off for the south.
The green duckweed lay on the water, and the white flag flowered.
Our road passed through Lu-jiang with Chang-bo on the right hand.

(*Zhao hun*, *ll.*133–5)

Since Lu-jiang was in southern Anhui, the southern expedition ('*nan zheng*') of *l.*133 could only have been from one of the 'eastern' capitals to which the Chu court had to move after the loss of the Jiang-nan territory in 278 B.C. The scholar Lu Kanru, who has discussed the dating of this poem at some length, is of the opinion that the capital in question must be Shou-chun, near modern Shou-xian in northern Anhui. In his view Chen, the first of the 'eastern' capitals (near what is now Huai-yang in eastern Henan), was too remote from Lu-jiang to have been the location of the court for which this poem was written; but I cannot myself see any very strong objection to understanding the 'southern expedition' as a journey of several days' duration, or to the notion that so long a journey should have been undertaken for the purpose of hunting. The 'student fellow' in the song, who kissed the young lady while the train was going through a tunnel, was returning from 'weeks of hunting in the fields of Maine', and ancient Chinese monarchs were no less addicted to the sport than young Americans of a more recent era. Moreover, for the king and the courtier-poet both to have had nostalgic memories of the lost Jiang-nan territory, as the anguished last line of the poem would seem to imply, the king *can* only have been King Xiang and the capital *can* only have been Chen, since the move to Shou-chun did not take place until the twenty-second year of King Kao Lie of Chu (241 B.C.).

I suggest, then, that *Zhao hun* was composed for King Xiang at the Chu court in Chen some time between 277 B.C., the first year after the sack of Ying and loss of the Jiang-nan territory, and 263 B.C., the last year of King Xiang's reign. And since an early-established tradition names Song Yu as the most important poet at the court of King Xiang, we might just as well continue to speak of him as the author of this poem.

[When I was young, I was pure and spotless;
My body was imbued with unfailing righteousness.
. . . . this perfect virtue,
Entangled in the world's affairs, grew foul with neglect.
Lacking the means to have this virtue tested,
I have long been unfortunate and full of bitter sorrow . . .]

The Lord God said to Wu Yang:
'There is a man on earth below whom I would help:
His soul has left him. Make divination for him.'
10 Wu Yang replied:
'The Master of Dreams . . .
The Lord God's bidding is hard to follow.'
[The Lord God said:]
'You must divine for him. I fear that if you any longer decline,
    will be too late.'
15 Wu Yang thereupon went down and summoned the soul, saying

'O soul, come back! Why have you left your old abode and fled
    to the earth's far corners,
Deserting the place of your delight to meet all those things of
    evil omen?

'O soul, come back! In the east you cannot abide.
There are giants there a thousand fathoms tall, who seek only f
    souls to catch,
20 And ten suns that come out together, melting metal, dissolving
    stone.
The folk that live there can bear it, but you, soul, would be
    consumed.
O soul, come back! In the east you cannot abide.

'O soul, come back! In the south you cannot stay.
There the people have tattooed faces and blackened teeth;
25 They sacrifice flesh of men and pound their bones for meat pas
There the venomous cobra abounds, and the great fox that can
    run a hundred leagues,
And the great nine-headed serpent, who darts swiftly this way
    and that,
And swallows men as a sweet relish.
O soul, come back! In the south you may not linger.

'O soul, come back! For the west holds many perils.

The Moving Sands stretch on for a hundred leagues.

You will be swept into the Thunder's Chasm, and dashed in
   pieces, unable to help yourself;

And even should you chance to escape from that, beyond is the
   empty desert,

And red ants as huge as elephants and wasps as big as gourds.

The five grains do not grow there; dry stalks are the only food;

And the earth there scorches men up; there is nowhere to look
   for water;

And you will drift there for ever, with nowhere to go in that
   vastness.

O soul, come back! Lest you bring on yourself perdition.

'O soul, come back! In the north you may not stay.

There the layered ice rises high, and the snowflakes fly for a
   hundred leagues and more.

O soul, come back! You cannot long stay there.

'O soul, come back! Climb not to the heaven above,

For tigers and leopards guard the nine gates, with jaws ever
   ready to rend up mortal men,

And one man with nine heads that can pull up nine thousand
   trees,

And the slant-eyed jackal-wolves pad to and fro;

They hang out men for sport and drop them in the abyss,

And only at God's command may they ever rest or sleep.

O soul, come back! Lest you fall into this danger.

'O soul, come back! Go not down to the Land of Darkness,

Where the Earth God lies, nine-coiled, with dreadful horns on
   his forehead,

And a great humped back and bloody thumbs, pursuing men,
   swift-footed:

Three eyes he has in his tiger's head, and his body is like a
   bull's.

O soul, come back! Lest you bring on yourself disaster.

'O soul, come back! and enter the gate of the city.

55   Skilled priests are there who call you, walking backwards to lead
     you in.

Qin basket-work, silk cords of Qi, and silken banners of Zheng:

All things are there proper for your recall; and with long-drawn
     piercing cries they summon the wandering soul.

O soul, come back! Return to your old abode.

'All the quarters of the world are full of harm and evil.

60   Hear while I describe for you your quiet and reposeful home.

High halls and deep chambers, with railings and tiered balconies;

Stepped terraces, storeyed pavilions, whose tops look on the high
     mountains;

Lattice doors with scarlet interstices, and carving on the square
     lintels;

Draughtless rooms for winter; galleries cool in summer;

65   Streams and gullies wind in and out, purling prettily;

A warm breeze bends the melilotus and sets the tall orchids
     swaying.

Beyond the hall, in the apartments, the ceilings and floors are
     vermilion,

The chambers of polished stone, with kingfisher curtains hanging
     from jasper hooks;

Bedspreads of kingfisher seeded with pearls, dazzling in
     brightness:

70   Arras of fine silk covers the walls; damask canopies stretch
     overhead,

Braids and ribbons, brocades and satins, fastened with rings of
     precious stone.

Many a rich and curious thing is to be seen in the furnishings of
     the chamber.

Bright candles of orchid-perfumed fat light up flower-like faces
     that await you;

Twice eight handmaids to serve your bed, each night alternating
     in duty,

75   The lovely daughters of noble families, far excelling common
     maidens.

Women with hair dressed finely in many fashions fill your
    apartments,
In looks and bearing sweetly compliant, each gently yielding to
    the other.
But, despite their soft looks, of strong and noble natures, lofty
    spirits.
Beauty and elegance grace the inner chambers:
Mothlike eyebrows and lustrous eyes that dart out beams of
    brightness,
Delicate colouring, soft round flesh, flashing, seductive glances.
In your garden pavilion, by the long bed-curtains, they wait your
    royal pleasure:
Of kingfisher feathers its purple curtains and the blue hangings
    that furnish its high hall;
The walls, red; vermilion the woodwork; jet inlay on the roof-
    beams;
Overhead you behold carved rafters, painted with dragons and
    serpents;
Seated in the hall, leaning on its balustrade, you look down on a
    winding pool;
Its lotuses have just opened; among them grow water-chestnuts;
And purple-stemmed water-mallows enamel the green wave's
    surface.
Attendants quaintly costumed in spotted leopard skins wait on
    the sloping bank;
A light coach is tilted for you to ascend; footmen and riders wait
    in position.
An orchid carpet covers the ground; the hedge is of flowering
    hibiscus.
O soul, come back! Why should you go far away?

'All your household have come to do you honour; all kinds of
    good food are ready:
Rice, broom-corn, early wheat, mixed with yellow millet;
Bitter, salt, sour, hot and sweet – there are dishes of all flavours:
Ribs of the fatted ox, tender and succulent;
Sour and bitter blended in the soup of Wu;

Stewed turtle and roast kid, served up with yam sauce;

Geese cooked in sour sauce, casseroled duck, fried flesh of the great crane;

100 Braised chicken, seethed terrapin, high-seasoned, but not to spo the taste;

Fried honey-cakes of rice flour and malt-sugar sweetmeats;

Jade-like wine, honey-flavoured, fills the winged cups;

Ice-cooled liquor, strained of impurities, clear wine, cool and refreshing;

Here are laid out patterned ladles, and here is sparkling wine.

105 O soul, come back! Here you shall have respect and nothing sha harm you.

'Before the dainties have left the tables, girl musicians take up their places.

They set up the bells and fasten the drums and sing the latest songs:

"Crossing the River", "Gathering Caltrops" and "The Sunny Bank".

The lovely girls are drunk with wine, their faces are flushed.

110 With amorous glances and flirting looks, their eyes like wavelet sparkle;

Dressed in embroideries, clad in finest silks, splendid but not showy;

Their long hair, falling from high chignons, hangs low in lovely tresses.

Two rows of eight, in perfect time, perform a dance of Zheng;

Their *xi-bi* buckles of Jin workmanship glitter like bright suns.

115 Bells clash in their swaying frames; the catalpa-wood zither's strings are swept.

Their sleeves rise like crossed bamboo stems, then slowly shimmer downwards.

Pipes and zithers rise in wild harmonies, the sounding drums thunderously roll;

And the courts of the palace quake and tremble as they throw themselves into the Whirling Chu.

Then they sing songs of Wu and ballads of Cai and play the D lü music.

Men and women now sit together, mingling freely without
   distinction;

Hat-strings and fastenings come untied: the revel turns to wild
   disorder.

The singing-girls of Zheng and Wei come to take their places
   among the guests;

But the dancers of the Whirling Chu find favour over all the
   others.

Then with bamboo dice and ivory pieces the game of Liu Bo is
   begun;

Sides are taken; they advance together; keenly they threaten each
   other.

Pieces are kinged and the scoring doubled. Shouts of 'five white!'
   arise.

Day and night are swallowed up in continuous merriment of
   wine.

Bright candles of orchid-perfumed fat burn in stands of delicate
   tracery.

The guests compose snatches to express their thoughts as the
   orchid fragrance steals over them;

And those with some object of their affections lovingly tell their
   verses to each other.

In wine they attain the heights of pleasure and give delight to the
   dear departed.

O soul, come back! Return to your old abode.'

LUAN

In the new year, as spring began, we set off for the south.

The green duckweed lay on the water, and the white flag
   flowered.

Our road passed through Lu-jiang with Chang-bo on the right
   hand.

I stood on the marsh's margin and looked far out on the
   distance.

My team was of four jet horses; we set out together a thousand
   chariots strong.

The beaters' fires flickered skyward, and the smoke rose like a
   pall.

I trotted to where the throng was, and galloped ahead to draw
   them,

140   Then reined as we sighted our quarry, and wheeled around to
   the right hand.

I raced with the King in the marshland, to see which of us
   should take it.

The King himself shot the arrow; the rhinoceros turned and fled

'The darkness yields to daylight; we cannot stay much longer.

Marsh orchids cover the path here: this way must be too
   marshy.'

145   On, on the river's waters roll; above them grow woods of maple

The eye travels on a thousand *li*, and the heart breaks for
   sorrow.

O soul, come back! Alas for the Southern Land!

Notes

*ll.*1–6   *When I was young . . . bitter sorrow*: not only these lines but the
   lines of the 'prologue' which follows them (7–15) are
fragmentary. I suspect that Liu Xiang had the text of *Zhao hun* copied
out from the 'Collected Works of Song Yu in 16 *pian*', which would
have been written on bamboo slips. The beginning of the bamboo
'book' containing the text of *Zhao hun* and the end of the preceding
'book' were probably both defective, i.e. slips had become detached
and parts of the writing on them defaced, and the copyist, in attempting
to reconstruct the beginning of the poem, must have erroneously
incorporated some lines belonging to the previous volume into the text
of *Zhao hun*.

*l.*7   *The Lord God said to Wu Yang*: Wu Yang occurs in a passage in the
   'Book of Seas and Mountains' describing the wonders of the West:

East of the Kai-ming are the shamans Wu Peng, Wu Di, Wu Yang,
Wu Li, Wu Fan and Wu Xiang, standing round the corpse of Ye Yu
with herbs of immortality in their hands, trying to bring him back to
life. Ye Yu has the body of a serpent and the head of a man. He was
slain by the servants of Er Fu.

The story of Ye Yu and Er Fu has long been forgotten, but the early fourth century commentator Guo Pu, in his verses on the pictures with which the 'Book of Seas and Mountains' was once illustrated, tells us that Ye Yu was the innocent victim of Er Fu's malice and that the shamans were commanded by God to go with life-restoring herbs to revive him. After they had done so, he dived into the Weak Water and turned into a human-headed dragon. (A very similar story was told about Gun. See 'Heavenly Questions', *ll.*73–6.) Wu Yang was evidently a divine shaman or Shaman Ancestor, whose life-restoring powers make him an appropriate choice as soul-summoner in this poem. The idea that God himself was concerned about the state of the king's health and personally arranged a soul-summoning to remedy it is, of course, a piece of courtly flattery by the poet.

*l.*13 *The Lord God said*: these words are not in the Chinese text, the fragmentary state of which can, however, be deduced from the obvious existence of a lacuna of uncertain length after the words 'The Master of Dreams' in *l.*11 above.

*ll.*114–15 *Their* xi-bi *buckles . . . strings are swept*: in the Chinese text these two lines come after *l.*126, where they are obviously out of place. The bamboo slip on which the sixteen characters of Chinese text were written must have got misplaced in the course of reconstruction or repair. *Xi-bi* is a word of non-Chinese origin. The northern Chinese adopted the custom of wearing these foreign-style buckles from their barbarian neighbours towards the end of the fourth century B.C.

*l.*135 *Our road passed through Lu-jiang*: in the Han dynasty Lu-jiang was the name of a town in southern Anhui and the name has been given to various places in that part of China up to the present day. In the 'Book of Seas and Mountains' it appears as the name of a river which eventually joins the Yangtze 'west of Peng-ze', i.e. near Jiujiang. Too little is known about Warring States geography to be quite sure where or what is indicated by the 'Lu-jiang' of this poem, but it seems reasonable to assume that it was somewhere in the southern half of Anhui. The name Chang-bo is altogether unknown. *Chang* means 'long' or 'tall' and *bo* could mean 'bush', 'scrub', 'jungle', 'thicket'. A possible rendering of this line might be 'We passed along the valley of the Lu-jiang with Longwood on our right hand', but that is only a guess.

*l.*137 *we set out together a thousand chariots strong*: the huge numbers seem less surprising if it is borne in mind that in ancient China kings and emperors used hunting as an opportunity for carrying out military manoeuvres. Much of the vast quantities of game slaughtered would go to feed the army which had helped to capture it.

Da zhao *'The Great Summons'*

Da zhao is remarkably like *Zhao hun* in its catalogue of threats and blandishments but differs from it in certain important respects. First of all it has no prologue or epilogue and therefore lacks any personal note from which deductions might be made about its date and authorship. In the second place the soul-summoning is much more sedate than in *Zhao hun*, ending not with a description of an orgy, but with a set of very fulsome verses in praise of the majesty and might of the ruler to whom it is addressed. A third peculiarity is that it repeatedly refers to Chu: 'Enjoy yourself in your land of Chu' (*l*.26), 'sauce of Chu' (*l*.34), 'clear Chu wine' (*l*.43), 'the "Lao Shang" of Chu' (*l*.46). In *Zhao hun*, except for 'the Whirling Chu' (*l*.118), which was the name of a dance, there is no mention of Chu. The king does not need to be reminded that he is a king of Chu, and products, unless their country of origin is specified, are naturally assumed to be of local make. Perhaps the strangest feature of all is the area defined in *ll*.98–9 as being the one over which the ruler to whom the poem's concluding panegyric is being addressed exercises his sway. Three of the limits which bound it, You-ling, Jiao-zhi (i.e. Tongking in Annam) and the eastern seaboard, were roughly speaking the northern, southern and eastern boundaries of the Qin empire. The Sheep's Gut Pass, however, named as the western limit, was in Shanxi and actually *excludes* the metropolitan area of Qin. My guess is that this summons was written for Xiong Xin, the grandson of King Huai of Chu, who in 208 B.C. was discovered working as a shepherd and raised up by Xiang Yu, commander of the insurgent forces fighting against Qin, to be a new King Huai of Chu. (He was actually called King Huai, to remind people of his grandfather, who had died a prisoner in Qin.) In the spring of 206 B.C., after the 'execution' of the last Qin ruler and the sack and burning of the Qin capital, Xiang Yu bestowed on him the title of 'emperor' but not long afterwards had him murdered. Although by no means a nonentity, Xiong Xin never had any more power than his generals were prepared to allow him; nevertheless, for two years or more he must have lived in some state and, in name if not in reality, had princes and dukes as his vassals (*ll*.107–8).

As regards the authorship of this poem, Wang Yi is for once undecided: '*Da zhao* is by Qu Yuan. Some say it is by Jing Cuo. It is impossible to be sure which of them wrote it.' The attribution to

Qu Yuan, though obviously erroneous, is interesting in view of Si-ma Qian's listing of *Zhao hun* among the writings of Qu Yuan. My own view is that it was probably *Da zhao* that he was referring to. '*Zhao hun*' is not a real title like '*Li sao*' or '*Tian wen*', but a mere description of the contents: 'Soul Summons'. In another context *Da zhao* could equally well be referred to as '*Zhao hun*'. It is called '*Da zhao*' in the context of this anthology to distinguish it from the other summons poem (not because it is longer – in fact it is a good deal shorter than *Zhao hun* – but because of its imperial pretensions). If my guess is correct, the fact that it was written for another King Huai of Chu may have contributed to the confusion over its authorship.

Nothing is known about Jing Cuo beyond the fact that he was one of the 'later Chu poets' who wrote in the style of Qu Yuan (see p. 59).

Green spring follows the old year and the bright sun shines,
And the breath of spring stirs, quickening all creation.
Dark winter's frosts melt away. O soul, do not flee!
O soul, come back! Do not go far away!

O soul, go not to the east!
In the east is the great sea, where the swelling waters billow
   endlessly,
And water-dragons swim side by side, swiftly darting above and
   below.
It is clammy with rain and fog, that glister white and heavy.
O soul, go not to the east, to the desolate Gulf of Brightness!

O soul, go not to the south!
In the south are a hundred leagues of flaming fire and coiling
   cobras;
The mountains rise sheer and steep; tigers and leopards slink;
The cow-fish is there, and the spit-sand, and the rearing
   python.
O soul, go not to the south! There are monsters there that will
   harm you.

15   O soul, go not to the west!
In the west are the Moving Sands stretching endlessly on and on
And beasts with heads like swine, slanting eyes and shaggy hair,
Long claws and serrated teeth, and wild, mad laughter.
O soul, go not to the west! In the west are many dangers.

20   O soul, go not to the north!
In the north are the Frozen Mountain, and the Torch Dragon,
  glaring red;
And the Dai river that cannot be crossed, whose depths are
  unfathomable;
And the sky is white and glittering, and all is congealed with
  cold.
O soul, go not to the north! There is no bourne there to your
  journeying.

25   O soul, come back to leisure and quietness!
Enjoy yourself in your land of Chu, tranquil and untroubled.
Indulge your fancies, fulfil your wishes, let your mind be at ease
Number your days out in lasting pleasure, to old age, full of
  years.
O soul, come back to pleasure that cannot be told!

30   The five kinds of grain are heaped six ells high, and the corn of
  zizania.
Cauldrons seethe to their brims, wafting a fragrance of well-
  blended flavours:
Plump orioles, pigeons and geese, flavoured with broth of jackal
  meat.
O soul, come back! Indulge your appetite!

Fresh turtle, succulent chicken, dressed with the sauce of Chu;
35   Pickled pork, dog cooked in bitter herbs, and ginger-flavoured
  mince,
And sour Wu salad of artemisia, not too wet or tasteless.
O soul, come back! Indulge in your own choice!

Roast crane next is served, steamed duck and boiled quails,
Fried bream, stewed magpies, and green goose, broiled.

O soul, come back! Choice things are spread before you.
Four kinds of wine have been subtly blended, not rasping to the
    throat:
Clear, fragrant, ice-cool liquor, not for base men to drink;
And white yeast has been mixed with must of Wu to make the
    clear Chu wine.
O soul, come back and do not be afraid.

Musicians from Dai, Qin, Zheng and Wei are ready with their
    pipes;
They play the 'Jia Bian' of Fu Xi and the 'Lao Shang' of Chu.
The singers chorus 'The Sunny Bank' to the music of Zhao
    flutes.
O soul, come back and tune the mulberry zither!

Two teams of eight join in a dance to the chanting of poetry;
Bells and stone-chimes sound in unison as the musicians move
    into the *luan*,
And the four trebles blow with all their might as they enter the
    final modulation.
O soul, come back! Listen to their songs and lays!

Ah, the vermeil lips and dazzling teeth, lovely and alluring!
The uniformity of excellence, skilful and imposing!
The well-rounded flesh and fine bones, elegant and pleasing!
O soul, come back to solacing and comfort!

And there are lovely eyes, flashing smiles from under long, moth-
    like eyebrows,
And faces of delicate refinement, glowing with the rosy flush of
    youth:
Beauty overflowing in abundance, goodness and grace to match
    it.
O soul, come back! Enjoy this in quietness!

There are plump cheeks and small tilted ears and eyebrows
    arched compass-fine;
The softness and grace of gesture that betokens a generous
    nature;

Small waists and necks long and slender as golden *xian-bei*
    buckles.
O soul, come back! Let resentful thoughts be banished!

65   There are those who bring ease for the heart in every one of
    their movements;
Whose powder and eyebrow black give off a rich perfume.
Half-hiding their faces behind long sleeves, well they know how
    to detain a guest!
O soul, come back and fill your night with pleasure!

Ah, the straight brows, jet in hue, the lovely eyes, large and
    lustrous!
70   The dimpling cheeks and fine teeth, flashing in winning smiles!
The well-rounded flesh and fine bones, the lithe and graceful
    limbs!
O soul, come back! Enjoy what gives you comfort!

The main hall is large and spacious; the audience chamber
    resplendent with scarlet woodwork;
A solar in the southern building rises high above the roof-eaves;
75   And loggias run round about, and covered walks for exercising
    beasts in . . .

Here you may gallop or amble at leisure, or hunt in the spring-
    quickened park.
Jade are the hubs of your chariot, and its chased yoke-bar
    splendid with patterned adornment.
Wild parsnip, orchid and cassia grow thickly beside the way.
O soul, come back! Indulge your heart's desire!

80   The gardens are stocked with peacocks; phoenixes too are found
    there;
The jungle-fowl chorus at dawn; bald crane are mixed among
    them;
Swans fly to and fro; green geese wander around.
O soul, come back! The phoenixes are hovering.

Come the sleek, happy face, and lusty, sanguine health:
85   A body that will maintain fitness to ripe old age.

Your family and household fill the court, distinguished, all, in
    rank and office.
O soul, come back, and dwell at peace in your household!

From all your land, by every road, like the clouds assembling:
The great lords of the three sceptres, godlike in giving dooms,
Watching over the young and meek, upholding the orphan and
    the widow.
O soul, come back! Let good governance shine forth!

In your lands and domains of a thousand fields your people teem
    and prosper;
Your benignity falls on all classes of men; glorious are your rich
    favours;
Dread goes before you; peaceful arts follow you; the beauty of
    your goodness is manifest.
O soul, come back! And rewards and punishments shall be justly
    meted.

Your fair fame, like the sun, shines over every land;
The report of your goodness equals Heaven's; myriads live in
    your peace.
North up to You-ling and south as far as Jiao-zhi;
West all the way to the Sheep's Gut Pass and eastward to the
    sea's edge.
O soul, come back! Raise up good men to office!

Proclaim your rule! Show forth your acts! Restrain the cruel
    oppressor!
Lift up excellence to the place of counsel! Punish the infamous
    and mean!
The Just and Good sits on the throne, most like Great Yu in his
    command.
The flower of chivalry hold governance, from whom flows favour
    over all.
O soul, come back, and let the state be ruled!

In glory and majesty your godlike power is revealed.
With stately mien your Dukes ascend and descend in the hall.
The Princes are all assembled; the Nine Ministers have taken
    their places;
The butts are clearly marked out; the leather targets are
    stretched:
110 Holding their bows and grasping their arrows, they bow and
    defer with ceremonial courtesies.
O soul, come back! Revive the ways of the Three Kings of old!

Note

*l.*63 xian-bei *buckles*: another 'spelling' of the foreign word which
    appears as *xi-bi* in *Zhao hun*, *l.*114; probably a reference to the
elongated animal shapes with which they were decorated.

Xi shi *'Sorrow for Troth Betrayed'*

In the original order *Xi shi* came between *Ai shi ming* and *Da zhao*,
after Liu Xiang's *Jiu tan*. In other words, it is unlikely to have
been part of Liu Xiang's *Chu ci* and must be thought of as a very
late addition to the anthology. Wang Yi's brief preface to it is at
first sight rather puzzling:

> The authorship of *Xi shi* is unknown. Some people say it is by
> Jia Yi, but I doubt whether this could be verified. '*Xi*' means 'to
> regret', 'to feel sorry about'; '*shi*' means 'promise' or
> 'undertaking'. The words '*xi shi*' are an expression of sorrow for
> King Huai's broken faith. In the old days, when a ruler engaged
> a minister to help him in government, he entered into a solemn
> covenant with him in order to establish a close relationship of
> mutual trust between them. *Xi shi* is an indictment of King
> Huai's failure to remain faithful to this agreement.

Since the only Chu poet known to have been a contemporary of
King Huai is Qu Yuan, it follows that the whole of this preface

from '"*Xi*" means "to regret"' onwards must have been written not by Wang Yi but by someone who thought that the author of *Xi shi* was Qu Yuan. Wang Yi incorporated this earlier preface by someone else in his new edition, merely substituting the two sentences about authorship for the original opening of the earlier preface. This is certainly not the only one of Wang Yi's prefaces which represents a mere recycling of pre-existing material. In the preface to *Tian wen* he indicates quite openly that he is quoting someone else.

But there is more that is puzzling in this preface than the contradictory statements about the poem's authorship. The statement that it is an indictment of a king's inconstancy (whether or not the king in question was King Huai) bears no relation to the actual content of the poem.

On the analogy of *Xi song* and *Xi wang ri* (Nos. I and VII of *Jiu zhang*) this poem ought to be called *Xi yu nian lao*, since these are the words with which the first line of the Chinese text begins. To judge from the occasional broken lines, missing rhymes and general disjointedness of the sense, the text of *Xi shi* appears to contain several lacunae. It therefore seems extremely likely that a section is missing from the beginning of it which did in fact begin with the words '*Xi shi*'. Like other poems we have already examined in this anthology, *Xi shi* turns out to be a fragment.

The opinion of 'some people', which Wang Yi mentions only to reject it, was probably based on the fact that *ll.*69–76 of *Xi shi* are partly a paraphrase and partly a copy of passages from Jia Yi's 'Lament for Qu Yuan' (see pp. 51–2). The reappearance of lines from Jia Yi's 'Lament' in *Xi shi* would seem to indicate, if anything, that Jia Yi was *not* the author of the latter, particularly in view of Wang Yi's unusual scepticism, yet two great twelfth-century editors, Hong Xing-zu and Zhu Xi, both decided that the literary merit of *Xi shi* was such that 'only Jia Yi could have written it'.

In spite of their formidable sponsorship, we must, I think, eliminate Jia Yi as a possible author of this poem. Its references to the Great Unity (*l.*10), to Bactria (*l.*20), and to the Qing Shang music (*l.*30) suggest a considerably later date than 168 B.C., the year of Jia Yi's death; and the repeated complaints of age and decrepitude seem unlikely to have come from one who was still in his thirties when he died. *Xi shi* must, I think, along with so much else in this anthology, be ascribed to Anon. Its date is probably the same as or a little later than that of *Yuan you*, with which it has a good deal in common. (Like *Yuan you*, it is heavily influenced by the ideas of Han Taoism.) Though unoriginal in theme, its description of air travel, written in a pre-aeroplane age, is exhilarating and rather impressive.

Oppressed by each day's new signs of age and decay,
By the swift, irreversible passage of the years,
I climbed the blue heaven, mounted up on high,
And, passing over a myriad peaks, farther and farther I flew.

5   I looked down on the meanders of great rivers,
Came where the four seas drenched me with their spray . . .
Then I climbed to Heaven's Pole and rested there a while,
Sucking dewy vapour to fill my emptiness.
I caused the Scarlet Bird to fly before me;

10 I rode in the ivory chariot of the Great Unity:
The coiling Green Dragon ran in the left-hand traces;
The White Tiger made the right hand of my team . . .
The sun and moon served me for carriage-awning;
I carried Jade Girls at the back of my chariot.

15 Galloping onwards through the midst of sombre shadows,
I came at last to rest on the mountain of Kun-lun.
Limitless bliss is there without surfeit.
But though I should have liked to stay and sport there with the
    spirits,
I crossed the Red Water and rode still onwards . . .

20 On my right the Bactrians with their foreign ways . . .

                                   ★

[I caused] the great swan to soar: at a single wing-clap
We saw every wind and bend of mountain and river . . .
[I caused the great swan to] soar a second time,
And we looked on the whole world, round heaven and square
    earth.

25 We gazed down on the Middle Land with its myriad people
As we rested on the whirlwind, drifting about at random.
In this way we came at last to the moor of Shao-yuan:
There, with the other blessed ones, were Red Pine and Wang
    Qiao.
The two Masters held zithers tuned in perfect concord:

30 I sang the Qing Shang air to their playing.
In tranquil calm and quiet enjoyment
Gently I floated, inhaling all the essences.
But then I thought that this immortal life of the blessed
Was not worth the sacrifice of my home-returning . . .

★

If the great swan is late on his journey and tries to alight
    somewhere,
He is mobbed by owls who prevent his rest.
If the godlike dragon is stranded on dry land,
His body becomes a prey to ants.
[If it is thus with the great swan and the godlike dragon,
then how much the more must this be true of the good man
    born in an age of disorder.]
Old age comes creeping on me and growing decrepitude;
And I turn this way and that and have no rest.
The vulgar crowd stream on, never stopping;
The crooked forgather to bend the straight.
You must seek advancement by sneakingly conforming
Or else you must live obscure and hide yourself far away.
It is hard that weights and measures should be judged with so
    little discernment,
And the beam and scraper be forced, and the true amount
    falsified.
Some sway this way and that in unprincipled compliance;
Some with straight speaking harshly voice their mind.
It grieves me that what is true and right should not be examined,
That straw and silk should be twisted into the one same rope.
Men's eyes are darkened in this present age,
Unable to tell black from white or foul from fair.
They reject tortoise-shell and jade, the treasure of hill and pool,
But all are agreed in prizing worthless pebbles.
Mei Bo, for his protests, ended in pickled pieces;
Lei Ge, by his compliance, held power in the land.
It grieves me that the good, who gave all their devotion,
Are, for their pains, undone by little men.
Bi Gan made loyal protest, and his heart was cut from his body;
Ji Zi let his hair loose and pretended to be mad.
If water is turned back at source, then the stream will run dry;
If a tree is sundered from its roots, it cannot grow.
I set no store by my body; I take no thought of danger;
But I shrink from suffering if it brings no results . . .

[LUAN]

Ah me!
Have you not seen the phoenix, soaring on high?
70   He roosts far away in the wild of the Great Outlands.
From pole to pole he wanders in hovering circuit,
And only where virtue is enthroned will he deign to alight.
Even so the Wise Man, with his godlike virtue,
Withdraws from an evil age and hides himself away.
75   For if the kylin could be constrained and bound,
What would distinguish him from common cattle?

Notes

*l.*14 *Jade Girls*: the Jade Girls or Jade Women were star spirits,
ethereal beings of great beauty and dazzling whiteness who
feature a good deal in Taoist mythology.

*l.*20 *the Bactrians with their foreign ways*: the mention of Da-xia
(Bactria), Tai Yi ('the Great Unity, *l.*10) and the Qing Shang
music (*l.*30) all in the same poem suggests that *Xi shi* is unlikely to
date from any earlier than the mid second century B.C.

*ll.*39–41 *If it is thus ... age of disorder*: this is obviously part of an old
commentary which got mistaken for part of the text. It must
have been interpolated before Wang Yi edited this text, since he treated
it as part of the poem and wrote several lines of commentary on it!

*ll.*58–63 *Mei Bo ... Lei Ge ... Bi Gan ... Ji Zi*: the same four names
are all mentioned in *Tian wen. ll.*143–8. See *Tian wen*, notes,
on p. 146. 'Lei Ge' is simply another version of the 'Lei Kai' of *Tian
wen*.

Zhao yin shi *'Summons for a Recluse'*

This charming poem is thought to have been written by a poet at the court of Liu An, Prince of Huai-nan (*c.*179–122 B.C.). Liu An was a great patron of learning and literature, and in intellectual distinction his court at Ġhou-chun in Anhui, capital of the last three kings of the Warring States kingdom of Chu, far outshone the Han imperial court. The collection of mainly Taoist treatises which goes by the name of *Huai nan zi* ('The Prince of Huai-nan's Book') and which a great modern authority* has described as 'one of the most important monuments of ancient Chinese scientific thought' was composed under his patronage, and Liu An was himself the author of an introduction to *Li sao* and of the earliest commentary on it. He wrote these at the invitation of his 'nephew' (really his cousin's son), the young Emperor Wu, who succeedèd to the imperial throne in 140 B.C. at the age of sixteen when Liu An was about thirty-nine and whose enthusiasm for Chu literature no doubt owed something to the older man's encouragement.

Liu An was described by his biographer as 'a man who loved books and music but took little pleasure in hunting, shooting or racing, and who sought by a kind of calculating benevolence to win the hearts of the people'. He was a highly ambitious man like his father before him, whose imperial pretensions and treasonable activities had led, in 174 B.C., when Liu An was still a small child, to his death by self-starvation in a sealed prison-carriage on the road to exile. Liu An was a surviving grandson of the Founding Emperor, and the accession of his young and childless 'nephew' led to the not unreasonable hope that illness or accident might one day seat him upon the imperial throne – a hope which was considerably strengthened when the all-powerful chancellor, the Marquess of Wu-an, went out of his way to assure him, during one of his visits to the capital, that in the event of 'anything happening to the emperor' the Prince of Huai-nan would have his best support. Later, as the chances of legitimate succession began to recede, the intrigues in which he and his family engaged became increasingly treasonable. At the time of his suicide in 122 B.C., when several thousand others lost their lives, he was said to have been planning a full-scale armed rebellion against the emperor.

---

* Joseph Needham in *Science and Civilisation in China*, Vol. 1, Cambridge University Press, 1954.

Traditionally the 'Prince' of this poem is supposed to be Liu An himself and the mountain forest from whose perils he is urged to return represents the jungle of political intrigue in which he had dangerously enmeshed himself; but the poem gains nothing by being taken as a political allegory and I see no reason why it should be understood in this way. Apart from its intrinsic beauty, which has inspired countless echoes and imitations by later poets, it has an importance out of all proportion to its exiguous size because of the corroboration it seems to lend by its presence and position (i.e. original position) in this anthology to the view that Liu An was the first editor of the *Chu ci* poems.

> The cassia trees grow thick
> In the mountain's recesses,
> Twisting and snaking,
> Their branches interlacing.
5 > The mountain mists are high,
> The rocks are steep.
> In the sheer ravines
> The waters' waves run deep.
> Monkeys in chorus cry;
10 > Tigers and leopards roar.
> One has climbed up by the cassia boughs
> Who wishes to tarry there.
> A prince went wandering
> And did not return.
15 > In spring the grass grows
> Lush and green.
> At the year's evening,
> Comfortless,
> The cicada sings with
20 > A mournful chirp.
> Wildly uneven,
> The bends of the mountain:
> The heart stands still
> With awe aghast.
25 > Broken and wild,
> Chilling the heart.

In the deep wood's tangle
Tigers and leopards spring.
Towering and rugged,
The craggy rocks, frowning.
Crooked and interlocked
The woods' gnarled trees.
Green cyprus grass grows in between,
And the rush-grass rustles and sways.
White deer, roebuck and horned deer
Now leap and now stand poised.
Sheer and steep,
Chill and damp:
Baboons and monkeys
And the bears
Seek for their kind
With mournful cries.
Tigers and leopards fight,
And the bears growl.
Birds and beasts, startled,
Lose the flock.
O Prince, return!
In the mountains you cannot stay long.

Qi jian *'Seven Remonstrances'*

In the original order in which the pieces in this anthology were arranged *Qi jian* came between the *Jiu huai* of Liu Xiang's contemporary Wang Bao and Liu Xiang's own *Jiu tan*. Dong-fang Shuo, to whom Wang Yi attributes these poems, was a jester at the imperial court in the early days of Wu Di's reign (140–87 B.C.) who mixed his drolleries with scathing criticisms of the emperor. His dates are unknown, but it is likely that he died before Wang Bao and Liu Xiang were born and therefore most unlikely that Liu Xiang would have placed these poems after Wang Bao's if he too thought that Dong-fang Shuo was their author. In any case, Liu

Xiang had a rather low opinion of Dong-fang Shuo, one of his reasons being that Dong-fang Shuo had belittled the saintly brothers Bo Yi and Shu Qi, who are extravagantly praised, it so happens, in the second of the *Qi jian* poems. Nothing that we know about Dong-fang Shuo leads us to suppose that he was particularly interested in Qu Yuan or that he is likely to have been a writer of poetry in the Chu style – or, indeed, of any poetry at all. In his catalogue of books in the Imperial Library Liu Xiang placed him not among the poets but among the 'miscellaneous writers'. Dong-fang Shuo's first-century biographer explicitly warns us that of all the works popularly attributed to Dong-fang Shuo (evidently there was already a large apocrypha) only those listed in the biography were authentic, and *Qi jian* is not in the list. Like so much else in this anthology, *Qi jian* should probably be ascribed to Anon. Liu Xiang must have placed it at the end of his own edition of the *Chu ci* anthology precisely because of its anonymity. Perhaps it was written by a courtier-poet belonging to the same group as Mei Sheng (see the introduction to *Ai shi ming* on p. 262), whose 'Seven Exhortations to Rise'* might have suggested the idea of a cycle of seven Chu-style poems.

The anonymous author of these poems assumes the persona of Qu Yuan as a poetic convention enabling him to rail with impunity against the injustice of his employer and the iniquity of the times. The poems are extremely derivative, drawing extensively on *Li sao*, *Jiu zhang*, *Jiu bian* and *Yuan you*, but totally lacking the magic, passion and movement of their originals. The conventions of Chu poetry – the symbolism of plant and flower and the parallels drawn from ancient history and mythology – seem in these poems to have become an end in themselves. The result is a long, almost unrelieved litany of complaint which progresses by mere accumulation and ends only when poet, reader and metaphor are all three exhausted.

I 'When First Exiled' (Chu fang)

I was born in the city,
But now I live in the wilds.
My speech was faltering,
And I had no strong supporters.

* See John Scott and Graham Martin (eds.), *Poems of Love and Protest: Chinese Poems from the Sixth Century B.C. to the Seventeenth Century A.D.*, Rapp and Whiting, 1972, pp. 36–48.

My knowledge was shallow, my talents small,
And my experience scant.
I spoke of what was fit,
And so was hated of courtiers.
The king would not see what was of lasting profit,
And in the end I was banished to the wilds.
When I look back and think of what is now past,
I see there is nothing that I could have changed.
The crowd all banded together,
And the king was gradually deluded by them.
The wily flatterer was ever before him;
The wise were forced to guard their silence.
Now that Yao and Shun are dead,
Who cares to be loyal and true?
Steep towers the high hill,
Deep flows the water:
My last day is coming;
I shall share a ditch with the wild deer.
Alone I'll crouch down
And sleep by the wayside.
The world's all the same:
To whom can I speak?
They chase off the swan
But let owls flutter near.
They cut down the orange tree
And plant rows of bitter peach.
The graceful long-leafed bamboo
Grows by the deeps of the river;
Above, the dense growth keeps off the dews,
Below, it is cool when the breezes come . . .
I know we can never be reconciled:
Like bamboo and cypress, we have different natures.
I cannot meet those who have gone before,
Nor wait for those who are yet to come.
Ah sad, blue Heaven!
No one will rescue me.
I am grieved that my prince will not awake;
And only with death will my grief end.

II 'Drowning in the River' (Chen jiang)

1   When I think of the history of bygone ages,
      I see how selfish narrowness is a man's undoing.
      Yao and Shun were sage and full of loving-kindness,
      So later times have praised them and not forgotten them.
5   Duke Huan of Qi was unwise in his appointments,
      But Yi Wu was loyal and his name is glorious.
      Duke Xian of Jin was by Li Ji besotted,
      And Shen Sheng, though filial, met an early end.
      King Yan showed only kindness and righteousness;
10 King Wen of Jing roused himself, and so Xu was lost.
      Zhòu lost his throne by his cruel tyranny;
      Ji Zi foresaw it and pretended to be mad . . .
      The king of Zhou had Lü Wang for his counsellor.
      He followed the ancient ways and acted mercifully,
15 And raised up a mound above the grave of Bi Gan.
      The wise and good admired him and gladly took his side;
      Daily they came streaming in and united with him.
      He made the laws clear and in accord with reason.
      Even the hidden orchid and iris in those days were fragrant.
20 It saddens me that the crowd should all be jealous of me . . .
      I neither care for lands nor hanker after glory,
      But my mind is overcast and afflicted within me.
      I made a chain of orchid and iris for my girdle,
      But it lost its fragrance when I passed through the fish market.
25 The true servant was honest and acted uprightly,
      But he met with detractors and found himself rebuffed.
      The world's ways change; everything is altered;
      I alone am pure and will not submit.
      Bo Yi starved himself on Shou-yang Mountain;
30 Shu Qi's name endures in ever-growing glory.
      The floating clouds spread out, darkening the sky,
      Causing the sun and moon to have no light.
      The loyal servant, true of heart, tries to protest,
      But the sycophant is ever at hand to traduce him.
35 The flowering herbs of autumn give promise of fruition
      When a fine frost falls on them, descending in the night.

Chill blows the autumn wind, bringing death with it,
And the flowers of the field fall before they are full-grown.
The crowd are united in their envy of a good man;
The wise man, isolated, is easily undone.
Though full of good counsels, he is given no employment,
And retires to hide himself away in some mountain cave.
Some have their achievements spoiled or left unconcluded,
Even as Zi Xu, who in death found no grave.
The world follow fashion and change themselves to suit it,
Bowing when the wind blows and falling into line.
The true withdraw themselves, defeated;
The false advance and win acceptance.
It is too late now to regret what is past:
Giving all one's loyalty never brings rewards.
The others reject all rules; they refuse to use them;
Diligent for private ends, but not the common weal.
I shall never change, though; I shall keep my honour;
Yet I grudge to die now, before my proper time.
I shall take a barge and go sailing down the river,
Lest by some good chance my lord should yet come to his
    senses.
It pains me that loyal words should always give offence,
That Shen Tu was driven to drown himself in the river.
I wanted to impart all the lore that I had gathered,
But my lot was to have a prince who would not listen to me.
He will not open his eyes, he will not be guided;
He cannot distinguish between warp and weft.
By listening to the idle talk of treacherous ministers
He has cut off his country's hope of a safe future.
He destroys square and compass; he will not use them;
He turns from the straight line that the inked string marks.
He will not awake until disaster overtakes him,
Till the fire is already loose in the autumn brushwood:
Already it will be too late; no chance of stopping it;
No time will be left for debating the disaster.
The others draw themselves apart and band themselves in
    factions;
The man that walks a lone course has no one he can turn to.

Slowly my lord was infected, till he no more knew himself,
Changed as the beasts in autumn when their winter coats grow
    through.
75 Many light things heaped up can at last break the axle;
The first fault, by complication, brings heavy consequences.
If I cast myself in the Yuan or Xiang's flowing waters,
The waves might carry me eastwards to the sea.
Let me fill my bosom with gravel and sink to the river's bottom
80 I can no longer bear to look on my prince's folly.

III 'Disgust with the World' (Yuan shi)

The world is sunk and foul and undiscriminating,
Its ways irregular as jagged rocks.
The pure and clear is stopped at source;
The turbid ever grows in volume.
5 The owls have gathered in a flock;
The black crane folds his wings and hides away.
Bramble and mugwort enter the very bedchamber;
The blue daisy shoots up and multiplies;
Yet peony, iris and spikenard are rejected.
10 What can I do if the world cannot tell what is fragrant?
How level and smooth the great highway was!
But foul weeds have choked it and made it hard to follow.
Gao Yang for no fault was compassed in dust of war;
Yao and Shun's reputations are besmirched by gossip.
15 Who can any longer tell what the truth was?
Even with the Eight Wise Helpers he could never do it.
Yet, notwithstanding, Heaven keeps its height;
And Earth retains its everlastingness.
I shall wear white and wander at my will;
20 Let them keep their dark finery, I'll be a different colour.
Xi Shi, for all her graces, gets no audience;
But Mo Mu, crooked and stunted, is ever in attendance.
The cassia grub has not the sense to stay in the cassia;
The bitter polygonum's grub will not move to the sweet mallow

Living in the darkness of an impure age,
How can my ambitions ever find fulfilment?
My thoughts have that in them which prompts me to travel far,
But it is not something that the crowd would understand.
Qi Ji was stumbling between the shafts of a broken cart;
Only when he met Sun Yang was he put to better use.
Lü Wang was poor and wretched and had no livelihood;
Then he met King Wen of Zhou, and at last he could have his
   wish.
Ning Qi sang the pedlar's song as he fed his ox;
Duke Huan heard it and did not reject him.
The girl at the hostelry was picking mulberry leaves:
Confucius came over and waited on her.
I alone am at odds with the world and have not met my match;
Therefore my heart is sore and my thoughts are in confusion.
I think what became of Bi Gan for all his loyalty;
I think what became of Zi Xu for all his care.
And I grieve, too, for Bian He, the man of Chu:
The jade he presented was judged worthless stone.
Both King Li and King Wu refused to examine it,
And he ended with both his feet cut off for his pains.
When it is a little man in the place of power,
See how he regards the loyal and true!
He changes the ordinances of the wise men of old,
Delights in whisperings, acts with abandon,
Is familiar with flatterers, distant with the good and wise,
But reproaches Lü Ju for being ill-favoured!
Since he sees only favourites and keeps the others hidden,
How can he ever tell which is black, which white?
I never shall find a way of showing what is in me;
Always it must be suppressed and never find an outlet.
I summoned all my subtlety to make my meaning clear to him,
But I was kept screened from him in darkness and obscurity.
Of the years of my life's span already half are numbered,
Yet still I stick fast, bogged in difficulties.
I wish I could fly up high and settle far away;
But I fear I might fall in his net and be destroyed.
Better to throw myself into the river's waters

And set my spirit hurrying across its swift currents.
I would rather become mud in the bed of the sea or the river
Than look any longer on this unclean age.

IV 'Embittered Thoughts' (Yuan si)

The good man is afflicted and lives in obscurity;
Scrupulous in honesty, he will not compromise.
Zi Xu protested and lost his life;
Bi Gan was loyal, but had his heart cut out;
5   Zi Tui carved his own flesh to feed his lord with,
But his service was forgotten; deeply he was wronged.
Though your acts are shining white, the world will call them
    black;
Thorns will crowd about you until they make a forest.
Gracillary is cast out into the alley-way;
10 Tribulus spreads over the eastern hall.
The good man is hidden and may not show himself;
The flatterer goes in and makes himself seen.
Owls go in together and hoot in a chorus,
But the phoenix flies off and soars up high.
15 Oh, if only once I could see him, could go hurrying straight to
    his side!
But the way to him is blocked and impassable . . .

V 'Oppressed by Grief' (Zi bei)

Living in misery, to whom can I make my plaint?
Alone I long ponder, sad and melancholy.
When I look within myself I am not ashamed:
My fortitude is firmer and knows no diminution.
5   Three years in obscurity – and still no remission!
My time runs out swiftly as a collapsing wall.
I grieve that I have not life enough left to fulfil my wish:

I long to return for a single glimpse of him.
Sad that my human lot is so unfortunate,
I leave these things to God's will and the stars of heaven.
My body is sick of a sickness that will not leave me;
My heart heaves with passion like boiling water.
Ice and hot coals cannot stay in the same place together;
And full well I know that my life will not be a long one.
Alas, that my lot should be so wretched and so joyless!
Alas, that the sum of my years should be foreshortened!
I grieve that I may not return to where I used to dwell;
I lament to be separated from my home.
When birds are startled and lose the flock,
They still fly aloft, calling with mournful cries.
The fox when he dies needs must lie towards his earth;
And all men, in the end, revert to their true natures.
The old courtiers grow strangers, each day more forgotten;
The new ones are ever near and growing in his favour.
None of them can walk straight in the gloom of darkness;
None can perform without hope of reward.
Grieved that the crowd should all be of this nature,
I mounted on the whirlwind and journeyed far away.
I swept over Heng-shan as though it were a molehill:
In such delights as this I would forget my sorrow.
Yet it vexed me to think of those idle, lying voices,
To think that mouths, being many, should have power to make
   metal molten.
As I passed over my old home, I took one look back at it,
And I sobbed until my coat-front was all wet with my tears.
But I must become as one made of hard white jade on the
   outside,
Having a *wan-yan* jewel inside him for a heart.
Then, when the breath of evil, entering, troubles my bosom,
The jade of my outward parts will but shine with a brighter
   radiance.
How the livid clouds spread out till they covered all the heavens!
How the fine frost fell till it mantled all the earth!
The soft wind blew in uncertain eddies;
The wild wind passed with a rushing blast.

I heard South Land music and wanted to go there,
And coming to Gui-ji I rested there awhile.

45   There I met Han Zhong, who gave me lodging.
I asked him wherein lay the secret of heaven's Tao.
Borrowing a floating cloud to take me on my journey,
With the pale woman-rainbow as a banner to fly over it,
I harnessed the Green Dragon to it for my swift conveyance,

50   And off in a flash we flew, at a speed that made the eyes dim.
Where would it take us to, this frenzied travelling?
Distractedly I wondered where I was going . . .
[Distressed that the mass of men are not to be trusted,
I wished to leave the crowd and remove far off.

55   Climbing a mountain peak, I looked into the distance,
Admired the cassia that flowers in winter time . . .]
I gazed at the glaring blaze of the Fire of Heaven;
I listened to the sound of waves in the Great Deep.
I clung to the Eight Cords to guide my progress;

60   I sipped the dewy vapours to give me long life.
I take no pleasure now in the things the world cares for.
My food is the autumn fruits of plants and trees;
My drink the morning dew on bamboo and azalea.
I have built myself a house of osmanthus wood;

65   I have planted an orchard of orange and pumelo,
And rows of lily-magnolia and pepper-privet.
The solitary jungle fowl cries all through the night,
Mourning the constancy of the dweller there.

VI 'Mourning My Lot' (Ai ming)

I mourn that my lot was cast in an unfit time;
I grieve for the many woes of the land of Chu.
My nature was one of spotless purity,
But I fell on a time of disorder and met with disgrace.

5   Hating the upright dealing of an honest man,
The muddy, impure world could not understand me.
My prince and I – we were so much at odds,

I removed myself from him to wander by Yuan and Xiang.
There I threw myself into the Mi-luo's waters,
For I knew there was no hope that the world might change.
Anguish of parting and broken hopes assailed me,
And I turned in the water, but already the current had carried
    me far.
I had entered the gloomy gates of the House of Darkness
Hidden in caverns under the rocky cliff-face.
Henceforth the water-serpents must be my companions,
And dragon-spirits lie with me when I would rest.
How sheer and awful were the towering rocks overhead!
My fainting soul shrank back, oppressed;
And as I lay, mouth full of water, deep below the surface,
The light of the sun seemed dim and very far above me.
Mourning for its body, dissolved now by decay,
My unhoused spirit drifted, disconsolate.
Remembering how Orchid and Pepper had lost their fragrance,
My soul was confused, it could see no way ahead.
If only I could be sure that my acts had been faultless
I could still be happy, even in my dissolution.
Yet I grieved that the land of Chu was sinking to destruction;
I was sad that the Fair One had advanced so far in error.
Truly the fashion of this present age is folly;
Foggy of purpose, they lack sense of direction.
I remembered how selfish men had taken charge of policy,
And I been forced into exile, far south of the River.
I remembered how Nü Xu had expostulated with me,
All the tears she had shed for me in sorrowful entreaty.
But I had resolved to die, to abandon the living:
There could be no returning now, even if I tried.
Standing in the pellucid water of the rushing shallows,
I gazed on the rugged peaks of high mountains;
Then, with sad memories of the red cliffs of Gao-qiu,
Plunged once more in the waters, never more to return.

VII 'Reckless Remonstrance' (Miu jian)

It angers me that the Fair One is so fickle.
How short-lived was his resolution!
Alas, that Tai-shan should have become a ditch!
And who would have thought that great rivers could run dry?
5   I wanted to wait on his leisure, to show him my intent;
But I feared to infringe some ban or prohibition.
In the end I restrained my feelings and kept silent;
And so I grieve still in bitter discontent.
Jades and pebbles are kept in the same box;
10 Fish-eyes and pearls are strung on the same string;
Old hacks and thoroughbreds are mixed indiscriminately;
Tired ox and mettled stallion are under the same yoke.
Swiftly the years pass, like flowing water;
Old age draws nearer; I more and more decay.
15 My heart is melancholy and full of troubles;
Tossed and unsettled, I have nothing left to hope for.
Truly this generation are cunning artificers!
They destroy the square and compass and alter all the
    measurements.
Qi Ji they reject and will no longer ride him;
20 Instead, they whip a broken hack when they would take the
    road.
What our present age lacks is not a horse like Qi Ji,
But a fancier like Wang Liang with the skill to drive him.
The good horse sees that the man at the rein is a tyro,
So he kicks up his heels and takes himself far off.
25 If you make the handle straight without regard to the chisel,
I fear it will never fit well in the socket.
And if you disregard the world and keep yourself above it,
The purity of your actions will be displeasing to them.
When the bow is loosened and unstrung,
30 What means is there of knowing how far it can shoot?
When there is no danger of imminent disaster,
How can you know what the good man would die for?
Custom advances the flatterer and promotes the rich man;
The man who acts honestly is shut out and unnoticed.

The wise and good man lives obscure and does not flock with
    others;
His enemies are linked in bands of close fraternity.
Their evil counsels are dressed up fair but full of crookedness;
Their government is selfish, not for the common good.
The righteous man withdraws and escapes into hiding;
The flatterer mounts up into the hall of judgement.
The delights of Peng Xian are discarded;
The inked line of Chui the Cunning is erased.
The good bamboo arrow is mixed with the kindling;
But a bolt of fleabane stalk is shot at a hide target.
If you harness a lame ass to your carriage and drive without a
    whip,
How can you hope to reach the end of your journey?
If you take a straight needle to use as your hook,
How can you hope to catch any fish?
Bo Ya broke the strings of his zither
Because there was no Zhong Zi-qi to hear him play.
Bian He clasps his block of jade and weeps tears of blood:
Where can he find a craftsman good enough to shape it?
Like sounds harmonize together;
Creatures mate with their own kind.
The flying bird cries out to the flock;
The deer calls, searching for his friends.
If you strike *gong*, then *gong* responds;
If you hit *jue*, then *jue* vibrates.
The tiger roars, and the wind of the valley comes;
The dragon soars, and the radiant clouds come flying.
Square and round, being of different shape,
Can by no force be fitted together.
Lie Zi hid away and lived in poverty,
Finding no one in the world worthy to work for.
The common birds have each their place in flock, skein or
    gaggle;
Only the phoenix soars alone and has no place to go to.
Passing through this evil age, my hopes all blighted,
I will go off to the mountain caves and find myself a home there.
I would gladly close my mouth and end my days in silence,

70 But in the past I received great favours from my lord:
So, alone, I nurse my anger and store up my bitterness,
And the darkness of sorrow remains with me, unending.
For three long years now I have locked up these thoughts:
I wish just once I could see him, to tell him all my mind.
75 For if, without seeing him, I told these things publicly,
Who in this generation would understand me?
I lie on my bed of sickness, consumed with constant sorrow;
My true feelings are submerged and may not be expressed.
One cannot with the vulgar crowd reason of higher things:
I grieve because my spirit can find no outlet.

VIII Luan

The phoenix and the phoenix' mate
Grow daily more and more remote;
The geese, the chickens and the ducks
Fill the courtyards and the halls;
5 Farmyard ducks and frogs and toads
Swim about in the lotus pool.
The horse Yao Niao has run off;
A clumsy camel is harnessed in his place.
A leaden knife is borne in with honour;
10 The Tai E sword is flung away.
The holy herb is weeded out;
The poison lily is planted in rows.
Orange and pumelo wither and die;
The bitter plum rustles with rich verdure.
15 The earthenware crock goes up into the audience hall;
The tripods of Zhou are sunk deep in the waters.
From of old things have always been the same:
Why should I complain of the men of today?

Notes

I 'When First Exiled'

l.17 Now that Yao and Shun are dead: i.e. now that there are no longer
good and wise kings, like Yao and Shun, capable of appreciating
honest courtiers.

II 'Drowning in the River'

l.6 But Yi Wu was loyal: Yi Wu was one of the names of the hegemon
Duke Huan of Qi's wise minister Guan Zhong. On his death-bed he
advised the duke against his favourites Shu Diao and Yi Ya, but Duke
Huan disregarded his advice and employed them, with disastrous
consequences.

l.7 Duke Xian of Jin was by Li Ji besotted: Li Ji was the name of Shen
Sheng's wicked stepmother. Cf. *Jiu zhang* I ('Grieving I Make My
Plaint'), *l.*61 and note.

l.9 King Yan showed only kindness and righteousness: a legendary ruler of
the little state of Xu whose benevolence and pacifism led to his
country's destruction by the King of Chu. 'Jing' was another name for
Chu. King Wen of Chu reigned from 689 B.C. to 677 B.C.

l.12 Ji Zi foresaw it and pretended to be mad: Ji Zi's pretended madness
is referred to in 'Heavenly Questions', *ll.*143–8.

l.15 And raised up a mound above the grave of Bi Gan: said to have been
one of King Wu's first acts after the conquest of Shang.

l.30 Shu Qi's name endures: both brothers starved themselves to death
and both won imperishable fame by doing so. Only metrical
considerations have produced this seeming distinction between them.

l.44 Zi Xu, who in death found no grave: because he was sewn up in a
sack and thrown into the river by the ungrateful king of Wu. See
Jiu zhang VII ('Alas for the Days Gone By'), *ll.*39–40 and note.

III 'Disgust with the World'

l.13 Gao Yang for no fault was compassed in dust of war: Gao Yang, *al.*
Zhuan Xu, is the 'high lord Gao Yang' of *Li Sao*'s opening line.
The demon Gong Gong disputed with him for possession of the world.
See note on 'Heavenly Questions', *ll.*7–10.

ll.21–2 Xi Shi ... Mo Mu: the same pair are mentioned in *Jiu zhang*
VII ('Alas for the Days Gone By'), *ll.*60–61.

*l.*30 *when he met Sun Yang*: another name for Bo Le, the great
       horse-fancier. See *Jiu zhang* V ('Embracing Sand'), *l.*64 and note.

*l.*36 *Confucius came over and waited on her*: sericulture, along with the
       spinning and weaving of silk, were among the traditional
occupations of the Chinese woman and collecting mulberry leaves to
feed the silk-worms one of the few occasions she had of going outside
the house. Chinese folk-song and story are full of mulberry-leaf pickers
being accosted by flirtatious or designing males. The girl referred to in
this story (source now unknown) was admired by Confucius for her
maidenly modesty because she did not even look up at his approach.

*l.*41 *Bian He, the man of Chu*: legendary discoverer of an actual,
       historical jade, as famous in Chinese antiquity as the Koh-i-noor
diamond is today. He presented his lump of uncut jade in two reigns,
but each king believed it to be worthless and cut off one of his feet as a
punishment for fraud. Only in the following reign was the great value of
the stone appreciated.

*l.*50 *But reproaches Lü Ju for being ill-favoured*: Lü Ju appears in Mei
       Sheng's 'Seven Exhortations to Rise' in a list of women
world-famous for their beauty. She is said to have been a mistress of the
fourth-century King of Liang whose court was visited by the
philosopher Mencius.

IV 'Embittered Thoughts'

(Only the first eight couplets of this poem have survived. The rest
appears to have been lost.)

*l.*5 *Zi Tui carved his own flesh*: i.e. Jie Zi-tui, the follower of Duke Wen
      of Jin in his years of exile. See *Jiu zhang* VII ('Alas for the Days
Gone By'), *ll.*41–6 and note.

V 'Oppressed by Grief'

*l.*29 *I swept over Heng-shan*: northernmost of the Five Sacred Peaks.
       Rather confusingly the southern one is also called Heng-shan –
written with a different character. The geography of this poem is
puzzling. Heng-shan (the northern one) is on the borders of Shanxi and
Hebei. Unless there is something wrong with the text, the poet must
have temporarily forgotten that he is pretending to be Qu Yuan.

*l.*45 *There I met Han Zhong*: for the Immortal Han Zhong, see note on
       Yuan you, *l.*30. I know of no particular reason why one would
expect to encounter him on the Gui-ji mountain in Zhejiang. A Taoist
adept once met a man riding on a white deer who claimed to be Han

Zhong on the slopes of Hua-shan, the westernmost of the Five Sacred Peaks.

l.52 Distractedly I wondered when I was going: the rhyming couplets break off at this point and the text becomes fragmentary. *Ll.*53–6 seem out of place in this context and are probably interpolated from another poem.

l.59 I clung to the Eight Cords: the Great Circles, which divide the 'fields' of the sky, are here thought of as actual cords radiating from the Celestial Pole.

VI 'Mourning My Lot'

l.33 I remembered how Nü Xu had expostulated with me: in *Li sao, ll.*129 et seq.

l.39 The red cliffs of Gao-qiu: the words *gao qiu* mean 'high hill'. Qu Yuan calls Kun-lun a '*gao qiu*' in *Li sao l.*216. Here it is certainly used as a proper name. I think Wang Yi's statement that 'there was a mountain called Gao-qiu in Chu' was based on a misunderstanding of *Li sao l.*216 – a misunderstanding which the anonymous author of this poem evidently shared.

VII 'Reckless Remonstrance'

l.49 Bo Ya broke the strings of his zither: a legendary musician. When he played, his friend Zhong Zi-qi knew what he was thinking about. He broke the strings of his zither when Zhong Zi-qi died because there was no one left to appreciate his playing. See Appendix III on p. 391 of *The Story of the Stone*, Vol. 4 (Penguin Books, 1982).

l.57 If you strike gong, then gong responds: *gong* and *jue* are two of the notes in the old pentatonic scale (*gong, shang, jue, zhi, yu* = do, re, mi, so, la). *Gong* was the name of the tonic note, so '*gong*-tuning' was the old Chinese name for a musical key.

l.59 The tiger roars, and the wind of the valley comes: the superstition that tigers had some sort of control over the wind had a long survival. In Chapter 23 of the novel *Shui hu zhuan* ('The Robbers of the Marshes') the arrival of the tiger which Wu Song kills with his bare hands is heralded by a fierce gust of wind.

l.63 Lie Zi: a half-legendary Taoist sage. The 'Book of Lie Zi', a collection of stories and sayings that goes under his name, is thought to date from as late as A.D. 300 (see A. C. Graham, *The Book of Lieh-tzu*, John Murray, 1960), but parts of it are very much older.

VIII '*Luan*'

l.7 The horse Yao Niao: one of two horses mentioned in the *Lü-shi chun qiu*, an encyclopedic work produced under the auspices of the First Qin Emperor's putative father, Lü Bu-wei, as 'famous in antiquity for their speed and endurance'.

l.10 The Tai E sword: according to legend, one of the iron swords made by the Wu swordsmith Gan Jiang for the King of Chu.

l.16 The tripods of Zhou: nine cauldrons believed to have been cast by the Great Yu. In the Zhou dynasty they were regarded as symbols of royal power and a vassal 'asking about the tripods' was assumed to be planning mischief against the sacred person of the king. Si-ma Qian's 'History' contains conflicting accounts of what happened to them on the death of the last Zhou king in 256 B.C. According to one of them they were carried off into Qin, according to the other they were lost in a river. A famous Han bas-relief shows servants of the First Qin Emperor engaged in an unsuccessful attempt to raise one of the cauldrons from the water.

Ai shi ming '*Alas That My Lot Was Not Cast*'

Not much is known about Zhuang Ji, the author of this poem. (Wang Yi calls him 'Yan Ji' to avoid the taboo on the personal name of the emperor Ming, who reigned from A.D. 58 to 75.) He was a native of Wu, in what is now southern Jiangsu. His fortunes were linked with those of Zou Yang and Mei Sheng, two poets at the court of Liu Pi, Prince of Wu. The three of them left Wu, probably in 157 B.C. when Liu Pi's treasonable activities, which were to culminate in the Vassals' Rebellion of 154 B.C., were beginning to grow dangerous. They found a new patron in Liu Wu, Prince of Liang, a younger brother of the reigning emperor. Life at the court of Liang soon became as stormy as it had been in Wu. Liu Wu was plotting to succeed his imperial brother, and Zou Yang's opposition to this scheme led to his imprisonment and almost to his death. Zhuang Ji and Mei Sheng, it is said, were too scared to protest. The poets appear to have remained in Liang, however. Mei Sheng once received a summons from the emperor, but seems to have preferred being a literary lion at the provincial court of Liang, to which he soon returned. Whether Zhuang Ji was still alive in 144 B.C. when the Prince of Liang died it is impossible to say.

Ai shi ming is an example of Sao poetry at a very low ebb. Here is all the apparatus of the Sao poet: the symbolism, the parallelism, the allusions, the introspective grief, even – in one brief, perfunctory passage – the spirit journey. But the inspiration is dead. Image is piled upon image in illustration of the same theme: virtue and talent are not recognized; I am virtuous and talented; therefore I am not recognized; therefore I am miserable. The effect of having this said in 160 lines of verse is monotonous and oppressive.

Yet Zhuang Ji was nicknamed 'The Master' by his contemporaries, and *Ai shi ming* was evidently esteemed by other writers sufficiently for them to want to plagiarize it. As in the case of *Qi jian*, the main reason for the discrepancy between modern and contemporary taste is that the poet's situation has lost its poignancy for us and we cannot, except in the most general terms, identify the objects of his scorn and hatred.

Alas that my lot was not cast to meet with the men of old!
How far I was born out of the proper time!
For those that are gone, I cannot reach back to;
And those yet to come, I cannot wait to see.
My mind is full of resentment that finds no outlet.
Only in these verses can I express my feelings.
All the night wakefully watching, I cannot get to sleep;
All through the year my heart is full of care.
My laden heart, to whom could I declare it?
With whom in the crowd could I share my deep counsels?
I am sunk in wretchedness, worn with weariness;
And old age draws near and soon will be upon me.

I dwell in the midst of gloom and sadness,
My high ambitions choked and repressed.
For the road to my lord is blocked and impassable;
The rivers are wide, and there is no bridge.
I wanted to go to the Hanging Garden of Kun-lun,
So I plucked the flower of jade that grows on Zhong Mountain.
Breaking a jewelled spray off from that precious tree,
I gazed on the mountains of Lang-feng and Ban-tong.

But the rushing Weak Water made a barrier
Blocking the road midway and making it impassable.
I had not the power to wade across its waters,
Nor had I wings to fly on high above it.
25 So, disappointed, unable to make the journey,
I wandered back and forth irresolutely.
Sad and disconsolate, I am full of longing;
My heart is constricted and wounded deeply.
Long I delay here, lingering in uncertainty:
30 Each day my hunger grows, for my food is exhausted.
Alone I sit with my shadow, dwelling in isolation,
And long I think with yearning of my old home.
Alone and deserted, without a single friend,
With whom can I enjoy the fragrance that I have got?
35 The bright sun reddens and soon will be setting,
And I mourn because a good old age will not be my portion.
My chariot broken down and my horses weary,
Helpless I hover, unable to go on.
And since I can find no place in this muddy world,
40 Go backwards or forwards – I do not know what I should do.
My towering hat cleaves the clouds;
The sword at my side swings over continents;
My garments seem to constrict and cramp me:
My left sleeve catches on the Fu-sang tree,
45 On the right my skirt brushes the Bu-zhou Mountain:
The world is too narrow for me to move in freely.
The chisel I hold is modelled on that of Fu Xi;
The lines I carve were measured with Yao's and Shun's
      instruments.
Honour I revere: I follow a high example:
50 Even Yu and Tang are unworthy, to my aspiring mind.
Yes, though I am in sore straits, my steadfastness will not alter
I will never harm the straight for the sake of the crooked and
      evil.
Men nowadays league together, each favouring his own friends:
They measure all men by the same corrupt measure.
55 The crowd stand together, shoulder pressed to shoulder;
But the wise draw far off and hide away in retirement.

If you make a quail's cage to put the phoenix in,
Though he fold his wings, it will still be too small for him.
If the Divine King will not wake up and see,
How can I state my case, how show him my loyalty?
The vulgar are jealous and obscure the wise:
Who, then, can understand my behaviour?
I want to unburden my mind, to vent my indignation;
But can I be sure of an auspicious outcome?
Jade sceptres are mixed with shards of pottery;
Long Lian and Meng Ju are lodged in the same palace.
Such now is the whole world's fixed custom:
That is why I am afflicted, and shall end my days in distress.
Alone I toss in the darkness and cannot get to sleep;
Trouble and indignation fill my breast.
My soul goes flying forth from my body,
And my troubled heart is sad and sore.

My mind is disappointed and knows no peace;
For my road is dark and full of difficulty.
Alone, forlorn, I keep to my little corner,
Torn with grief and racked with perpetual sighing.

I mourn through the long nights, tossing and turning,
The breath in me heaving like waves in water.
I have grasped the graver's knife but cannot use it;
I hold the measuring tools, but have nothing to measure.

If you trot Qi Ji in a little courtyard,
How can he show off his long-distance paces?
If you put a monkey inside a narrow cage,
How can you hope to test his agility?

If you try to climb a mountain with a team of lame tortoises,
It seems to me obvious that you will not reach the top.
If, rejecting Guan and Yan, you give office to worthless slaves,
It seems obvious that you will not have a wise administration.

The tough arrow-bamboo is mixed up with the kindling,
While a quarrel of fleabane is shot at the leather target.
Bent double under my load like one that measures his paces,
I could not straighten my back up even if I tried.

Did I go outside, there were spring-traps threatening me;
If I flew up aloft, the barbed line would drag me down.
95   By no twist or turn could I find a place of safety:
Small wonder my insides are cramped so that I scarce can
    breathe!

Wu Guang threw himself in the deep water,
Unable to accept the dust and dirt of the world.
Since no one can last long who is so much beleaguered,
100   I shall withdraw myself and live in poverty.
I shall carve a house for myself between the mountain's pillars;
I shall bathe in the river below before I put on my clothes.
There the foggy dew falls thick in the early morning;
The heavy clouds begin at the very roof-tops;
105   Rainbows shine in the morning mist,
And in the evenings the rain comes drizzling down.
Far and forlorn, with no hope of return:
Sadly I gaze in the distance, over the empty plain.
Below, I fish in the valley streamlet;
110   Above, I seek out holy hermits.
I enter into friendship with Red Pine;
I join Wang Qiao as his companion.
We send the Xiao Yang in front to guide us;
The White Tiger runs back and forth in attendance.
115   Floating on cloud and mist, we enter the dim height of heaven;
Riding on white deer we sport and take our pleasure.

On and on my soul speeds, seeking a lonely dwelling;
Swiftly it goes forth, never to return.
Aloft and aloft we go, ever more distant,
120   Till my mind is unsettled and my heart repines.

The phoenix soars up into the azure clouds,
Where the fowler's barbed cord can never reach him.
The dragon lies low in the swirling waters,
Where the fisherman's nets can never entangle him.
125   He knows he would court death by hankering for bait,
And so he prefers to swim below, in the crystal wave.
It is better to be obscure and keep from misfortune,

Than endure to meet with shame and disgrace.
Zi Xu died to fulfil the right;
Qu Yuan drowned himself in the Mi-luo.
They would not change, even when faced with bodily
   destruction;
For loyalty and faith admit no alteration.
My mind is honest and my heart is true;
I keep my feet unswervingly to the ink-line;
I hold the balance with impartiality,
And measure the true weight without any error.

I have brushed away the dust and disorder,
Purged unclean attachments and returned to the True.
I am clean in body and pure in substance;
My soul within is dazzling in its spotless purity.
Yet the world turns from me in disgust and will not employ me,
And so I will hide myself far away from it.
I will creep away and conceal my traces;
I will keep silent, I will not make a sound.
Alone and ill at ease and full of bitterness:
How can I vent my anger and give my thoughts expression?
The day grows dark and draws towards its ending;
I shall go into the silence, leaving no name behind.
Bo Yi died on Shou-yang Mountain;
He ended in obscurity, distinguished by no honour.
And if Tai Gong had not had the luck to meet King Wen,
He might have gone all his life without finding an opening.
I have gems and ivory at my breast and precious stones at my
   girdle:
I want to show off my treasures, but there are none to judge
   them.
My life here on earth passes rapidly to its ending:
Soon oblivion will come, while I still have no achievements.
The breath of evil penetrates my body,
And diseases sprout up to rack and torment me.
I long for but one more glimpse of the blessed spring's bright
   sun;
But I fear I shall not last until the coming year.

Notes

*ll.*18–20 *Zhong Mountain ... Lang-feng ... Ban-tong*: these names
belong to mythological geography. Zhong Mountain was
supposed to be somewhere in the neighbourhood of the magic
mountain of Kun-lun, and Lang-feng and Ban-tong were often said to
be parts of Kun-lun itself.

*l.*47 *The chisel I hold is modelled on that of Fu Xi*: a mythical 'emperor',
often represented as a consort of Nü Wa, with a serpent's body.
Usually it is a carpenter's square that he holds in his hand.

*l.*66 *Long Lian and Meng Ju are lodged in the same palace*: as members
of the royal harem. The first was a very ugly, the second a very
beautiful woman.

*l.*87 *Guan and Yan*: i.e. Guan Zhong and Yan Ying, two famous
ministers of Qi, the first of Duke Huan, the second of Duke Jing
(*reg.* 547–490 B.C.).

*l.*94 *the barbed line would drag me down*: Chinese fowlers combined the
arts of hunting and fishing by attaching a long silk cord to their
arrows, particularly when hunting water-fowl, which could then be
shot over water and retrieved by hand.

*l.*97 *Wu Guang threw himself in the deep water*: a legendary wise man, so
unworldly that he went off in a rage and drowned himself when
Tang the Successful offered him the world to rule.

*ll.*111–12 *Red Pine . . . Wang Qiao*: Taoist Immortals mentioned in
Yuan you. See the introduction to *Yuan you* and the notes on
Yuan you, *ll.*23 and 54.

*l.*113 *the Xiao Yang*: an anthropoid monster whose upper lip covers
his face when he laughs. His laughter was sinister, it was said,
being an indication that he was about to eat human flesh. He seems a
strange sort of choice for a guide. Perhaps he was chosen because he
inhabits solitary places and Zhuang Ji wanted to emphasize how far he
had withdrawn from the haunts of men.

Jiu huai *'Nine Regrets'*

Wang Bao, the author of *Jiu huai*, came from what, in those days, was a rather remote part of China. Like the famous Si-ma Xiang-ru – one of the greatest poets of the Han dynasty – he was a native of Shu, in what is now the province of Sichuan. He owed his success to his gifts as a song-writer and to a somewhat unamiable talent for turning flatteries into beautiful verse.

He was first heard of by a local official who commissioned him to write panegyrics in praise of the government which were then set to music and performed. One of the performers eventually made his way to the capital, and in the course of time the emperor heard Wang Bao's songs and was charmed by them. In about 58 B.C. Wang Bao received an imperial summons to court, where he was given further commissions and rewarded with an honorary appointment. The emperor took Wang Bao and a number of other poets with him on hunting expeditions and made them write verses about the various palaces and lodges which they visited, awarding prizes for the poems which pleased him most. On one occasion, when the heir apparent was suffering from some sort of melancholia, Wang Bao was sent to cheer him up with recitations from his writings and stayed with him until he was better. Two of Wang Bao's *fu*, 'The Flute' and 'The Gan-quan Palace', particularly delighted the heir apparent, who was constantly asking his concubines and harem attendants to recite them to him.

Wang Bao was not only a poet and musician but also a humorist. 'The Slave's Contract', in which he gets his own back on a curmudgeonly old slave by pretending that he wants to buy him and intimidating him with an immense and comical catalogue of all the duties he will be expected to perform after his purchase, though humour of a somewhat cruel kind, is still quite funny.

Within a year or two of Wang Bao's début as a court poet, news came from Yi-zhou in Sichuan of a green cock and a golden horse which had appeared to many people in the nearby mountains, and Wang Bao, since he came from those parts, was judged a suitable person to invite the golden horse to the capital. He fell ill and died on his way to Yi-zhou, to the great sorrow of the emperor. If the fragment of the invitation which he proposed to read to the theriomorphic apparitions of Sichuan is authentic, it would appear to have been somewhat on the lines of the 'Summons' poems of *Chu ci*.

Jiu huai is written throughout in the Song style. Prosodically, that is, it resembles the 'Nine Songs' rather than *Li sao* or *Jiu zhang*. It is a little strange to find this past master in the art of courtly flattery giving utterance in these poems to the passionate outcries against injustice and corruption which were expected of a Sao poet, but it will be observed that these make up only a small fraction of the whole, which is mostly devoted to 'spirit journeys' of the *Yuan you* variety and contain several indications of that interest in supernatural phenomena which was a feature of the second half of Emperor Xuan's reign. The 'God of the Great Jewel' mentioned in the third poem was later the subject of a long memorial to the throne by Wang Bao's contemporary and colleague Liu Xiang.

Wang Bao's biography is devoid of dates and it is impossible to say when he wrote these poems. Probably it would have been some time between 60 and 50 B.C.

I *'Release from Worldly Contrivings'* (Kuang ji)

My lot was cast in a luckless time:
I must submit to lifelong hardship.
Deep is my sorrow, bitter is my torment.
Oh, but once to tell! – but there is no way.
5   Riding the sun and moon, I travel aloft,
Wishing to divert myself in Hao and Feng.
All over I scan them, in every corner:
I wander up and down in the orchid palaces,
The iris gates, the peony halls,
10   That waft abroad a myriad scents,
The bamboo pavilions and melilotus chambers.
I gaze on the streets each way intersecting:
Bright gold lies in heaps there,
Fine jade fills their halls.
15   Cassia-scented waters bubble,
Gushing in a copious stream.
The ancient turtles leap and sport;
The great cranes circling soar.
I lean on a casement and gaze into the distance,
20   Thinking of my prince, whom I cannot forget.
Gloomy, because I cannot address him,
Long I brood on my inward pain.

ii 'A Road to Beyond' (Tong lu)

The Gate of Heaven, the Door of Earth
Yield no admittance to the wise.
The lawless soil the seat of power;
The virtuous are not looked upon.
Brooding on this, still clothed I sleep;
To whom can I utter words of awakening?
The phoenix, soaring, removes far off;
The fattened quail draws near.
The whale and the sturgeon hide in the deeps;
But frogs are left to sport in the islets.
With team of dragons I mount the heavens,
In ivory chariot borne aloft.
We start from Cong-ling in the morning;
We come to Ming-guang in the evening.
In the north I drink from the Flying Spring;
In the south I pluck flowers of the Holy Herb.
I wander through all the constellations;
I roam about round the Northern Pole.
My upper garment is of red stuff;
Of green silk is my under-robe.
I loosen my girdle and let my clothes flow freely;
I stretch out my trusty Gan-jiang sword.
The Leaping Serpent follows behind me,
The Flying Horse trots at my side.
I caught a glimpse of the Flying Garden,
Surveyed the Bright Shiner, Benetnasch.
I opened a box and drew out divining slips,
And grieved to see what fate was to be mine.
I have plaited orchids and will take my leave for ever;
I will depart from those I love.
The floating clouds that idly drift
Lead me on I know not whither.
Far I gaze into the darkening distance;
I hear the thunder rumble loud.
Melancholy steals upon me;
Disappointed, I mourn my lot.

III 'Dangerous Heights' (Wei jun)

The woods receive not the singing cicada;
How can I stay in the Middle Lands?
In a good month I'll harness my chariot;
I'll pluck the jade flower to bedeck myself with;
5   Then, knotting flowering iris, I'll fare on my journey.
I shall leave the crowd and wander far off,
Through the dreadful heights of the Dai Mountain,
Past the Nine Points and the Cowherd star.
Stealing a little time to wander,
10   I shall roam all round, leaving trails of brightness.
Seeing the Great Unity I stop awhile,
Tie up my bridle and take a rest.
I glance at the bright sun in his dazzling splendour.
Far my way stretches, onward and onward.
15   I turn to watch comets as they rush past me,
Observe the dark clouds as they float by in squadrons.
The God of the Great Jewel moves with a rumble,
And all the cock pheasants cry out to greet him.
Over vast spaces flies my questing spirit;
20   The fear at my heart fills me with unquietness.
I walk my horse up the Flying Pillars,
Looking for one who could be my companion;
But never a glimpse of one do I find,
And long I ponder in deep dejection.

IV 'A Light on the World' (Zhao shi)

The world was dirty and dark:
I left my lord and turned to the truth.
Driving a dragon, twisting and coiling,
Soaring in circles, I mounted on high.
5   Wearing a flowered coat, flame-bright in colour,
And a flowery robe under it, sweetly perfumed,
I mounted on the upward eddies of the whirlwind,

And I had good sport floating on Heaven's River.
Then, calming my spirits, composing my bearing,
I joined the company of the Immortals.
Falling stars descended in a shower
And alighted, glittering, on the hill-tops.
I gazed on my old home, shrouded in darkness:
'How can I stay here much longer?' I thought.
My mind bade me go, but my heart was afraid.
I tied up my bridle and stood hesitating.
I could hear the White Maiden softly singing;
I listened to the Queen blowing on the reed organ.
My soul was troubled and stirred to sadness;
My bowels were twisted into writhing knots.
I fingered my girdle, richly decked with flowers,
And I heaved a huge sigh from the depths of my sadness.
I made Zhu Rong go on before me;
I commanded Zhao Ming to open the gates.
Driving six dragons I ascended,
Riding my chariot into heaven's dim heights.
Through all the world I go, seeking a mate;
But who is there worthy to spend all my days with?
Suddenly I looked back on the West Garden,
And saw the piled mountains' overhanging crags.
The tears in streams came coursing down my cheeks,
As I grieved that my king had lost Heaven's blessing.

v 'Honouring the Good' (Zun jia)

In the late spring warm and bright,
All the flowers grow, row on row:
But I grieve for the orchid and iris
Piled stalk across stalk in dead heaps,
And gracillary, cast away unwanted,
And lily-magnolia, stifled and obscured.
I think then of the good men of old:
How many of them met with an evil end.

Wu Xu floated down the Great River;
10   Qu Yuan drowned himself in the Xiang.
     My thoughts revolve over these things, pondering,
     And my heart is pained within me.
     I look on the Huai river's seething waters,
     And go to my hiding, racing along their stream.
15   My boat slips downstream in the current
     That eastwards flows amidst boom of boulders.
     Water-dragons lead the way;
     Striped fish jump across the rapids.
     Rushes I pluck for mats to sit on,
20   Water-grasses to make an awning.
     The water leaps up at my pennant
     And gives it a fine trail of water-weed.
     Banners of cloud advance like the lightning
     As, swiftly darting, I speed on my way.
25   The Lord of the River opens his gates
     And comes to meet me with glad welcome.
     My thoughts turn back to my homeland's city:
     I am full of sorrow for its troubles.
     And I am sad for the floating duckweed
30   That floats about, rootless, on the water.

VI 'Stored Blossoms' (Xu ying)

The autumn wind blows chill and keen,
Loosing the blossoms and shaking the boughs.
When the small frost falls, fine and light,
The singing cicada sickens and dies.
5   The swallows, leaving for their return,
     Fly circling round the Holy Hill.
     I look down on the mist-shrouded valley
     And hear the snarl and roar of bears.
     Yao and Shun are now no more:
10   What reason have I long to stay?
     I look down on the racing waters;

Glance back at the deserted woods.
Gathering my robe about me,
I bestride the rainbow and mount on high
And on the clouds I ride around;
Then, exhausted by my labours,
Come to rest on a bank of orchid.
Despondent at my hopes' frustration,
Dark with a black cloud of stored sorrow,
Listlessly I think of my lord:
My body has left, but my thoughts stay with him,
And melancholy fills my breast.

VII 'Thoughts on Loyalty Bent' (Si zhong)

Climbing the heavens, my soul wanders free.
In the pale dawn the Virgin is singing.
I grieve for the arrowroot heaped on the hill,
All mixed together in promiscuous confusion.
The straight stems are crushed down to wither and die.
The crooked ones raised up to the sky's bright vapours.
My mind is pierced with a pang of grief;
My heart for pity sadly sorrows.
Driving black dragons, I travel northwards,
Directing my course towards the Cong-ling mountains.
Linking the Five Constellations to make a pennant,
Waving the vapours of air as my banner,
Through the vast tracts of the sky I go rushing,
The Middle Land in the distance below me.
Xuan Wu and the Water Mother go
To meet me in the verdant south.
I climb to the Flowery Awning and chariot on the brightness:
Let me wander here for a while diffusing radiance.
I lay hold of Ku-lou to ladle my wine with,
Seize hold of the Melon to eat with my food.
Having rested, I start again on my far journey,
Take off the jade brake and make towards the west.

I think how the world is averse to righteousness,
And I know I cannot stay in these parts for long.
25   Waking, I beat my breast and brood,
And my heart is troubled and grieves within me.

VIII 'Raising Barriers' (Tao yong)

When I watch this benighted world's devices
I despair; but where else can I go?
Grieved by the disorder of their manners,
I shall shake my wings and fly high above them.
5   Harnessing an eightsome of writhing dragons,
Raising a fluttering rainbow banner,
I gaze down on the mid-world's vastness,
And mount aloft in noble array.
I float over the Weak Water, radiating brightness;
10   On its high banks then, halting hesitantly,
I rest my chariot, seeking a companion.
I visit the Lord of Heaven and ask him for instruction:
He says, 'No Way is more precious than Returning to the True
Those who love my teachings shall find tranquillity.'
15   So I pursue my journey to the world's southern shore,
Taking a gloomy road through Doubting Mountain.
I cross ten thousand miles of flaming fire,
Pass over ten thousand towering mountain peaks.
Fording seas and rivers, I slough off my old body;
20   Leaving North Bridge behind, I take my leave for ever.
The floating clouds gather and darken the day;
The dust storm rises suddenly, blinding.
I rest in the great halls of the Summer City.
My face is haggard, my spirit is weary;
25   But my mind is illumined with understanding:
Here in this place I shall find self-knowledge.
I think of Yao and Shun transmitting their great heritage,
Favouring Gao Yao and adopting his counsels.

It grieves me that in all the earth's nine lands there is no worthy
   master.
Sighing I lean on my chariot rail and compose these verses.

IX 'Quenching the Light' (Zhu zhao)

Woe and alas! my heart within is torn.
The winter heliotrope is dead, its leaves and stems blighted.
Shards and stones are prized as jewels, Sui and He rejected.
The leaden knife is praised for sharpness, Tai E discarded as
   blunt.
The thoroughbred droops his ears; for a long time now no one
   has used him.
A lame ass draws the chariot and stumbles half-way up the hill.
The pure are in hiding; the favoured are fools.
The phoenix may not soar; but quails vaunt their flight.
Harnessing steeds of the rainbow to my chariot, I ride
   transfigured above the clouds.
The *jiao-ming* bird clears the way before me; green snakes follow
   in my train.
We gallop through the cassia woods, we vault over dangerous
   places.
The mountain peaks leaped and danced, the valleys sang for joy,
And the words of the sacred books were chanted in harmony to
   the tune.
I alone was there to enjoy it: such pleasure none could add to.
I turned and looked back at the foolish world, lost in
   destruction's nets.
I twisted my girdle, preparing to depart, and my tears fell in
   streams.

x Luan

Heaven opens up its gates and shines down on the world.
Stumps and weeds are cleared away; orchid and iris are
    disclosed.
When the four Evil Ones were banished, after them came Yu.
Sage Shun held the power, making Yao's tradition bright.
Who could be like them? Him would I serve!

Notes

I 'Release from Worldly Contrivings'

*l.*6 *Hao and Feng*: ancient cities of Shaanxi where the early Zhou kings
    Wen and Wu are said to have had their capitals. In Wang Bao's
time they were no more than a memory. He means, I think, that he
wishes to return in spirit to a long-vanished Golden Age. His vision of it
is a purely fanciful one and in any case soon recedes.

II 'A Road to Beyond'

*ll.*13–14 *Cong-ling ... Ming-guang*: Cong-ling (the Onion Peaks) was
    the Han name for the Pamirs. Ming-guang (Bright Light) is
unidentified. I suspect that Wang Bao sometimes uses exotic or even
made-up names because they sound good and with no particular
location, either real or imaginary, in mind.

III 'Dangerous Heights'

*l.*17 *The God of the Great Jewel moves with a rumble*: refers to a cult of
    Qin origin extremely popular during the Former Han dynasty.
The god worshipped was an anthropomorphic figure with a pheasant's
head, and his name was Chen Bao or Tian Bao ('Heavenly Jewel': the
'Great Jewel' of this text). His coming was heralded by a shower of
lights like falling stars and a crashing sound like stones being knocked
together. This sound was answered by the crowing of all the cock
pheasants in the neighbourhood.

*l.*21 *the Flying Pillars*: a magic mountain.

IV 'A Light on the World'

l.8 floating on Heaven's River: the Milky Way.

ll.17–18 the White Maiden ... the Queen: the White Maiden is a fairy lady who makes frequent appearances in Taoist texts as an interlocutor of the Yellow Ancestor. The Queen is, I think, Nü Wa, whose servant Sui invented the mouth-blown reed organ or *sheng* (Japanese *shō*).

l.23 Zhu Rong: Spirit Guardian of the South. Cf. *Yuan you, l.143*.

l.24 I commanded Zhao Ming to open the gates: Zhao Ming was the name of one of the pre-dynastic ancestors of the Shang kings, but I do not think he is meant here. Wang Yi's commentary on this line glosses 'Zhao Ming' as 'the Fiery God' (whoever that is). Since Zhao Ming occurs in one of his own poems, it must be assumed that he is speaking with some knowledge. Perhaps it is the sun.

V 'Honouring the Good'

l.9 Wu Xu floated down the Great River: i.e. Wu Zi-xu, the unfortunate minister of the King of Wu, generally referred to as Zi Xu.

VII 'Thoughts on Loyalty Bent'

l.15 Xuan Wu and the Water Mother: Xuan Wu is the turtle guardian of the north. The Water Mother is a kind of naiad.

ll.17–20 the Flowery Awning ... Ku-lou ... the Melon: these are all names of constellations.

VIII 'Raising Barriers'

l.16 Doubting Mountain: where Chong Hua (Shun) lies buried.

l.20 Leaving North Bridge behind: North Bridge here and the Summer City of *l.23* are unidentifiable.

IX 'Quenching the Light'

l.3 Sui and He rejected: two priceless jewels – the pearl of the Marquess of Sui and the jade of Bian He. The Marquess of Sui cured a wounded snake which some time later emerged from a river with a pearl in its mouth and presented it to him as a token of its gratitude. For Bian He's jade, see *Qi jian* III ('Disgust with the World'), *l.41* and note.

*l.*4 *Tai E*: the famous sword which the legendary smith Gan Jiang made for the King of Chu.

*l.*10 *The* jiao-ming *bird*: this appears to be another name for the jiao-peng, explained by glossarists as 'a phoenix-like bird which inhabits the South'.

'Luan'

*l.*3 *the four Evil Ones*: identified as the demon Gong Gong, Yu's father Gun (more unlucky, one would have thought, than evil), a somewhat obscure villain called Huan Dou, and the San Miao, from whom the Miao tribes are supposed to be descended.

Jiu tan *'Nine Laments'*

Liu Xiang (77–6 B.C.), the author of *Jiu tan*, is known to scholars chiefly as a bibliographer of prodigious industry and achievements. Indeed, so many and varied were his accomplishments that few would think of him as a poet – though it was in fact as a poet that he began his career at the emperor Xuan's court (not counting his boyhood years as a page) at about the same time as Wang Bao.

Liu Xiang was a very different sort of person from Wang Bao. In the first place he was nobly born, a member of the imperial Liu clan. His father was a marquess, and great-grandson of the first Han emperor's younger brother, the Prince of Chu. And though engaged throughout his life in scholarship and letters and almost always unsuccessful as a politician, Liu Xiang undoubtedly regarded himself first and foremost as a statesman.

His career began disastrously. He had somehow obtained possession of a 'pillow-book' of Liu An, the unfortunate Prince of Huai-nan, called 'Secrets of the Garden of Great Treasures', which purported to show how gold could be made alchemically and life indefinitely prolonged. Aware of the emperor Xuan's growing interest in the occult, the youthful Liu Xiang (he was about twenty-one at the time) thought to win favour by presenting the recipe for gold to the emperor. Unfortunately the experiments were not only unsuccessful but vastly expensive, and Liu Xiang found himself in prison and facing a death sentence. He was saved from this only by the exertions of his elder brother, the new marquess, who obtained a pardon for him by making over half his estates to the central government.

Liu Xiang's talents were too great to remain neglected for long. Next year he was given an academic post, followed, four years later, by appointments to advisory posts in the government. He rose to even higher position under the auspices of the great Confucian scholar Xiao Wang-zhi at the beginning of Emperor Yuan's reign in 48 B.C. Unfortunately the new emperor was a weak and vacillating person, more interested in music than in statecraft, and increasingly under the influence of his mother's and great-grandmother's relations, the Shi and Xu clans, and the unscrupulous eunuch secretaries Hong Gong and Shi Xian. News of a secret conference between Liu Xiang and the other Confucian members of the government on the subject of limiting the powers of the emperor's maternal relatives somehow leaked out before it had reached any conclusion, and the Confucians were imprisoned. Liu Xiang was soon released from this second imprisonment, but he was stripped of rank and office and held no further appointment for nearly fifteen years. He was soon to see his learned patron, Xiao Wang-zhi, driven to suicide. A few years later the eunuchs and maternal relatives gained complete control of the government with the suicide of Liu Xiang's friend Zhang Meng, hounded to his death by the implacable eunuch secretary Shi Xian. Liu Xiang voiced his despair and anger in a number of pamphlets. In 33 B.C. he exercised his right as a former minister to protest against the disgraceful treatment of Chen Tang, newly returned from his amazing exploits in central Asia.

The accession of the emperor Cheng in 32 B.C. saw the fall of the hated eunuch Shi Xian. Liu Xiang was given rank and office once more and a few years later began his immense labours on the collation and cataloguing of books in the Imperial Library. He was now a respected elder statesman. But the learned memorials in which he repeatedly warned the throne against the latest threat to it – the rise of the empress Wang's family – though politely enough received, were invariably unheeded; and his three collections of stories, 'The New Preface', 'A Garden of Tales', and 'Lives of Famous Women', which were designed to promote the emperor's moral regeneration, were, one suspects, admired more for their entertainment value than for the morals they pointed.

The official biography of Liu Xiang gives us the following picture of him in his last years: 'A man simple in his tastes and caring little for the fashions of the time; by day he studied his books and by night he observed the stars, sometimes not sleeping until dawn.' He died in 6 B.C. at the age of seventy-two. Thirteen years later a member of the Wang clan usurped the imperial title.

From this brief outline of Liu Xiang's life it can be seen that the folly of princes and the evil power of flatterers against which the Sao poets so often declaimed were to him no mere figure but a burning reality. Frequently the words of *Jiu tan* can be found paralleled in Liu Xiang's memorials to the throne. *Jiu tan* is written mostly in the persona of Qu Yuan, but often Liu Xiang speaks for himself through Qu Yuan's mouth, and sometimes he drops the mask altogether and speaks of Qu Yuan in the third person.

However, though *Jiu tan* was undoubtedly written with passionate feeling, I doubt whether many people read it nowadays for enjoyment. Liu Xiang is perhaps too learned a writer to be enjoyable, and he cannot always escape the charge of dullness. Yet sometimes there is a nobility and grandeur in these poems which atones for the surrounding flatnesses and infelicities. The nine poems are modelled on *Jiu zhang*, with regular Sao-style couplets and *luan* in a different metre.

A great revival of interest in Chu poetry occurred during the reign of Emperor Xuan at about the time when Wang Bao and Liu Xiang were starting their careers as court writers, but I prefer to believe that Liu Xiang wrote these poems during the bitter years out of office when his friends and patrons were being undermined and destroyed by the hostile clique surrounding the emperor Yuan.

Liu Xiang used to be (and often still is) thought of as the compiler and editor of the whole *Chu ci* anthology as we read it today except for the set of his own poems which the later editor Wang Yi appended when he made his annotated edition a century later. In fact, as I have suggested elsewhere, Liu Xiang's *Chu ci* probably contained only thirteen of the seventeen titles which make up the present anthology, viz: 1. *Li sao*; 2. *Jiu bian*; 3. *Jiu ge*; 4. *Tian wen*; 5. *Jiu zhang*; 6. *Yuan you*; 7. *Bu ju*; 8. *Yu fu*; 9. *Zhao yin shi*; 10. *Zhao hun*; 11. *Jiu huai*; 12. *Qi jian*; 13. *Jiu tan*. I have also suggested that the nucleus of this anthology was a pre-existing collection of Chu poems edited by Liu An consisting of the first nine of the above titles. It is interesting in this connection to note that the first outstanding event in Liu Xiang's life implies that he already, at the age of twenty or so, had access to Liu An's surviving writings.

1 *'Encountering Troubles'* (Feng fen)

Thus speaks the last scion of Bo Yong's line,
Qu Yuan, the truly faithful-hearted:
Tracing my ancestry from Gao Yang,
I am the kindred of King Huai of Chu.

A virtuous nature I received at birth,
And exalted with fair fame my life's long road.
My name made me equal of the earth and sky;
In brightness I rivalled the starry firmament.

I sucked pure essences and spewed out earthy humours:
Thrown on an evil world, I held no truce with it.
And for sounding men's metal without fear or favour
I was turned out, and lies were told about me.

My prince gave ear to falsehood and spurned the truth,
Rejected my counsels and followed his own bent.
My proud heart, burning, was choked with rage;
My high hopes, shattered, came tumbling down.

His feckless mind could find no place for me;
His person freezingly withdrew from me.
Crestfallen, I took leave of my dear prince,
To sigh by marsh's edge and river's brink.

Though Pepper and Cassia were snared and overthrown,
They still kept faith and turned towards the truth.
Then, though slanderers everywhere thrive like a creeping weed,
Why should not I still bare my soul to him?

He had plighted troth with me in the temple hall;
Then, in mid-course, he went back on his word.
The orchids and asarum which I held in my bosom
I scattered away as I walked in the wilderness.

With loud lament I yearned for my native mountains;
With grieving heart I longed for my native land.
I wished I could find him alone and speak my heart;
But the path to him was dark and the road was blocked.

33   With looks all leaden and ravaged over,
     With spirit broken and aged before my time;
     With a skirt that flapped, bellying in the breeze,
     With robe dragging heavily in the dew,

37   I went down to the rushing flood of the River,
     Followed the waves' crests, ever downwards,
     Threading my way round the curves of the mountains,
     Till the whirlwind came with blusterous roaring.

41   I drove my chariot to the Black Rock Mountain,
     Trotted my horses by the Dong-ting lake.
     At daybreak I started out from Cang-wu,
     At evening I sheltered at Castle-in-the-Rocks.

45   Hibiscus was my awning, of water-caltrops my car,
     My tower was of spotted shells, my hall of jade,
     Fig-leaves were my hangings, my mats were of *lu-li* stone,
     My coat was of fish-scales, my skirt of the rainbow.

49   I climbed up Feng-long and looked downwards
     And saw how far behind I had left the city.
     Longing for the old ways of my home in Nan-ying,
     My bowels in a single night turned nine times over.

53   Far and wide the great waves roll,
     Swelling and curving towards the east.
     My heart is desolate with long yearning;
     My mind is clouded over and daily growing feebler.

57   Thick falls the frost and mantles all things over,
     And keen the autumn wind blows, mournful and chill.
     While my body wanders on, never returning,
     My soul flies far from it, vexed with constant sorrow.

LAMENT

61   Even as the rushing water roars with the crash of boulders,
     And the waves sweep up and surge, and the rapids boil and rac
     Whipped to wild frenzy, plunging in foaming flood, dashing on
         jagged rocks,

Swirling and circling, whirling and eddying, hurling frustrated at
    that which confines them –
So Qu Yuan, meeting with many misfortunes, falling on dire
    disgrace,
Poured out his wondrous words in writing, to leave to posterity.

II *'Leaving the World'* (Li shi)

The Loved One does not know me,
The Loved One hears me not;
I went to the Loved One's fathers,
And spoke to the Loved One's ghosts.

The Loved One turned himself from me,
But lent ear to the flatterer.
I made Heaven and Earth bear witness,
And the Four Seasons testify.

I commanded the sun and moon to shine on me a little longer,
And held the Dipper's Handle as pledge of my good faith.
I appointed Shi Kuang to sound the truth of my words,
And ordered Gao Yao to listen as his assessor.

I was given, by shell-crack, the name of True Exemplar,
And by yarrow stalks, the title of Divine Balance.
The lofty virtues I had in my youth already,
I strengthened and refined when I grew to manhood.

I would not follow the halting gait of the vulgar:
I made my direction straight, and was faithful to my purpose,
Not taking my line off the true to follow the crooked,
Or humbling my pure mind in my daily dealings.

My actions were as true as flawless jade is,
As I followed in the tracks of the chariot of state;
But the crowd made dark the light with their sycophancies,
And the chariot of state was overturned in the murk.

25   In mid-career the chariot swerved from its course;
     The team of four took fright and ran amuck.
     With the driver no more able to control them,
     The yoke was bound to break and the box of the car to be
        smashed.

29   Bridles from bits snapped as they raced on wildly:
     At the stage-stops none dared stand and try to halt them.
     And so, with the road clear ahead and no human interference,
     They could gallop on unchecked for a thousand *li*.

33   Cast rudely down into low obscurity,
     Unable ever to mount up again:
     I nothing cared about my own degradation,
     I only grieved that the coach of state should founder.

37   I passed from the city gate and took my bearings,
     Still hoping my prince would change his mind and recall me.
     Alas, that the driver's life should be so afflicted!
     Sorrow often his lot, calamity his portion.

41   Nine long years went by without my recalling.
     I thought of Peng Xian on his watery wanderings,
     Of Shi Yan floating among the river's eyots,
     And went down into the Mi-luo's flowing waters.

45   I tried to follow the river's mazy windings,
     But dashed on the jagged rocks and was driven athwart my
        course.
     The roaring waves, curving their broken crests above me,
     Spun me drifting through the long shallows' turbid waters.

49   As I rode the Huang-tuo downwards towards the sea,
     How I wished the flood would reverse and carry me homeward
     But the waves' black chariots, swiftly thronging,
     Bore me drifting on, ever farther from it.

53   I rowed my boat across the river,
     Crossed the Xiang's waters and journeyed to the south.
     Standing by the river's brink, I lifted my voice in mourning,
     Sigh on sigh heaving in my sorrow.

My mind is distraught; I forget where I am going;
My soul goes wandering off, high into the air;
The heart within me yearns in sadness;
My longing spirit speeds on its way alone.

LAMENT

When I think of my native land, my heart uncertain falters.
The daylight turns to dusk; my mind with sorrow darkens.
I have left the city for the east: what have I now to hope for?
Slanderers have banded together to bring me to this pass.
To go ever onwards like the river: that shall my heart's desire
    be.
I turn and gaze on the road to the city, to which I shall never
    return.

III *'Embittered Thoughts'* (Yuan si)

My thoughts are overcast with bitter care;
My will frustrated, but unyielding.
I lie in wretchedness until the dawn,
And, at the sunset hour, begin long griefs.

I pity the orphan child in an empty house.
I grieve for the piteous fledgeling, trapped in a blasted willow.
The mother bird, bereaved, cries out on the high wall;
While pigeons coo content, roosting in bosky trees.

Like a monkey lost in the dark depths of the forest,
I have been cast off and banished far away.
The traveller wearily walks along the highway,
While his wife eats out her heart in anxious longing.

I have shown good faith and truth without ever failing,
My nature was as pure as silk from the bleaching,
My brightness rivalled that of the sun and moon,
My art excelled in lustre the brilliance of jade and gems.

17   My pain is smothered and may not be told;
      My thoughts submerged and not to be expressed.
      The lingering fragrance in the end must die:
      The fame I had, dispersed, its lustre dimmed.

21   Headlong I drove away from the Gate of Jade
      To find instead ill fame and bring on myself derision,
      Like Guan Long-feng, whose head fell from his body,
      And Prince Bi Gan, who was cut up and made into pickles.

25   I, who cared only for my country's safety,
      Earned only enmity and hatred for my pains;
      Concerned that the state was falling to destruction,
      I reaped reproach and wove a chain of woe.

29   Since the filth of the bluebottle cheats the eye with its hue,
      And Li Ji of Jin turned devotion into hate,
      I feared that by climbing the steps I might be endangered
      And drew back to the farthest end of the hall.

33   The afflicted courtier lifts up his voice in plaint;
      For this present reign is rank, its weeds neglected.
      Braving displeasure, I boldly expostulated,
      But, for my pains, was held guilty, and looked on with
            suspicion.

37   Parsley and pollia are choked with weeds,
      Nothosmyrnium soaked in a muddy ditch,
      Fragrant angelica drowned in a stinking pool,
      Carved rhinoceros horn is left in a bamboo box.

41   Tang-xi is grasped now for chopping straw with,
      And Gan-jiang wielded for carving meat.
      Foul marsh-weeds are treasured in pouches of leopard-skin,
      While Jing He's jade is smashed up for builder's rubble.

45   The times are foul and turbid, past purifying;
      The age is in confusion that none can see a way through.
      I wish I could calmly wait for a better time to come,
      But I fear that my years are too far advanced already.

I would bend my principles and go with the stream,
But my heart cleaves tightly to them and will not let me.
Better, perhaps, to float on the Yuan and ride along its waters,
And go down the Xiang and the River, tossed and turned by the
    current.

LAMENT

The cart-wheels creak in the mountains: my heart is torn with
    longing.
The traveller hurries, distracted, not knowing where he can rest.
Aimlessly roaming in the wilds, in lonely desolation,
I will race my stallions a while, to ease my sorrowful feelings.
If I carried my old bones back to my homeland, there are none
    there I could talk to:
Taking a long farewell, I leave on my far journey and drift away
    on the the Xiang.

IV *'Going Far Away'* (Yuan shi)

My thoughts are gloomy and dejected;
In loneliness I grieve, nursing my bitter wrongs,
My bosom confused like a tangled skein,
My tears running fast like meal from the grinders.

Choking with long-suppressed emotion,
I look to High Heaven to justify me:
Convoke the Five Peaks and the gods of the Eight Quarters,
Question the Nine Bright Shiners and the Six Holy Ones.

I summon the fixed stars to present my case,
Charge the Five Lords to take my deposition.
The North Star is my arbitrator,
And the Great Unity is my assessor.

13   They bade me keep to the true course of the Yin and Yang,
To cleave to the central harmony of Earth,
To hang at my girdle the coiling Green Dragon,
To wear at my belt the sinuous rainbow serpent.

17   I must trail behind me the flashing Broom Star,
Cling to the Fire Bird and the Bird of Paradise,
Rove the clear void of pure divinity,
Dress in flowing garments of cloud.

21   Jade should my whip be, my banner scarlet
Fringed with the dusky Moon Bright pearls,
A great rainbow flag like an awning above me,
And pennants dyed in the hues of the sunset.

25   My body was pure and without blemish,
After my peerless father's fashion.
Grieved by the failure of all my past endeavours,
I breasted the Mi-luo, to pass beneath its waters.

29   But the swelling billows bore me to the south side:
I drifted along the Jiang and Xiang with the current,
Entered the Marquess of Yang's deep-surging waters,
Passed down the rocky rapids and climbed a little island.

33   The steep-towering banks shut off my view of heaven,
The lowering clouds hid the prospect before me,
And the mountains rose up sheer, seeming to have no end;
Towering height upon height, they seemed to press down upon
    me.

37   Snow fluttered thickly down, blanketing the trees;
The massed clouds gathered more densely as they descended;
The narrow cliffs rose up sombre and threatening,
Their rocks, sharp and jagged, shutting off the sun's light.
41

    I sorrowed for my old home, and anger rose within me:
Too long, oh too long, I had left my native land!
I turned my back on the Dragon Gate and entered the Great
    River,
Climbed a high mound and looked out to Xia-shou.

Turning my boat athwart the stream, I crossed the Xiang river.
There was a singing in my ears; my mind was dazed.
The waters billowed all about me,
And the swell rose up, heaving and boiling.

The journey was so long, there seemed to be no ending:
I wandered this way and that, not knowing where I went.
I took the sun and moon as guides to find where the north lay,
And rested a little while to clear my thoughts.

The waves rolled onwards into the dark distance:
To east and west nothing could be discerned in the gloom;
So, following wind and waves, I drifted southward.
The mists closed about me with the darkness of night.

Sombrely the sun in the west was declining:
The road stretched far ahead, full of difficulties
I thought with a stoup of wine to solace my care,
But my throbbing anxieties would not leave me.

LAMENT

The wandering wind whirls and the dust flies up in eddies;
Flowers and trees wave and fall; the season grows sere and sad.
Ruin and disaster are my lot, not to be averted.
Long I sigh and moan and my tears fall unconstrained.
By unburdening my heart in verse, I hoped I might escape;
But my powers fail and I drift farther and farther in exile.

v 'Lament for the Worthy' (Xi xian)

When I read the Li sao of Master Qu,
My heart is heavy with sorrow for him;
My voice complains in the lonely silence,
And I turn to my groom, plunged, too, in gloomy sadness.

5   He struck out at slander and righted infamy,
    Cut out the foul canker from current custom,
    Washed off the stains of sinful impurity,
    Wiped out the vile and brutish uncleanness.

    He laid sweet scents in his bosom, melilotus he held in his hand,
10 Wore at his girdle the fragrant hemlock parsley.
    Pepper and pollia filled his hands;
    His virtue raised him above the floating clouds.
    He climbed up Chang-ling and surveyed the world about him,
    Gazed down on beds of angelica, row on row.
15 He wandered through banks of orchids and clumps of melilotus
    And glanced up at the jagged rocks of jade.
    The choice flowers he flaunted shone with glittering radiance,
    Rich and heavy their perfume, spotless their beauty.
    He wove the cassia branch's delicate spray
20 With melilotus and lily-magnolia.
    Such were his blossoms, yet they found no favour:
    Cast out in the wilds, they wilted and died.

    He pursued Zi Qiao to become his acolyte
    And Shen-tu Di who cast himself in the deeps.
25 He was like Xu You and Bo Yi in unspotted goodness,
    Or Jie Zi-tui who hid himself in the mountain,
    Or Shen Sheng of Jin who met a hapless end,
    Or Jing He who wept tears of blood,
    Or Shen Xu of Wu who had his eyes gouged out,
30 Or Prince Bi Gan who was wrongfully rejected.

    He wished to humble himself and abase his body,
    But his mind recoiled and never would submit.
    Since square and round are unlike and do not fit together,
    The angle and the line have different dispositions.

35 I should like to wait a little until a better time comes,
    But the day is getting dark and draws towards the evening.
    Time steals on, remorseless, with ever-advancing step;
    The years pass swiftly by in perpetual revolution.

Would I falsely compromise, and make my peace with the world?
The way within is closed and will not open to me.
Would I wait for the world's ways to grow pure and clean?
The fog only grows the denser, until it is like a dust-storm.
If I advance with the pigeon's timorous movements,
Slanderers rise up like a screen to bar me.
If I quietly follow the fashion's fluctuations.
They are still suspicious and force me to retire.

My mind is distracted and in a turmoil;
My feelings disordered and full of bitter grief.
I pluck the wild fig on the mountain moorland,
Gather wild persimmons in the river islet.

Sighing and weeping, I gaze towards Gao-qiu,
Sobbing with grief and ceaselessly yearning.
Who more anxious than I to shoulder the burden?
But the red sun is sinking to his setting.

LAMENT

The Jiang and Xiang with teeming waters race ever onwards on
  their way.
In a great turmoil they heave their waves up, surging with a
  sudden fury.
With careworn heart I toss and turn, afflicted with heavy
  sadness.
My resentments find no outlet; always I must hide my anger.
It is my lot to meet misfortunes; there is nothing that I can do.
My labouring heart is full of woe and my tears fall down in
  streams.

VI 'Saddened by Sufferings' (You ku)

Alas! my heart is heavy,
Mourning for my native land's misfortunes.
Nine years now I have left it without returning.
Alone I go on my lonely way to the south.

5 When I think of the ways that are now my country's fashion,
My mind rejects them with shame and confusion.
I wander beside the wilderness, crying into the wind,
Walk slowly through the mountain glens.

9 I follow the marsh flats' winding channels,
Silent in sombre desolation;
I rest on a rocky ledge and weep,
Sad and distressed; there is no joy in my life.

13 I climb a high peak and long stand staring,
Straining for a glimpse of Nan-ying.
The mountains continue far into the distance;
Long, long is my road – it seems to go on for ever.

17 I hear the black cranes crying in the morning
On the towering summits of the lofty mountains.
Alone with my growing anger, by turns glad and grieving,
I hover through the islets, singing softly.

21 Three birds came flying from the south;
I marked their constancy and wished to follow northwards.
I wanted the three birds to take a message for me,
But they left with a start and I was too late to catch them.

25 I should like to abandon my resolve, to forget my constancy,
But my heart is bound fast and has never yet been shifted.
Outwardly idle wanderer, gazing on the passing scene,
Inside I am all regrets and pent-up grief.

29 I should like for a little while to forget my sorrow,
But my heart is too impregnated with care.
I should like by music's aid to find relief from sadness,
But my thoughts are tied in a tangle that nothing can untie.

33 Sadly I sang the *Li sao* to give vent to my feelings,
But I could not get to the end of *Jiu zhang*,
For the long sobs rose in my throat and choked me,
And the tears collected and ran down in streams.

It grieves me that shining pearls should be cast out in the mire,
While worthless fish-eye stones are treasured in a strong-box.
Proud stallions are treated as if they were pack-mules,
And Dapple Grey classed as a broken-down hack.

Weeds overrun and choke the cassia bushes;
Owls roost in the magnolia trees.
Stupid bigots hold forth in hall and temple,
While the great and magnanimous are banished to the mountains.

The Xiao-shao music of Shun is execrated;
The vulgar Whirling Chu is held in high esteem.
The cauldrons of Zhou are sunk in southern rivers;
A clay pot is heated in the midst of the hall.

The good man's heart cleaved to the old ways,
But he was not able to maintain them. .
Turning into the southward-going highway,
A traveller now, he journeys through the night.

Homesick, he thinks of the road to Ying,
And turns his head back with longing glances.
The streams of snivel join in one channel,
And the tears run down his face like rain.

LAMENT

I climbed a mountain and long stood gazing, grieving in my
    inmost heart.
Verdant were the greens of the landscape, but I wept as though
    my heart would break.
Loth to tear myself away, I looked back northwards, all bedewed
    with my tears.
My spirit is broken and my pride crushed; I am stuck fast
    beneath the flood.
I think of my loneliness: whom can my soul seek?
My groom is bewildered; we drift like wandering water.

VII *'Grieved by This Fate'* (Min ming)

1 Of old, my noble father in his magnanimity
Loved to raise the able and glorify the good.
Unblemished was his heart, without impurity;
Lofty was his nature, without any blame.

5 He banished the glib-tongued and the sycophantic,
Reproved the slanderers and the fawning favourite;
But ever he loved the loyal and true and esteemed the honest:
He summoned the good to him, the wise and intelligent.

9 Great was his mind, beyond estimation;
Calm was his heart, like a deep pool.
The crooked fled from him and could find no entrance;
The true could not leave, even if they sought retirement.

13 He drove the paramours out of the council chamber,
But welcomed the goddess Fu Fei from the Yi-luo river.
He rooted out slanderous knaves from the central courtyard,
But chose Lü Wang and Guan Zhong out of the bushland.

17 Under the greenwood was no wronged gentleman;
On the river's banks were no exiles in hiding.
The San Miao and their kind were driven into banishment;
Yi and Gao and their sort filled the king's houses.

21 But now the clothing's outsides are worn as a lining,
And the lower garment goes on the upper body.
Song Wan is cherished between the two pillars,
And Zhou and Shao cast out among the far barbarians.

25 The wonder horse is sent away and put to work the mill;
The ass and mule are harnessed for post-swift travelling.
The maiden of Cai is dismissed from the bedchamber;
The Rong wife installed and dressed in embroidered silks.

29 Qing Ji is imprisoned in a deep dungeon;
Chen Bu-zhan goes to war and is sent to raise sieges.
The Sounding Bell *qin* of Bo Ya has been broken;
They hold a Qin *zheng* now and strike its jangling strings.

Chips of white marble are treasured in brazen coffers;
Jacinth is thrown out into the courtyard.
Han Xin is hidden among the rank and file,
While a private commands and leads assaults on cities.

Flowering rush and hemlock parsley are cast away in the marsh's
    eyots;
Gourds and calabashes lie worm-eaten in baskets.
The unicorn flees into the marshes;
Bears gather and romp inside the palace gardens.

The fragrant bough and the jewelled spray are broken;
Thorn bushes and kindling wood are planted in their stead.
Iris, melilotus and freesia are uprooted;
Wild bean and zingiber assiduously hoed.

Sad that the men of this age are so unequal,
Some so short-sighted and some so far-seeing:
Some so obtuse that they have no comprehension;
Some of clear vision who cannot win a hearing:

It grieves me that I was born out of my time,
To endure afflictions and meet with reproach.
Even though I fearlessly utter all my mind,
My prince is ill disposed and sure to silence me.

Truly I grieve that my delicate-scented blossoms
Should be by him accounted evil-smelling.
Because of the fragrant cassia I cherished in my bosom
I have fallen upon troubles and had to bear insults.

LAMENT

The good old king is dead and will return no more.
In the mountains, dark and precipitous, the road to Ying is long.
After the slanderer's subtle words, who can win a hearing?
The traveller without a bourn has no one he can talk to,
But at each step he heaves a sigh, each sound more dolorous
    than the last,
Sadness and grief inside his breast, utterly disconsolate.

VIII 'Sighing for Olden Times' (Si gu)

1 How dark the deep forest is
Beneath the trees' dense shade!
And the serried mountains are broken and sheer,
Their peaks obscuring the light of day.

5 Alas! my heart is in despair,
And my eyes are blinded with brimming tears.
The wind whistles sadly, swaying the trees,
And the scurrying clouds are crooked and curled.

9 Sad that my life is bereft of gladness,
I sorrow, afflicted, in mountain and wild.
In the morning I wander on the long hill's bluff;
In the evening I fearfully go to my lone rest.

13 My hair hangs dishevelled and tangled on my shoulders,
My body is sick and spent with toil;
My soul in wild haste goes fleeting southwards;
Tears soak my bosom and wet my sleeves.

17 My longing heart finds none to unburden to;
My mouth is stopped up: I cannot speak.
I have left behind my old quarter in Ying city,
Crossed the Yuan and Xiang, and moved to a distant region.

21 I think how my homeland has been brought to ruin,
And the ghosts of my ancestors robbed of their proper service.
I grieve that the line of my father's house is broken;
My heart is dismayed and laments within me.

25 I shall wander a while upon the sides of the mountain,
And walk about upon the river's banks.
I shall look down, whistling, on the deep waters,
Wander far and wide, looking all about me.

29 By composing the subtle words of the *Li sao*,
I hope to recall the Fair One to his senses,
So that he summons my chariot back to Nan-ying
To drive once more in the tracks we used to follow.

The road is long, the removal difficult;
But alas! my poor heart will not desist.
The others have turned their backs on the laws of the Three and
the Five,
Abandoned the Great Plan's mighty rules,

Discarding square and compass, falsifying measures,
Casting aside the balance and weighing as they fancy.
He who cleaves to the ink-line finds himself rejected;
Those who stoop are favoured and kept in close attendance.

The pear tree withers among the tall grasses;
The thorn bush is planted in the midst of the court.
Xi Shi is banished to the north chambers;
The ill-favoured cluster at each side of the throne.

Wu Huo is cherished and drives the royal horses;
Duke Shao of Yan is made to work in the stables.
Kuai Gui mounts up in the holy temple;
Gao Yao is cast out into the wilds.

Observing these things, I heave a long sigh:
I should like to mount the steps but feel too uncertain.
So I ride the white waves, my high-stepping coursers,
Bidding a long farewell as I float into the distance.

LAMENT

Up and down I wander on the black hillside: underneath are the
mere's deep waters.
A long time I pause on the banks of the Han, my tears all the
while in torrents falling.
Now that Zhong Zi and Bo Ya are dead, for whom can one
make music?
Now that Xian E will no more drive, how can one show one's
feelings?
Sadly I sigh, with mounting grief; my heart is reft and torn.
I look back at Gao-qiu and my tears fall in a shower.

IX 'The Far-off Journey' (Yuan you)

1 Alas! my nature cannot be altered;
Repeated punishments cannot sway it.
Clothed in bright raiment, different from the vulgar,
Lofty in mien, towering above the rest,

5 Like Wang Qiao riding upon the clouds,
Or charioting the sunset across the courts of heaven:
My years shall equal those of the earth and sky,
My splendour be like that of the sun and moon.

9 I ascended Kun-lun and turned my face northwards
And bade the Immortals muster and come to visit me.
I chose attendant spirits in the Land of Great Darkness,
Mounted to heaven's portals by the Dark Gate mountain.

13 I turned about my chariot and guided it to westward;
I raised up my rainbow flag at the Jade Gate.
I drove my six dragons to the mountain of Three Perils,
And assembled the Four Gods on the ninefold shore.

17 I raced my chariot on the Western Mountains,
Crossed the Flying Valley and journeyed to the south,
Traversed the Great Plain and sped straight onwards,
Passed by Zhu Rong in the Scarlet Sea.

21 My jade yoke-bar buckled in the burning heat,
My two hub-guards bent in the Pool of Heaven.
I plunged through the towering spray, making my way
        eastwards,
Tethered my six dragons to the Fu-sang tree.

25 When I had seen all the sights within the Four Seas,
I determined to fly aloft, ascending and descending.
I summoned all the gods together at the revolving pole;
To marshal them, I raised up the many-coloured rainbow.

Drawn by phoenixes, skywards I soared,
Leading a train of black cranes and *jiao-ming* birds.
Peacocks came flying to welcome and escort us.
I sent off a flight of swans to the Dipper's Handle.

I flung open God's palace and his heavenly park,
Ascended the Hanging Garden, whose brightness blinded me.
I twisted a jewelled branch to twine in my girdle.
I stood Chang Geng above us, to replace the daylight.

I trampled the startling thunder, banished the dreadful
    lightnings,
Bound up the evil spirits and tied them to the Pole Star.
I lashed the Wind God and made him ride before me,
Imprisoned the Dark Spirit in the Pit of Night.

I rode in the high wind's face, hither and thither;
I wandered, gazing, all over the north.
There I came to Zhuan Xu and laid my plaint before him,
And examined Xuan Ming on Kong-sang Mountain.

I turned my chariot about and journeyed to Chong-shan
And made my report to Yu Shun at Cang-wu;
Crossed in a willow boat to Gui-ji,
And came upon Shen Xu among the Five Lakes.

Then, when I saw the ways that prevailed in Nan-ying,
I cast my body into the Yuan's waters.
I gaze on my native land so blackly benighted:
The turbulence of the times shows no abatement.

I held in my bosom fragrant orchids and iris,
But they enviously plucked them from me and crushed them.
I spread out crimson hangings for my lord's greater splendour,
But a puffing wind blew them up and concealed me from his
    eyes.

The sun in a red glow goes to his western lodgings,
And from his fiery brightness looks back on the world.
I wish I could steal some time for a little pleasure;
Yet with what anxieties I am afflicted!

LAMENT

61   He was as the cloud dragon, floating in watery vapours, like a
         dense mist;
       Billowing formlessly, with thunder-roll and lightning-flash, high
         aloft he races;
       Mounting the void, treading the dark sky, spurning the turbid
         vapours, swimming in the clear ones, he enters the House of
         God;
       Shaking his wings and beating with his pinions, racing the wind,
         driving the rain, he wanders without end.

Notes

1 'Encountering Troubles'

l.1 the last scion of Bo Yong's line: in *Li sao, l.2*, Qu Yuan refers to Bo
    Yong as his *huang kao*, a term meaning something like 'sainted sire'
    which is frequently found in inscriptions dating from the Zhou dynasty
    in the sense of 'late father'. I have translated it 'father' in *Li sao*, but it is
    evident that Liu Xiang must have understood it in the more general
    sense of 'forefather'. A distinguished modern scholar, Professor Rao
    Zongyi of the Chinese University of Hong Kong, advanced the view, in
    an early work of his, that 'Bo Yong' is an alternative form of 'Zhu
    Rong', the name of the fire god from whom the kings of Chu were
    descended. I am not wholly convinced by this view, but it is certainly a
    very plausible one. Qu Yuan was, after all, born on Zhu Rong's
    feast-day. See note on *Li sao, l.4*.

l.41 I drove my chariot to the Black Rock Mountain: the geography of
    this poem is largely fanciful, so there is little point in trying to
    identify the place-names. Cang-wu is, of course, the name of the area in
    which Shun, or Chong Hua, was buried. Cf. *Li sao, l.185*, where Qu
    Yuan begins his journey to Kun-lun from that area.

l.51 my home in Nan-ying: literally 'South Ying' or 'Southern Ying'.
    The kings of Chu gave the name of 'Ying' to whichever city
    happened to be their capital at any particular time. During the last
    three reigns they moved their capital to Shou-chun in Anhui and Qu
    Yuan's old capital had to be called 'South Ying' to distinguish it from
    the new one. Throughout the Han dynasty Qu Yuan's Ying and the
    metropolitan area around it continued to be referred to as 'Nan Ying'
    and 'Nan Chu'.

II 'Leaving the World'

*l.*1 *The Loved One*: the Chinese is 'Ling Huai', a name invented by Liu
Xiang on the analogy of 'Ling Xiu' (see note on *Li sao, l.*44). A
word-play is intended on the name of Qu Yuan's king, King Huai.
Unfortunately it cannot be reproduced or suggested in translation.

*l.*11 *Shi Kuang*: a famous blind musician who was Master of Music or
Kapellmeister to the Duke of Jin in the sixth century B.C. In a
well-known story demonstrating the effects of music on the natural
environment he attempts to prevent the Music Master of a visiting ruler
from playing some ghostly music that the latter had heard while
camping beside a river. Shi Kuang had realized, after hearing only a few
bars of it, that the music had destructive properties. His apprehensions
were justified when the duke insisted on the performance continuing
and a tremendous storm arose which blew the tiles off the roof of the
palace. This was followed by three years of drought and, in the case of
the duke himself, by a debilitating illness from which he never
recovered. Liu Xiang assumes that a man with so sensitive an ear would
make a good lie-detector.

*ll.*13–14 *by shell-crack ... by yarrow stalks*: turtle shells and yarrow
stalks were used in the two chief methods of divination. It
was with reference to the latter kind of divination that the *Yi jing* or
'Book of Changes' was written. The purpose of the divination referred
to here was to make sure of choosing a lucky name. Like Mr Shandy,
Chinese fathers thought that the name a child was given would have a
good deal to do with his success or failure in later life.

*l.*43 *Shi Yan floating among the river's eyots*: another blind musician, he
was Master of Music to Zhòu, the last Shang king. On Zhòu's
death he embraced his instrument and jumped into the River Pu. It was
there, centuries later, that the ghostly music was heard which Shi
Kuang (*l.*11 above) so feared to hear repeated.

*l.*49 *the Huang-tuo*: another name for the Yangtze in one part of its
course.

III 'Embittered Thoughts'

*l.*21 *Headlong I drove away from the Gate of Jade*: not the pass of that
name from which the silk caravans began their journey across
Central Asia to the West, but the gate of the king's palace. In fact the
characters for 'jade' and 'king' differ by only a single dot, so perhaps it
is 'king's gate' that Liu Xiang really wrote.

*l.*23 *Guan Long-feng*: loyal minister of the wicked Xia king Jie. Jie
beheaded him for his outspokenness.

l.30 Li Ji of Jin: Shen Sheng's wicked stepmother.

l.41 Tang-xi is grasped now for chopping straw with: Tang-xi was the
    name of a place in Henan famous for its swords – hence a sword
made in Tang-xi, or, by extension, any good sword. Similarly, Gan
Jiang (in *l.*42) was the name of a famous swordsmith, but 'a Gan Jiang'
came to mean, first, a sword made by Gan Jiang, and later, by
extension, any sword good enough for Gan Jiang to have made.

l.44 Jing He's jade: i.e. the jade of Bian He of Jing (= Chu).

IV 'Going Far Away'

l.7 the Five Peaks: the five sacred mountains of China (the two
    Heng-shans, Hua-shan, Song-shan and Tai-shan) were themselves
deities.

l.31 the Marquess of Yang's deep-surging waters: i.e. the waters of the
    Yangtze, in which the legendary Marquess once drowned himself.
He is said to have become a water spirit responsible for stirring up the
waves. Chinese seldom refer to the Yangtze itself by his name (they
usually call it *Chang Jiang*, 'Long River', rather than *Yang-zi Jiang*,
'Lord Yang's River'), but writers and poets often speak of 'Yang-hou's
(i.e. the Marquess of Yang's) waves' when they are thinking of the river
in its more violent aspect.

V 'Lament for the Worthy'

l.23 Zi Qiao: i.e. Wang Zi-qiao or Wang Qiao, the Taoist Immortal.
    See note on *Yuan you*, *l.54*.

l.25 Xu You: a legendary recluse to whom Yao unsuccessfully offered
    the government of his empire. The proposal so horrified him that
he had to go off and wash his ears out after listening to it.

l.29 Shen Xu of Wu: i.e. Zi Xu, *al.* Wu Zi-xu. Liu Xiang is here
    showing off his formidable learning in a way which contemporary
readers would almost certainly have found confusing. Few of them
would have read the ancient text in which it says that when Zi Xu
arrived as a refugee in Wu and offered his services to the king there he
was given an estate in Shen. Most readers would probably identify
'Shen Xu' with Shen Bao-xu, the name of Zi Xu's famous rival. See
note on *Jiu bian* VII, *l.1*.

l.51 I gaze towards Gao-qiu: like Wang Yi and the anonymous author
    of *Qi jian*, Liu Xiang evidently misunderstood the 'high hill' of *Li
sao*, *l.216*, as the name of a mountain in Chu.

VI 'Saddened by Sufferings'

l.14 Straining for a glimpse of Nan-ying: the poem begins with Qu Yuan
on his way from Ying, the old Chu capital near Jiangling, to his
exile in the south. Here he is gazing *northwards* towards the city from
which he has been banished. (In *ll.21–3* he expresses a hope that the
northward-flying birds will carry a message for him.) Nan-ying
('Southern Ying') is not 'in the south' from Qu Yuan's point of view. As
in 'Encountering Troubles' *l.51*, above, Liu Xiang's use of this form
when speaking in the persona of Qu Yuan is strictly speaking an
anachronism. He does so merely to remind his readers that he is talking
about the ancient Ying, not the later one in Anhui.

l.46 The vulgar Whirling Chu: this was the dance that found special
favour with the diners in 'Summons of the Soul'. See *Zhao hun*,
ll.117–23.

VII 'Grieved by This Fate'

l.14 the Yi-luo river: an archaic name for the River Luo. Fu Fei, the
goddess of the Luo, was the first of the mythological ladies
courted by Qu Yuan in *Li sao*. See *Li sao, ll.221 et seq.*

l.20 Yi and Gao: Yi Yin and Gao Yao, wise ministers of Tang the
Successful and the Great Yu.

*ll.23–4 Song Wan is cherished between the two pillars ... Zhou and
Shao*: Song Wan (Nan-gong Wan) murdered Duke Min of
Song and two of his ministers in 682 B.C. To 'stand between the pillars'
meant to hold high office, since this was where ministers ranged
themselves when a ruler held court. Zhou and Shao are the Duke of
Zhou and the Duke of Shao, the wise and loyal regents of their nephew,
the young Zhou king Cheng, after the death of their elder brother,
King Wu.

l.28 The Rong wife installed: the Rong were a barbarian tribe
constantly at war with the early Chinese. Liu Xiang may have a
particular story in mind, but I cannot trace it.

l.29 Qing Ji: Qing Ji of Wu fled to Zheng when He Lü assassinated his
nephew Wang Liao. (See note on *Tian wen, ll.169–70*, for further
details.)

l.30 Chen Bu-zhan: a minister of Duke Zheng of Qi. He was so
nervous that when he took the field against Duke Zheng's
murderers, he died of a heart-attack as soon as the war-drums began to
roll.

*l.*35 *Han Xin*: one of the great generals of Liu Bang, the founder of the
       Han dynasty. He is the subject of one of the riddles in Chapter 50
of *The Story of the Stone*. S.v. 'Huai-yin' on p. 590 of Vol. 2 (Penguin
Books, 1977).

VIII 'Sighing for Olden Times'

*ll.*35–6 *the laws of the Three and the Five ... the Great Plan's mighty
         rules*: the Three and the Five are sage rulers of antiquity,
variously identified by different authorities. The poet of *Jiu zhang* IV
('Outpouring of Sad Thoughts') points to the Three and the Five as
examples which he had hoped his ruler might follow. I have suggested
there (note on *ll.*33–4) that the 'Three' and 'Five' in that context refer
to the dynastic founders Yu, Tang and King Wu and the Five
Hegemons; but I suspect that Liu Xiang, writing at a much later date,
would, like most of his contemporaries, have identified the Three and
the Five as mythical 'emperors'. The 'Great Plan' is the name of a book
in the Confucian *History Classic*. In this book a collection of precepts
designed to give guidance to rulers in the government of their kingdoms
are arranged in groups in accordance with the numbers of a magic
square.

*l.*45 *Wu Huo*: professional strong man at the court of King Wu of Qin
       (*reg.* 310–307 B.C.) who patronized anyone proficient in
weight-lifting – an art which he practised himself and died from the
effects of.

*l.*46 *Duke Shao of Yan*: this is the Duke Shao or Duke of Shao who was
       joint regent with the Duke of Zhou of the boy-king Cheng. See
note on 'Grieved by This Fate', *ll.*23–4, above.

*l.*47 *Kuai Gui*: celebrated political émigré and trouble-maker who was
       a contemporary of Confucius. He was exiled from Wei after an
abortive attempt to kill his mother, Nan Zi. Confucius' disciple Zi Lu
was killed in the coup d'état by means of which Kuai Gui eventually
returned to Wei and made himself duke. His reign was short, for he was
soon driven into exile once more.

*l.*56 *Xian E*: Wang Yi glosses this as the name of a 'good charioteer',
       the symbol of an able ruler. Elsewhere, however, Xian E appears
as the charioteer of the moon, said to be a beautiful woman – possibly a
variant form of the name of the moon goddess, Chang E. Once again
Liu Xiang's passion for recondite allusions proves self-defeating.

IX *'The Far-off Journey'*

*l.*46 *Yu Shun*: i.e. Shun. Yu was the name of an ancient kingdom in Shanxi from which Shun is said to have originated.

*l.*48 *Shen Xu*: i.e. Zi Xu, as above. His spirit was said to be responsible for storms and flood-tides in the lower Yangtze region. Lake Tai-hu, source of the grotesque rocks favoured by Chinese gardeners, is sometimes called 'the Five Lakes'.

Jiu si *'Nine Longings'*

Wang Yi is better known as the author of the earliest extant commentary on *Chu ci* than as the author of these poems. Hardly anything else has survived of his writings, and very little is known of his life except that he came from Yicheng in Hubei, in the territory of the ancient kingdom of Chu, that he was employed in the Imperial Library some time between A.D. 114 and 119, and that he was appointed a gentleman-in-waiting in the reign of the emperor Shun (A.D. 126–142). He does not seem to have been a particularly distinguished or talented person. Indeed, the frequent imbecilities of his commentary tend to make one forget that, because of his familiarity with the dialect and local traditions of Chu, he often provides us with the only key to what would otherwise be insoluble difficulties.

Wang Yi rigorously applied the Confucian principles of *Shi jing* exegesis in his interpretation of *Chu ci*, sometimes with peculiar results. The chief interest of his *Jiu si* poems is that they enable us to see these principles given a practical demonstration.

Wang Yi's somewhat mechanical use of symbolism often produces a near-comic effect when he is at his most serious. Thus in *Yuan shang* ('Resentment against the Ruler') the picture of the poet standing in a storm of thunder, lightning, hail, sleet and wind (all 'bad' symbols) and covered from head to foot with a wide variety of insects (also 'bad' symbols) is both ludicrous and repellent. Sometimes the words, if taken at their face value, do not make any picture at all – even a ludicrous one. For instance, clouds and rainbows, according to Wang Yi, are both 'bad' symbols: and so we find, in *Zao e* ('Running into Danger'), that rainbows, as well as clouds, *darken* the sky. Wang Yi's brilliant son, Wang Yan-shou, is

deservedly more famous as a poet. A fine translation of his poem
'The Nightmare' is to be found in Arthur Waley's *Chinese Poems*.

Like Wang Bao's *Jiu huai*, all of these poems by Wang Yi are
written in the Song style. In a brief preface to the poems he tells us
that it was in emulation of Liu Xiang's and Wang Bao's
contributions to this genre that he wrote them and also because,
being a fellow-countryman of Qu Yuan, he was 'more than
commonly sympathetic' to him.

I *'Meeting with Reproach'* (Feng you)

Woe and alas! Sorrow and welladay!
Heaven gave me life in a dark time,
Guiltless to bear blame, through the tongues of slander.
With heart in a turmoil and joyless mind
5   Heavily I yoked my car and went forth to wander.
I roamed to the world's ends, passed through all the Nine Land
Seeking for a Xuan Yuan, searching for a Chong Hua.
Soon the world receded far away behind me.
Clasping my girdle-jades, I paused in mid-course,
10   Longing, like Gao Yao, to establish ordinances,
Envying Feng Hou, who received the Magic Chart,
Grieved that fate had brought me all the Six Sorrows,
To lay down my jade-like worth low in the mud.
Wildly I galloped on through woodlands and marshes,
15   Coasting at frantic pace the mountains' winding spurs.
My chariot-bar broke and my horses sank exhausted;
Stricken I stood then, my face bathed in tears.
I thought of the wisdom of Wu Ding and King Wen;
I lamented Ping and Fu Cha's misguided folly:
20   Raising Yue and Lü Wang, Yin and Zhou prospered;
With Wu Ji and Pi in power, Ying and Wu were desolate.
Looking up, I sighed, the breath within me choking:
Only when my passion passed could I breathe again.
Tiger and wild ox fight in the king's court;
25   Jackals and wolves bicker at my sides.
Clouds and mists gather and darken the sun's light,

And the whirlwind rises, lifting up the dust.
Staggering to free myself, I run this way and that:
I would creep into hiding, but where can I go?
To my prince's chamber? But it is inaccessible.
I wish to prove my honour, but am shut off from him.
I look back on my country, remote now in the distance;
Sadness tears my heart and my mind is worn with worry.
My soul is too restless to let me sleep at night,
And I lie all the morning in staring wakefulness.

II 'Resentment against the Ruler' (Yuan shang)

How the king's chief minister mouths his malice,
And all his officers spitefully chatter!
Alas, that confusion is grown so sordid!
High and low, all join in the same rout.
The bean-vine everywhere spreads its creepers,
But fragrant heracleum is broken and withered:
Scarlet and purple are mixed in confusion,
No one is left who can tell the difference.
Here I lie in my cave in the mountains,
Long pondering, in my far retreat,
Grieving for Huai in his foolish blindness,
Who used his mind with so scant clarity.
Soon he will lose the jewel of authority,
And forfeit the kingly keys of power.
My heart within is scorched and burning
For the grief it gives me to think of this.
Serving, I emulated Chou Mu and Xun Xi;
Retiring, I mused on Peng Xian and Wu Guang,
Resolving to follow their twin examples.
Not knowing where I can go for refuge,
I wander lamenting in the wilds.
Overhead I descry the Armill,
While the Great Fire dips to westward
And She Ti swings down low.

25 The thunder rolls with dreadful rumble;
Hail and sleet fall fiercely and fast;
The darting lightning flashes fierily;
The cold wind mournful shrills.
Birds and beasts with terror startled
30 Fly to shelter in nest and lair.
The love-ducks quack their tender affection;
Foxes cleave to their mates.
But I, alas! am lone and forlorn,
Solitary, with none to lean on.
35 On this side the crickets cry,
On that side the corn-grubs squeak;
The caterpillar creeps up my skirt,
The green worm into my bosom.
With creeping and crawling things all about me,
40 In heavy sadness I lament.
Standing in sorrow,
My heart perplexed and broken.

III 'Impatience with the World' (Ji shi)

Wandering back and forth on the banks of the Han,
I seek the Holy Maid, goddess of the waters;
For, alas! in this land there is no good match for me,
And my matchmaker is stupid and tongue-tied.
5 Quails and pies in high places senselessly chatter;
The mynah's shrill cries deafen my ears.
I hold the Flower of Light, the precious sceptre,
Peddling it for sale; but there are no offers.
I have resolved to hurry off, to journey northwards,
10 Summoning my friends to bear me company.
The sun is overcast, giving no light:
Peering in the deep gloom I can see nothing.
Faster I drive my coach and ride into the distance
To seek advice of the high lord Fu Xi.
15 Along by the banks of the river I travelled:

The way was now changed and the times were disjointed.
Fording the Sky Water, I wandered eastwards.
I bathed myself in the Pool of Heaven,
Then I called on Tai Hao to learn Life's Secret.
He said, 'Love and duty are of all things most precious.'
With rejoicings I set out on my homeward journey.
I came to King Wen of Zhou in Qi of Bin country:
Clasping the Flower of Jade, I made a solemn compact.
But the day was ending and my heart grew heavy:
For Heaven's favour never comes a second time,
And to go back on my word would be against my nature.
I crossed the Long-dui mountains and traversed the desert,
Passed underneath the foot of Gui-ju and He-li.
And so, with faltering steps, I arrived at Kun-lun
And rested awhile in Lu Ao's company.
I sucked jade nectar to quench my thirst
And ate the immortal flower to assuage my hunger.
I live in desolation with few companions;
Far I have fallen; my wits are distracted.
I gaze on the endless flood of the river,
And my heart is strangled with pain and sorrow.
The sky begins to lighten as dawn approaches,
But the dust that hangs over all is not dispersed.
Care has deprived me of sleep and of appetite,
And my groans of rage reverberate like thunder.

IV 'Pity for the Ruler' (Min shang)

Woe to this servile generation!
To whispered words from sycophantic tongues,
The multitude who fawn and please,
The flattering smile that is now in fashion!
Corrupt men band in league together,
But the good man stands alone.
The swan creeps into a thorny thicket,
While pelicans flock in the royal apartments.

Burry catch-clothes grows lush and green;
10 Sweet-smelling nothosmyrnium wilts and falls.
When I look upon such rank impostures,
My heart is by them quite unmanned.
I retreat into the parks and woodlands,
Making my way along the footpaths.
15 How deep are the gullies where the streams run!
How high and forbidding are the mountains!
How tall and thickset the forest grows!
How close and impenetrable the undergrowth!
Layered and thick lie the frost and snow;
20 Hard and brittle is the ice.
North or south or east or west,
There is nowhere I can go.
I skulk beneath a withered tree;
I crawl into the mountain caves.
25 Dwelling alone, my thoughts unspoken,
Cowering and shrinking with the cold,
My years are numbered; death presses near.
Bowed down and broken, always humiliated,
Brooding in joyless melancholy on old age come too soon,
30 My hair is in disarray, my temples are whitening:
Oh for one anointing of Heaven's favour!
Orchid flower in my bosom and jewelled bough in my hand,
I stand in indecision, waiting for the daylight.
The clouds lower heavily, the lightning flashes,
35 The orphan bird, terrified, utters plaintive cries.
My thoughts are melancholy, my vitals pierced and torn.
Choking with my anger, to whom can I protest?

v 'Running into Danger' (Zao e)

I lament for the tragic fate of Qu Yuan,
Who in the Mi-luo cast his precious body.
Ever intractable is the land of Chu:
Even to this day it remains the same.

Not on the 'Sheepskin Coat' do its gentry set their hearts,
But vie in flatteries and slanders.
Pointing to the straight and true, they call it crooked;
They slander the jade disk, calling it a stone.
The vultures play freely in the painted chamber,
While the Bird of Paradise perches on the wood-pile.
Swiftly I will rise up and hurry on my business,
Leaving behind the taunts of the crowd of petty men.
Riding an azure cloud I ascend the heavens
And come to the place where the Bright Shiner dwells.
Over Heaven's Highway a long way we gallop;
Treading the Ninefold Light, wildly we sport;
Fording the Milky Way I cross to the southward
And feed my horses at the River Drum.
Clouds and rainbows crowd up, darkening the heaven,
Shen and Chen circle round out of their true positions.
Meeting a falling star, I ask him the way:
He looks back and points for me to take the left hand,
And I pass by Ju-zi and so straight onwards.
My driver has lost his way in the confusion
And, lurching blindly, he runs us far astray.
Our path is a different one from the sun's and moon's.
My mind is frantic: which way shall we go?
Grieving that those I seek will not befriend me,
I climb the Stair of Heaven and look down below.
I see my old home in the city of Ying.
Freely my thoughts range; I long to return;
But the crowd of evil things gathers darkly.
My longing thoughts are stifled, twisted and warped inside me;
And my streaming tears run down like a shower of rain.

VI *'Grieving over Disorder'* (Dao luan)

Alas! ah, sorrow!
What turbulent confusion!
Silk and rushes in the same skein;

Hats and shoes tied up together;
5 Hua Du and Song Wan serve at the feast,
While Dukes Zhou and Shao carry loads of hay.
The white dragon was shot,
The sacred turtle seized,
Zhong Ni in distress,
10 Zou Yan in dark dungeon laid.
I, mindful of this,
Fly off and lie hid.
I would climb the high mountains,
But on them are apes;
15 Or enter the deep valleys,
But in them are serpents.
On my left I see the screaming shrike,
On my right glimpse the hooting owl.
In terror I faint,
20 Or leap and stamp in rage,
Walk about on the plain
And look heavenward, sighing.
Wild wheat and marsh grass make a jungle;
Rushes and cottonweed grow dense and matted.
25 The fallow deer step lightly,
The badgers swiftly shuffle,
The swooping hawks hover,
The fluttering quails flap.
But I, alas, am desolate
30 And have no companion.
I would sing softly to myself,
But the sun hastes to his setting.
The black crane flies up high,
Swiftly speeding to heaven's vault,
35 The orioles sing their liquid song,
The magpies utter their piercing cry,
The king swan strikes his wings,
The homing goose is on his way.
My thoughts are awakened
40 To longing for my Holy City.
I slip my shoes on to begin the journey,
But stand awhile first, waiting for the coming dawn.

VII *'Distressed by These Times'* (Shang shi)

See, in the summer sky, the Spirit of Brightness!
The Power of Light comes forth, pure and clear.
The wind blows gently with a grateful warmth,
And all the plants burst into glory of flower.
Bitter-herb and fool's lettuce verdantly luxuriate,
But asarum and iris have bleakly wilted;
And I grieve that the good should have to suffer,
To be cut off and crushed before their time.
But the age is turbid with violent confusion.
Sad that in my own day no one can know me,
I look back at the heroes of former ages
And see how they, too, were disgraced and entangled.
Guan Zhong was bound in gyves and fetters,
Bo-li Xi was bartered and sold;
Yet meeting with Huan and Mu, they were recognized and raised
    up,
Their talents were given use and their fame assured.
Let me be easy, then, and take some comfort,
Seeking diversion in my books and music.
But the narrowness of the Middle Land oppresses me:
I will go to live among the barbarians.
Crossing the sheer heights of the Wu-ling range,
I gazed on the lofty peak of Fu-shi,
Climbed Cinnabar Mountain up to the Fiery Plateau
And halted my chariot at Huang-zhi.
I called on Zhu Rong to have my doubts resolved,
But he would do nothing, wrapped in his own affairs.
And so I turned from him and journeyed northwards.
I met the god there with joy and gladness,
Hoping to dwell in peace and find happiness;
But my heart was wretched and I found that I could not.
I gave my team the reins and whipped them up again,
Leapt like a whirlwind, floated like a cloud,
Treading an airy passage across the sea,
Following An Qi to the Isle of Bliss.
Then, ascending heaven's ladder, I mounted the northern sky,
Climbed the jade terrace of the King of Heaven,

Bade the White Maiden strike the keys of her organ.
Cheng Ge sweetly sang to her playing;
The notes joined in harmony, liquid and pure,
40 The music rose, sensuous and languishing,
And all were merry, all drunk with pleasure:
I alone grieved in heavy sadness.
With a sigh I looked back at the Zhang-hua palace,
And my mind was sick with longing for it.

VIII *'Lament for the Year'* (Ai sui)

Clear and cool is the autumn sky,
High and bright the deep blue ether.
The north wind is blowing keen and chill,
And the trees and plants all shrivel.
5 Mournfully the cicada sings,
And the centipede grows sluggish.
Swiftly the year draws towards its close.
I too feel the season's melancholy,
Distressed at the impurity of the world's ways.
10 Nothing illuminates their blindness:
They prize as jewels those worthless pebbles
And throw away this Shiner of the Dark.
The bloom of pepper is trampled in the mire,
And thorny xanthium fills the royal chambers.
15 I lift up my robe and loosen my girdle,
Grasp in my hand the Mo Yang sword,
Mount my chariot and order my groom
To drive me away to the world's end.
Going down from the hall I see scorpions;
20 Going out of the gate I run into wasps;
In the alleyways there are millipedes;
In the town there are many mantises.
And when I look on these baneful pests,
My heart by the sight is sorely stricken.
25 I cast my eyes down and remember Zi Xu,

Raise them up and pity Bi Gan.
I throw my sword aside, I tear off my hat,
Bow down my body and writhe in humility.
I will hide away in the hills and marshes,
Or creep into the close-set thicket.
I have looked down into the mountain torrent
Where the water gushes in swift commotion:
Turtles and water-lizards happily disport themselves,
Sturgeons and catfish gregariously throng,
Moving in shoals up and down the river,
Swimming abreast or marshalled in their ranks.
It grieves me that I have got no such companions,
But live all alone, gloomy and desolate.
The winter night drags on endlessly:
Rain and snow fall, darkening the sky.
Red glow the spirit lights,
And the ghost fires flash.
Fair virtue is grievously oppressed:
My sorrow makes me weary of my life.
Obsessed with smothering griefs,
I have no way of venting my feelings.

IX 'Maintaining Resolution' (Shou zhi)

I climbed the jade peak and dallied there,
Gazed on the serried range of hill-tops
Which cassia trees clothe with their rich verdure,
Bursting with purple flowers, laden with foliage,
Truly a place for phoenixes to nest in!
Yet now the owl alone roosts in them,
Or rooks and pies that startle with their clamour.
Looking on this, I am filled with sorrow.
The sun and moon are overshadowed,
And the sky obscured with malignant vapours.
Alas, that my king is so unperceptive!
How can I prove my honesty or demonstrate my truth?

I will unfurl my pinions and soar beyond the rude world,
Wandering untrammelled, for my soul's nurture.

15 Driving six dragons, writhing and curvetting,
Off I race, mounting into the clouds,
Waving a bright comet for my banner,
Grasping the lightning to lash my steeds with.
In the early morning I departed from Yan-ying;
20 At dinner-time I came to the many-channelled stream.
I circled its tortuous banks and rested in the north,
Then drove my chariot to its southernmost extremity.
I called on the Lord of Heaven and offered him tribute,
The loyalty I prized grown yet more strong within me.
25 I passed through the Nine Palaces and looked all over them,
Viewed their hidden stores of treasure.
I visited Fu Yue, bestriding a dragon,
Joined in marriage with the Weaving Maiden,
Lifted up Heaven's Net to capture evil,
30 Drew the Bow of Heaven to shoot at wickedness,
Followed the Immortals fluttering through the sky,
Ate of the Primal Essence to prolong my life.
I gazed on the Tai Wei palace, rising in majesty;
I glimpsed the Three Steps, brilliantly discernible.
35 I would share with God's ministers the labours of creation,
Establish a glorious work and win great reputation.
But the sun is sinking in the west, half-veiled by the horizon:
My mind no longer functions beneath its load of care;
And so I grieve, encompassed by great sorrows.

x *Luan*

The court of Heaven appears in brightness; clouds and rainbow
    vanish;
The Three Lights shine radiantly over all the world.
The lizards are banished; the turtle and dragon are installed;
Wise counsels prosper, with Armill and Balance for aids.
With Ji and Xie beside him, Yao's works won greatness;
But alas! such choice spirits have no counterpart today.

Notes

I 'Meeting with Reproach'

l.7 Seeking for a Xuan Yuan, searching for a Chong Hua: looking for a good and just ruler like the Yellow Ancestor (Xuan Yuan) or Shun (Chong Hua).

l.11 Envying Feng Hou: said to have been adviser to the Yellow Ancestor.

l.18–21 I thought of the wisdom of Wu Ding, etc.: the names in this passage are those of two good and two bad kings and their respective ministers. Wu Ding of Shang employed Fu Yue ('Yue') after seeing him in a dream (see note on *Li sao*, *ll.*291–2); King Wen of Zhou discovered Lü Wang, who was once a butcher; King Ping of Chu, whose capital was Ying, made Zi Xu an implacable enemy by killing his father and brother – a deed to which he was prompted by the wicked minister Fei Wu-ji (the 'Wu Ji' of *l.*21). King Fu Cha of Wu, He Lü's successor, forced Zi Xu to kill himself. His favourite minister was Zai Pi ('Pi', *l.*21). King Fu Cha lost his kingdom and his life through refusing to listen to Zi Xu.

II 'Resentment against the Ruler'

l.11 Grieving for Huai: King Huai of Chu, Qu Yuan's king.

l.17 Chou Mu and Xun Xi: each of these statesmen died loyally with his master, as the feudal code of honour prescribed. Chou Mu was killed by Song Wan, murderer of the Duke of Song (see *Jiu tan* VII, 'Grieved by This Fate', *l.*23), and Xun Xi was killed by the murderer of the two luckless successors of Duke Xian of Jin.

l.18 I mused on Peng Xian and Wu Guang: who both drowned themselves rather than suffer dishonour.

ll.22–4 the Armill ... the Great Fire ... She Ti: names of constellations.

III 'Impatience with the World'

l.19 Then I called on Tai Hao: Tai Hao was the god of the eastern sky. In Wang Yi's day he was identified with the legendary 'emperor' Fu Xi (see *l.*14, above). Fu Xi is supposed to have invented the eight trigrams after observing the tracks and markings of birds and animals. He was the first civilizer and gives a typically Confucian reply to Wang Yi's inquiry. (*Ren* = 'love' or 'benevolence' and *yi* = 'duty' or 'righteousness' were the terms most frequently heard on Confucian lips.)

l.22 *King Wen of Zhou in Qi of Bin country*: King Wen lived under Mt Qi in the land of Bin in what is now Western Shaanxi. Wang Yi is now half-way on his journey from Tai Hao at the eastern end of the world to Kun-lun in the far west.

l.30 *And rested awhile in Lu Ao's company*: Lu Ao was a man of Yan, in Hebei, sent by the Qin First Emperor to look for Immortals. He never returned from his quest, but such failures were accounted successes by the faithful, who assumed that the missing searcher had become an Immortal himself and gone to paradise.

v 'Running into Danger'

l.5 *'Sheepskin Coat'*: name of a song in *Shi jing* (No. 146) which praises the good men of old.

l.18 *River Drum*: a constellation more usually called the Oxherd or the Ploughboy. (He is separated from his lover, the Weaving Maiden, by the Milky Way, which Chinese call the River of Heaven.) Shen, Chen, Ju-zi and the Stair of Heaven in *ll.*20, 23 and 29 are also the names of constellations.

vi 'Grieving over Disorder'

l.5 *Hua Du and Song Wan*: both murderers. Hua Du killed Duke Shang of Song in 710 B.C. for particularly sordid reasons.

l.9 *Zhong Ni*: this was Confucius' 'style', the name by which, in his lifetime, his equals and superiors addressed him.

l.10 *Zou Yan in dark dungeon laid*: famous fourth-century B.C. philosopher. He never suffered imprisonment, that I know of, any more than the Dukes of Zhou and Shao ever portered hay. Wang Yi presumably means that that is the sort of fate which befalls people of their calibre in these disordered times. It is, however, just possible that he is confusing Zou Yan with Zou Yang (see introduction to *Ai shi ming*). Zou Yang *was* imprisoned, for giving loyal but unacceptable advice to his employer, the Prince of Liang, in the second century B.C. Zou Yang's 'Letter from Prison' was a favourite anthology piece.

vii 'Distressed by These Times'

ll.13–15 *Guan Zhong ... Bo-li Xi ... Huan and Mu*: Guan Zhong was taken prisoner by the Duke of Lu. He was sent back to Qi in chains, in the expectation that he would be executed, for he had offended the new Duke Huan; but Duke Huan freed him and raised him to high office. Duke Mu of Qin purchased Bo-li Xi in exchange for five sheepskins when he was a captive in Chu. See *Jiu zhang* VII ('Alas for the Days Gone By'), *l.*33, note.

*l.*24 *halted my chariot at Huang-zhi*: a barbarian state of somewhat uncertain location. In the second century A.D. it sent a rhinoceros to the Chinese court. Kanchipura in south India and Malaya have both been suggested by scholars for its whereabouts.

*l.*34 *Following An Qi to the Isle of Bliss*: An-qi Sheng, a magician from the Shandong coast favoured by the First Qin Emperor. He disappeared, leaving a letter in which he invited the emperor to meet him in two years' time in the fairy island of Peng-lai. The impostor Li Shao-jun boasted to the emperor Wu of the Han dynasty that he had been to sea and seen An-qi Sheng on one of the islands eating dates as big as melons.

*ll.*37–8 *the White Maiden . . . Cheng Ge*: fairy maidens.

*l.*43 *the Zhang-hua palace*: name of a famous pavilion of the kings of Chu.

IX 'Maintaining Resolution'

*l.*19 *I departed from Yan-ying*: in texts emanating from the Warring States period 'Yan-ying' seems often to refer to two cities: the royal capital near present-day Jiangling on the Yangtze and a sort of secondary capital some 180 miles north of it on the River Han. In some cases it is possible that 'Yan-ying' refers only to Yan. There is considerable uncertainty about this because our knowledge of Warring States history is so fragmentary. I suspect that Wang Yi thought that 'Yan-ying' in early texts was simply another way of referring to Ying and that he uses 'Yan-ying' here as he does 'Nan-ying' elsewhere.

*l.*27 *I visited Fu Yue, bestriding a dragon*: Fu Yue, the convict who became chief minister of the Shang king Wu Ding, was translated after his death into a star.

*ll.*28–34 *the Weaving Maiden . . . Heaven's Net . . . the Bow of Heaven . . . Tai Wei . . . the Three Steps*: these are all names of constellations.

X *Luan*

*l.*2 *The Three Lights*: i.e. the three sources of brightness, the sun, the moon and the stars.

*l.*5 *Ji and Xie*: ancestors of the Zhou and Shang royal houses who worked for the legendary sage-king Yao. Ji is Hou Ji, 'King Millet'.

Glossary of Names

AN-QI SHENG Magician employed by the Qin First Emperor, believed to have become an Immortal.

ARMILL Name of a constellation.

BAN GU (A.D. 32–92) Historian and man of letters. He completed the 'History of the Former Han Dynasty', which his father Ban Biao had begun. He wrote a preface to *Li sao* which survives. His brother was a famous general and his sister a very learned woman who supplied some of the missing parts of the 'History' after his death.

BAN-TONG Name of one of the peaks or terraces (accounts differ) in the magic mountain of Kun-lun.

BAO SI Unsmiling queen of King You (*reg.* 781–771 B.C.), the last ruler of Western Zhou. His attempts to amuse her by lighting the beacon fires in time of peace are said to have led to the fall of his kingdom.

BI GAN Uncle of the last Shang king, Zhòu, universally admired for his wisdom. Zhòu had his heart cut out to see if it was true that a sage's heart had an extra chamber. He was honoured posthumously by King Wu, the founder of the Zhou dynasty.

BIAN HE Man of Chu who found the uncut stone from which one of the most famous jades of Chinese antiquity was made. The first two kings to whom he offered it believed that it was worthless and each cut off one of his feet as punishment for attempted fraud. Only the third king recognized its great value and had it, rather than its unfortunate discoverer, cut.

BO LE Legendary charioteer and horse-fancier, often taken as a symbol of the discerning ruler able to recognize talent and give it suitable employment.

BO-LI XI Minister of the Lord of Yu, taken captive by Duke Xian of Jin in 664 B.C. and sent in the train of a Jin princess being married in Qin. He escaped on the way, but was seized by the inhabitants of a Chu frontier town. Duke Mu of Qin, impressed by reports of his cleverness, bought him from them for the price of five sheepskins and made him his counsellor.

BO YA Legendary musician who broke his instrument when his friend Zhong Zi-qi died because no one was left to understand his music.

BO YI One of two princely brothers who left their kingdom of Gu-zhu to serve King Wen of Zhou, but withdrew when they found that

Wen's son Wu was taking up arms against his overlord and starved to death on Shou-yang Mountain rather than 'eat the corn of the usurper'.

BO YONG Father or ancestor of Qu Yuan, according to the way in which the second line of *Li sao* is understood. Modern scholars almost unanimously say father, but Liu Xiang (q.v.) certainly thought otherwise.

BO-ZHONG A mountain in which the River Han rises.

BOOK OF SEAS AND MOUNTAINS A book, some parts of which may date from the fourth century B.C. but some parts from a century or even two centuries later, containing accounts, usually fabulous, of the mountains, rivers and lakes of China, with particular regard to the monsters, gods and spirits which inhabit them, the myths with which they are associated, and appropriate ways in which they may be propitiated by the traveller who encounters them. The text of the book was originally meant to accompany an illustrated *mappa mundi* and is nowadays generally thought to have been compiled by Chu shamans. *Shan hai jing* (as it is called in Chinese) is the most important text to have survived on the subject of ancient Chinese mythology and is indispensable to any study of the early poems of *Chu Ci*.

BU-ZHOU The name of the north-western of the eight mountain pillars which in Chinese mythology were said to have supported the sky. It was broken by the demon Gong Gong in a cosmic battle with the *di* Gao Yang, with the result that the sky was dislodged and the earth tilted downwards to the south-east. 'Bu-zhou' means 'Not-fitting' or 'Incomplete'.

CANG-WU An area in south Hunan where the *di* Shun (*al.* Chong Hua) was said to be buried.

CAO FU Driver of King Mu of Zhou's remarkable team of horses when the latter made his fabulous journey to the West.

CHANG *al.* 'Lord Chang'. Name of King Wen of Zhou. See WEN.

CHEN Chu capital from 278 to 241 B.C., once capital of the sovereign state of Chen, whose rulers traced their ancestry from Shun.

CHEN BU-ZHAN Minister of a sixth-century B.C. Duke of Qi, so timid that he died of fright on the field of battle as soon as the drums began to beat.

CHENG GE A fairy maiden.

CHONG HUA Name of the *di* Shun, said to have died in the far south while campaigning against the Miao tribes and to have been buried in Doubting Mountain. His sorrowing queens, who went south to look for him, became the tutelary goddesses of the River Xiang.

CHOU MU Minister of a seventh-century B.C. Duke of Song who died at the hands of his master's murderer.

CHUI Legendary carpenter of superhuman skill said to have been employed by the sage-king Yao.

CONFUCIUS Latinized form of Kong-fu-zi; *al.* Kong Zi ('Master Kong'), Kong Qiu, Kong Zhong-ni, Zhong Ni. His traditional dates are 551–479 B.C. His interpretation of the songs of *Shi jing*, which played an important part in his teaching, had a powerful influence on subsequent literary theory.

CONG-LING 'The Onion Peaks'. Chinese name for the Pamir mountains, not known about before the Han exploration of Central Asia in Emperor Wu's reign.

DAN *al.* 'Shu Dan'. The name of King Wu's younger brother, the Duke of Zhou. See ZHOU.

DONG-FANG SHUO Writer and humorist, famous for his outspoken criticisms, at the court of the Han emperor Wu during the early years of his reign. Traditionally held, but probably in error, to be the author of 'Seven Remonstrances'.

DONG-TING Large lake to the south-east of the ancient Chu capital, into which the River Xiang and several other rivers drain. The ancient Dong-ting is thought to have been vastly greater in extent than the modern lake. The shrine of the Xiang goddesses was on an island in the north-east corner of it.

DRAGON GATE The water-gate of the old Chu capital of Ying.

DU AO Sometimes referred to as 'Zhuang Ao', he became king of Chu in 676 B.C. In the fifth year of his reign his brother Xiong Yun, whom he was plotting to kill, fled to the little state of Sui. Returning with a Sui army, he killed Du Ao and reigned in his stead as King Cheng of Chu.

E-ZHU Probably near modern E-cheng on the River Yangtze. A 'Prince of E' is referred to in Chu inscriptions dating from 323 B.C.

FA Name of King Wu of Zhou (see WU) who overthrew the last of the Shang kings towards the end of the second millennium B.C. and founded the Zhou dynasty.

FEI LIAN The wind god, sometimes represented as a winged deer. 'Fei' means 'flying', but the meaning of 'Lian' is uncertain. The character with which the word 'wind' is written suggests a great bird.

FEI WU-JI Wicked minister of King Ping of Chu who prompted the king to put the father and elder brother of Wu Zi-xu to death.

FENG Ancient Shaanxi capital of King Wu of Zhou.

FENG HOU Legendary adviser of the Yellow Emperor.

FENG LONG Variously identified as the Thunder God or Master of the Clouds. Probably the god who makes the rain. He is chosen by Qu Yuan to be his emissary to a river goddess.

FLOWERY AWNING A constellation.

FORD OF HEAVEN A constellation.

FU CHA King of Wu who forced his father's adviser Wu Zi-xu to kill himself and lost his kingdom and his life through his refusal to follow Zi Xu's advice.

FU FEI Goddess of the River Luo. According to Wang Yi, she was the daughter of Fu Xi. Her consort was the god of the Yellow River, of which the Luo is a tributary.

FU-SANG Mythical tree: a giant mulberry tree in the eastern ocean in whose branches the ten suns roost and from which one sets out every morning on its journey across the sky.

FU XI A mythical 'emperor'. Sometimes represented as the consort of Nü Wa, with a serpentine lower half.

FU-YAN Place where Yue, the convict-labourer chosen by the Shang king Wu Ding to be his counsellor, was discovered. Hence his surname.

FU YUE The Shang king Wu Ding first saw him in a dream. Later kings are known to have sacrificed to a 'Dream Father', along with other distinguished ministers of a former age, who may perhaps be Fu Yue.

GAN JIANG Legendary Wu swordsmith. The fact that the metal he used was iron rather than bronze probably had something to do with the superiority and fame of the swords that he and his wife made together.

GAO-QIU Supposedly the name of a Chu mountain, but the place-name may be due to misunderstanding of a line in *Li sao*.

GAO-TANG The Lady of Gao-tang was the goddess of Shaman Mountain, a fertility goddess who manifested herself in the form of clouds and rain and who once offered her favours to a king of Chu.

GAO XIN High lord or *di*, also known as Di Ku or simply Ku. He sent the Shang ancestress Jian Di the swallow by whose egg she became pregnant.

GAO YANG High lord or *di* from whom the royal houses of Chu, Qin, Qi and Zhao all traced their descent. He was also known as Zhuan Xu.

GAO YAO One of the 'ministers' (each of them the first ancestor of one or other of the ancient ruling families) at the courts of Yao, Shun and Yu, esteemed for the wisdom of his judgements, and therefore a patron, in later times, of judges and magistrates.

GOU MANG Guardian spirit of the east. His name 'Hooked Sprout' or 'Curly Sprout' presumably describes the appearance of seedlings as they push through the earth in spring, the season associated with the eastern heavens. The somewhat confusing association of Gou Mang with Zhu Rong (q.v.) in one early source presumably reflects the part that fire once played in agriculture.

GREAT FIRE A constellation: σ, α and τ Scorpii.

GREAT JEWEL The name of a god whose cult seems to have been popular in north-west China during the Former Han dynasty. He was represented as a human figure with a pheasant's head and his coming was heralded by a thunderous rumbling and the crying of all the cock pheasants in the neighbourhood.

GREAT UNITY *al.* Tai Yi, a god sometimes identified with a star; chief among those invoked by the shamans whom the emperor Wu patronized and whom he worshipped in spectacular nocturnal ceremonies.

GREAT YU See YU.

GREEN DRAGON Theriomorphic guardian of the eastern sky, i.e. of the constellations in that quadrant of the heavens (the 'Palace of Spring') which was associated with the east.

GU GONG The 'Old Duke'. See TAN FU.

GUAN LONG-FENG Loyal minister of the wicked Xia king Jie, who beheaded him for his outspokenness.

GUAN ZHONG Famous minister of the hegemon Duke Huan of Qi in the first half of the seventh century B.C. Before Huan's accession he was tutor to a rival claimant and was captured while fighting against Huan on the other side. Huan recognized his loyalty and ability and, instead of executing him, made him his adviser. Confucius gives high praise to him in the 'Analects' (XIV, 18). An ancient collection of essays on statecraft, economy, etc. goes under his name.

GUANG Wu prince who later became King He Lü (q.v.).

GUI-JI Name of a mountain and also of a city in the same area, i.e. Shao-xing in Zhejiang province. This was part of the ancient kingdom of Yue which was annexed by Chu in 333 B.C.

GUN Mythological character, father of Yu and said by some sources to be the son of Gao Yang, i.e. God. He was told by Yao to control the flood-waters, but failed to do so because of his obstinate attachment to outmoded methods and was executed. His exposed body did not rot and after three years was cut open, whereupon his son Yu emerged and the corpse turned into a bear – other accounts say a turtle or a dragon – and dived into a nearby lake. The character for 'Gun' is analysable into elements meaning 'dark' and 'fish'.

HAI Said to have been the First Herdsman: an early ancestor of the Shang kings, who sacrificed to him along with his brothers Heng and Wei ('Tai-jia Wei') and his father Ji.

HAN XIN (d.196 B.C.) Foremost among the insurgent generals who helped Liu Bang to become founder of the Han dynasty. Liu Bang made him a marquess, but later grew suspicious of him. He was executed by Liu Bang's savage empress in her husband's absence.

HAN ZHONG One of the *fang-shi* from the Hebei-Shandong area sent off by the Qin First Emperor at the end of the third century B.C. to look for herbs of immortality. He failed to come back.

HAN ZHUO Legendary character; said to have been a servant of Lord Yi, the Mighty Archer, who usurped the empire of the Xia. Han Zhuo committed adultery with Lord Yi's wife and had Lord Yi killed and cooked on his return from the hunt.

HANGING GARDEN An earthly paradise on the magic mountain of Kun-lun in the west.

HAO Ancient capital in Shaanxi of the Zhou king Wen.

HE BO The 'River Earl': god of the Yellow River.

HE LÜ King of Wu from 514 to 496 B.C. after assassinating his nephew Wang Liao. Under his able rule and with the help of foreign advisers and superior arms, Wu became militarily powerful and He Lü was able to invade and defeat his great neighbour, the kingdom of Chu.

HENG One of the early ancestors of the Shang kings, son of Ji and brother of Hai (q.v.).

HENG-SHAN The name of *two* of the Five Sacred Peaks of China. The two Hengs are written with completely different characters and their identity in our spelling is fortuitous. The North Peak Heng-shan is on the borders of Hebei and Shanxi; the South Peak Heng-shan is west of the River Xiang in Hunan.

HONG XING-ZU Song scholar active in the early twelfth century who wrote an excellent 'Amplification' of Wang Yi's commentary on *Chu ci*. It includes textual notes which incorporate the earlier work of Su Dong-po and other Song scholars. The text of *Chu ci* with Wang Yi's 'Commentary' and Hong Xing-zu's 'Amplification' is the edition which scholars most often use today.

HOUSE OF SPRING One of the four equatorial 'palaces' of ancient Chinese astronomy: the one presided over by the Green Dragon.

HUA DU Nobleman of Song who murdered Duke Shang of Song in 710 B.C. Hua Du first stirred up popular feeling against Kong Fu, the Minister of War, whose wife he coveted, and then attacked and killed him. When the Duke reacted angrily to this outrageous behaviour, he killed him, too. The murdered Kong Fu is thought to have been an ancestor of Confucius.

HUAI King of Chu (*reg.* 328–299 B.C.) By all accounts a violent and superstitious man, disastrously lacking in judgement. Tradition represents him as the dupe of the diplomat Zhang Yi and of his corrupt and jealous queen, Zheng Xiu. His imprisonment and death in Qin, however, turned him into a royal martyr, like our King Charles, and his name was a rallying cry for the insurgents who rose against the hated tyranny of Qin in the closing years of the third century B.C.

HUAI-NAN One of the 'kingdoms' into which the founder of the Han dynasty divided the eastern half of his newly won empire and in which, after he had finally eliminated all his old comrades-in-arms, he installed members of his family as all but autonomous rulers. Huai-nan had Shou-chun, which had been the last Chu capital, as its seat of government and to begin with occupied a large section of what had formerly been the kingdom of Chu. Liu An, best known of the Han princes who held court at Shou-chun, was a grandson of the founder. The Taoist classic compiled under his patronage (a work much consulted by students of *Chu ci*) is named *Huai nan zi* – the 'Prince of Huai-nan's Book' – in his honour.

HUAN Duke of Qi from 685 to 643 B.C. The most powerful ruler of his day and also the wealthiest (his inscribed knife-coinage was China's first real currency). Duke Huan organized a confederacy of Zhou states which he led in battle against external enemies. The hegemony of Qi did not, however, survive him.

JADE GIRL The Jade Girls were star spirits conceived of as ethereal beings of great beauty and dazzling whiteness. They appear to have been a Taoist invention.

JI *al.* 'Lord Ji' or 'Hou Ji'. See MILLET.

JI An early ancestor of the Shang kings, nowadays identified by scholars with the ancestor whom Si-ma Qian's 'History' calls 'Ming'. The father of Hai, Heng and Tai-jia Wei.

JI ZI A prince of the Shang royal house who protested, along with other dissident noblemen, against the cruel tyranny of King Zhòu, but escaped their grisly fate by pretending to be mad. After the Zhou conquest he withdrew to Korea and is said to be buried in the North Korean capital of Pyongyang.

JIA KUI (A.D. 30–101) A descendant of Jia Yi in the ninth generation. A contemporary of Ban Gu, he is said, like him, to have written a commentary on *Li sao*, which has not, however, survived. Jia Kui was a great authority on the Confucian classics, particularly on the ancient chronicle history *Zuo zhuan*.

JIA YI (201–168 B.C.) Brilliant young statesman and writer. He advised the emperor Wen on ways of reducing the power of the princes but was dismissed from the imperial service because of their enmity. He wrote a 'Lament for Qu Yuan' while travelling south to Changsha, whither he had been demoted.

JIAN DI Legendary first ancestress of the Shang people. Imprisoned in a tower, like Danaë, she was made pregnant by an egg which was brought to her by a swallow sent by the *di* Ku (*al.* Gao Xin).

JIAO Son of Han Zhuo and the Mighty Archer Lord Yi's adulterous wife. His exploits appear to have included carrying a boat over dry land. He killed most of the Xia princes, but in the end was himself killed by Shao Kang.

JIAO-ZHI The ancient name for Tonkin in what is now Vietnam.

JIE The last Xia king in about the middle of the second millennium B.C. Said to have been hated for his misrule. He was supplanted by Tang the Successful, founder of the Shang dynasty, whom he had once imprisoned but later released. He died in exile at a place called Ming-tiao 'among the southern barbarians'.

JIE YU The madman of Chu, famous for his mockery of the sage Confucius.

JIE ZI-TUI *al.* Zi Tui. One of the followers of Chong Er, who later became Duke of Jin, during his years of exile. Once, in an extremity, he fed Chong Er with a piece of his own flesh. Later, when rewarding his followers, Duke Wen (as he now was) forgot Zi Tui, who retired in pique to live on Jie Mountain. He refused to come down when Duke Wen finally remembered him, and when the Duke's followers tried to smoke him from his hideout, he clung to a tree and was burned to death.

JING CUO A Chu poet in the generation after Qu Yuan, contemporary of Song Yu and Tang Le. The traditional attribution of *Da zhao* to him is unverifiable as nothing whatsoever is known about him.

JING HE See BIAN HE.

KONG-SANG A name (the meaning of the words is 'hollow mulberry tree') given to various places. There was a Kong-sang in Henan and another in northern Shanxi. The associations are mainly mythological or legendary.

KU The name of a *di*. See GAO XIN.

KU-LOU The name of a constellation.

KUAI GUI The heir apparent of Duke Ling of Wei, forced to flee in 486 B.C. because of the failure of his plot against the life of his father's consort, the duchess Nan Zi. In 480 B.C., after intrigues and broils, in one of which Confucius' disciple Zi Lu lost his life, he became Duke of Wei, but only for three years, after which time he was once more driven into exile.

KUN-LUN A mythical mountain in the west on the top of which there was said to be a doorway into the sky. It was sometimes conceived of as a sort of ziggurat with a terrestrial paradise called the Hanging Garden on one of its terraces.

LANG-FENG One of the terraces of Kun-lun. One authority identifies it with the Hanging Garden.

LEI GE *al.* Lei Kai. A toadying courtier of the Shang king Zhòu who, when honest men were being killed and tortured, won lands and titles by his obsequious flatteries.

LI JI Barbarian consort of the senile Duke Xian of Jin. She set the Duke against his presumptive heir Shen Sheng, his son by another wife, by making it appear that Shen Sheng was trying to poison him.

LI LOU Legendary character whose eyesight was so keen that he could see a fine hair at a distance of a hundred paces. A large section of the 'Book of Mencius' is named after him. Li Lou is also frequently mentioned by the Taoist philosopher Zhuang Zi.

LING FEN A shaman whom Qu Yuan meets in his travels and asks to make divination for him. Possibly – since *ling* in the Chu dialect was sometimes used to mean 'shaman' – the same person as the Wu Fen mentioned in the 'Book of Seas and Mountains' as one of ten shamans living in a holy mountain in the west.

LIU AN (*c.* 170–122 B.C.) Prince of Huai-nan from 164 B.C. Alchemist, philosopher and poet. The great Taoist work *Huai nan zi* was written under his patronage, as well as many poetical works which are now lost. He communicated his enthusiasm for Chu poetry to the young Emperor Wu, for whom he wrote an 'Introduction to *Li sao*', part of which survives in quotation. His ambitious nature drove him to ever more treasonable activities and resulted in his death and the deaths of hundreds, perhaps even thousands, of his followers.

LIU BANG (247–195 B.C.) Founder of the Han dynasty. Of humble origins, he fought as a subordinate general under Xiang Yu, commander-in-chief of the insurgents in the rebellion against Qin, but managed to unite most of the other generals against Xiang after the latter's cynical liquidation of King Huai's grandson, the new 'emperor'.

LIU PI Prince of Wu from 196 to 154 B.C. Son of Liu Bang's elder brother. His 'kingdom' became rich from the minting of copper from its own mines and the manufacture of salt, and Liu Pi himself became the first great literary patron of the new age. The Chu poets Zou Yang, Zhuang Ji and Mei Sheng first found employment at his court. He played a leading part in the Vassals' Rebellion, which involved his own and six other princely states.

LIU WU Prince of Liang from 168 to 144 B.C. He was a son of the emperor Wen and younger brother of the emperor Jing by the same mother, the formidable Dowager Empress Dou. Many of the Chu writers transferred their allegiance to his court when it became clear that the Prince of Wu was plotting a rebellion.

LIU XIANG (77–6 B.C.) A cadet member of the imperial Liu clan whose father was a marquess. A man of prodigious learning: poet, bibliographer, astronomer, historian and man of affairs. His best-known work was the editing and cataloguing of books in the Imperial Library. Known to have had access to the books that had belonged to Liu An and a keen student of *Chu ci* poetry, which he himself wrote and edited.

LIU XIE (A.D. 465–522) His 'Literary Mind and the Carving of Dragons' is the most comprehensive and penetrating work of literary criticism to have survived from the medieval period. Liu Xie ended his days as a Buddhist monk, but his literary theories are essentially Confucian in spirit.

LIU XIN (d. A.D. 23) Son of Liu Xiang, whose catalogue of books in the Han Imperial Library he completed. It appears as a chapter of the 'History of the Former Han Dynasty' by Ban Gu.

LONG LIAN Said to be a hideously ugly woman. Only mentioned in Zhuang Ji's *Ai shi ming*.

LU AO One of the *fang shi*, like Han Zhong, who was sent by the Qin First Emperor to look for Immortals but never returned.

LUO-YANG City in Henan, capital of the Zhou kings from 771 B.C. and, centuries later, of the emperors of the Later Han period.

LÜ BU-WEI (?–235 B.C.) Immensely wealthy Qin merchant. He gave pecuniary and other assistance to a hard-up prince whose son was to become Qin First Emperor, but many believed Lü Bu-wei to be the real father. The encyclopedic work *Lü shi chun qiu* ('Mr Lü's Book of the Four Seasons') was compiled under his patronage.

LÜ JU A famous beauty, said to have been the mistress of a fourth-century B.C. king of Liang.

LÜ WANG Elderly commoner of great sagacity said to have been discovered by King Wen of Zhou while working as a butcher in the market. King Wen made him his counsellor, and he continued to act as adviser to Wen's son, King Wu, playing a leading role in the campaign against the Shang tyrant Zhòu. After the victory he was made first Duke of Qi, which continued to be ruled by his descendants until 379 B.C.

MEI BO A Shang nobleman whose body was cut up and pickled by the Shang tyrant Zhòu as a punishment for having too outspokenly protested against the king's cruelty. The pickled pieces were distributed among the king's vassals as an example of what was likely to happen to critics.

MEI SHENG Poet of uncertain date but thought to have died in 141 B.C. He was with the poets Zhuang Ji and Zou Yang at the court of Liu Pi, Prince of Wu, and later at the court of Liu Wu, Prince of Liang, whom Si-ma Xiang-ru served for a time. His best-known work is the 'Seven Exhortations to Rise', a series of seven descriptive *fu* linked together by a connecting narrative.

MELON The name of a constellation.

MENCIUS Latinized form of Meng Zi: 'Master Meng'. A Confucian philosopher active in the fourth century B.C. The *Book of Mencius* dating probably from the third century B.C. consists of a number of dialogues in which he is the principal interlocutor.

MENG JU Probably the same person as Lü Ju (q.v.).

MI Surname of the kings of Chu and various other noble houses. Mi was one of the 'Eight Lineages of Zhu Rong'. One tradition traced the descent of the Mi clans from the sixth and youngest son of Zhu Rong's son Lu Zhong.

MI-LUO River of Hunan in which Qu Yuan drowned himself. It is a tributary of the Xiang which it joins near the point where the latter debouches into Lake Dong-ting.

MILLET King Millet ('Ji' or 'Hou Ji') was the legendary First Ancestor of the Zhou people. His mother Jiang Yuan conceived him by stepping in a giant's footprint (presumably God's). All efforts to get rid of him were unsuccessful and he soon grew to a great size and began sowing grain. In the first book of *Shu jing* he appears, along with other First Ancestors, as a 'minister' at the court of the sage-kings Yao and Shun.

MO MU A sort of female bogle of hideous aspect. She is said by one authority to have been one of the Yellow Ancestor's wives.

MO XI Queen of the wicked Xia king Jie. She was a captive princess, taken on one of Jie's expeditions. His infatuation with her is said to have hastened his overthrow by the heroic Tang.

MO YANG Wife of the Wu swordsmith Gan Jiang. The pair of swords which Gan Jiang made for He Lü, King of Wu, are said to have been named after him and her. But there were other explanations of how the Gan Jiang and Mo Yang swords came to get their names.

MO ZI Late fifth-century B.C. philosopher whose followers were the chief rivals of the Confucians. The book that goes by his name is much later and contains both essays in which his utilitarian theories are expounded and dialectical chapters in which the logical and other principles of the late third century B.C. Mohists are demonstrated.

MOVING SANDS The Chu poets give this name to an unlocatable area in the mythical geography of the west, but no doubt it derives ultimately from travellers' tales of the Takla Makan desert.

MU Duke of Qin (d. 621 B.C.) The lament for the three young warriors who followed him into the grave is one of the few datable pieces in the 'Book of Songs'. Duke Mu married a Jin princess in whose train Bo-li Xi (q.v.), later to become his trusted adviser, was sent.

MU Zhou king, the fourth after King Wu, who was famous for his travels and for the horses which drew him on these prodigious journeys. A fictitious account of these travels called 'Mu, Son of Heaven' was among the bamboo books found at Ji-jun, Henan, in the tomb of a fourth-century B.C. king of Wei in A.D. 229.

NAN-YING 'Southern Ying': the name by which Han writers usually referred to the old Chu capital on the central Yangtze to distinguish it from the later Chu capital at Shou-chun. During the brief Qin period this city was referred to simply as 'Nan-jun' ('the Southern Commandery').

NING QI A travelling merchant who was chosen by Duke Huan of Qi to be one of his ministers. Duke Huan heard him singing while he tended his ox (or ox-team) one evening and was impressed by the content of his song.

NÜ QI Sister-in-law of the strong man Jiao who was killed by the Xia prince Shao Kang.

NÜ WA Mythical world-ruler generally represented as serpentine from the waist down; sometimes spoken of as a creator-goddess, sometimes associated with a brother/consort, Fu Xi, as the inventor of marriage and various other civilized institutions.

NÜ XU Female personage in *Li sao* traditionally, though without foundation, taken to be Qu Yuan's elder sister.

OXHERD A constellation, also called the River Drum. It consists of the stars β, α and γ of Aquila. The Oxherd and Weaving Maiden constellations lie one on either side of the Milky Way and were thought of by the Chinese as lovers separated by a river across which they gaze at each other with longing. They represent between them the traditional male and female occupations of the Chinese peasantry: ploughing and weaving.

PENG KENG Possibly the same as Peng Zu, third son of Lu Zhong (s.v. MI), who was supposed to have lived for several hundred years.

PENG XIAN A Shaman Ancestor several times referred to by Qu Yuan. Wang Yi says he was the minister of a Shang king and that he drowned himself. Some modern authors understand 'Peng Xian' as not one name but two: Shaman Peng and Shaman Xian, legendary 'inventors' of different shaman skills.

PING Name of the Rain God; also called Ping Yi or Feng Yi. (Ancient Chinese is thought to have had no labio-dentals, so 'Feng' and 'Ping' would have sounded pretty much the same.)

PING Tyrannical sixth-century B.C. king of Chu who put Zi Xu's father and elder brother to death. When the Wu army captured Ying in 506 B.C., Zi Xu exhumed him and took vengeance on his remains.

POOL OF HEAVEN Name of a constellation, said by *Huai nan zi* to be 'the fish-pond of Tai Yi'.

QI Son of the Great Yu and a mountain nymph called the Lady of Tu-shan. The Lady of Tu-shan turned into stone, but burst open at Yu's request to yield up their unborn child: hence his name 'Qi', which means 'open'. Yu left the kingship to Gao Yao's son, but the people preferred Qi. He is said to have brought down the 'Nine' music (Nine Songs, Nine Changes, etc.) from heaven.

QI JI Legendary horse said to have been rescued from drudgery by the horse-fancier Bo Le.

QIAN LEI Said by the commentators to be the name of a 'creator spirit': referred to in 'Far-off Journey' and in Si-ma Xiang-ru's 'Mighty Man' but, as far as I know, nowhere else.

QIN FIRST EMPEROR King Zheng of Qin became King of Qin in 246 B.C. The last of the rival kingdoms was eliminated in 221 B.C., the twenty-sixth year of his reign, and he became emperor of a unified China. He called himself 'the First Emperor' in the belief that he was founding a dynasty that would last for ten thousand generations, but it lasted no more than two, and the Second Emperor, who acceded in 209 B.C., reigned for only three years.

QING JI Prince of Wu, the son of Wang Liao; said to have possessed superhuman strength and courage; nevertheless, he fled to Zheng when his great-uncle He Lü murdered his father in 515 B.C. Qing Ji is mentioned in *Mo zi*, in the 'Prince of Huai-nan's Book' and in the *Lü shi chun qiu* but not in *Zuo zhuan* or the 'History' of Si-ma Qian.

QING XIANG King Xiang of Chu (q.v.). 'Qing Xiang' is the formal, more correct version of his name, but most sources refer to him as 'Xiang'. These king-names are posthumous titles like 'the August', 'the Bold'. Their somewhat limited range had been exhausted by the fourth century B.C. and it became the universal practice to use combinations of them.

QIONG-SHI Home of Lord Yi, the Mighty Archer. Its exact location is uncertain.

RED PINE Legendary Taoist Immortal, one of several spoken of by the ascetics of the late third century B.C. as evidence of the efficacy of their régimes.

RED WATER One of several mythical rivers, each of a different colour, said to flow out of the magic mountain of Kun-lun.

RIVER DRUM Another name for the Oxherd constellation (q.v.).

RU SHOU Guardian spirit of the west. His name means 'plenteous harvest' and is evidently meant to suggest the autumn, which is associated with the western sky.

RUO TREE Mythical tree at the edge of the world whose leaves give off a red light visible when the sun is going down in the west.

SANG HU An eccentric Taoist recluse, said by some to have been a contemporary of Confucius.

SCARLET BIRD Theriomorphic guardian of the south.

SHANG Name of a dynasty of kings ruling from various centres in Henan over a large area of north China during the second half of the second millennium B.C. Their existence has been verified by the discovery and decipherment of vast numbers of inscribed fragments of bone used for divinatory purposes. The traditional dates 1766–1122 B.C. are probably too early, the first by perhaps as much as two centuries.

SHAO The Duke of Shao was one of the two younger brothers of King Wu of Zhou (q.v.) who acted as regents of the young King Cheng. His descendants continued to hold high office at the Western Zhou court and in some cases to be governors of the conquered lands in the south.

SHAO KANG Only surviving Xia prince when the sons of Qi and their offspring were killed. His mother escaped to her own people when she was still pregnant with him. Shao Kang worked as a cook for the Lord of Yu, who subsequently gave him his two daughters in marriage and the wherewithal to go back and claim his patrimony.

SHE TI A constellation, consisting of some of the stars of Boötes, which ancient Chinese astronomers used as a marker for calendrical purposes.

SHEN BAO-XU A minister of Chu in the sixth century B.C., rival of Wu Zi-xu. When the armies of Wu entered Ying and Zi Xu desecrated the tomb of King Ping, Shen Bao-xu fled to Qin and, by weeping in the Qin court continuously for seven days, persuaded the Duke of Qin to go to Chu's assistance.

SHEN SHENG Prince of Jin who hanged himself as a result of his wicked stepmother's machinations. He preferred to take his own life rather than distress his father by revealing her wickedness to him. His ghost appeared to a Jin shaman some years after his death and threatened the country with dire retribution, which was only averted when his body was reburied with fitting ceremony.

SHEN-TU DI Contemporary, according to one tradition, of the wicked Shang king Zhòu, who drowned himself in disgust when his remonstrances were ignored.

SHI JING Known as the 'Book of Songs' or 'Poetry Classic'. A collection of ancient songs, many of them dating from the ninth, eighth and seventh centuries, and probably arranged in its present form some time in the sixth century B.C.

SHI KUANG Master of Music to the Duke of Jin in the sixth century B.C. who warned his master against the dangerous consequences of listening to the ghost-music of a defeated state.

SHI YAN Music Master of Zhòu, the last Shang king. He jumped into the River Pu, clasping his instrument, after Zhòu's death. His ghost was heard playing music there some five centuries later.

SHOU-CHUN City near present-day Shou-xian in Anhui which was the capital of the Chu kings from 241 to 223 B.C. and of the Han imperial princes who governed the 'kingdom' of Huai-nan during the second century B.C. Various archaeological finds have been made there, including that of the 'Prince of E's' bronze tallies.

SHOU-YANG Mountain near present-day Luoyang to which the two princes Bo Yi and Shu Qi withdrew and starved themselves to death rather than 'eat the corn of Zhou'.

SHU JING The 'Book of History' or 'History Classic'. A collection of ancient documents (including the *Yao dian*, purportedly an account of proceedings at the court of the sage-kings Yao and Shun), which later became a Confucian classic. Covert references to *Shu jing* may be found in the early poems of *Chu ci*.

SHU QI Younger of the two princes of Gu-zhu who starved themselves on Shou-yang Mountain. The elder brother was Bo Yi.

SHUN Legendary sage-king supposed to have been chosen by Yao as his son-in-law and successor because of the exemplary patience with which he bore the oppression of his appalling family. Said to have died on a campaign against the Miao and to be buried in the far south on Doubting Mountain. The Chu poets refer to him as 'Chong Hua'. The ruling house of the little state of Chen, which Chu annexed, regarded themselves as his descendants. (It was to Chen that the Chu king moved his capital after the fall of Ying in 278 B.C.)

SI-MA QIAN (145–86 B.C.) Author of a history of China from ancient times to his own day: our principal source of information for the two centuries preceding the founding of the Han dynasty.

SI-MA XIANG-RU (?179–118 B.C.) Born and bred in the part of China now called Sichuan. He was at the court of Liang with Zhuang Ji and other poets until the Prince of Liang's death in 144 B.C., when he returned to Sichuan. Summoned to the imperial court by the emperor Wu *c*. 138 B.C. His *fu* 'On the Imperial Hunting Park' and 'The Mighty Man' were both written for the emperor. Generally regarded as the greatest poet of the Han dynasty.

SONG WAN Minister of Duke Min of Song. In 681 B.C. he and the Duke fell out over a board-game they were playing and he killed the Duke with the board. After several other murders he fled to Chen, but was sold by his hosts and sent back drugged to Song, where he was dismembered and pickled.

SONG YU Most distinguished Chu poet in the generation after Qu Yuan. He is sometimes spoken of as Qu Yuan's 'disciple'. Traditionally said to have been a contemporary of King Xiang of Chu (*reg.* 298–263 B.C.). *Jiu bian* and *Zhao hun* are both usually attributed to him, as well as a number of *fu* which are almost certainly by later authors. Nothing whatever is known about his life.

SUI Name of a small principality: originally one of the Ji states, it was early on annexed by Chu and its marquesses became vassals of the Chu king. One of them, of unknown date, was given a large pearl by a grateful snake whose life he had saved. This was said to have been the origin of a famous jewel, the Marquess of Sui's Pearl.

SUN YANG Another name of Bo Le the horse-fancier (q.v.).

TAI 'Duke Tai' was the name posthumously given to Lü Wang (q.v.) as first Duke of Qi.

TAI 'King Tai', *al.* Gu Gong ('the Old Duke'), is the same as Tan Fu (q.v.).

TAI E One of the swords made by the legendary Wu swordsmith Gan Jiang.

TAI HAO The *di* of the east. Later mythographers sometimes identified him with Fu Xi.

TAI-SHAN Eastern and holiest of the Five Sacred Peaks of China.

TAI YI See GREAT UNITY.

TAN FU Zhou ancestor, the grandfather of King Wen. It was he who first led his people to settle on the 'plain of Zhou' under Mount Qi.

His two elder sons realized that their younger brother had fathered a
sage and went off in order to make way for him.

TANG Called Cheng Tang: 'Tang the Successful'. The founder of the
Shang dynasty. He was instructed by God that it was his duty to
overthrow the Xia tyrant Jie, who had briefly imprisoned him,
and proceeded to do so with the help of his faithful counsellor Yi
Yin.

TANG LE One of the Chu poets in the generation after Qu Yuan.
Nothing is known about him.

TU-SHAN The name of a mountain. The Lady of Tu-shan was a
mountain goddess whom the Great Yu married but visited
infrequently. She became literally petrified with fright on seeing Yu
when he had changed himelf into a bear, but the rock she had
turned into burst open when Yu called to it to deliver up his unborn
child.

WANG BAO Poet from Sichuan who made his début at the court of the
emperor Xuan. One of the poets of the *Chu ci* revival, he died long
before his contemporary Liu Xiang, probably some time before
49 B.C.

WANG CHONG Sceptical philosopher of the first century A.D. Because
so many of his criticisms are directed against what he regarded as
superstitions, his book, *Lun heng*, is an important repository of
information about ancient Chinese beliefs.

WANG QIAO *al.* Master Wang, Wang Zi-qiao, Zi Qiao, etc. Legendary
Taoist Immortal. According to Taoist hagiography he was a son
of King Ling of Zhou (*reg.* 571–545 B.C.) who flew away on a great
bird, after which he was never seen again; but he is not mentioned
in any pre-Han source.

WANG SHU Said to be the charioteer of the moon. *Wang* means 'full
moon' and *shu* means 'develop' or 'disclose', so perhaps 'Wang Shu'
is simply a 'kenning' for the moon itself.

WANG YAN-SHOU Brilliant but neurasthenic son of Wang Yi, already a
well-known poet when he was drowned at the age of twenty.

WANG YI Second-century editor and commentator of *Chu ci*: speaks
of himself as a 'fellow-countryman' of Qu Yuan, who lived some
four centuries before his time. First employed in the Imperial
Library some time between A.D. 114 and 119.

WEAK WATER Name of a river, part of the mythical geography of the
west, so called because it was said that nothing would float in it.

WEAVING MAIDEN Name of a constellation, separated from the
Oxherd constellation (q.v.) by the Milky Way. Its principal star was
Vega in our Lyra.

WEI 'Dark Wei' or 'Tai-jia Wei': one of the pre-dynastic ancestors
worshipped by the Shang kings. He was in fact the first ancestor to
be known by a cyclical day-name, *Jia*. (The Shang gave their

ancestors posthumous names like 'Great Tuesday', 'Warlike Wednesday', etc.)

WEI-LÜ A name belonging to the geography of myth, sometimes explained as the name of a mountain, sometimes that of a great vortex in the Eastern Sea.

WEN Posthumous title of Chong Er, who was Duke of Jin from 636 until 628 B.C. The saga of his wanderings, attended by a band of faithful followers, during his years of exile before he became Duke must have been a favourite of the story-tellers of ancient China, to judge from the number of references to it in early sources.

WEN King Wen, father of King Wu who founded the Zhou dynasty. His name was Chang and he was the son of Ji or Ji Li, younger brother of Tai Bo and Yu Zhong, who are said to have founded the state of Wu. King Wen served Zhòu of Shang as a vassal. He is said to have composed the omen-text of the 'Book of Changes' while he was Zhòu's prisoner.

WEN Seventh-century B.C. king of Chu who is said to have extinguished the pacific kingdom of Xu.

WEN CHANG The name of a constellation, part of our Ursa Major. In later times it was thought to control the destinies of officials and was regarded as a sort of patron saint by those taking the Civil Service examinations.

WHITE MAIDEN A Taoist fairy.

WHITE TIGER Theriomorphic guardian of the west.

WU King Wu, founder of the Zhou dynasty (the traditional date of 1122 B.C. may be more than a century too early). His short reign was followed by a regency of the Dukes of Zhou and Shao. Confucius regarded the Duke of Zhou as the moral and cultural founder of the Zhou dynasty.

WU The Han emperor Wu Di, in his long reign (140–87 B.C.), presided over an expansive age as remarkable for its cultural achievements as for its conquests and explorations. Under the influence of his 'uncle' Liu An, he was for a time an avid patron of Chu poetry.

WU DING Shang king thought to have reigned from 1238 to 1180 B.C. Said to have been guided in his choice of Fu Yue as minister by a dream.

WU GUANG A sage who is supposed to have drowned himself in disgust when Tang, after defeating and banishing the Xia tyrant Jie, offered him the government of the world.

WU HUO Professional strong man at the court of King Wu of Qin (*reg.* 310–307 B.C.). The Charles Atlas of his time, he is frequently referred to in contemporary sources.

WU XIAN A Shaman Ancestor, sometimes identified with an historical person. In one of the books of *Shu jing* the Duke of Zhou, while listing for his brother the Duke of Shao's benefit the famous men who had helped various Shang kings to achieve greatness, mentions 'Wu Xian, who put the royal house in order' in the time of Tai Wu, the seventh Shang king.

WU YANG One of the six shamans said in the 'Book of Seas and Mountains' to be engaged in reviving the corpse of Ye Yu with magic herbs. In *Zhao hun* God directs him to revive the sick king.

WU ZI-XU *al.* Wu Yuan, Zi Xu, Shen Xu. Late sixth-century B.C. nobleman of Chu who fled to Wu when his father and elder brother were unjustly killed by King Ping. He advised King He Lü throughout the latter's successful campaigns but was rejected by He Lü's successor, Fu Cha, who forced him to kill himself and threw his body into the river. In the Han dynasty he was worshipped as a water god.

XI HE Charioteer of the sun. One tradition makes Xi He mother of the ten suns who bathes one of them in the sea each morning before sending it on its way across the sky.

XI SHI Village maiden of great beauty sent by the King of Yue to the King of Wu in order to hasten his demoralization and ensure his defeat: the original 'kingdom-toppling beauty'.

XIA River which was anciently part of the geography of the now much-altered area north of Lake Dong-ting. It is thought to have left the Yangtze a little below Jiangling and rejoined it near modern Wuchang. (The lower part of the Han seems to have been thought of as part of it.)

XIA Traditionally the name of a dynasty supplanted by the Shang. Some modern scholars have questioned whether any of the tradition is historical.

XIAN Duke of Jin (*reg.* 676–651 B.C.) besotted by his barbarian consort Li Ji (q.v.).

XIAN E A beautiful fairy woman; some say the charioteer of the moon, or perhaps even the moon herself.

XIANG The principal river of Chu. The temple of its tutelary goddess(es) on Goddess Island in Lake Dong-ting was evidently an important shrine, since it was visited by the Qin First Emperor in his travels.

XIANG King of Chu who reigned from 298 to 263 B.C. He became king during the lifetime of his father, King Huai, when the latter was detained in Qin. In 278 B.C. the entire western half of his kingdom, including the capital Ying, was overrun by Qin armies and he and his court fled eastwards and set up a new capital in Chen.

XIANG YU Member of an old aristocratic Chu family who commanded the insurgent forces against Qin until defeated by his rival Liu Bang in 202 B.C.

XIAO YANG A hideous man-eating demon living in solitary places.

XIE First Ancestor of the Shang people whose mother Jian Di (q.v.) conceived him by eating the swallow's egg sent her by Gao Xin. He appears, along with various other tribal ancestors, as one of the 'ministers' at the court of Yao and Shun described in the first book of *Shu jing*, but is otherwise a fairly colourless figure, unlike King Millet, the First Ancestor of the more patriarchal Zhou people.

XIONG XIN Grandson of King Huai of Chu. He was taken from obscurity and used as a figurehead by the insurgents in 208 B.C., first as a new 'King Huai of Chu' and then briefly, in 206 B.C., as 'emperor'. He was murdered on Xiang Yu's orders in 205 B.C.

XU YOU Recluse who washed his ears out after they had been tainted by Yao's suggestion that he should take over government of the empire.

XUAN MING Attendant spirit of the God of the North.

XUAN WU The tortoise and snake guardian of the north. Perhaps originally the theriomorphic avatar of Xuan Ming.

XUAN YUAN Name of the Yellow Ancestor; sometimes also of one of the circumpolar stars.

XUN XI Nobleman of Jin to whom Duke Xian entrusted the sons of Li Ji and her younger sister and who laid down his life when they were killed by the partisans of Chong Er in 651 B.C.

XUN ZI Third-century B.C. Confucian philosopher who is believed to have held office as a local magistrate in the north-eastern part of Chu some time in the middle period of King Xiang's reign.

YAN King of the little state of Xu whose pacifism failed to appease his powerful neighbour, the King of Chu.

YAN Chu city on the River Han, roughly where Yicheng is today. It served as a secondary capital and as such was sometimes referred to as 'Yan-ying'. Rather confusingly, 'Yan-ying' in some contexts refers to both cities, Yan and Ying.

YAN-ZI A mountain behind which the sun was said to pass beneath the earth.

YANG Marquess Yang, a legendary nobleman who posthumously became a water deity responsible for stirring up waves on the River Yangtze, which is now named after him.

YANG XIONG (53 B.C.–A.D. 18) Han scholar, philosopher and poet. Like Si-ma Xiang-ru and Wang Bao, he came from Sichuan. Admired Qu Yuan as a poet but was critical of his character. His Chu-style poems included an 'Anti-*Li sao*' which is still extant and imitations of five of the *Jiu zhang* poems.

YAO Legendary sage-king. He and Shun, who are the central characters in the *Yao dian* section of *Shu jing*, were chosen by Confucius and his followers as ideal models of kingship. Outside Confucian sources, however, Yao, unlike Shun, is very little heard of.

YAO NIAO A legendary horse famous for its speed and endurance.

YELLOW ANCESTOR Legendary common ancestor of Gao Yang and Gao Xin and hence of the entire Chinese race. Unknown in the earliest Chinese sources, he seems to have been an invention of later euhemerizing writers on mythology. He plays an important part in Taoist writings. In the Han period Taoism was in fact sometimes referred to as 'the teachings of Lao Zi and the Yellow Ancestor'.

YI (Written with a different Chinese character from the 'YI' below.) The son of Gao Yao (q.v.) chosen by the Great Yu to succeed him. He was, however, displaced by Yu's son Qi, traditions varying as to whether this was done by peaceful or violent means.

YI Lord Yi, the Mighty Archer, an ambivalent figure in Chinese mythology and legend. According to one tradition, he appears as a sun hero sent by God to deliver mankind from various plagues and monsters. One of his wives, according to this tradition, was the consort of the god of the Yellow River whom Yi had shot through the eye; another was the moon goddess who fled to the moon with the herb of immortality which she had stolen from him. Another tradition makes him out to be a tyrannical usurper who wrested kingship from the quarrelling sons of Qi, only to have it wrested from himself in turn by his servant Han Zhuo, the paramour of his wife, who murdered him and his sons. One form of his name suggests that he may have been a hero of the eastern Yi people, a 'barbarian' tribe with whom the early Chinese were frequently in conflict.

YI JING The 'Book of Changes': an ancient handbook originally written for use in conjunction with the yarrow-stalk type of divination and enlarged by commentaries of later date. The earliest part was traditionally supposed to have been composed by King Wen of Zhou when he was a prisoner of the Shang king. *Yi jing* became a sacred text of the Confucians a good deal later than *Shi jing* and *Shu jing*.

YI LI Early work on ritual, laying down in great detail the order of ceremonial to be observed by Zhou aristocrats on various important occasions (birth, death, marriage, initiation, archery contests, etc.).

YI WU Another name for Guan Zhong (q.v.).

YI YIN Wise counsellor of Tang the Successful, founder of the Shang dynasty. When an infant he was, like Moses, found beside a river and brought up in a princely household, in which he later served as a cook. He won his way to Tang's heart by his cooking and was requested as part of the dowry when Tang was negotiating for the hand of the daughter of Yi Yin's employer.

YI ZHI Another name for Yi Yin (q.v.).

YIN An alternative name for the Shang (dynasty). Chinese historians sometimes reserve this name for the period beginning with the Shang king Pan Geng's removal to the capital of Yin in 1300 B.C. I consistently use 'Shang' for the whole dynasty. The text of *Chu ci*, like other ancient texts, seems to use the two names quite haphazardly.

YING Name given (rather confusingly) by the Chu kings to a whole series of capitals. Qu Yuan's capital was undoubtedly the one near present-day Jiangling in Hubei and this is quite clearly the 'Ying' of the *Jiu zhang* poems, whoever their author was. In 278 B.C. the Chu court moved to Chen in Henan and in 241 B.C. it moved again to Shou-chun in Anhui, where it remained until what was left of Chu was annexed by Qin in 223 B.C.

YOU The last king of Western Zhou (*reg.* 781–771 B.C.). His downfall is said to have been hastened by his infatuation with the unsmiling Bao Si.

YOU YI An ancient chieftaincy somewhere in the Yellow River valley. According to a legend which only partly survives, Mian Chen, the Lord of You Yi, allowed the Shang ancestor Wang Hai to pasture his flocks and herds in his territory but killed him in revenge when he discovered his adultery with his wife.

YU Mythological hero said to have been born as a result of a Caesarean section performed on the corpse of his father, Yu succeeded in controlling the flood which his father had failed to control. The accounts of how he did this – shifting mountains, changing the courses of rivers, etc. – are supernatural and make him out to have been a demiurge; but it is clear that what he really invented was drainage and irrigation. This, combined with the fact that he is associated with the beginnings of hereditary kingship (he is regarded as the 'founder' of the Xia dynasty, in spite of the fact that it was not his wish that his son Qi should succeed him), shows that he is a 'culture hero' and represents a stage in the development of primitive society similar to what took place in Egypt and the Middle East, when water control was felt to necessitate a very much larger scale of social organization than had previously been known.

YU XIONG The earliest Chu king or chieftain known to us by name. He is said to have been a contemporary of King Wen of Zhou. All subsequent Chu kings called themselves 'Xiong' in remembrance of him.

YUAN One of the rivers of Chu which flow into Lake Dong-ting.

YUE See FU YUE.

ZAI PI Chu émigré who, like Zi Xu, took service under He Lü, King of Wu. He became Chief Minister under He Lü's successor, Fu Cha, in which position he had frequent differences of opinion with Zi Xu about the policy that should be adopted towards the neighbouring state of Yue. Fu Cha favoured Zai Pi's policies and eventually compelled Zi Xu to kill himself, but historical accounts give no indication that Zai Pi was to blame.

ZHANG HENG (A.D. 78–139) Han poet and scientist (he was a learned astronomer and the inventor of a seismograph). Wrote an immense, panoramic '*Fu* on the Two Capitals' in imitation of an earlier work by the historian Ban Gu.

ZHANG YI Machiavellian diplomat and politician of the Warring States period who dedicated his energies to promoting the aggressive expansionism of Qin. A contemporary of Qu Yuan, he features as one of the principal villains in Si-ma Qian's fictional 'Biography of Qu Yuan'.

ZHAO Fourth of the Zhou kings, said to have died while on an expedition against the Chu people.

ZHAO-GE Ancient city of Henan which was at one time a Shang capital and was still of some importance in the late third century B.C. Supposed to be where King Wen of Zhou first met Lü Wang (q.v.).

ZHENG XIU Jealous and scheming queen of King Huai of Chu.

ZHI See YI YIN.

ZHONG ZI-QI Appreciative friend of the legendary musician Bo Ya.

ZHOU Name of a people living on the western borders of the Shang 'empire' who believed themselves to be descendants of King Millet, the divine inventor of agriculture. The Zhou chieftains were employed by the Shang kings as Guardians of the Western Marches but ultimately joined in alliance with a number of other discontented vassals and defeated the Shang king in battle. King Wu, the Zhou conqueror, became the founder of a Zhou dynasty which lasted through the greater part of the first millennium B.C.

ZHÒU Rather confusingly, the name of the last Shang king overthrown by King Wu of Zhou. In Chinese 'Zhou' and 'Zhòu' are written with quite different characters and are pronounced in different tones. Zhòu was traditionally represented as a monster of cruelty and depravity, partly, no doubt, as a result of Zhou propaganda which aimed to persuade the conquered populace that the Shang kings had forfeited their role as priestly mediators between Heaven and the people by their misbehaviour.

ZHU RONG Originally a fire god, euhemerized as a Master of Fire and said to be First Ancestor of a number of lineages, including the Mi clan from which the Chu nobility were all descended. He was identified with Zhong Li, sometimes thought of as two persons, Zhong and Li, and also with the guardian spirit of the south, whose theriomorphic avatar was the Scarlet Bird.

ZHU XI (A.D. 1132–1200) Great Neo-Confucian philosopher. Author of a commentary on *Chu ci* which rivals Hong Xing-zu's in importance and has become one of the two standard editions in which the anthology is usually read today.

ZHUAN XU Early identified with Gao Yang (q.v.). Third-century cosmologists identified Zhuan Xu with the God of the North.

ZHUANG JI Sometimes incorrectly referred to as 'Yan Ji', which perpetuates a long-obsolete taboo on the personal name of the Later Han emperor Ming. A writer of poetry in the Chu style who lived, with the poets Zou Yang and Mei Sheng, at the provincial courts of Wu and Liang in the mid second century B.C. Author of *Ai shi ming*.

ZHUANG JIAO Veteran Chu general whose career began in the reign of King Huai's father. In spite of numerous contemporary references, it is hard to work out the exact circumstances of his rebellion in 300 B.C. It appears to have been a sort of military take-over of the capital following a series of catastrophic defeats of Chu armies in the field. Zhuang Jiao had opened up large areas of Sichuan and Yunnan, to which he must have withdrawn again when his rebellion proved unsuccessful. Later, when Qin conquests severed his communications with Chu, he set up as an independent king of Dian, in Yunnan. A descendant of his became a tributary of the Han Court in the reign of Emperor Wu.

ZHUANG ZI al. Zhuang Zhou. Fourth-century B.C. Taoist philosopher, part author and part inspirer of the book which bears his name.

ZHUO See HAN ZHUO.

ZI CHAN Nobleman of Jin in the sixth century B.C., famous for his wisdom, learning and eloquence.

ZI LAN Traditionally said to be the name of one of King Huai's sons who subsequently became Chief Minister to his elder brother, King Xiang.

ZI QIAO See WANG QIAO.

ZI TUI See JIE ZI-TUI.

ZI WEN Famous Chief Minister of King Cheng of Chu in the seventh century B.C. He is said to have been exposed in infancy and suckled by a tigress.

ZI XU See WU ZI-XU.

ZOU YAN Famous fourth-century B.C. philosopher, one of the cosmological school who explained both history and natural phenomena in terms of the interaction of Yin and Yang and the five primal forces or 'elements'.

ZOU YANG One of the group of poets and writers to which Zhuang Ji and Mei Sheng belonged, who lived at the provincial courts of Wu and Liang in the mid second century B.C. Author of a famous 'Letter from Prison' addressed to the Prince of Liang, against whose treasonable activities he had protested.

ZUO ZHUAN Ancient chronicle history covering the period 722–481 B.C. conceived in the form of an extended commentary on the court annals of the state of Lu which were believed (probably erroneously) to have been edited by Confucius.

Chronological Table

B.C.
2000

The Xia kings

1500

The Shang kings

1000   The early Zhou kings

771   The fall of Western Zhou
658   First year of Duke Huan of Qi, first of the Five Hegemons
551   Confucius born (551–479 B.C.)
328   First year of King Huai of Chu
323   Defeat of Wei army by Chu general Zhao Yang
318   King Huai leads allied armies against Qin: a fiasco
312   Chu defeat at Dan-yang
301   Chu defeat
300   Chu defeat. Rebellion of Zhuang Jiao
299   King Huai detained in Qin
298   First year of King Xiang of Chu
296   Death of King Huai in Qin
278   Qin general Bo Qi sacks Ying. Chu court moves to Chen
262   First year of King Kao Lie of Chu
246   First year of King Zheng of Qin, later First Qin Emperor
241   Unsuccessful allied attack on Qin. Chu court moves to
       Shou-chun
237   First year of King You of Chu
235   Qin and Wei attack Chu. Death of Lü Bu-wei, putative father
       of First Qin Emperor
227   First year of King Fu Chu of Chu
223   Chu annexed by Qin
219   First Qin Emperor visits shrine of Xiang Goddesses
210   First Emperor sacrifices to Shun on Doubting Mountain; dies
       later that year
209   First year of Second Qin Emperor. Risings against Qin
208   Insurgents make King Huai's grandson 'King of Chu'
206   King Huai's grandson proclaimed emperor after 'execution'
       of Second Qin Emperor and installed in Jiang-nan
205   King Huai's grandson, the new 'emperor', murdered by order
       of the insurgent leader, Xiang Yu

202	The insurgent general Liu Bang defeats his rival Xiang Yu and becomes founder of the Han dynasty
c.200	Liu Bang, the first Han emperor, installs shaman cults in Chang-an
196	First year of Liu Pi, Prince of Wu (196–154 B.C.)
179	First year of Wen Di (the emperor Wen)
176	Probable date for composition of Jia Yi's 'Lament for Qu Yuan
168	First year of Liu Wu, Prince of Liang (d. 144)
164	Liu An (ae. c. 15) becomes Prince of Huai-nan
156	First year of Jing Di (the emperor Jing)
154	The Vassals' Rebellion
150	Si-ma Xiang-ru probably in Liang at this date
145	Approximate date of composition of 'Sir Fantasy'. Si-ma Qian born
140	First year of Wu Di (the emperor Wu) ae. 16; Liu An ae. c. 39
138	Liu An often at court about this time
135	Appearance of comet
130	The impostor Li Shao-jun influential at court
126	Zhu Mai-chen at court (said to be expert in *Chu ci*)
124	Probable date of composition of 'The Imperial Hunting Park'
122	Death of Liu An, Prince of Huai-nan
120	Big sacrifice to Tai Yi
118	Death of Si-ma Xiang-ru
87	Death of Emperor Wu
86	Death of Si-ma Qian
77	Liu Xiang born
73	First year of Xuan Di (the emperor Xuan)
53	Yang Xiong born
52	Liu Xiang ae. 25. He and Wang Bao active at imperial court. Elderly *Chu ci* expert 'Mr Pi' summoned to court from Jiujiang
49	Wang Bao died before this date
48	First year of Yuan Di (the emperor Yuan)
32	First year of Cheng Di (the emperor Cheng)
20	Yang Xiong's Chu poems probably written around this date
6	First year of Ai Di (the emperor Ai). Death of Liu Xiang
A.D.	
18	Death of Yang Xiong
23	Death of Liu Xiang's son Liu Xin (who completed his father's catalogue of books in the Imperial Library)
30	Jia Kui born
32	Ban Gu born
92	Death of Ban Gu
101	Death of Jia Kui
114	Wang Yi active between A.D. 114 and 142

The Provinces of Modern China

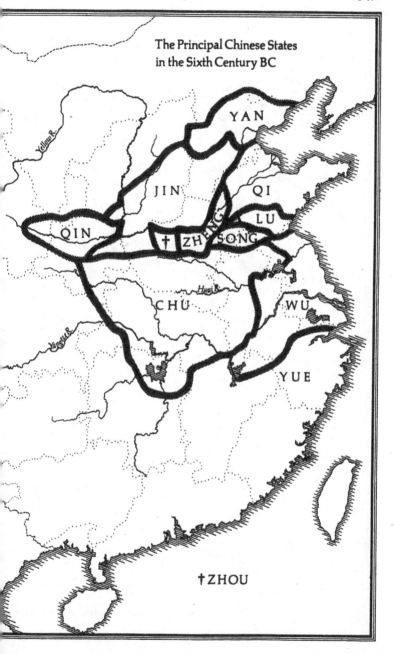

The Principal Chinese States
in the Sixth Century BC

YAN

JIN

QI

QIN

† ZHENG SONG LU

Huai R.

CHU

WU

YUE

†ZHOU

Yellow R.

Yangtze R.

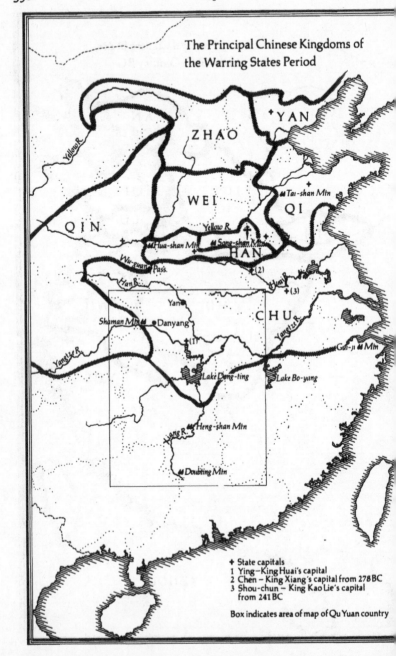

The Principal Chinese Kingdoms of the Warring States Period

YAN

ZHAO

WEI

QI

Tai-shan Mtn

QIN

Yellow R.

Hua-shan Mtn

Song-shan Mtn

HAN

(2)

Wu-guan Pass.

Han R.

Yan

Shaman Mtn ● Danyang

(1)

CHU

Yangtze R.

Gui-ji Mtn

Yangtze R.

(3)

Huai R.

Lake Dong-ting

Lake Bo-yang

Heng-shan Mtn

Xiang R.

Doubting Mtn

+ State capitals
1 Ying—King Huai's capital
2 Chen—King Xiang's capital from 278 BC
3 Shou-chun—King Kao Lie's capital
   from 241 BC

Box indicates area of map of Qu Yuan country

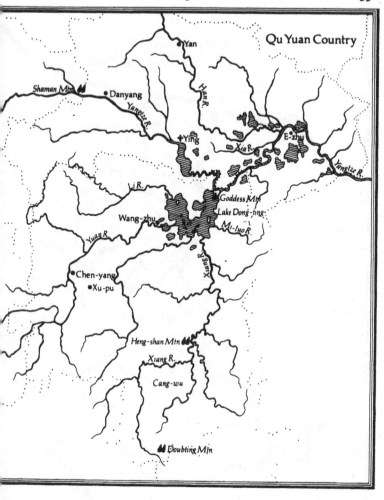

Qu Yuan Country

Yan

Han R.

Shaman Mtn

Danyang

Yangtze R.

Ying

Xia R.

E-zhu

Yangtze R.

Li R.

Goddess Mtn

Wang-zhu

Lake Dong-ting

Mi-luo R.

Yuan R.

Xiang R.

Chen-yang

Xu-pu

Heng-shan Mtn

Xiang R.

Cang-wu

Doubting Mtn

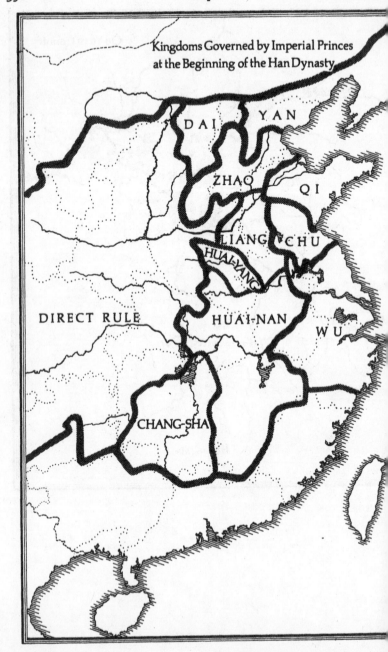

Kingdoms Governed by Imperial Princes
at the Beginning of the Han Dynasty

DAI   YAN

ZHAO   QI

LIANG   CHU

HUAI-YANG

DIRECT RULE   HUAI-NAN   WU

CHANG-SHA